ALSO BY L

MW00849426

Authored Books

Caught Up: 1 Thessalonians 4 and the Truth About the Rapture (Alliance of Confessing Evangelicals)

Content Yet Contending: Jude (EP Books)

How Can Justification Make Me Joyful? (Reformation Heritage Books)

From the Pen of Pastor Paul: 1–2 Thessalonians (EP Books)

God in Our Midst: The Tabernacle and Our Relationship with God (Reformation Trust Publishing)

God With Us: Knowing the Mystery of Who Jesus Is (Reformation Heritage Books)

In Defense of the Descent: A Response to Contemporary Critics, Explorations in Reformed Confessional Theology (Reformation Heritage Books)

In Living Color: Images of Christ and the Means of Grace (Reformed Fellowship)

Jesus Loves the Little Children: Why We Baptize Children (Reformed Fellowship)

The Good Confession: An Exploration of the Christian Faith (Wipf & Stock)

The Nursery of the Holy Spirit: Welcoming Children in Worship (Wipf & Stock)

Welcome to a Reformed Church: A Guide for Pilgrims (Reformation Trust Publishing)

What to Expect in Reformed Worship: A Visitor's Guide (Wipf & Stock)

With Heart and Mouth: An Exposition of the Belgic Confession (Reformed Fellowship)

Why Believe in God? (P&R Publishing)

Why Should I Fast? Cultivating Biblical Godliness (Reformation Heritage Books)

Why We're Protestant: A Reformation 500 Declaration (Alliance of Confessing Evangelicals)

Co-Authored Books

A Well-Ordered Church: Laying a Foundation for a Vibrant Church [with William Boekestein] (Evangelical Press)

Edited Books

Planting, Watering, Growing: Planting Confessionally Reformed Churches in the 21st Century, ed. Daniel R. Hyde and Shane Lems (Reformation Heritage Books)

GRACE WORTH FIGHTING FOR

GRACE WORTH FIGHTING FOR
RECAPTURING THE VISION OF GOD'S GRACE IN THE CANONS OF DORT

By Daniel R. Hyde

ISBN: 1-949716-92-9

ISBN-13: 978-1-949716-92-4

Cover design by Rachel Rosales, Orange Peal Design.

Arial and Sarah were on either side of the bed. Ruth was sitting up at a forty-five-degree angle, a nurse fixing a cannula under her nose for oxygen.

'She just snapped out of it about an hour ago, they said,' Sarah said, moving to Arial's side of the bed so we could get closer.

'A miracle,' the nurse said. 'We've taken out her breathing tube.'

'Thank you,' the patient mumbled in a low tone. 'Privacy?'

'Of course,' the nurse said, giving the cannula a last tweak.

'I'm very glad to see you're doing better,' Pavlik said, as the door closed. 'Was there something you needed to tell me?'

'Yes, I—' Ruth was convulsed with a coughing fit.

'Sorry,' she said, as she caught her breath. 'But I need to tell you—'

The coughing again.

'I think I know what you want to say,' I said, stepping closer. 'I'm Maggy Thorsen, Sarah's friend and Arial's too.'

'The detective,' she said breathily. 'You . . . you know?'

'I think I do,' I said. 'And you can correct me if I go astray, OK?'

She nodded.

I turned to the rest of the assembly. I didn't wish Ruth ill, but I was glad I was getting my big reveal. 'This all dates back to the day Arial was conceived, Saturday, December nineteenth.'

'So not the twentieth,' Arial said.

Ruth shook her head and pointed for me to go on.

I did. 'Ruth met a man named Jonathan Springbok at a conference in Monterey and went up to his room.'

'Where he raped her,' Sarah injected impatiently. 'We know this.'

My eyes met Ruth's and I shook my head. 'I don't think she was raped.'

'But that was the night before Jonathan was run down . . . oh.' Arial's eyes were big.

Ruth's eyes, for her part, were brimming with tears.

I continued. 'I think the sex was consensual. I even think that, in that intoxicating moment, Ruth might have believed she'd found the one.'

'But "the one" was married,' Sarah said.

'That was the problem,' I said, turning to Ruth. 'He told you, didn't he?'

She nodded. 'After . . . he said I had to leave. That he was flying back to his wife and kids the next morning. He made me feel like a . . . a . . . slut.'

The last word was barely audible.

'So you pulled on your clothes and ran,' I said. 'Ran home and maybe your mother—'

'She was there,' Ruth said, pulling herself up a bit. 'And my grandmother. I was a mess, tears running down my face. Edna said . . . she said I smelled like . . . sex.'

'So, you told them you'd been raped,' Arial said. 'Did you also tell them that you'd run the man down in a fit of jealousy?'

Ruth was shaking her head, back and forth, trying to speak.

I held up a hand. 'May I?'

She nodded.

'First of all, I don't think Springbok necessarily lied about being married. I think he just didn't say.'

'Lie of omission.' This was the first time Pavlik had spoken.

'Yes,' I said, watching Ruth for any signals I was wrong. 'I also don't think Ruth killed him. I think it was Edna.'

A famous portrait of the Synod of Dort
By Pouwels Weyts in 1621

To all my confessional Anglican friends on both sides of "the pond":
Fighting to preserve,
Laboring to propagate,
An inheritance rich in grace.

"As for the aspersion of Arminianism, I can testify that in our joint employment at the Synod of Dort you [Joseph Hall] were as far from it as myself. And I know that no man can embrace it in the Doctrine of Predestination and Grace but he must first desert the Articles agreed upon by the Church of England, nor in the point of perseverance but he must vary from the common Tenet and received opinion of our best approved Doctors in the English Church."[1]

—John Davenant, 1629

---

[1] In Joseph Hall, *The Reconciler, or An epistle pacificatorie of the seeming differences of opinion concerning the true being and visibilitie of the Roman Church Enlarged with the addition of letters of resolution, for that purpose, from some famous divines of our Church* (London: Printed for Nath: Butter, 1629), 84–85.

CONTENTS

A NOTE ON ABBREVIATIONS

IN THE following work I will abbreviate the Canons of Dort as "CD." As I'll explain below, there are five heads or points of doctrine (*doctrinae caput*) and each has multiple positive articles as well as rejections of the errors of the Remonstrants (Arminians). When I'm referring to a point of doctrine and one of its *articles*, I will abbreviate as 1.1 (first point of doctrine, article 1). When referring to a point of doctrine and of its *rejection of errors*, I will abbreviate 1.RE 1 (first point of doctrine, rejection of errors 1).

ACKNOWLEDGEMENTS

ACCORDING TO one recent survey, after the initial 90% of manuscript proposals are weeded out, of the remaining 10% only 13.4% were successful in being accepted by a traditional publisher.[1] I know the feeling; nearly all my book proposals have been rejected *at least* once before finding a publisher who says yes. This book's story includes being rejected by five publishers—"A book on what? That won't sell." Each rejection became an opportunity for me to sharpen its focus. In God's providence, this led me to the Davenant Institute. I thank Joseph Minich, editor in chief, for reaching out to me and encouraging a proposal and Brad Littlejohn, president, who ultimately had a vision for bringing this work to the public. And since all books require a lot of behind the scenes work that never gets mentioned on an acknowledgments page, I thank Michael Lynch and Chase Vaughn for their historical theological insights and April LeHoullier, whose editorial assistance was invaluable in making this a more readable book.

With every book I write I am reminded of my congregation, the Oceanside United Reformed Church. You are a model of being "hearers and doers" (Jas. 1:22) of the Word of God's grace that comes to you week in and week out. May the Lord continue to pour out his grace upon us that we might demonstrate that grace to the lost!

Last but certainly not least is my wife, Karajean, who holds the army of children at the gate of my study at bay so that I may write! I pray all four of you—Cyprian, Caiden, Daxton, and Sadie—never know a day outside the grace of the triune God in whose name you were baptized. You're why grace is worth fighting for!

---

[1] https://medium.com/publishizer/calculating-the-odds-of-getting-a-traditional-publisher-798b1c7b94b0 (Accessed February 9, 2019).

PREFACE

THE END of 2018 through the beginning of 2019 will mark the four hundredth anniversary of the Synod of Dort (held November 13–May 29) and its greatest achievement: the Canons of Dort.[1] These words may not mean much to you—yet. This **synod**[2] or ecclesiastical assembly was "one of the most remarkable gatherings of protestant divines ever assembled"[3] as professors, pastors, and politicians from throughout Reformed regions in Europe gathered in the city of **Dort** in the Netherlands to debate and deliberate how to respond to the teachings of Jacobus (James) Arminius (1559–1609) and his followers. The result was its **canons**[4] or theological rules. While there is increasingly a wealth of English material already in print on Reformation and post-Reformation confessions of faith such as the Belgic Confession (1561),[5] Heidelberg Catechism (1563),[6] and Westminster Standards (1648),[7] there is scant material on the Canons.[8]

---

[1] Also spelled Dordt or Dordrecht.

[2] From the Greek συνοδία, "a caravan, a group of travelers." *A Greek-English Lexicon of the New Testament and Other Early Christian Literature,* trans. William F. Arndt and F. Wilbur Gingrich (Second edition, 1958; Chicago: University of Chicago Press, 1979), 791.

[3] Anthony Milton, "Introduction," in *The British Delegation and the Synod of Dort (1618–1619),* ed. Anthony Milton, Church of England Record Society 13 (Woodbridge, UK: Boydell, 2005), xvii.

[4] From the Greek κανών, which originally referred to a straight rod and therefore a rule or standard. By the second century AD, Christians used this word to speak of "the rule of faith." *A Greek-English Lexicon of the New Testament,* 403.

[5] See Daniel R. Hyde, *With Heart and Mouth: An Exposition of the Belgic Confession* (Grandville, MI: Reformed Fellowship, 2008), and especially the bibliography on pp. 533–43.

I don't precisely recall the first time I encountered the Canons of Dort, but what I do know is that ever since they have been fascinating to me. Over the course of many years I've read what I could when I could on them, researching their history and theology to equip myself to teach and even occasionally preach their doctrines. Knowing the four hundredth anniversary year of 2018–2019 was on the horizon, I began consolidating notes. Having written a commentary on the Belgic Confession of Faith, I desired to do something similar for the Canons. Since four hundredth anniversaries don't occur often for those of us whose "span" is but "seventy or even by reason of strength eighty" (Ps. 90:10), I would like to guide you who long for a greater knowledge and deeper application of what it means to say "by grace [I] have been saved" (Eph. 2:5, 8). To do this we'll delve into the Reformed vision of God's grace presented in the Canons of Dort.[9]

We sing hymns about grace: "Amazing grace, how sweet the sound, that saved a wretch like me." For those who prefer Psalm-singing: "O Lord, my God, most earnestly my heart would seek thy face, within thy holy house once more to see thy glorious grace."[10] Nowadays it's a cottage industry to talk about "gospel-centered" everything related to Christianity, but

---

[6] For bibliographies of primary and secondary works on the Heidelberg Catechism, see: Lyle D. Bierma, *The Theology of the Heidelberg Catechism: A Reformation Synthesis*, Columbia Series in Reformed Theology (Louisville, KY: Westminster John Knox, 2013), 231–42, and *A Faith Work Teaching: The Heidelberg Catechism's Enduring Heritage*, ed. Jon D. Payne and Sebastian Heck (Grand Rapids, MI: Reformation Heritage Books, 2013), 263–69.

[7] For bibliographies of primary and secondary works on the Westminster Standards, see J. V. Fesko, *The Theology of the Westminster Standards: Historical Context and Theological Insights* (Wheaton, IL: Crossway, 2014), 399–414, and Robert Letham, *The Westminster Assembly: Readings Its Theology in Historical Context* (Phillipsburg, NJ: P&R, 2009), 369–80.

[8] The most up-to-date scholarship is found in *Revisiting the Synod of Dordt (1618–1619)*, ed. Aza Goudriaan and Fred van Lieburg, Brill's Series in Church History 49 (Leiden: Brill, 2011).

[9] I will not spend time in this book defending the practice of writing and confessing creeds and confessions. I've done that elsewhere and refer you to the following: *The Good Confession: An Exploration of the Christian Faith* (Eugene, OR: Wipf & Stock, 2006); *Welcome to a Reformed Church: A Guide for Pilgrims* (2010; Orlando, FL: Reformation Trust, eighth printing 2017). See also Carl R. Trueman, *The Creedal Imperative* (Wheaton, IL: Crossway, 2012).

[10] A versification of Psalm 63 in *Trinity Psalter Hymnal* (Willow Grove, PA: Trinity Psalter Hymnal Joint Venture, 2018), 63B.

do we know what we're singing when "grace" leaves our lips? Our Reformation forefathers at Dort did.

Whether you're a pastor, member of a historic Reformed denomination, part of a network of "new Calvinist" churches and church plants, or even a person who thinks "Calvinism" is bunk, I'm going to assume you're unfamiliar with the material in the Canons. So I'll open up by giving you a lay of the land to know the "who, what, when, where, and why." History is full of material, so I'll try to keep the story going with applications to recapture your attention. Since God's grace proclaimed in the Word of God is always under assault, it's important to go back in history to the theological and spiritual battle that led to the Synod and Canons of Dort back in the late sixteenth to early seventeenth centuries. The only cure for our "chronological snobbery," as Oxford University professor C. S. Lewis (1898–1963) described us, is to engage history.[11] Grace was worth fighting for back then; it still is!

The heart of this book is to follow the contours of the Canons themselves to get into their content, which describe the beauties and depths of God's grace. I have two aims as we go through this material. First, each chapter on the positive articles (chs. 1, 3, 5, 7) will open by explaining the teachings of the followers of Arminius that led to the synod, show how these teachings have contemporary analogies today, and then trace the history of Western Christian thought on these subjects. I do this in an attempt to reassess the popular view that the Canons are "Reformed *distinctives*" by recapturing and retrieving their catholicity. My second aim in these chapters on the articles and rejections (chs. 2, 4, 6, 8) is to recapture and retrieve the riches of God's grace so that we're built up. There's no sense in recapturing and retrieving something if you're not going to use it! Carl Trueman said, "The past is the church's past and something from which we need to draw help for the present in an appreciative, thoughtful and critical manner."[12] As a pastor myself, I'll lay out the material with plenty of headings and division so that whether you're a pastor, study group leader, or just reading for personal edification, this material can be useful in various settings.

---

[11] C. S. Lewis, *Surprised by Joy: The Shape of My Early Life* (1955; New York: Harcourt Trade Publishers, reprinted 1966), 204, 205, 211, 214.

[12] Carl R. Trueman, "Foreword," in *Beyond Calvin: Essays on the Diversity of the Reformed Tradition*, ed. W. Brad Littlejohn and Jonathan Tomes, Proceedings of the 4th Annual Convivium Irenicum (Lincoln, NE: Davenant Trust, 2017), viii.

Throughout the Canons we'll see how God's grace in predestination must be preached and understood by God's people in the context of our sinfulness and God's free grace in Jesus Christ. We'll study how God's grace in Christ's satisfaction on the cross is necessary to satisfy God's wrath toward our sins and that this message of "It is finished" (John 19:30) must be preached indiscriminately. We'll consider how God's grace in the Holy Spirit's work of regeneration is understood best against the backdrop of our original state and subsequent depravity, which means that human reason and the law of God cannot bring us new life. Therefore a work no less powerful than creation and resurrection is necessary. We'll conclude by seeing how God's grace in the preservation/perseverance of the saints is vital to us because of our continual struggles with sin and our and our propensity to sin so heinously that we might temporarily feel lost again. Yet God is faithful to renew to repentance and restore to his grace. Weaved in and out of this material are various practical aspects of the doctrine of God's grace that we need to apply to our lives: why evangelize if God predestines; the response of humility by the awestruck sinner; the use of means of grace, especially the Word, sacraments, and prayer; striving for godliness; and the important perennial topic of assurance.

In sum, although the following description is anachronistic, what we'll see is that "the main focus of the Canons is on the *Missio Dei* (the mission of God): God's redemption of the cosmos through the saving work of Jesus Christ, applied to the hearts of his people by the Holy Spirit."[13] That's how grand and great God's grace is; that's why it was and still is worth fighting for against all enemies "foreign and domestic."

It's "amazing grace!"

---

[13] Anthony Hoekema, "The Missionary Focus of the Canons of Dort," *Calvin Theological Journal* (November 1972): 210.

TIMELINE

INTRODUCTION:
WHY GRACE WAS (AND STILL IS) WORTH
FIGHTING FOR

WIJ STRIJDEN voor de Dordtse leer, omdat die is van God de Heer! Translated into English from Dutch, this means, "We fight for the doctrine of Dort, because it is from God the Lord!" These words from the pen of Lambertus G. C. Ledeboer (1808–1863) became a rallying cry of early nineteenth-century Reformed Christians in the Netherlands as they struggled against the tide of theological indifference and liberalism. It's a launching point for us to say that regardless of where or when you live, the doctrines of God's grace found in the Word of God are always under assault. Paul fought against the legalism of neonomianism in his letter to the Galatians (e.g., 2:21; 5:4) and against antinomianism is his letter to the Romans (e.g., 5:20–6:2). It sounds strange to put the two words, "fight" and "grace," side by side. Yet this is precisely what Jude did: "*contend* for the faith…for certain people have crept in unnoticed…who pervert the *grace* of our God into sensuality and deny our only Master and Lord, Jesus Christ" (vv. 3–4).[1] Historic Reformation baptismal services even go so far to say that in baptism we are called "manfully to fight under his banner against sin, the world, and the devil, and to continue Christ's faithful soldier and servant unto his life's end."[2]

---

[1] On Jude, see Daniel R. Hyde, *Content Yet Contending: Jude* (Welwyn Garden City, UK: EP Books, 2017).

[2] "The Ministration of Publick Baptism of Infants to Be Used in the Church," in the Book of Common Prayer (1662; repr., Cambridge: Cambridge University Press, 2012), 263. This language is also a part of the historic Dutch Reformed liturgy for

In this book I want to go back with you to the beginning of the seventeenth century to a major theological and spiritual fight about grace that culminated at the Synod of Dort and its major result: the Canons of Dort. If we never go back and learn the lessons of history, we'll remain perpetually infantile in our faith. Since this same spiritual fight for the doctrine of God's grace to sinners continues today, going back and learning from the experiences of those who have gone us before will equip and inspire us to "fight the good fight of the faith" (1 Tim. 6:12).

The Netherlands in the sixteenth century

THE REFORMATION GOES DOWN TO THE NETHERLANDS

The strife at the Synod of Dort was just one episode in a larger drama that hit the scene of Europe in what we know as the sixteenth-century Protestant Reformation. The Reformation, though, didn't come out of nowhere or even start on October 31, 1517, with Martin Luther but was rooted in a series of lengthy medieval debates.[3] In this book, though, we'll focus our attention on late sixteenth- and early seventeenth-century Netherlands.[4]

---

baptism: *Psalter Hymnal* (Grand Rapids, MI: Board of Publications of the Christian Reformed Church, 1976), 125, 139.

[3] See especially the works of Heiko Oberman: *The Harvest of Medieval Theology: Gabriel Biel and Late Medieval Nominalism* (1963; rev. ed., Grand Rapids, MI: Eerdmans, 1967); *Forerunners of the Reformation: The Shape of Late Medieval Thoughts Illustrated by Key Documents*, trans. Paul L. Nyhus (New York: Holt, Rinehart and Winston, 1966); *The Dawn of the Reformation: Essays in Late Medieval and Early Reformation Thought* (1986;

At the time of the sixteenth-century Reformation, the Netherlands ("Low Countries") consisted of seventeen independent territories in what today are the Netherlands, Belgium, northern France, and Luxembourg.[5] In those days the Holy Roman emperor Charles V (1500–1558) ruled these lands and was very popular. Proving that all politics is local, his popularity stemmed from his having been raised in the Netherlands, his ruling as the count of each of the seventeen territories individually, rather than as emperor, and his appointing local men to stand in his place as *stadhouder* ("steward") since he could not be in every place at once.

For a century and a half before *the* Reformation, "reformation" movements

Charles V with Armor by Juan Pantoja de la Cruz (1605)

found a home in the Netherlands. The Waldensians who formed in the late twelfth century in Lyon, France, spread into northern Italy, and then when mercilessly persecuted by Rome sought refuge in the Netherlands. The Lollards or lay preaching movement who formed in fourteenth-century England escaped persecution in the Netherlands. Also in the fourteenth century

---

repr., Grand Rapids, MI: Eerdmans, 1992); *The Two Reformations: The Journey from the Last Days to the New World* (New Haven, CT: Yale University Press, 2003). On late medieval catholic "reformers," see also David C. Steinmetz, *Reformers in the Wings: From Geiler von Kaysersberg to Theodore Beza*, 2nd ed. (Oxford: Oxford University Press, 2001), 9–46.

[4] On the Reformation in general, see Euan Cameron, *The European Reformation* (Oxford: Clarendon, 1991); Diarmaid MacCulloch, *The Reformation: A History* (New York: Penguin, 2003). On the Reformation in the context of the history of the Netherlands, see Alastair Duke, *Reformation and Revolt in the Low Countries* (London: Hambledon and London, 2003); Jonathan I. Israel, *The Dutch Republic: Its Rise, Greatness, and Fall 1477–1806* (1995; repr., Oxford: Clarendon, 1997).

[5] For more detail on what follows, see Hyde, *With Heart and Mouth*, 7–24; Karel Blei, *The Netherlands Reformed Church, 1571–2005*, trans. Allan J. Janssen (Grand Rapids, MI: Eerdmans, 2006), 9–18; Peter Y. De Jong, "The Rise of the Reformed Churches in the Netherlands," in *Crisis in the Reformed Churches: Essays in Commemoration of the Great Synod of Dort, 1618–1619*, ed. Peter Y. De Jong (Grand Rapids, MI: Reformed Fellowship, 1968), 1–21.

there was an indigenous group to the Netherlands who sought a simple life of faith known as the Brethren of the Common Life. It's said that on the eve of the Reformation, even the Friesland fishermen who lived in huts could read, write, and discuss biblical interpretation.[6] Soon after Martin Luther's (1483–1546) translation of the Old Testament (1522) and complete

Bible (1534) was finished in German, they were translated into Dutch and used by Augustinian monks in preaching in the Netherlands. Among these were the first Protestant martyrs in the Netherlands, Johann Esch and Heinrich Voes, burnt at the stake on July 1, 1523, in Brussels. Especially moving is Luther's hymn "A New Song Shall Now Be Begun," memorializing them:

The Martyrdom of Johann Esch and Heinrich Voes by Ludwig Rabus (1554)

1. A new song now shall be begun,
Lord, help us raise the banner
Of praise for all that God has done,
For which we give Him honor.
At Brussels in the Netherlands
God proved himself most truthful
And poured his gifts from open hands
On two lads, martyrs youthful
Through whom He showed His power.[7]

In the 1530s "radical" reformation came in the form of the Anabaptist movement (from the Greek words *ana*, "again," and *baptizo*, "baptize," meaning "re-baptizers"). Soon after, Reformed theology infiltrated the southern Netherlands around the year 1544 most likely from French Re-

---

[6] De Jong, "The Rise of the Reformed Churches in the Netherlands," 6.

[7] In *Martin Luther: Hymns, Ballads, Chants, Truth* (4-CD set; St. Louis, MO: Concordia, 2004), 8–13.

formed missionaries via Geneva. It wasn't until the 1560s that Reformed theology spread to the northern provinces.

As we see today all over the world, in places like China, Egypt, and Iran, this struggle for religious freedom coincided with a newfound political struggle for independence.[8] In a surprise move, in 1556 Charles V did what honorable men whose political life had ended in those days: he retired out of public life to the Monastery of Yuste in Spain and abdicated his rule over the Netherlands. The rule of these provinces moved to his son Philip II of Spain (1527–1598). But the apple fell very far from the tree. While his father was respected, Philip was despised. The peasants despised him because he raised taxes and didn't speak Spanish. The Catholic nobility despised him. He wasn't raised in the Netherlands, so when he "reformed" the church by adding bishoprics this lessened the territories of existing ones, thereby shrinking the nobles' coffers and hereditary inheritance. This showed how out of touch he was. "Follow the money," as we say. Protestants despised him for his persecution.

Philip as Prince by Titian (1554)

While Charles enacted laws outlawing Protestantism, he never strictly applied them. One such law was the 1550 *Edict*, which Philip reenacted and applied. It forbade reading and possessing forbidden books, worshipping outside the Roman Church, talking or disputing openly or secretly the Scriptures and especially difficult doctrines, and reading, teaching, or expounding the Scriptures unless a graduate of a university. The penalty for confessors was the sword for men and being buried alive for woman, while for those who would not confess, the fire awaited.[9] There even was a law conscripting the citizenry into Philip's information apparatus that said if

---

[8] See W. Robert Godfrey, "Calvin and Calvinism in the Netherlands," in *John Calvin: His Influence in the Western World*, ed. W. Stanford Reid (Grand Rapids, MI: Zondervan, 1982), 95–120.

[9] De Jong, "The Rise of the Reformed Churches in the Netherlands," 18n5.

you failed to inform the authorities of someone later found to be a heretic, *you* would be guilty of treason.

The pressure upon and persecution of the Reformed led Guido de Brès (1522–1567), primary author of the Belgic Confession, to toss over the wall of the Castle of Tournai a copy of the Confession and a letter from his faithful Reformed subjects on November 2, 1561, which was then passed on to the king. In the letter, de Brès described the situation:

> But our enemies have stopped your ears with so many false accusations and reports that we are not only prevented from appearing before you, but driven from your territories, murdered and burnt wherever we may be. Therefore grant us at least, most gracious Lord, in the name of God that which no one can deny even to the animals, namely to hear from afar our cries. If your Majesty, having heard us, judges us to be guilty, let the burnings increase and the tortures and torments multiply throughout your kingdom. And contrariwise, if our innocence is manifest to you, may you be for us a support and refuge against the violence of our enemies.

He went on to describe the many "banishments, prisons, racks, exiles, tortures and countless other persecutions" of the Reformed and that "we would lead a far easier life if we did not embrace and maintain this doctrine." In words reminiscent of the ancient martyr Polycarp, de Brès then said in the name of the Reformed churches throughout the Netherlands:

> But having the fear of God before our eyes, and being in dread of the warning of Jesus Christ, who tells us that He shall forsake us before God and His Father if we deny Him before men, we suffer our backs to be beaten, our tongues to be cut, our mouths to be gagged and our whole body to be burnt, for we know that he who would follow Christ must take up his cross and deny himself.[10]

---

[10] For this letter, see Hyde, *With Heart and Mouth*, 499–504.

***Destruction of the Church of Our Lady in Antwerp, August 20, 1566,* by Frans Hogenberg**

Tensions boiled over in 1566 with a revolt over images and statues in the churches called the *beeldenstorm*, "the statue storm." This led to a vicious inquisition known as the "Council of Blood" led by the Duke of Alva known as "the Bloody Duke." Philip is reported to have said that he would rather see the Netherlands destroyed than to rule over heretics. Reports vary, but the number of Protestants martyred was somewhere between two thousand and one hundred thousand.

With every political action there is an equal and opposite reaction. Resistance to Philip's reign began to coalesce in 1572 under the leadership of William of Orange (1533–1584), the leading noble in the Netherlands.[11] Thus began the Eighty Years' War. One irony of William was that he was the son of the Count of Nassau in a German-speaking region while he ruled over the House of Orange, a small principality in France, yet he would become the leader of a new Dutch nation. The Dutch national anthem enshrines this irony in its opening words: "*Wilhelmus van Nassouwe ben ick, van Duytschen bloet,*" that is, "William of Nassau am I, of German blood."

---

[11] Image found at
https://en.wikipedia.org/wiki/William_the_Silent#/media/File:William_I,_Prince
_of_Orange_by_Adriaen_Thomasz._Key_Rijksmuseum_Amsterdam_SK-A-
3148.jpg.

William "the Silent" of Orange

The question for a God-fearing man was exactly how to revolt, since Romans 13 teaches that God ordained even Emperor Nero. The solution was to unite the nobles politically, not religiously. In proper medieval revolts those who did the revolting would convince people the king's advisors had duped him. It was political, not religious, freedom that was sought—at least officially. All this talk of freedom must have been exhilarating! But the reality is that if you poke a bear, expect to get bitten. Spain was the most powerful country in Europe at the time. William asked the neighboring German Lutheran princes for aid, but they required the Netherlands to become Lutheran. So William asked his next closest neighbors the Huguenots in France, led by the powerful Admiral Gaspard II de Coligny (1519–1572). He agreed, but had to go to a wedding first on St. Bartholomew's Day between Margot, sister of Charles IX, king of France, and Henri de Bourbon, king of Navarre.[12] This wedding was supposed to end the religious strife in France between Roman Catholics and Protestants. Since all is fair in love and war, this wedding became the occasion for Catholics to rise up in mass murder against Protestants in the St. Bartholomew's Day massacre. With the death of Coligny and over six thousand Huguenots, help from France was out. Where would William turn? He asked Elizabeth I of England (1533–1603). She was already at war with Philip. She succeeded his wife Mary I (1516–1558), who was her half sister and known as "Bloody Mary" by English Protestants. Elizabeth agreed to give just enough aid to keep the Spanish occupied in the Netherlands away from her own borders.

---

[12] An excellent film on these parts of Reformation history is *Queen Margot* (1994).

In January 1579 the ten southern provinces united in the Union of Arras, which led the seven northernmost provinces to form the Union of Utrecht. In response Philip's army besieged Leiden, a city right in the middle of the northern union that would have divided the seven provinces in two. Since William's army wasn't large enough to end the siege by direct assault, he came up with a plan that is the stuff of military legend: he convinced the city officials to put out the fires of war by breaking the dikes and letting the city flood so that William could fight the Spanish with his navy in the city! After this victory, William offered the city perpetual nontaxation. Instead, the city asked for a university to be founded and built. Cue the foreboding music, as we'll see this university again soon.

In the aftermath, the new United Provinces rejected Philip's rule in 1582. William held the title of *stadhouder* of the entire Netherlands. When he was assassinated in 1584, his son Prince Maurice of Nassau (1567–1625), a strong military leader, became *stadhouder* while Johan van Oldenbarneveldt (1547–1619) became its *landsadvocaat* ("land's advocate") or the chairman of the republican government.

Prince Maurice

In a brief time of political peace for the new republic, the Reformation took root. It's always important to keep in mind, though, that the Reformation wasn't a golden age that occurred in a vacuum apart from the same problems we face. It occurred in real history, with real people. For example, even as Reformed theology began to take root and grow, some ministers questioned and outright contradicted the Reformed teaching of predestination. We have to recognize the possibility of this happening was real; many who formerly were Roman priests or laymen became ministers almost overnight with a

Johan van Oldenbarneveldt

minimum of training.[13] The minutes of the earliest synod meetings in the Netherlands leading up to the Synod of Dort reveal that what to do with former priests who desired to become Reformed ministers was a recurring issue.[14] Reformation was not static; it was a process. It still is.

EVERY STORY NEEDS A BOGEYMAN

Decades of struggle within the Dutch Reformed churches came to a head in the person of Jakob Hermanszoon, who Latinized his name to Jacobus Arminius.[15] Born in Oudewater in South Holland, he was orphaned at a young age then raised by Theodorus Aemilius, a converted Roman priest. When he, too, died in 1574, Arminius went to grammar school in Marburg under the well-known philosopher Rudolph Snellius (1546–1613), himself a native of Oudewater.[16] Returning to the Netherlands, he became the twelfth student at the newly created University of Leiden (1576–1581),[17] which was to become one of the great Reformed universities along with Geneva, Heidelberg, and Cambridge. After Arminius completed six years of study, the merchant guild of Amsterdam funded what was then known as a *peregrinatio academica* or academic pilgrimage in Geneva, Basle, and Padua. In 1582 he studied in Geneva under Theodore Beza (1519–1605), John Calvin's (1509–1564) successor. He had some philosophical troubles with at least one professor at Geneva. While in Marburg, Arminius had been taught a modified

---

[13] See Fred van Lieburg, "Gisbertus Samuels: A Reformed Minister Sentences by the Synod of Zeeland in 1591 for His Opinions on Predestination," in Goudriaan and van Lieburg, *Revisiting the Synod of Dordt*, 1–22.

[14] See P. Biesterveld and H. H. Kuyper, *Ecclesiastical Manual*, trans. Richard R. De Ridder (Grand Rapids, MI: Calvin Theological Seminary, 1982), 63, 81, 129, 141–42.

[15] For works on Arminius, see Carl Bangs, *Arminius: A Study in the Dutch Reformation* (Grand Rapids, MI: Zondervan, 1985); Richard A. Muller, *God, Creation, and Providence in the Thought of Jacob Arminius* (Grand Rapids, MI: Baker, 1991); *Arminius, Arminianism, and Europe: Jacobus Arminius (1559/60–1609)*; William den Boer, *God's Twofold Love: The Theology of Arminius (1559–1609)*, trans. Albert Gootjes, Reformed Historical Theology 14 (Göttingen, Germany: Vandenhoeck & Ruprecht, 2010); Keith D. Stanglin and Thomas H. McCall, *Jacob Arminius: Theologian of Grace* (Oxford: Oxford University Press, 2012).

[16] Richard A. Muller, "Arminius and Arminianism," in *The Dictionary of Historical Theology*, ed. Trevor A. Hart (Grand Rapids, MI: Eerdmans, 2000), 33.

[17] Bangs, *Arminius*, 47.

Aristotelian philosophy along the Ramist line; Geneva, though, was strictly Aristotelian.[18]

Jacobus Arminius

This led Arminius to move on to Basle for studies from September 1583 to August 1584 then back to Geneva in 1585, on to Padua from summer 1586 to summer 1587 where he heard the famous Aristotelian Jacopo Zabarella (1533–1589), and finally back to Geneva to finish his education in 1587. The earlier drama between the young seminary student and one of his professors abated as Beza wrote a glowing letter of recommendation for Arminius's ordination, saying, "God has gifted him with an apt intellect both as respects the apprehension and the discrimination of things" and that "unquestionably, so far as we are able to judge, [is] most worthy of your kindness and liberality."[19] After studying in Geneva he took a detour through Italy to return to the Netherlands. When he was later embroiled in theological controversy, Arminius's opponents evidenced their own practice of total depravity by spreading the rumor that during his time in Italy he went to see the pope and even kissed his toes.

In August 1588 Arminius became one of the pastors of the Reformed church in Amsterdam. In those days cities were served by one consistory or ruling body including several pastors who would rotate from congregation to congregation. Being a minister in the Dutch Reformed Church meant signing the Form of Subscription, a document pledging adherence to the Heidelberg Catechism and Belgic Confession.[20] The church-

---

[18] See Muller, *God, Creation, and Providence in the Thought of Jacob Arminius*, 15–16.

[19] Casper Brandt, *The Life of James Arminius, D.D.*, trans. John Guthrie (London: Ward, 1854), 24.

[20] Van Lieburg, "Gisbertus Samuels," 2. For easy access to a faithful and modernized version of this text, see "Form of Subscription" at https://www.urcna.org/1651/custom/23867. For a study of its history, see W. Robert Godfrey, "Subscription in the Dutch Reformed Tradition," in *The Practice of Confessional Subscription*, ed. David W. Hall (Oak Ridge, TN: Covenant Foundation, 1997), 67–75.

es had adopted these in subsequent synods: 1571 (Emden),[21] 1574 (Dordrecht),[22] 1578 (Dordrecht),[23] 1581 (Middleburg),[24] and 1586 (The Hague). At The Hague it was decided that all professors, ministers, elders, deacons, and even schoolteachers had to sign this Form of Subscription. Any minister who would not sign would be deposed from office.[25]

Like all good young Reformed preachers, Arminius began his preaching ministry in the book of Romans. His preaching didn't take long to cause strife. No doubt a comment on his own angst as a young pastor looking for fruit in his ministry, Arminius said that his hearers "would have been better off if they had remained in the Roman Catholic Church, because then at least they would be doing good works in the hope of eternal reward while now they did none at all."[26] On Romans 5 he said death was inevitable even if Adam had obeyed the Lord's command.[27] By 1591 Arminius had really stepped in it. On Romans 7 he evidenced his moving away from the Augustinian tradition by suggesting that Paul was speaking of the unregenerate man, meaning that even after the Fall man had free will.[28] By 1592 he made it to Romans 9 and got into even more trouble by suggesting that "Jacob I loved and Esau I hated" meant not the individuals but classes of people.[29] It was around this same time that there was a larger controversy on the doc-

---

[21] Biesterveld and Kuyper, *Ecclesiastical Manual*, 43.

[22] Biesterveld and Kuyper, *Ecclesiastical Manual*, 59.

[23] Biesterveld and Kuyper, *Ecclesiastical Manual*, 82.

[24] Biesterveld and Kuyper, *Ecclesiastical Manual*, 115.

[25] Biesterveld and Kuyper, *Ecclesiastical Manual*, 149. See van Lieburg, "Gisbertus Samuels," 1.

[26] Louis Praasma, "The Background of the Arminian Controversy (1586–1618)," in De Jong, *Crisis in the Reformed Churches*, 27.

[27] Peter G. Feenstra, *Unspeakable Comfort: A Commentary on the Canons of Dort* (Winnipeg: Premier, 1997), 7; Cornelis P. Venema, *But for the Grace of God: An Exposition of the Canons of Dort* (Grand Rapids, MI: Reformed Fellowship, 1994), 11.

[28] Muller, "Arminius and Arminianism," 33; Venema, *But for the Grace of God*, 11. See his posthumously published "Dissertation on the True and Genuine Sense of the Seventh Chapter of the Epistle to the Romans," in *The Works of James Arminius: Volume 2*, trans. James Nichols (1828; repr., Grand Rapids, MI: Baker Books, 1999), 471–683.

[29] Van Lieburg, "Gisbertus Samuels," 7. See his posthumously published "Friendly Conference with Dr. F. Junius," in *The Works of James Arminius: Volume 3*, trans. William Nichols (1875; repr., Grand Rapids, MI: Baker Books, 1999), 1–235.

trine of predestination within the Reformed churches in England and the Netherlands as well as the Roman Catholic Church. As Muller notes,

> The view of grace and election expressed by Arminius was not some new invention brought about by a close analysis of problems in the Reformed doctrine, but a doctrinal perspective similar both to late medieval doctrines of grace and election and to the views of several British writers who protested against the Reformed doctrine of predestination at Cambridge only a decade before Arminius and profoundly akin to the views expressed by Roman Catholic opponents of Michael Baius during the same period.[30]

Arminius's senior colleague Petrus Plancius (1552–1622) protested to the consistory, which investigated and found out that Arminius asserted his agreement with the words of the Belgic Confession article 16 on predestination, but held his right to interpret them for himself.[31]

In 1602–1603, the Plague took the lives of thousands in the Netherlands, including two of the three theological faculty at the University of Leiden: Lucas Trelcatius (1542–1602) and Franciscus Junius the Elder (1545–1602). Only Franciscus Gomarus (1563–1641) survived. Never wanting a good crisis to go to waste, the avant-garde members of the government appointed Arminius to the faculty, which concerned the "strict" Calvinist ministers. Gomarus agreed to interview Arminius as a precaution, and was satisfied. Arminius's first series of lectures were on theological prolegomena in the same vein as his predecessor Junius.[32] Within a couple of years, though, questions began to surface about Arminius's theology because his reading list contained too many Roman Catholic books, his public lectures didn't match rumors of his private conferences with some students, and some of those students he was turning out didn't fare well on ecclesiastical exams. One student in 1608–1609, Caspar Sibelius, said, "I observed among a number of fellow students enrolled in the private theological class

---

[30] Muller, *God, Creation, and Providence in the Thought of Jacob Arminius*, 13.

[31] Van Lieburg, "Gisbertus Samuels," 2.

[32] See Arminius's "Orations" on the object, author and end, and certainty of theology in *The Works of James Arminius: Volume 1*, trans. James Nichols (1825; repr., Grand Rapids, MI: Baker Books, 1999), 1:321–401. For Junius, see Franciscus Junius, *A Treatise on True Theology*, trans. David C. Noe (Grand Rapids, MI: Reformation Heritage Books, 2014).

of doctor Arminius, many things that, had I been ignorant, might easily have led me into dark and abominable error."[33] Beginning in 1607 in letters, meetings, and speeches, Gomarus became convinced that Arminius was undermining the chief article of the church: the doctrine of justification by faith alone.[34] Arminius's teaching that God elected those to salvation based on their foreseen faith turned faith into a work by which we are justified. Arminius responded by saying that Gomarus misrepresented him and was attacking him because he didn't hold to a supralapsarian view of the decrees of God. Gomarus, though, insisted that his attack had nothing to do with supralapsarianism but with justification and the gospel.[35] Thus Gomarus said, "I would not dare to appear before God's throne if I believed what Arminius does."[36]

Many ministers in the Netherlands began to call for a national synod. The last national synod was nearly two decades before in 1586 in The Hague, which adopted a Church Order that called for these meetings every three years.[37] But this was an ideal; the reality was that most of the nobles and politicians were on the side of Arminius, so nothing was done. This reminds us that in the seventeenth-century world, all theological struggle was political struggle. There was no "invisible wall of separation" as we're used to in the United States. Not only were Reformed ministers seeking to determine Arminius's confessional status,[38] they were also seeking to assert the right of the church to decide and depose, if necessary, without interference from the state. This, in fact, was one of the key purposes of the classic Reformed view of the so-called two kingdoms.[39] Those who believed the government had authority over the church were called *politieken* ("politi-

---

[33] Cited in Muller, *God, Creation, and Providence in the Thought of Jacob Arminius*, 27.

[34] See Aza Goudriaan, "Justification by Faith and the Early Arminian Controversy," in *Scholasticism Reformed: Essays in Honor of Willem J. van Asselt*, ed. Maarten Wisse, Marcel Sarot, and Willemien Otten (Leiden: Brill, 2010), 155–78.

[35] W. Robert Godfrey, *Reformation Sketches* (Phillipsburg, NJ: P&R, 2003), 128.

[36] Feenstra, *Unspeakable Comfort*, 8.

[37] Church Order, article 44 in Biesterveld and Kuyper, *Ecclesiastical Manual*, 148.

[38] On the historiographical and theological issues related to whether Arminius was Reformed according to the confessions of his church, see Richard A. Muller, "Arminius and the Reformed Tradition." *Westminster Theological Journal* 70, no. 1 (Spring 2008): 19–48.

[39] See W. Bradford Littlejohn, *The Two Kingdoms: A Guide for the Perplexed*, Davenant Guides (Lincoln, NE: Davenant Trust, 2017).

cals") while those who believed the church had its own authority over its matters were called *kerkelijken* ("ecclesiasticals").[40] In 1607 the Regional Synod of South Holland dealt with complaints about his theology. The political commissioner to the assembly conveyed the grievances to Arminius, who agreed to a friendly conference under leadership of the government. This led to a private conference between Gomarus and Arminius later that year, but nothing was settled. In July of 1607, Sibrandus Lubbertus (1555–1625) sent a letter to various churches warning that Arminius and Johannes Uytenbogaert[41] were seeking a synod to revise the Belgic Confession and Heidelberg Catechism on the doctrines of original sin, the freedom of the will, predestination, faith, justification, sanctification, and regeneration.[42] In 1609 a second meeting was held, and again, no resolution was found. He was asked to write out his views, which were finally published in his *Declaration of Sentiments*.[43] He said there were three Reformed views of predestination, then proceeded to give his own, in which God made four decrees: a general decree appointing Christ as mediator; a second decree to save those who would repent and believe; a third decree to set up the conditions and means of this salvation (preaching and sacraments); and a fourth decree in which those God foreknew would repent, believe, and persevere would be saved; those he foreknew wouldn't repent, believe, and persevere would be damned.[44] From all accounts, Arminius was a humble and godly man who did not seek controversy. He said in a letter about various theses he wrote on the issue of free will that he "composed [them] in [a] (guarded) manner, because I thought that they would thus conduce to peace." His desire for peace is evidenced in his further comment "I know that it is one thing to be silent respecting a truth and another to utter a falsehood, that latter of

---

[40] Herman J. Selderhuis, "Introduction to the Synod of Dordt (1618–1619)," in *Acta of the Synod of Dordt: Acta et Documenta Synodi Nationalis Dordrechtanae (1618–1619), Volume 1*, ed. Donald Sinnema, Christian Moser, and Herman J. Selderhuis (Göttingen, Germany: Vandenhoeck & Ruprecht, 2015), xvii.

[41] Also Jan or Hans, Wtenbogaert or Uitenbogaert.

[42] Nicolas Fornerod, "'The Canons of the Synod Has Shot Off the Advocate's Head': A Reappraisal of the Genevan Delegation at the Synod of Dordt," in Goudriaan and van Lieburg, *Revisiting the Synod of Dordt*, 188.

[43] See W. Stephen Gunter, *Arminius and His Declaration of Sentiments: An Annotated Translation with Introduction and Theological Commentary* (Waco, TX: Baylor University Press, 2012).

[44] Muller, "Arminius and Arminianism," 34.

which it is never lawful to do, while the former is occasionally, nay very often, expedient."[45] Here we are four hundred years later with our labels "Arminian" and "Calvinist," but these were real men. The men we vilify as heretics could be just as godly as the heroes we praise. The investigation had to be suspended when he became sick, and then he died in 1609 of tuberculosis.[46]

THE REMONSTRANTS REMONSTRATE WITH A REMONSTRANCE

The death of Professor Arminius did not end the strife. It never does, as the problems are never merely with a professor but with his loyal students who go out to change the world. On January 14, 1610, forty-three ministers who followed Arminius's teaching gathered in the city of Gouda and "crossed the Rubicon." Arminius became "one of the dozen or so theologians in the history of the Christian church who has given lasting direction to the theological tradition and who, as a result, has stamped his name upon a particular doctrinal or confessional viewpoint."[47] Led by Uytenbogaert (1557–1644), the court preacher, and supported by the aforementioned powerful statesman van Oldenbarneveldt, they were convinced that their views should be tolerated in the church and prepared a document to this effect called the *Remonstrance*, which contained five points.[48] A "remonstrance" is a public protest and petition. This party of ministers became known as the Remonstrants, those who protested. Since all theology was politics, they branded themselves the *rekkelijken* or moderates while their opponents were called the *preciezen* or precisionists.[49]

---

[45] Cited in Carl Bangs, *Arminius: A Study in the Dutch Reformation* (Nashville, TN: Abingdon, 1971), 269.

[46] On the heart of Arminius's theology being the justice of God (*iustitia Dei*), see William den Boer, "Defense or Deviation? A Re-examination of Arminius' Motives to Deviate from the 'Mainstream' Reformed Theology," in Goudriaan and van Lieburg, *Revisiting the Synod of Dordt*, 23–47.

[47] Muller, *God, Creation, and Providence in the Thought of Jacob Arminius*, 3.

[48] See the Remonstrant articles at the beginning chapters 1, 3, 5, and 7 as well as in appendix 1: The *Remonstrance* of 1610.

[49] Fred van Lieburg, *The Synod of Dordrecht 1618–1619*, trans. Dick Swier, ed. Herman A. van Duinen and Cees Esseboom (Dordrecht: Stichting Historisch Platform Dordrecht, 2017), 5.

Soon after the Remonstrants published their *Remonstrance* others responded in 1611 with the *Counter-Remonstrance*. Theological tensions increased, leading to political and societal tensions to grow as well. The United Provinces were a young republic that had just come out of war and was facing inevitable war again. In 1609 the Twelve Years' Truce was signed between the republic and Spain. Twelve years meant 1621 was just around the corner and war was in its wake. And while the state-sponsored church was the Reformed church, only about 20 percent of the population were members of Reformed congregations.

This led to a meeting between the sides March 10–25 and then again May 11–20, 1611, in The Hague known as the *Collatio Hagiensis*. But again, this was to no avail. The Arminians knew that they were a minority so they didn't want a synod; therefore they sought the support of van Oldenbarneveldt. Because a synod was not called, many people in the pews who considered themselves *preciezen* moved from one congregation to another to avoid Arminian preachers, only leading to the political and theological tensions in the republic. In 1615 there were riots, *preciezen* believers met for worship outside the cities, and rumors began of a secret synod to leave the state-supported church.[50] As Petrus Cunnaeus (1586–1638), a philosopher at the University of Leiden, said, theologians introduced this strife into the

Maurice disbands Oldenbarneveldt's *waardgelders* by Joost Cornelisz Droochsloot (1625)

---

[50] Godfrey, "Calvin and Calvinism in the Netherlands," 106.

social media platforms of their day: barbershops, boats, wagons, and thea-ters.[51] Sir Dudley Carleton (1573–1632), English ambassador to the Nether-lands, would later refer to this time as "our civil warre; which is prose-prosequuted with much incivilitie, as appeares by many rayling and scoffing libels."[52]

By summer 1617, under the influence of Carleton, Prince Maurice aligned himself with the *preciezen* by worshipping with them in The Hague on July 23.[53] It's reported that up to this point Maurice said he didn't know whether predestination was blue or green but that he was going to make it orange.[54] In response, van Oldenbarneveldt rallied the two provinces of Holland and West Friesland to issue "The Sharp Resolution" (*De Scherpe Resolutie*), which stated among other things that no national synod would be held and that local magistrates were allowed to raise militias called *waardgeld-ers* to keep one from meeting. But Maurice showed that it was better to speak softly and carry a big stick. Unlike van Oldenbarneveldt, he had a standing army, which disarmed these local militias on July 31, 1618, paving the way for the synod. The fledgling republic and fractured Reformed church was on the verge of civil war, all while Spain was preparing for the resumption of war in 1621. Under this pressure, Prince Maurice convinced the States General to hold a synod. Van Oldenbarneveldt was arrested and later executed as a traitor on May 14, 1619, eliciting the grim play on words from the Genevan theologian Giovanni Diodati (1576–1649): "The Canons of the Synod had shot off the Advocate's head" (*Dat de Canons van de Synode den Advocaet het hooft hadden afgeschooten*).[55] The Dutch *canons* is a homonym of

---

[51] Cited in Henri A. Krop, "Philosophy and the Synod of Dordt. Aristotelianism, Humanism, and the Case Against Arianism," in Goudriaan and van Lieburg, *Revisit-ing the Synod of Dordt*, 49.

[52] Milton, *The British Delegation and the Synod of Dort*, 63 (2/5).

[53] Due to Elizabeth's aid of the Netherlands mentioned above, the English con-trolled the towns of Flushing and Brill until 1616 while the English ambassador was a sitting member of the States General. Milton, introduction to *The British Dele-gation and the Synod of Dort*, xxii.

[54] Milton, introduction to *The British Delegation and the Synod of Dort*, xvii, citing K. H. D. Haley, *The Dutch in the Seventeenth Century* (New York: Harcourt Brace Jo-vanovich, 1972), 105.

[55] Gerard Brandt, *The History of the Reformation and other ecclesiastical transactions in and about the Low-Countries*, 4 vols. (London, 1720–1723), 3:371. For the Dutch, see Brandt, *Historie der Reformatie en andre kerkelyke geschiedenissen in en ontrent de Nederland-en* (Rotterdam: Barent Bos, 1704), 3:741.

kanons: the former referring to canons, as in rules; the latter referring to cannons, as in guns.

THE SYNOD OF DORT (NOVEMBER 13, 1618 – MAY 29, 1619)

The decision to hold a *national* synod to deal with this strife within the Dutch Reformed Church soon became an opportunity for an *international* synod at the urging of King James I of England (1566–1625).[56] While he had called for "mutual tolerance" (*mutuelle tolerance*) early in 1613, by early 1617 he was advocating a national synod.[57] On behalf of the king, Ambassador Dudley Carlton addressed the States General with the reason: "It is a Nationall Synode; I say Nationall, because the evill being passed from Province to Province, a Provinciall Synode is not sufficient, but onely for so much it serveth for a preparative to the Nationall Synode."[58]

This national and international character is what made Dort "not just an important event in Dutch history, but in the history of the church."[59] Europeans were connected via students like Arminius who traveled across Europe to study in the common language of Latin. In fact, the aforementioned Gomarus and synod president Johannes Bogerman (1576–1637) studied in England at Oxford and Cambridge, Gomarus even graduating from Cambridge in 1584. Invitations were then sent on July 25, 1618, to Reformed principalities across Europe to send their best theologians to help settle the strife. But not even this went off without a hitch as the letter to Geneva did not arrive until October 9, over two months late, due to the Remonstrants' obstruction in the government.[60]

---

[56] On the political and religious rationale for English involvement, see Milton, introduction to *The British Delegation and the Synod of Dort*, xvii, xxii–xxvii.

[57] See the documents in Milton, *The British Delegation and the Synod of Dort*, 3–4 (1/1), 6–8 (1/3).

[58] Milton, *The British Delegation and the Synod of Dort*, 18 (1/9).

[59] Milton, introduction to *The British Delegation and the Synod of Dort*, xvii.

[60] See Fornerod, "The Canons of the Synod," 189–91.

Invitations were sent to King James himself in England,[61] France, Brandenburg, the Palatinate, Hesse, Nassau-Wetterau, Bremen, Emden, Geneva, and several Swiss cantons. The French were forbidden by King Louis XIII from attending while Brandenburg did not attend for fear of damaging its relationship with surrounding Lutheran princes.[62] There were other Reformed churches that were *not* invited. There were Dutch Reformed "strangers" churches in England as well as in western German border regions of Lingen-Bentheim-Steinfurt-Tecklenburg and Cleves-Gulik-Berg-Mark-Moers. Fred van Lieburg helpfully reminds us of the political tensions such churches were in: presbyterial Dutch churches under the protection of the episcopal Church of England as well as the churches within German regions surrounded by Lutherans and the Holy Roman Empire.[63] The Hungarian Reformed Church at the other end of Europe was not invited. Its churches in the western Kingdom of Hungary were under Catholic Hapsburg rule while those in the eastern Principality of Transylvania were under Muslim Ottoman rule. With the Defenestration of Prague in 1618, what became known as the Thirty Years' War was under way, eventually engulfing all of Europe.[64]

The next issue was where to hold the synod. Prince Maurice preferred The Hague where the States General met. Others suggested Utrecht. King James "dislike[d]" Utrecht because it was "a towne which hath ben allwayes given to sedition and mutiny, is now wholly inclyned to the Armin-

---

[61] On the British delegation, see Anthony Milton, "A Distorting Mirror: The Hales and Balcanquahal Letters and the Synod of Dordt," in Goudriaan and van Lieburg, *Revisiting the Synod of Dordt*, 135–61.

[62] Milton, introduction to *The British Delegation and the Synod of Dort*, xviii.

[63] Fred van Lieburg, "The Participants at the Synod of Dort," in *Acta of the Synod of Dordt*, lxvii.

[64] On the Hungarian Reformation, see Katalin Péter, *Studies on the History of the Reformation in Hungary and Transylvania*, ed. Gabriella Erdélyi, Refo500 Academic Studies 45 (Göttingen, Germany: Vandenhoeck & Ruprecht, 2018); Márta Fata, "The Kingdom of Hungary and Principality of Transylvania," in *A Companion to the Reformation in Central Europe*, ed. Howard Louthan and Graeme Murdock, Brill's Companions to the Christian Tradition 61 (Leiden: Brill, 2015), 92–120; Graeme Murdock, "Reformed Orthodoxy in East-Central Europe," in *A Companion to Reformed Orthodoxy*, ed. Herman Selderhuis, Brill's Companions to the Christian Tradition 40 (Leiden: Brill, 2013), 293–321.

ian faccion."[65] Dordrecht eventually became the location. Its political importance was highlighted as it was the oldest city in the province of Holland, where in 1572 the first meeting of the free provinces that formed the Netherlands met and where in 1578 the first national synod assembled. It was also a stronghold of orthodox Reformed belief so there would be little disturbance. They met in the retrofitted *kloveniersdoelen*, the musketeers' shooting range. Perhaps the irony didn't escape them!

The synod hosted eighty-four delegates: fifty-eight *theologi interi* (Dutch and Walloon) and twenty-six *theologi exteri* (international).[66] The *interi* were divided according to importance and prestige. The political delegates plus secretary, treasurer, and liaison to the city of Dordrecht from the States General sat on one side and at the front. These men ranged in age from just twenty-two all the way up to seventy years old. On the same side were seated the delegates of the Dutch theological faculties, and finally the provincial delegates from the eight Dutch-speaking provincial synods, the Walloon-speaking synod representing churches also under the cross in the Spanish-ruled southern Netherlands, and the independent territory of Drenthe.

King James I by Daniël Mijtens (1621)

I'll focus here on the *exteri*, who were a "who's who" of theologians and preachers, that Johannes van den Berg called "a muster of the forces of Calvinism."[67] I'll list these delegates in their order of precedence according to the synod.

---

[65] Milton, *The British Delegation and the Synod of Dort*, 20 (1/10); van Lieburg, *The Synod of Dordrecht 1618–1619*, 11.

[66] For a list of delegates, see van Lieburg, "The Participants at the Synod of Dort," in *Acta of the Synod of Dordt*, lxiii–cvii. See also De Jong, *Crisis in the Reformed Churches*, 213–21. See also Simon Kistemaker, "Leading Figures at the Synod of Dort," in ibid., 39–51.

[67] Johannes van den Berg, "The Synod of Dort in the Balance," in *Religious Currents and Cross-Currents: Essays on Early Modern Protestantism and the Protestant Enlightenment*,

From England King James sent "some selected Theologians and grave divines, who if there be cause may with temper and moderacon assist."[68] King James sent the synod's only bishop, George Carleton of Llandaff in Wales (1559–1628), who was referred to in various notes of the synod merely as "the Bishop."[69] He had an entourage of eight to ten, stayed in his own lodging,[70] and always spoke first when the British delegation was called upon in public sessions. In some of the artwork of the synod in session "the Bishop" sat under a canopy, and when the synod processed at its conclusion, it was "the Bishop" who was at the head of the foreign delegates.[71] After the synod he was made bishop of Chichester. King James also sent Joseph Hall (1574–1656), who was dean of Worchester and afterward bishop of Exeter and Norwich; John Davenant (1572–1641), who was master of Queen's College, Cambridge, and after the synod became bishop of Salisbury; and Samuel Ward (1572–1643), who was master of Sidney Sussex College, Cambridge, and afterward became Lady Margaret professor at Cambridge. After the synod began, King James also sent Walter Balcanquahall (1586–1645), who was fellow of Pembroke Hall, Cambridge, and afterward restored as master of the Savoy and made dean of Rochester and Durham. The reason was that "it was his Majesties purpose to have sent ever unto their Synode some Ministers of the Scottish nation."[72] Although he conferenced with the English, Balcanquahall was the de facto representative of the Church of Scotland and called *Scotus* in various diaries.[73] Soon after the synod began, Joseph Hall became ill as "the ayre of these parts

---

ed. Jan de Bruijin, Pieter Nanne Holtrop, and Ernestine G. E. Van Der Wall (Leiden: Brill, 1999), 1.

[68] Milton, *The British Delegation and the Synod of Dort*, 93 (2/9). For John Davenant's nephew's account of the at-times arduous journey, see ibid., 105–8 (3/1).

[69] Milton, introduction to *The British Delegation and the Synod of Dort*, xxxv. On Carleton's Reformed episcopacy, see Andre Gazal, "George Carleton's Reformed Doctrine of Episcopal Authority at the Synod of Dort," in *Beyond Calvin*, 107–26.

[70] He even used his private lodging as the location of what he called "a little synod" of representatives from all the foreign delegations to calm tensions. Milton, *The British Delegation and the Synod of Dort*, 198–99 (5/2).

[71] Milton, introduction to *The British Delegation and the Synod of Dort*, xxxv; van Lieburg, "The Participants at the Synod of Dort," in *Acta of the Synod of Dordt*, lxxviii. On his separate lodging, see ibid., 107n7 (3/1).

[72] Milton, *The British Delegation and the Synod of Dort*, 148 (4/1).

[73] Milton, introduction to *The British Delegation and the Synod of Dort*, xxviii n43.

doth so ill agree, that he is fallen into a languishing indisposition."[74] Because of this, he requested to return to England. The remaining delegation requested the king replace him with Thomas Goad, chaplain to the archbishop of Canterbury who afterward became prebendary of Wolverhampton and Winchester.[75] Behind the scenes Ambassador Carleton campaigned for John Prideaux not only "for the sufficiency of the man" but also "for the reputation of the University of Oxford, which is not yet so much as named in this Synod: but Davenantius Cantabrigiensis, Wardus Cantabrigiensis, and now Balcanquallus Cantabrigiensis."[76] Cheerleading for our alma mater is nothing new! King James's instructions to his delegates included nine points:

> 1. "…inure yourselves to the practise of the Latin tongue, that…you may deliver your mindes with the more readinesse and facility."

> 2. "…resolve among yourselves before hand what is the true state of the question, and jointly and uniformly agree thereupon."

> 3. "…if…any thinge be emergent whereof yow thought not before, yow shall meet and consult thereupon againe, and so resolve among yourselves ioyntly what is fit to be maintained; And this to be done agreable to Scriptures and the doctrine of the Church of England."

> 4. "Your advise shall be to those Churches, that their Ministers do not deliver in the Pulpit to the people those thinges for ordinary doctrines, which are the highest points of Schooles, and not fitt for vulgar capacity, but disputable on both sides."

> 5. "That they use no innovation in doctrine, but teach the same thinges which were taught twentie or thirtie yeares past in their owne Churches: And espetially that which contradicteth not their owne Confessions so long since published and knowne unto the world."

---

[74] Milton, *The British Delegation and the Synod of Dort*, 155 (4/4).

[75] Milton, introduction to *The British Delegation and the Synod of Dort*, xxviii, lii; see also ibid., 155 (4/4).

[76] Milton, *The British Delegation and the Synod of Dort*, 157 (4/5).

6. "That they conforme themselves to the publick Confessions of the Neighbour reformed Churches, with whom to hold good correspondence…"

7. "That if their be manie oppositions betweene any who are overmuch addicted to their owne opinions, your endeavor shall be that certaine positions be moderatly layd downe, which may tend to the mitigation of heat on both sides."

8. "That as you principally looke to Gods glory, and the peace of those distracted Churches, so you have an eye to our honour…and at all times consult with our Ambassador…"

9. "…in all other thinges which wee cannot forsee yow shall carry your selves with that advise, moderacion & discretion, as to persons of your quality and gravity shall appertaine."[77]

From the National Synod of France were delegated four men, the celebrated Pierre Du Moulin (1568–1658), who had taught at Leiden from 1592 to 1598 before returning home as minister of Charenton and chaplain to Catherine de Bourbon; André Rivet (1572–1651), who was minister of Thouars at the time of the synod and would become professor at Leiden afterward; the Geneva-educated Jean Chauve, who at the time was minister of Sommieres; and finally Daniel Chamier (1565–1621), also trained at Geneva and minister and professor at Montauban. These four men, in fact, had already been delegated by the National Synod of 1617 held in Vitré to a commission tasked with bringing about a decade-and-a-half-long desire for an international synod to unify the Reformed churches and then the Reformed and Lutherans.[78] Five different meetings between the Dutch ambassador to the French Court and Louis XIII seemed to be successful until the king ultimately reneged. While Du Moulin and Rivet awaited approval to

---

[77] Milton, *The British Delegation and the Synod of Dort*, 93–94 (2/9).

[78] Karin Maag, "Impact amid Absence: The Synod of Dordt and the French Huguenots," *In die Skriflig* 52, no. 2 (2018): a2340, https://doi.org/10.4102/ids.v52i2.2340, see pp. 2–3; Donald Sinnema, "The French Reformed Churches, Arminianism, and the Synod of Dort (1618–1619)," in *The Theology of the French Reformed Churches: From Henri IV to the Revocation of the Edict of Nantes*, ed. Martin I. Klauber (Grand Rapids, MI: Reformation Heritage Books, 2014), 100–102.

travel in Paris, Chamier and Chauve were notified in Geneva while traveling that they couldn't attend because they wouldn't be allowed back into France.[79] Du Moulin, in fact, wrote in his autobiography, "I had already made my pack to go to Dordrecht, when an officer of the Council of the king was sent to me, who prohibited me, on penalty of death, from leaving the realm; it was necessary to obey."[80] In lieu of their presence, the French sent their advice via letters and treatises. As late as December 20, 1618, Ambassador Carleton spoke of them being "daily expected."[81] Only a week later he reported that "those which were now on the way being returned to their homes upon new inhibition from the King, which they mett with at Geneva."[82] In their honor an empty set of benches stood between the British and the Palatinate and above where the Brandenburg delegates were to sit.

From Brandenburg Margrave Georg Wilhelm delegated two men: Johannes Bergius (1587–1658), professor at Frankfurt an der Oder, and Christoph Pelargus (1565–1633; also known as Storch), also professor at Frankfurt and general superintendent of the region known as the Mark of Brandenburg. On January 10, 1619, though, Georg wrote that Pelargus was ill and he did not want to press an already tense relationship with his Lutheran neighbors that surrounded Brandenburg. Their bench was left vacant just in front of the empty French bench.

From the Palatinate was sent Drs. Abraham Scultetus (1566–1625), minister and professor at Heidelberg, and the royal chaplain, Johann Heinrich Alting (1583–1644), professor at Heidelberg and inspector of the *Collegium Sapientiae*, and in place of the aged and most eminent of the Palatinate's theologians, Dr. David Paraeus (1548–1622), who still was able to correspond with the synod,[83] Paul Tossanus (1572–1634), minister in Heidelberg and councilor in the ecclesiastical Senate of the Palatinate.

---

[79] Milton, introduction to *The British Delegation and the Synod of Dort*, 156n25; Maag, "Impact amid Absence," 3–4.

[80] Sinnema, "The French Reformed Churches, Arminianism, and the Synod of Dort (1618–1619)," 108.

[81] Milton, *The British Delegation and the Synod of Dort*, 150 (4/2).

[82] Milton, *The British Delegation and the Synod of Dort*, 156 (4/4).

[83] His review of the five points of the Remonstrants was sent to the synod and later published as "Epitome of Arminianisme: or, The Examination of the Five Articles of the Remonstrants, in the Netherlands," in *The Summe of Christian Religion, Delivered by Zacharias Ursinus*, trans. A. R. (London, Printed by James Young, 1645), 817–44.

From Hesse were sent Dr. Georg Cruciger (1575–1634), rector and professor of logic at the Marburg Academy; Paul Stein (1585–1643), former court chaplain and at the time of the synod dean and professor of theology at Collegium Adelphicum Mauritianum at Cassel; Daniel Angelocrator (1569–1635), archdeacon of Marburg and superintendent of the churches in Upper Hessia along the Laen and Eder Rivers; and finally the eldest member of the synod, Rudolph Goclenius the Elder (1547–1628), who was seventy-one when the synod began. He had served as professor of physics, logic, mathematics, and ethics at the Marburg Academy since 1581.

From the four Swiss Republics were sent Johann Jakob Breitinger (1575–1645), "Antistes" or chief preacher of the Grossmünster of "Great Church" of Zurich; Sebastian Beck (1583–1654), professor of Old Testament and then New Testament in Basel; Wolfgang Mayer (1577–1653), minister of St. Alban's Church and professor of dogmatics in Basle; Markus Rütimeyer (1580–1647), rector of the Berne Academy; and Johann Konrad Koch (1564–1643), minister of the Schaffhausen Cathedral.

From the churches of Nassau-Wetteravia Duke John of Nassau sent Johannes Bisterfeld, rector and professor of theology at the University of Siegen. He was also the only foreign delegate to die at the synod on January 18, 1619. Duke John also sent Johann Heinrich Alsted (1588–1638), professor of theology at Herborn. When Bisterfeld died, Georg Fabricius, minister at Windecken, took his seat.

From the Republic of Geneva were sent two ministers and professors: the well-known Jean (Giovanni) Diodati (1576–1649), pastor and successor to Theodore Beza, and the lesser-known Théodore Tronchin (1582–1657), pastor and professor of theology.[84] The advice of the Company of Pastors was that they make known the sentiment of the Genevan Church, promise not to demean the names of John Calvin or Theodore Beza, nor were they authorized to accept a new confession of faith.[85] Although such a clear charge was given, implementing it wasn't always so easy, as Diodati com-

---

[84] On this delegation, see Fornerod, "'The Canons of the Synod Had Shot Off the Advocate's Head,'" 181–215; William A. McComish, *The Epigones: A Study of the Theology of the Genevan Academy at the Time of the Synod of Dort, with Special Reference to Giovanni Diodati*, Princeton Theological Monograph Series 13 (Eugene, OR: Pickwick, 1989).

[85] Fornerod, "'The Canons of the Synod Had Shot Off the Advocate's Head,'" 194.

plained in letters that Tronchin did not collaborate nor do his fair share of work.[86]

From the Republic of Bremen were sent Matthias Martinius (1572–1630), rector and professor of the *Gymnasium Illustre* ("Illustrious School"); Heinrich Isselburg (1577–1628), minister of Church of the Virgin Mary and professor of theology; and Ludwig Crocius (1586–1653), minister of St. Martin Church and professor of Old Testament and philosophy.

From the Republic of East Frisia (aka *Emden*) were sent Daniel Eilshemius (1555–1622), the oldest minister of Emden, whose son was a delegate from the Synod of Friesland, and Ritzius Lucas Grimersheim (1568–1631), minister of Emden.

The States General paid for the entire cost of the foreign delegates including supplies: each desk was covered in green cloth, had inkwells, sand-pots, paper, pens, and during winter a foot-warmer (*stoofie*) filled with glowing clay for each member.[87] Many candles and three great chandeliers illuminated the *kloveniersdoelen,* and during the winter a continual fire was kept. There were two large galleries, which could hold up to five hundred people interested in observing this gathering of celebrities. The cost was so great that a Remonstrant quipped that each canon written at Dort cost one ton of gold.[88] The high profile of this synod internationally is exemplified in the self-proclaimed prophetess Anna Walker, who traveled from England to Dordrecht because she claimed the Holy Spirit sent her to speak about predestination.[89] For ease of organization, the work of the synod is divided up into several sections.

The *opening ceremony* of the synod occurred on Monday November 12 with prayer services in Dutch by Dordrecht pastor Balthasar Lydius and in French by Middleburg pastor Jeremias de Pours. The first session was Tuesday morning, November 13. It opened with a speech and prayer by

---

[86] Fornerod, "'The Canons of the Synod Had Shot Off the Advocate's Head,'" 193.

[87] On the practical issues of housing the delegates and paying for the synod, see van Lieburg, *The Synod of Dordrecht 1618–1619,* 12–21. On issues with lodging, see Milton, *The British Delegation and the Synod of Dort,* 107n7 (3/1).

[88] Van Lieburg, *The Synod of Dordrecht 1618–1619,* 19.

[89] Jürgen Beyer and Leigh T. I. Penman, "The Petitions of 'A Supposed Prophetesse': The Lübeck Letters of Anna Walker and Their Significance for the Synod of Dordt. A Linguistic and Contextual Analysis," in Goudriaan and van Lieburg, *Revisiting the Synod of Dordt,* 107–33.

Lydius[90] then another speech by Martinus Gregorii on behalf of the States General. The elected president of the synod was Bogerman, who made the public vow, "I will use no human writing, but only the word of God, which is an infallible rule of faith...I will only aim at the glory of God, the peace of the Church, and especially the preservation of the purity of doctrine."[91] This is echoed in the preface to the canons when it says the synod itself was

> fired with the love of God and for the salvation of the church, and after having invoked the name of God, having bound itself by a sacred oath that it would take the Holy Scriptures alone as the rule of judgment, and engage in the examination and decision of this cause with a good and upright conscience.[92]

Bogerman's personal theological advisor was the exiled English Puritan and anti-Remonstrant polemicist, William Ames (1576–1633). The synod's two vice presidents were Jacobus Rolandus (1562–1632) and Hermannus Faukelius (1560–1625). The two secretaries were Festus Hommius (1576–1642) and Sebastianus Dammannus (1578–1640).

The *pro-acta* ("before the acts") took place from November 14, 1618, to December 5, 1619, while the synod awaited the late-arriving Remonstrants who were meeting privately in Rotter-

Johannes Bogerman

---

[90] For the Latin text see *Early Sessions of the Synod of Dort: Acta et Documenta Synodi Nationalis Dordrechtanae (1618–1619): Volume II/2*, ed. Donald Sinnema, Christian Moser, and Herman J. Selderhuis (Göttingen, Germany: Vandenhoeck & Ruprecht, 2018), 4–8. For an English translation see Douglas J. Kuiper and H. David Schuringa, "Prayer of Balthasar Lydius," *Protestant Reformed Theologica Journal* 52, no. 1 (November 2018): 3–18.

[91] Fred H. Klooster, "The Doctrinal Deliverances of Dort," in De Jong, *Crisis in the Reformed Churches*, 57.

[92] *The Articles of the Synod of Dort*, trans. Thomas Scott (Philadelphia: Presbyterian Board of Publication, 1856), 172.

dam as a countersynod to strategize since, in a sense, they were predestined to lose.[93] During this time the synod dealt with catechism instruction,[94] preparation for the ministry, the baptism of slaves throughout the Dutch colonies, book censorship, and a new Dutch Bible translation. The result of this translation work was the *Statenbijbel* of 1637.[95]

The *acta* ("acts") dealt with the main issue. Once the Remonstrants arrived, they were present from December 6, 1618, to January 14, 1619. Their strategy was an attempt to divide and conquer by beginning discussion with reprobation, the most controversial topic between the delegations.[96] And when a full frontal assault was ineffective, they used delay tactics, eliciting from Ambassador Carleton: "the Remonstrants have bin remorantes [delaying]."[97] Their leader, Simon Episcopius (1583–1643), gave several long speeches including the argument that the synod had no right to judge. The irony was not lost on Bogerman who reminded them the synod had been convened by the States General, which they believed was the highest authority in church matters![98] Seeing that the proceedings were being bogged down, on January 1, 1619, the States General stated that if the Remonstrants would not cooperate with the synod, then their doctrines would be judged on the basis of published writings.[99] On January 3 a committee met to decide how to implement this decision. The result was a series of theses drawn up from Remonstrant writings.[100] When Ambassador

---

[93] John R. de Witt, "The Arminian Conflict and the Synod of Dort," in *Puritan Papers: Volume 5, 1968–1969*, ed. J. I. Packer (Phillipsburg, NJ: P&R, 2005), 16; Muller, "Arminius and Arminianism," 35.

[94] See Daniel R. Hyde, "The Principle and Practice of Preaching in the Heidelberg Catechism," *Puritan Reformed Journal* 1, no. 1 (January 2009): 97–117.

[95] See Marten H. Woudstra, "The Synod and Bible Translation," in De Jong, *Crisis in the Reformed Churches*, 95–114. An English translation of this version as well as its marginal notes can be found in *The Dutch annotations upon the whole Bible, or, All the holy canonical scriptures of the Old and New Testament*, trans. Theodore Haak (London: Printed by Henry Hills, 1657). It is available via http://eebo.chadwyck.com.

[96] Milton, *The British Delegation and the Synod of Dort*, 166 (4/11).

[97] Milton, *The British Delegation and the Synod of Dort*, 189 (4/19).

[98] See also Milton, introduction to *The British Delegation and the Synod of Dort*, xxvi.

[99] Cited in Donald W. Sinnema, "The Canons of Dordt: From Judgment on Arminianism to Confessional Standard," in Goudriaan and van Lieburg, *Revisiting the Synod of Dordt*, 314.

[100] Milton, *The British Delegation and the Synod of Dort*, 173–76 (4/13); Sinnema, "The Canons of Dordt," 314–15.

Carleton sent these back to England to keep the king informed, Archbishop George Abbot (1562–1633) replied:

> I stand amazed at their absurdnesse…for they make a hotch-potch of religion, borrowing some few things from some few Lutherans, but many things from the Papists, the Semi-pelagians and the Pelagians themselves. And it is certain true that they are not learned nor acquainted with the antiquityes of the Church.

He even reported that King James himself was "marvelously inflamed against these graceless positions."[101]

With the synod seemingly getting nowhere, President Bogerman famously ordered them out on January 14, 1619, with the words *Dimmittimini, Exite*, "You are dismissed! Get out now!" Ambassador Carleton remarked that while this was a right course of action, "yet the manner of their dismission is very ruffe and uncivill."[102] This, as well as other reasons, has led to the synod being caricatured and vilified throughout history as prejudicial.[103] Recently, though, this picture has begun to be reassessed not only theologically but also politically.[104]

Without the Remonstrants, the *acta* continued from January 15, 1619, to May 12, 1619. The Remonstrants continued playing a role by answering questions in writing while the various delegations were divided as "colleges" with each writing their own response to the five points of the Remonstrants. After this there was a three-week "shadowy period" without public sessions from March 25, 1619, to April 16, 1619, as the drafting committee worked to produce the canons.[105] The committee was made up of three foreign delegates (Bishop Carleton, Diodati, Scultetus), three Dutch theologians (Polyander, Trigland, Walaeus), the president (Bogerman), and the

---

[101] Milton, *The British Delegation and the Synod of Dort*, 183 (4/16).

[102] Milton, *The British Delegation and the Synod of Dort*, 185 (4/17). See also ibid., 190 (4/20).

[103] See the comments of the Arminian historian, Brandt, *The History of the Reformation*, 3:152–54. For the Lutheran response, see Nicolaus Hunnius, *Diaskepsis theologica: A Theological Examination of the Fundamental Difference between Evangelical Lutheran Doctrine and Calvinist or Reformed Teaching*, trans. Richard J. Dinda and Elmer Hohle (1999; repr., Malone, TX: Repristination, 2001).

[104] See the already cited Goudriaan and van Lieburg, *Revisiting the Synod of Dordt*.

[105] Milton, *The British Delegation and the Synod of Dort*, 296.

two vice presidents (Faukelius, Rolandus).[106] They worked over eight hours a day for these three weeks.[107] On April 26, 1619, the canons were presented to the States General. On May 6, 1619, the delegates processed down the street to the Grote Kerk ("Great Church") of Dordrecht for a public reading of the canons aloud in Dutch. Each signatory's name was read, after which each tipped his hat.[108]

Finally the *post-acta* ("after acts") took place from May 13, 1619, to May 29, 1619. While synod reconvened, Oldenbarnevelt was beheaded by the States General. This session dealt with standardizing the Dutch Church Order and its existing confessions—the Belgic Confession and Heidelberg Catechism—and internal issues such as Sabbath observance.[109] In total, there were 180 half-day sessions.[110]

THE CANONS, OR THERE'S NO SUCH THING AS "THE FIVE POINTS OF CALVINISM"

This decades-long strife in the Netherlands led to the synod's greatest work, the canons. There are several main things I want to communicate about the canons. Foremost is that it was the Remonstrants who put forward *five* points; the synod responded with counterpoints. This means that what Reformed churches believe is *not* summarized in the Canons of Dort or in their modern overly simplified acronym, TULIP (total depravity; unconditional election; limited atonement; irresistible grace; perseverance of the saints).[111] This acronym is a product of the early twentieth century,[112] reor-

---

[106] On the debate of whether to have such a committee, see Donald W. Sinnema, "The Drafting of the Canons of Dordt: A Preliminary Survey of Early Drafts and Related Documents," in Goudriaan and van Lieburg, *Revisiting the Synod of Dordt*, 297–98.

[107] Sinnema, "The Drafting of the Canons," 299.

[108] Cited in Sinnema, "The Canons of Dordt," 325.

[109] See Daniel R. Hyde, "*Regulae de Observatione Sabbathi*: The Synod of Dort's (1618–19) Deliverance on the Sabbath." *Puritan Reformed Journal* 4, no. 1 (January 2012): 161–83.

[110] On the recording of the Acts of Synod, see Donald Sinnema, "Introduction to the Acta Authentica, Acta Contracta and Printed Acta," in *Acta of the Synod of Dordt*, xxxix–lii.

[111] De Witt, "The Arminian Conflict and the Synod of Dort," 22–23.

ders the actual points of both the Remonstrants and response in the canons, plus it would have been impossible to come up with since the Dutch word for tulip is *tulp*.[113] According to Richard Muller:

> Just as it is improper, however, to identify Calvin as the sole progenitor of Reformed theology, so also is it incorrect to identify the five points or the document from which they have been drawn, the Canons of Dort, as a full confession of the Reformed faith, whole and entire unto itself. In other words, it would be a major error—both historically and doctrinally—if the five points of Calvinism were understood either as the sole or even as the absolutely primary basis for identifying someone as holding the Calvinistic or Reformed faith. In fact, the Canons of Dort contain five points only because the Arminian articles, the Remonstrance of 1610, to which they responded, had five points. The number five, far from being sacrosanct, is the result of a particular historical circumstance and was determined negatively by the number of articles in the Arminian objection to confessional Calvinism.[114]

Reflecting on Festus Hommius's (1576–1642) summary *Specimen controversiarum Belgicarum*,[115] intended for delegates on the eve of the synod, Aza Goudriaan explained: "The notion that the whole controversy was about nothing other than these five particular issues was rather, Hommius argued, an inadequate Arminian description of what was actually going on."[116]

---

[112] For the documentary evidence, see Kenneth J. Stewart, *Ten Myths about Calvinism: Recovering the Breadth of the Reformed Tradition* (Downers Grove, IL: IVP Academic, 2011), 291–92.

[113] Richard A. Muller, "Was Calvin a Calvinist? Or, Did Calvin (or Anyone Else in the Early Modern Era) Plant the 'TULIP'?" As found at https://www.calvin.edu/meeter/Was%20Calvin%20a%20Calvinist-12-26-09.pdf (accessed April 6, 2018). See also Selderhuis, "Introduction to the Synod of Dordt," in *Acta of the Synod of Dordt*, xxxi.

[114] Richard Muller, "How Many Points?" *Calvin Theological Journal* 28, no. 2 (November 1993): 426.

[115] Festus Hommius, *Specimen controversiarum Belgicarum* (Leiden, 1618). Available at https://books.google.com/books?id=1HhJAAAAcAAJ&printsec=frontcover#v=onepage&q&f=false (accessed July 25, 2018).

[116] Aza Goudriaan, "The Synod of Dordt on Arminian Anthropology," in Goudriaan and van Lieburg, *Revisiting the Synod of Dordt*, 81.

What Reformed churches in the Dutch tradition believe is most fully confessed in the thirty-seven articles of the Belgic Confession and 129 questions and answers of the Heidelberg Catechism.[117] Before Dort there was "166-point Calvinism"; after Dort added its ninety-three articles and rejections there is "259-point Calvinism." And we think being a "five-pointer" is really flexing some theological muscle! Again, Muller says:

> There are, therefore, more than five points and—as far as the confessions and the Reformed dogmaticians from Calvin to Kuyper are concerned—there cannot be such a thing as a "five-point Calvinist" or "five-point Reformed Christian" who owns just those five articles taken from the Canons of Dort and who refuses to accept the other "points" made by genuinely Reformed theology.[118]

A second main thing is that contrary to popular belief, the canons are a moderate and mediating document meant to unify. Late into the twentieth century the prevailing interpretation of the Reformation was that it was perverted by the Post-Reformation. In relation to the Synod of Dort we find statements like "the Synod of Dort in 1619 where the *extreme form of scholastic 'Calvinism'* was achieved in the Five Articles which *broke the unity of Calvin's theology* and *replaced his biblical dynamism by formulae.*"[119] Another example from this era of scholarship said, "The hyper-Calvinist majority at Dort skewed Reformed theology in a scholastic direction by their dependence on Aristotelian notions of causality, by making predestination the central doctrine to be defended in Reformed Christendom."[120] The sources and best research, however, show that the unity of doctrine at Dort allowed diverse ways of expression.[121] Nicolas Fornerod said the canons were:

---

[117] On the subject of historic Protestant churches being confessional churches, see Daniel R. Hyde, *The Good Confession: An Exploration of the Christian Faith* (Eugene, OR: Wipf & Stock, 2006), 7–28, and *Welcome to a Reformed Church: A Guide for Pilgrims* (Orlando, FL: Reformation Trust, 2010), 1–34.

[118] Muller, "How Many Points?" 427.

[119] Basil Hall, "Calvin against the Calvinists," in *John Calvin*, ed. G. E. Duffield (Grand Rapids, MI: Eerdmans, 1968), 28. Emphasis mine.

[120] Jack Rogers and Donald McKim, *The Authority and Interpretation of the Bible: An Historical Approach* (San Francisco: Harper and Row, 1979), 164.

[121] One example on the particular issue of "scholasticism" is Donald Sinnema, "Reformed Scholasticism and the Synod of Dort (1618–19)," in *John Calvin's Institutes:*

the expression of a laborious theological compromise worked out between the various Calvinist traditions represented at Dordt, and not simply the triumph of the most rigid forms of Dutch Contra-Remonstrant thought achieved with the backing of the most doctrinaire foreign delegations, notably Geneva's.[122]

A third main thing is that the canons were written as much as possible in a nonscholastic manner intended to edify believers. By scholastic (*scholasticus*) was meant a mode of teaching appropriate for theological debate and instruction in schools in contrast to how it was to be taught and preached in the church.[123] This is contrary to the opinion of the well-known nineteenth-century Reformed historian Philip Schaff, who said the canons "prepared the way for a dry scholasticism which runs into subtle abstractions, and resolves the living soul of divinity into a skeleton of formulas and distinctions."[124] The aforementioned committee that met on January 3, 1619, envisioned a document being drawn up in which the Remonstrants' five articles would be "solidly and vigorously treated at the capacity of the church, and in which it would be shown to the whole church that the Synod had kept far clear of strange and blasphemous doctrines and does not approve of the hard sayings of some Doctors."[125] Several foreign delegations emphasized this as well. Then on January 4, 1619, a letter arrived from the leader of the French Huguenots, Philip DuPlessis Mornay (1549–1623),

---

His Opus Magnum, ed. B. J. Van de Walt (Potchefstroom, South Africa: Potchefstroom University for Christian Higher Education, 1986).

[122] Fornerod, "'The Canons of the Synod," 183. See also Lee Gatiss, *For Us and for Our Salvation: "Limited Atonement" in the Bible, Doctrine, History, and Ministry* (London: Latimer Trust, 2012), 78; Godfrey, "Did the Canons Misfire?," 20. On the overall theme of diversity within the unity of Reformed theology, see *Drawn into Controversie: Reformed Theological Diversity with Seventeenth-Century British Puritanism*, ed. Michael A. G. Haykin and Mark Jones (Göttingen, Germany: Vandenhoeck & Ruprecht, 2011).

[123] On this distinction, see Sinnema, "Reformed Scholasticism and the Synod of Dort," 472–73; "The Distinction between Scholastic and Popular: Andreas Hyperius and Reformed Scholasticism," in *Protestant Scholasticism: Essays in Reassessment*, ed. Carl R. Trueman and R. S. Clark (Carlisle, UK: Paternoster, 1999), 127–43.

[124] *The Creeds of Christendom*, ed. Philip Schaff, rev. David S. Schaff, 3 vols. (1931; repr., Grand Rapids, MI: Baker Books, 1993), 1:515.

[125] Cited in Sinnema, "The Canons of Dort," 315. For Diodati's urging in this later at the synod, see Fornerod, "'The Canons of the Synod,'" 206.

advising a scriptural mode of speaking with succinctness, not subtlety.[126] The Palatinate theologians advised that the synod "draw up in the Dutch idiom some popular, moderate writing, appropriate for edification and peace...to be published for the use of the church."[127] The delegates from Hesse advised similarly, adding that synod's response be "constructed as much as possible from the very words of Scripture."[128] As we saw in King James's instructions to his delegates above, The British delegation also made this same recommendation.[129] President Bogerman went on to state the distinction clearly: the canons should not be scholastic but ecclesiastical.[130] While the delegates were thoroughly versed in Reformed orthodox scholasticism, they were also churchmen.[131]

At the same time, the canons were drafted *as much as possible* this way. This doesn't mean there were no academic issues addressed or mentioned. In theological schools the categories of fourfold causation were utilized to clearly define and expound doctrine: efficient cause (the author of something), material cause (the matter of something), formal cause (the form of something), and the final cause (the end or goal of something).[132] This language, either explicit or implicit, was impossible to avoid completely. Canon 1.5 speaks of "the *cause* or blame for this unbelief." Canon 1.6 says those

---

[126] Cited in Sinnema, "The Canons of Dort," 315.

[127] Cited in Sinnema, "The Canons of Dort," 316. At the end of their judgment (*judicium*) concerning the Remonstrants' teachings they even inserted an appendix on teaching predestination popularly: *modus docendi populariter doctrinam de Praedestinatione* ("The manner of teaching the doctrine of Predestination popularly"). Cited in W. Robert Godfrey, "Popular and Catholic: The *Modus Docendi* of the Canons of Dordt," in Goudriaan and van Lieburg, *Revisiting the Synod of Dordt*, 246. The Swiss simply advised a judgment "at the capacity of the church."

[128] Cited in Sinnema, "The Canons of Dort," 316.

[129] Sinnema, "The Drafting of the Canons," 296; "Reformed Scholasticism and the Synod of Dort," 476–77.

[130] Sinnema, "The Drafting of the Canons," 295–96. His fellow Netherlanders advised the same. From the Zeeland delegation came the advice to treat everything "at the capacity of the people and for the common use of the Church" while the Utrecht delegates called for a document that "the uneducated may be instructed." Cited in Sinnema, "The Canons of Dort," 317.

[131] On the use of "scholasticism" in service to the churches at Dort, see Andreas J. Beck, "Reformed Confessions and Scholasticism: Diversity and Harmony." *Perichoresis* 14, no. 3 (2016): 17–43.

[132] See Sinnema, "Reformed Scholasticism and the Synod of Dort," 499–500.

who "receive from God the gift of faith within time…stems (*provenit*; proceeds) from [God's] eternal decision." In other words, the cause of faith is God's eternal decree. Canon1.7 defines election in terms of its subordinate final cause being our salvation and its ultimate final cause being God's own glory. Canon 1.9 denies there are prerequisites in us that cause election; instead, faith and holiness are effects of election. Canon 1.15 denies God is the "author" or cause of sin. Canon 2.9 speaks of God's plan being "powerfully carried out," meaning, its effectual cause. Canon 3/4.14 says God "produces (*efficiat*; effects) in man both the will to believe and the belief itself." Canon 3/4.17 says God brings forth supernatural life in us by the use of the means of his Word as instrumental cause.[133]

A fourth point to stress is the catholicity of the canons. In the words of Seán F. Hughes, "Virtually every Christian tradition in this period, including the Roman Catholic and Eastern Orthodox Churches, had profound debates on the doctrine of grace."[134] Concerning the so-called five points of Calvinism debated prior to and settled at Dort, "the theological issues underlying them are not exclusively 'Calvinist' and comparable ideas can be found in many other Christian traditions."[135] As I mentioned above, each chapter below on the positive articles of the Canons of Dort, therefore, trace the history of Western catholicity on the doctrine at hand to show how the canons are "mainstream." The Palatinate delegates even advised the synod to form their response like ancient church councils had done so in writing brief and vigorous canons.[136] The benefit of emphasizing this catholicity is expressed by the Dutch theologian Arnold Huijgen: "The Reformed world has not always been an example of this catholic spirit that could bridge major theological differences."[137]

One last main thing is how the canons are structured. Each point or "head" (*caput*) of doctrine contains several positive articles of what is con-

---

[133] On causality in the Canons, see Sinnema, "Reformed Scholasticism and the Synod of Dort," 499–504.

[134] Seán F. Hughes, "The Problem of 'Calvinism': English Theologies of Predestination c. 1580–1630," in *Belief and Practice in Reformation England: A Tribute to Patrick Collinson by his Students*, ed. Susan Wabuda and C. J. Litzenberger, St. Andrews Studies in Reformation History (Aldershot, UK: Ashgate 1988), 232.

[135] Hughes, "The Problem of 'Calvinism,'" 233.

[136] Cited in Sinnema, "The Canons of Dort," 316.

[137] Arnold Huijgen, "The Theology of the Canons of Dort: A Reassessment after Four Hundred Years." *Unio Cum Christo* 4, no. 2 (October 2018): 116.

fessed and then several rejections of errors.[138] At the beginning of the positive articles in each point are several catholic consensus doctrinal points (1.1–4; 2.1–7; 3/4.1–2, 4–5; 5.1–2) then one article that defines the doctrine at hand (1.7; 2.8; 3/4.3, 6; 5.3).[139] Within the articles of each point, the implications of the theological issues are drawn out concerning God's justice and the fault of sin, the responsibility of man in salvation, assurance of faith, godliness, and the importance of the means of grace.[140]

THE FIGHT THEN, THE FIGHT NOW

Recounting this struggle above, I don't intend for you to now look at the canons like you would a museum piece. Paul's fight against the neonomians and antinomians, Augustine's fight with Pelagius, Luther's fight with Rome, and the canons' fight with the Arminians continues. Schaff said, "The Arminian controversy is the most important which took place within the Reformed Church," and should at least be important to us four hundred years later.[141]

We need the canons in our fight to preserve and propagate a pristine doctrine of God's grace in the salvation of sinners like you and me. Here we are plunged to the depths of depravity then raised to behold the eternal love of God. Here we are taken to the cross where we bow before the satisfaction made for us but then arise because it is so sufficient that we must promiscuously publish its news to all tribes, in every nation, on every continent. Here we experience the uncontrollable power of the Holy Spirit (John 3) efficaciously applying the infinite merit of the Son of God to the hearts of sinners like us. Here we feel the pain and struggle that comes with being Christian, loved by the Father but struggling to love, buried with Christ but constantly digging up our sins, filled with the Holy Spirit but being led astray by our own passions. Yet God the triune God is powerful to preserve us in his loving arms and to bring us to the Celestial City.

---

[138] See appendix 1.

[139] Godfrey, "Popular and Catholic," 257–60.

[140] Godfrey, "Popular and Catholic," 253–57.

[141] Schaff, *Creeds*, 1:509.

We need the canons in our fight because they echo the Holy Spirit's voice, being saturated article after article with the language of his inspired Scriptures proclaiming to us what it means to be saved by grace.[142]

We need the canons in our fight because unlike any other historic creed or confession, they pastorally apply Scripture to some of the most pressing problems in the Christian life: assurance of salvation (1.12–13, 16; 5.9–13), being simultaneously justified yet sinful (5.1, 4–6), the death of infants of believers (1.17), the weekly reception of the means of grace (1.14; 2.5; 3/4.8–9, 17; 5.10, 14), and the imperative of Christian holiness (1.18; 5.12).

We need the canons in our fight because they are the production of the first and last ecumenical Reformed synod.[143] Philip Schaff called Dort "the only Synod of a quasi-œcumenical character in the history of the Reformed Churches. In this respect it is even more important than the Westminster Assembly of Divines, which was confined to England and Scotland, although it produced superior doctrinal standards."[144] As an international synod, "the Synod of Dort functioned as an ecumenical Reformed council in a way that no Reformed gathering has before or since. The Canons of Dort therefore are not a Dutch production, but they represent an ecumenical consensus of the best minds in the whole Reformed community."[145] After the synod, when the Reformed church in France had its own struggles of issues of grace, it made the canons binding upon all its ministers at its twenty-third National Synod at Alais (1620) and again at its twenty-fourth Synod at Charenton (1623). Everywhere else they were at a minimum initially received with respect.[146] This international Reformed theology of the

---

[142] As a confession of faith, the canons are not *formally* the rule of faith, but because they exhibit the Word *materially*, they are a confession of true faith. Bernardinus De Moor, *Continuous Commentary on Johannes Marckius' Didactico-Elenctic Compendium of Christian Theology*, 1.32, trans. Steven Dilday. As cited at http://www.bernardinusdemoor.com/?p=377 (accessed November 27, 2013).

[143] Contrary to the opinion of Homer C. Hoeksema, who argued it was not ecumenical. *The Voice of Our Fathers: An Exposition of the Canons of Dordrecht* (Grand Rapids, MI: Reformed Free Publishing Association, 1980), 20–21.

[144] Schaff, *Creeds*, 1:514.

[145] Godfrey, "Did the Canons Misfire?," 19. See also "Calvin and Calvinism in the Netherlands," 107.

[146] Schaff, *Creeds*, 1:514. On the debates after the synod in England over whether the canons were binding, see Milton, *The British Delegation and the Synod of Dort*, 381–

early seventeenth century was expressed via a "diversity of views within a churchly consensus [that] produced at Dort a document which was far from extreme and quite representative of the Reformed theology of its day."[147] Afterward, Dr. John Jacob Breitinger of Zurich said that if ever the Holy Spirit was present in a council, he was present at Dort. Whenever Wolfgang Meyer of Basle would afterward speak of the synod, he uncovered his head and exclaimed, *Sacrosancta Synodus!*[148] Of this synod, the English Puritan John Owen (1616–1683) said, "The divines of that assembly…were esteemed of the best that all the reformed churches of Europe (that of France excepted) could afford."[149] After the synod concluded, the States General of the Netherlands desired to continue strengthening the networks of Reformed principalities throughout Europe by sending printed copies of the Acts of Synod to their sovereigns.[150]

We need the canons in our fight in our day and age of creedless Christianity. Over one hundred years ago, J. C. Ryle prophetically spoke of our day:

> The tendency of modern thought is to reject dogmas, creeds and every kind of bounds in religion. It is thought grand and wise to condemn no opinion whatsoever, and to pronounce all earnest and clever teachers to be trustworthy, however heterogeneous and mutually destructive their opinions may be. Everything forsooth is true, and nothing

---

402; Jay T. Collier, *Debating Perseverance: The Augustinian Heritage in Post-Reformation England* (Oxford: Oxford University Press, 2018).

[147] Muller, "Arminius and Arminianism," 35.

[148] Schaff, *Creeds*, 1:514–15.

[149] John Owen, "The Nature of Apostasy from the Profession of the Gospel and the Punishment of Apostates Declared," in *The Works of John Owen*, ed. William H. Goold, 16 vols. (1850–1853; repr., Edinburgh: Banner of Truth, fifth printing 1993), 7:74. See also Richard Baxter, *Reliquiae Baxterianae* (London, 1696), 1.73; William Cunningham, *The Reformers: And the Theology of the Reformation*, Collected Works: Volume 1 (Edinburgh: T&T Clark, 1862), 367.

[150] Janika Bischof, "The Printed *Acta Synodi Nationalis Dordrechti* as a Networking Tool," in *Material Moments in Book Cultures: Essays in Honour of Gabriele Müller-Oberhäuser*, ed. Simon Rosenberg and Sandra Simon (Frankfurt am Main: Peter Lang, 2014), 177–87.

is false! Everybody is right and nobody is wrong! Everybody is likely to be saved and nobody is to be lost![151]

We need the Canons of Dort because grace is worth fighting for. As the delegates who traveled from Geneva explained:

> What is this other than a disparagement of the glory due God in free election, of the praise due to Christ for redemption, and of the power of the Holy Spirit in conversion? It is also a weakening of Christian comfort in life and death and a tearing up of the certainty of our salvation. Finally it is an enervating of filial fear and trust in the hearts of believers. Rather it inflames the pride of man against God, so that he glories not in God or in Christ, but in himself.[152]

---

[151] J. C. Ryle, *Holiness: Its Nature, Hindrances, Difficulties, & Roots* (1879; repr., Moscow, ID: Charles Nolan, 2001), 13.

[152] Cited in Godfrey, "Popular and Catholic," 243–44. See also Cornelis P. Venema, *But for the Grace of God: An Exposition of the Canons of Dort* (Grand Rapids, MI: Reformed Fellowship, 1994), 17.

OUTLINE OF THE CANONS OF DORT

I. **First Point of Doctrine: Redemption Planned**
   A. *Common Christian Convictions (arts. 1–6)*
      1. Humanity's sin and condemnation (art. 1)
      2. God's love in Christ (art. 2)
      3. God's mercy in preaching (art. 3; cf. RE 9)
      4. Faith in Christ delivers from condemnation (art. 4)
      5. Humanity is guilty for unbelief (art. 5)
      6. Faith is given according to God's plan (art. 6; cf. RE 8)
   B. *Election Defined (art. 7; cf. RE 1, 9)*
   C. *Elaborations on Election (arts. 8–11)*
      1. One kind of election, not many (art. 8; cf. RE 2)
      2. Not based on foreseen qualities (art. 9; cf. RE 4, 5)
      3. Persons, not conditions (art. 10; cf. RE 3)
      4. Unchangeable (art. 11; cf. RE 6)
   D. *Answers to Alleged Problems Caused by Election (arts. 12–14)*
      1. Attainment of assurance (arts. 12–13; cf. RE 7)
      2. Preaching election (art. 14)
   E. *Reprobation Defined (art. 15)*
   F. *Answers to Alleged Problems Caused by Reprobation (arts. 16–17)*
      1. Reprobation and assurance (art. 16)
      2. Reprobation and children (art. 17)
   G. *Conclusion: Man's Response to God's Revelation (art. 18)*

II. **Second Point of Doctrine: Redemption Accomplished**
   A. *Common Christian Convictions (arts. 1–7)*
      1. God's justice requires satisfaction for sin (art. 1)

2. God gives His Son who alone can provide satisfaction (arts. 2–3)
3. Christ satisfies as God and man (art. 4)
4. Call to believe is to be preached to everyone (art. 5)
5. Cause of unbelief is in unbeliever, not in Christ (art. 6)
6. Christ is cause of faith (art. 7)

B. *Christ's Satisfaction Defined (art. 8; cf. RE 1–5, 7)*

C. *Elaboration on Satisfaction: Christ Will Always Have a Church (art. 9; cf. RE 6)*

III. **Third & Fourth Points of Doctrine: Redemption Applied**

A. *Common Christian Convictions on Depravity (arts. 1–2)*
1. Man was created good, but has become wicked in mind, will and affections (art. 1; cf. RE 2)
2. Original sin from Adam (art. 2; cf. RE 1)

B. *Depravity Defined (art. 3; cf. RE 3, 4)*

C. *Common Christian Convictions on Regeneration (arts. 4–5)*
1. Nature cannot regenerate sinners (art. 4; cf. RE 5)
2. The Law cannot regenerate sinners (art. 5)

D. *Regeneration Defined (art. 6)*

E. *Elaborations on Regeneration (arts. 7–17)*
1. Sovereignly to whom He will (art. 7)
2. Through a sincere call to believe (arts. 8–9)
3. As a gift to the elect (art. 10)
4. Renewing the elect in mind, will and affections (art. 11; cf. RE 6)
5. As a completely efficacious act of God alone (art. 12; cf. RE 7)
6. Ineffably (art. 13)
7. Actually creating faith (art. 14; cf. RE 9)
8. Believers & unbelievers respond differently to regeneration (art. 15)
9. God works faith in a personal way, not a mechanical way (art. 16; cf. RE 8)
10. God works our response through the means of grace (art. 17)

V.   Fifth Point of Doctrine: Redemption Preserved

A. *Common Christian Convictions (arts. 1–2)*
1.   Regeneration does not mean the end of sin or suffering (art. 1)
2.   The regenerate must strive for holiness (art. 2)

B. *Perseverance Defined (art. 3)*

C. *Perseverance and the Continuing Problem of Sin (arts. 4–8)*
1.   Weakness of the flesh can result in serious sins (art. 4; cf. RE 7)
2.   Such sins seriously disturb one's relationship with God (art. 5)
3.   God does not permit the destruction of that relationship (art. 6; cf. RE 3, 4)
4.   God renews a disturbed relationship (art. 7; cf. RE 8)
5.   Man is weak but God is steadfast (art. 8; cf. RE 1, 2, 9)

D. *Perseverance and Assurance (arts. 9–13)*
1.   Assurance of perseverance is possible for believers (art. 9)
2.   Assurance is found in the promises of the Word and in holy living (art. 10; cf. RE 5)
3.   Assurance is attacked, but overcomes (art. 11)
4.   Assurance produces humility and piety (art. 12; cf. RE 6)
5.   Assurance after serious sin produces more care in the future (art. 13)

E. *Perseverance and the Means of Grace (art. 14)*

F. *Perseverance and Consolation (art. 15)*

IVDICIVM
SYNODI
NATIONALIS,
REFORMATARVM
ECCLESIARVM BELGICARVM,

habitæ

DORDRECHTI,

Anno 1618. & 1619.

Cui etiam interfuerunt plurimi insignes Theologi Reformatarum Ecclesiarum Magnæ Britanniæ, Palatinatus Electoralis, Hassiæ, Helvetiæ, Correspondentiæ VVedderavicæ, Genevensis, Bremensis, & Emdanæ,

DE

QVINQVE DOCTRINAE

Capitibus *in Ecclesiis Belgicis Controversis.*

Promulgatum VI. May, cIɔ. Iɔc. XIX.

Cum Privilegio.

THE GRACE OF PREDESTINATION

I:

WHAT WE CONFESS

ARTICLES 1-18

THE REMONSTRANT DOCTRINE

BY THE TIME of the Synod of Dort, the *Remonstrance* of 1610 was somewhat outdated. Although individual theologians had moved beyond it, it remained a public statement by which to evaluate their teaching. On the doctrine of predestination its first article opened, reflecting the language of Ephesians 1: "That God by an eternal and immutable decree has in Jesus Christ his Son determined before the foundation of the world to save out of the fallen sinful human race those in Christ, for Christ's sake, and through Christ who by the grace of the Holy Spirit." So far; so good. David Paraeus even advised the synod, "At first sight, this Article seemes to have no question or inconvenience in it, but to deliver the summe of the Gospell."[1] It's the next statement, though, that was the issue: "who...*shall* be-lieve in this his Son Jesus Christ and [*shall*] persevere in this faith and obedience of faith."[2]

---

[1] David Paraeus, "Epitome of Arminianisme: or, The Examination of the Five Articles of the Remonstrants, in the Netherlands," in *The Summe of Christian Religion, Delivered by Zacharias Ursinus*, trans. A. R. (London, Printed by James Young, 1645), 817.

[2] As cited in "The *Remonstrance* of 1610," appendix C in De Jong, *Crisis in the Reformed Churches*, 208. Emphasis added.

THE ISSUE

The key issue was that the Remonstrants understood God's act of election to salvation to be *conditional*. They said God's eternal and immutable purpose in Christ to save was conditioned and dependent on those whom God foreknew "*shall* believe…and [*shall*] persevere."[3] While the Reformed distinguished God's unconditional act of electing from God's decreeing to use various conditions to bring about that salvation such as faith and perseverance, the Remonstrants defended their position at the synod in a list of theses. The first said, "God has not decided to elect anyone to eternal life, or to reject anyone from the same…without any consideration of preceding obedience or disobedience." The seventh said, "The election of particular persons is decisive, out of consideration of faith in Jesus Christ and of perseverance; not, however, apart from a consideration of faith and perseverance in the true faith, as a condition prerequisite for electing."[4] In other words, God took into account a person's obedience when he elected.

At the synod, the British delegation considered the Remonstrant thesis of election to salvation under the condition of faith *the* fundamental issue.[5] Their Collegiate Suffrage to the synod illustrated the difference between them and the Remonstrants this way: "For the Decree of God predestinating cannot bee conceived after this forme, I will choose *Peter* to eternall life, if it shall so happen that he doth believe, and persevere. But rather after this manner: I doe choose *Peter* unto eternall life, which that he may infallibly obtaine, I will give unto him persevering faith."[6] What makes the decree of election unconditional is that there is nothing antecedent to it that caused and compelled God to act. He acted of grace. All the aspects of the elect's salvation—faith, perseverance, and final glory—are consequent effects of election. This is still the issue. One of the men I first listened to after I was converted was Chuck Smith of Calvary Chapel Costa Mesa. Here's how he explained Ephesians 1 and God's predestination:

---

[3] Paraeus, "Epitome of Arminianisme," 817–18.

[4] See appendix 2: The Opinions of the Remonstrants (1619). As cited in "The Opinions of the Remonstrants," appendix H in De Jong, *Crisis in the Reformed Churches*, 222–29.

[5] *Thesis de electione huius vel illius ad salutem sub conditione fidei, fundamentalis est.* Milton, *The British Delegation and the Synod of Dort*, 175 (4/13).

[6] Milton, *The British Delegation and the Synod of Dort*, 230 (6/1).

Now imagine if you had that kind of capacity that you knew everything in advance before it ever happened. You knew exactly how it was going to turn out. You could sure go back and improve your lot, couldn't you? I have made some choices in my life that I was sorry that I made afterwards. I have made some poor decisions in my life. I sold too quickly. I bought at the wrong time. Oh, if I only had foreknowledge when I made my decisions I wouldn't have chosen the losers. That would be sort of stupid to choose losers, wouldn't it? If you knew in advance. If you knew who was going to win the ball game. Or better yet, you could go to the racetracks with this kind of knowledge. Imagine what you could do, having foreknowledge, knowing every horse what he was going to do in that race, and you would go to the racetrack with this kind of knowledge. Now, if you could, do you think you would go there and pick out a ticket of losers? I don't know what you do at racetracks. Would you pick out a bunch of losers? You would be stupid if you did. Of course, you wouldn't. You would pick the winners, because you know in advance who is going to win the race. What the outcome is going to be. And so you make your choices predicated on what the outcome is, because you already know in advance what it is going to be. That is just using your head. Now that is what thrills me about God choosing me. Because He don't choose no losers. God has only chosen winners. And by virtue of the fact that I have been chosen, that ensures that I am going to win.[7]

The elect, then, are a class of people who meet certain conditions, not individuals chosen by God in his love.[8] Men like Gomarus saw through this issue with Arminius and said this jeopardized the whole reason for the Reformation in the first place: God's gracious work of justifying sinners by faith alone, not because of anything in them or done by them.[9]

---

[7] "Ephesians 1." https://calvarychapel.com/pastorchuck/c2k/ephesians-1 (accessed May 9, 2018).

[8] Paraeus, "Epitome of Arminianisme," 818.

[9] See on Rejection of Errors 3 in chapter 2 below. For a comparison of similarities and differences in the doctrine of predestination between the Lutheran Book of Concord and the Reformed canons in the context of both affirming justification *sola fide*, see Joel R. Beeke, *Debated Issues in Sovereign Predestination: Early Lutheran Predestination, Calvinian Reprobation, and Variations in Genevan Lapsarianism,* Reformed

HISTORICAL BACKGROUND

In the history of Western catholic theology we distinguish three great camps when it comes to the relationship between God's grace and the salvation of sinners: Pelagianism, what is popularly called Semi-Pelagianism, and Augustinianism.

The British monk Pelagius (360–418) ended up in Rome and was scandalized by the state of morality among professing Christians. In one of his letters he reflects his struggle with what he saw:

> Do you consider him a Christian in whom there is no Christian act, in whom there is no righteous conduct, but evil, ungodliness and crime? Do you consider him a Christian who oppresses the wretched, who burdens the poor, who covets others' property, who makes several poor so that he may make himself rich, who rejoices in unjust gains…and a man of this kind has the audacity to go to church.[10]

Pelagius and his followers developed a theology with several features. First, created human nature was to have a body and soul with the power of contrary choice between good and evil called "free will" (*liberum arbitrium*). Since sin has no essential existence of its own, it cannot be part of human nature that is passed down from one man to another. Sin is merely imitating the sins of others. Thus subsequent humans are born unaffected by Adam's sin and in a similar situation as Adam, capable to exercise the power of contrary choice in fulfilling God's moral will. The "grace" of God is his giving humans inherent free will to determine right from wrong, revelation such as the law, and Jesus as an example to emulate. When man uses his will aright in following this revelation he does good, which is the ground of acceptance with God. In fact, it is possible for a human being even after Adam's sin to live a sinless life.[11]

Historical Theology 42 (Göttingen, Germany: Vandenhoeck & Ruprecht, 2017), 55–69.

[10] "On the Christian Life," in B. R. Rees, *Pelagius: Life and Letters* (1988, 1991; repr., Woodbridge, UK: Boydell, 1998), 119.

[11] For helpful summaries of Pelagius, see Justin S. Holcomb, *Know the Creeds and Councils* (Grand Rapids, MI: Zondervan, 2014), 87–88; F. H. Woods, *Canons of the Second Council of Orange, A.D. 529* (Oxford: James Thornton, 1882), 5–7; David F.

In 418 the Council of Carthage condemned various teachings of Pelagianism, including that infants do not have original sin, that God's grace is only effectual for past sins and not for avoiding sins in the future, that grace merely helps the believer learn what to desire and avoid, that the believer apart from grace can exercise free will to fulfill God's commands, and that believers only acknowledge "forgive us our debts" out of humility not reality.[12]

Then there were those like the monk John Cassian (360–435) who also rejected Pelagianism but thought Carthage (under the influence of Augustine) went too far. They were later named *"Semi*-Pelagians" in the seventeenth century.[13] It's important for us to be clear here. As Irena Backus and Aza Goudriaan have recently shown, neither Augustine nor that later Council of Orange (529) speak of those they opposed as "semipelagian." Further, neither Cassian, Vincent of Lérin, nor Faustus of Rietz identified their positions in any way with Pelagius. In fact, Augustine distinguished the monks of Marseille, whom he called the "Massilians" (*Massilienses*) from the Pelagians. It was Augustine's defender, Prosper, who labeled some of the Massilians' views as "remnant of the Pelagians" (*reliquiae Pelagianorum*). The term "Semi-Pelagian" was first used by Theodore Beza, whom Backus and Goudriaan say "seems to be the inventor of the terms 'Semipelagianism' and 'semipelagian.'" Beza used it as a synonym of Roman Catholic theology that teaches humanity is prone to sin yet not totally reliant on grace for conversion. Later it was used by Lutherans to refer to the followers of Philip Melanchthon, who asserted that man's free will unaided by grace was primary in man's conversion. Finally, among Roman Catholics it was first used as a label for the Massilians in the fifth century, no doubt as a polemic against being labeled themselves a la Beza.[14]

Wright, "Pelagianism," in *New Dictionary of Theology*, ed. Sinclair B. Ferguson, David F. Wright, and J. I. Packer (Downers Grove, IL: InterVarsity, 1988), 499–501.

[12] "Canons of the Council of Carthage May 1, 418," http://www.seanmultimedia.com/Pie_Council_Of_Carthage_May_1_418.html (accessed May 9, 2018). See Holcomb, *Know the Creeds and Councils*, 90–92.

[13] Justin Holcomb says, "Calling these theologians Semi-Pelagians is much akin to calling those who lived in post–World War II Germany Semi-Nazis, strictly on the basis of their historical location." *Know the Creeds and Councils*, 93.

[14] Irena Backus and Aza Goudriaan, "'Semipelagianism': The Origins of the Term and Its Passage into the History of Heresy," *Journal of Ecclesiastical History* 65, no. 1 (January 2014): 25–46.

While it's anachronistic to call Cassian et al. "Semi-Pelagians" themselves, the category is helpful as a way of distinguishing the various theologies of Augustine, Pelagius, and others in the fifth century. The problem with Cassian and others was that while they rejected Pelagianism, they also rejected important features of Augustine. Within the monastic community, the concern was lethargy among Christians in prayer and evangelism. The main point at issue between Cassian and Augustine was the beginning of faith (*initium fidei*), which Augustine's critics believed was the result of unaided human freedom, while grace strengthened it *after* its inception.[15] Perhaps, then, they are better called *Semi-Augustinians?*[16] This movement, too, was condemned over one hundred years later at the Second Council of Orange in 529. We'll look at its decisions in more detail when dealing with the third and fourth points of doctrine,[17] but for now, I'll mention the summary confession of faith from the Council of Orange that "we ought by God's mercy both to teach and believe" the following against both Pelagianism and Semi-Pelagianism:

- "...that through the sin of the first man free choice (*liberum arbitrium*) was so biased and weakened (*inclinatum et attenuatum*) that no one can afterwards either love God as he ought, or believe in God, or work for God's sake what is good, unless the grace of Divine mercy prevents (*praevenerit*, precedes) him."[18]

- "...the whole multitude of old fathers, we believe, had not that glorious faith which the Apostle Paul praises

---

[15] Wright, "Pelagianism," 636–37.

[16] For the most recent scholarship on the terminology, see Rebecca Harden Weaver, *Divine Grace and Human Agency: A Study of the Semi-Pelagian Controversy*, Patristic Monographs Series 15 (Macon, GA: Mercer University Press, 1996), 40–41; Weaver, introduction to *Grace for Grace: The Debates after Augustine and Pelagius*, ed. Alexander Y. Hwang, Brian J. Matz, and Augustine Casiday (Washington, DC: Catholic University of America Press, 2014), xiv–xv.

[17] See chapter 5.

[18] Woods, *Canons of the Second Council of Orange*, 45. On the history of this council, see Charles Joseph Hefele, *A History of the Councils of the Church from the Original Documents: Volume 4, A.D. 451 to A.D. 680*, trans. William R. Clark (Edinburgh: T&T Clark, 1895), 152–69; Weaver, *Divine Grace and Human Agency*, 225–34; Ralph W. Mathisen, "Caesarius of Arles, Prevenient Grace, and the Second Council of Orange," in *Grace for Grace*, 208–34.

through natural goodness which was first implanted in Adam, but that it was bestowed upon them by the grace of God. This grace, even after the advent of our Lord, we know and believe that all who desire to be baptized have, not as dependent on free choice (*libero arbitrio*), but that it is bestowed upon them by the bounty of Christ."[19]

• "We also profess and believe this wholesome doctrine, that in every good work it is not ourselves who begin and are afterwards helped by the mercy of God, but God Himself first, without any precedent good merits, inspires us with His faith and love, that we faithfully seek the sacred ordinances of baptism, and after baptism may by His help accomplish those things which are pleasing to Him."[20]

The major features of *Augustine's* doctrine (354–430) triumphed at Carthage and Orange. One of the delegates to Dort, John Davenant, approvingly cited the decisions of Orange as consistent with our Reformed Catholic faith.[21] Augustine succinctly stated his theology: "God elected believers; but He chose them that they might be so, not because they were already so."[22] Helpfully stating Augustine's ministry, Holcomb says, "Having dealt with the Donatist disappointment of how the institution of the church looks in real life, Augustine now turned to Pelagius' disappointment with how sinners look in real life."[23] This history of Christian reflection brought to the fore by Augustine, rejected by the Pelagians and Semi-Pelagians, was in turn responded to by Prosper of Aquitaine (ca. 390–after

---

[19] Woods, *Canons of the Second Council of Orange*, 45.

[20] Woods, *Canons of the Second Council of Orange*, 49, 51.

[21] John Davenant, *A Dissertation on the Death of Christ, as to Its Extent and Special Benefits*, in *An Exposition of the Epistle of St. Paul to the Colossians*, 2 vols., trans. Josiah Allport (London: Hamilton, Adams, 1832), 2:445–46, 490.

[22] "On the Predestination of the Saints," in *Nicene and Post-Nicene Fathers: First Series*, Volume 5 (1887; repr., Peabody, MA: Hendrickson, fourth printing 2004), 515. See also Peter Brown, *Augustine of Hippo: A Biography*, rev. ed. (Berkeley: University of California Press, 2000), 340–407; Matthew Levering, *The Theology of Augustine: An Introductory Guide to His Most Important Works* (Grand Rapids, MI: Baker Academic, 2013), 71–87; David F. Wright, "Augustine and Augustinianism," in *New Dictionary of Theology*, ed. Sinclair B. Ferguson, David F. Wright, and J. I. Packer (Downers Grove, IL: InterVarsity, 1988), 58–63.

[23] Holcomb, *Know the Creeds and Councils*, 89. On Augustine's theology, see Woods, *Canons of the Second Council of Orange*, 7–12.

455) and Fulgentius of Ruspe (467–533) culminating in the Second Council of Orange in 529. This Augustinian consensus continued through the centuries in men like Isidore of Seville (ca. 560–636), Gottschalk of Orbais (ca. 803–869),[24] Peter Lombard (ca. 1095–1160), Alexander of Hales (1170/1180–1245), Albert the Great (1200–1280), Bonaventure (ca. 1217–1274), Thomas Aquinas (1225–1274), Duns Scotus (ca. 1266–1308), William of Ockham (1285–1347), Nicholas of Lyra (1270–1349), and in the *schola Augustiniana moderna* of Thomas Bradwardine (ca. 1300–1349), Gregory of Rimini (ca. 1300–1358), Etienne Brulefer (d. ca. 1499), and John Eck (1486–1543).[25] Therefore van Asselt concluded, "The *theological* struggle at Dordt concerned the kernel of the Augustinian tradition within the whole of the Western church."[26]

This brings us to the first counterpoint or head (*caput*) of doctrine in the Canons of Dort on predestination. Christians need to talk about it; pastors need to preach it. It's offensive to unbelievers; it's even offensive to believers. To be effective witnesses for Jesus Christ and his grace we need to grow in the knowledge of his truth; we also need to grow in the wisdom of "speaking [his] truth in love" (Eph. 4:15).

COMMENTARY

Predestination is like a beautiful painting. Before an artist applies paint he or she needs a canvas. Then the painting can begin. The first point of doctrine opens with a canvas of six articles that are the common inheritance of

---

[24] See *Gottschalk and a Medieval Predestination Controversy: Texts Translated from the Latin*, ed. & trans. Victor Genke & Francis X. Gumerlock, Mediaeval Philosophical Texts in Translation 47 (Milwaukee, WI: Marquette University Press, 2010).

[25] See Heiko A. Oberman, *Masters of the Reformation: The Emergence of a New Intellectual Climate in Europe* (Cambridge: Cambridge University Press, 1981); *The Harvest of Medieval Theology: Gabriel Biel and Late Medieval Nominalism* (1963; rev. ed., Grand Rapids, MI: Eerdmans, 1967); Donald W. Sinnema, "The Issue of Reprobation at the Synod of Dort (1618–1619) in the Light of the History of This Doctrine" (PhD diss., University of St Michael's College, 1985), 8–51; David C. Steinmetz, *Luther and Staupitz: An Essay in the Intellectual Origins of the Protestant Reformation* (Durham, NC: Duke University Press, 1980).

[26] W. J. van Asselt, "No Dordt without Scholasticism: Willem Verboom on the Canons of Dordt," *Church History and Religious Culture* 87, no. 2 (2007): 205. Emphasis in original.

all Christians. After this canvas is laid out, the paint of predestination is applied.

Article 1

As all men have sinned in Adam, lie under the curse, and are deserving of eternal death, God would have done no injustice by leaving them all to perish, and delivering them over to condemnation on account of sin, according to the words of the apostle, "that every mouth may be stopped, and all the world may become guilty before God" (Rom. 3:19). And verse 23: "For all have sinned, and come short of the glory of God." And Romans 6:23: "For the wages of sin is death."

The first Christian conviction you need to know *before* saying a word about predestination is your sin and God's justice because of it.

YOUR SINFUL CONDITION

As all *people* (*homines*) have sinned in Adam and have come under the sentence of the curse and eternal death... Unlike the *Remonstrance* that began with God's eternal decree, the canons begin with biblical history:[27] the universal sinfulness of humanity and the justice of God.[28] In Romans 5, Paul explains the narrative of Genesis 1–3, saying, "Therefore, just as sin came into the world through one man, and death through sin, and so death spread to all men because all sinned" (v. 12). The point of verses 13–14 that follow is to say that even after Adam broke God's law and before Israel would break God's law again under Moses, everyone was still sinful. Why? Because of Adam. Notice the progression: Adam, sin, death. God created Adam (Gen. 1:26–27; 2:7); God gave Adam a command (Gen. 2:16–17); Adam violated the command (Gen. 3:1–6). What you have to understand is

---

[27] Jason Van Vliet points out this obvious contrast: "Election: The Father's Decision to Adopt," *Unio Cum Christo* 4, no. 2 (October 2018): 132–33.

[28] On Bishop Carleton's desire to begin this way, see Sinnema, "Reformed Scholasticism and the Synod of Dort," 496. See also Matthew Barrett, *The Grace of Godliness: An Introduction to Doctrine and Piety in the Canons of Dort* (Kitchener, ON: Joshua, 2013), 31; Feenstra *Unspeakable Comfort*, 13; cf. 24; Hoeksema, *The Voice of Our Fathers*, 135; Cornelis Pronk, *Expository Sermons on the Canons of Dort* (St. Thomas, ON: Free Reformed, 1999), 16. *1980 Acts of Synod* (Grand Rapids, MI: Board of Publication of the Christian Reformed Church, 1980), 517–18.

that what Adam did affected everyone else who was to come into the world. He was what our forefathers called "a public person," a representative of everyone else.[29] Just like what our president does matters to the rest of us because he represents us, so too Adam represented you and me way back in the Garden of Eden.

So "sin came into the world through" Adam, and notice that it's because of that one sin that "death" came into the world, "spread[ing] to all men" (v. 12). But the question is how did death come to everyone born into the world when everyone born had yet to sin? The last phrase in Romans 5:12 is the key: "because all sinned." When? When Adam sinned. All sinned in the one man's sin.[30] "But that's not fair." Before you say that, know that whatever you say of your involvement in Adam you will say of your involvement in Christ. Thus we are born "dead in trespasses and sins" (Eph. 2:1) and "in iniquity, and in sin...conceive[d]" (Ps. 51:5); therefore we're powerless to save ourselves. "But aren't children born good and without sin?" Paul says we are all "children of wrath" (Eph. 2:3). Jeremiah asks, "Can the Ethiopian change his skin or the leopard his spots?" (Jer. 13:23). No! Can anyone come to Christ on their own accord, from their own will? No! For the Lord himself tells us, "No one can come to me unless the Father who sent me draws him" (John 6:44). "No one seeks for God" (Rom 3:11). "The natural person does not accept the things of the Spirit of God, for they are folly to him, and he is not able to understand them because they are spiritually discerned" (1 Cor. 2:14). "Everyone who practices sin is a slave to sin" (John 8:34).

Because of Adam's sin and our participation in it, we **lie under the curse** mentioned in Genesis 2:15. The day Adam ate of the tree of the knowledge of good and evil he would surely die, both bodily and spiritually. Of course, we see God's grace in preserving Adam's bodily life and in preserving the human race. But Adam and we are now under a curse of spiritual death, and one day we shall all experience physical death: "it is appointed for man to die once, and after that comes judgment" (Heb. 9:27). In Romans 5 again we read in verses 15–19 a series of three great contrasts between Adam and Jesus with the result that we "have come under the

---

[29] See for example, John Owen, "The Doctrine of Justification by Faith," in *Works*, 5:220.

[30] On the exegesis of Romans 5:12, see John Murray, *The Imputation of Adam's Sin* (1959; repr., Phillipsburg, NJ: P&R, n.d.), 5–21.

sentence of…eternal death." Sin, curse, death. You can see this in the progression of Paul's words in Romans 5: in the beginning there was "one man," Adam; what Adam did is described with three terms: he "sinned" (ἁμαρτία; vv. 12, 16), he "trespassed" (παράβασις; v. 14; παράπτωμα; vv. 15, 16, 17, 18), and he was "disobedient" (παρακοή; v. 19). Because of this God pronounced his "judgment"; this judgment led to his "condemnation"; his condemnation led to his spiritual and eventual physical "death." As Paul says in Galatians 3:10 and 3:13: "For all who rely on works of the law are under a curse; for it is written, 'Cursed be everyone who does not abide by all things written in the Book of the Law, and do them'…Christ redeemed us from the curse of the law."

So we begin with the common Christian conviction of the doctrine of universal original sin in Adam against the condemned teaching of Pelagius before we talk about predestination. We do not begin with the mind of God. We do not begin with the eternal decree of God. We do not begin with things beyond our comprehension. We begin where the Scriptures begin; we begin from our vantage point: sin. We begin with the revealed God, not the hidden God. We begin with history then work our way backward to the eternal decision of God.

GOD'S JUST CONDEMNATION

God would have done no injustice by leaving them all to perish, and delivering them over to condemnation on account of sin. Offended people, though, say, "God sends no one to hell, they send themselves there." We're told, "God doesn't send anyone to hell because of their sinfulness but because of what they didn't do with Jesus Christ." We're told, "We all have an equal opportunity to get to heaven." The justice of God, though, is so hard in a multicultural, pluralistic, so-called postmodern world. But the modern objection that says, "God is unjust," is not modern at all. In Romans 9 this was one of the ancient objections Paul responded to: "What shall we say then? Is there injustice on God's part? By no means!" (Rom. 9:14). This is an objection of those in a sinful condition.

Instead, the Word of God tells us that we are sinners and God is just. Scripture tells us that because of our sins "every mouth may be stopped." Scripture tells us that because of our sins "the whole world may be held accountable to God" (Rom. 3:19). Scripture tells us that "all have sinned" and therefore all have "fall[en] short of the glory of God" (Rom. 3:23). Utilizing the imagery of falling short, which was used for a runner who lost a race, the *Dutch Annotations* say, "All men come too short who seek to obtain the glory of God, that is, eternal life by their works."[31] Scripture also tells us that "the wages of sin is death" (Rom. 6:23)—a death "not only temporal but also eternal, as appears from the following" phrase, "but the gift of God is eternal life."[32]

So what does this all mean? It means don't say a word about predestination until you have first humbled yourself under the mighty hand of God. It means don't say a word about predestination until you have confessed original, inborn sin. It means don't say a word about predestination until you have confessed your own actual, personal sins. It means don't say a word about predestination until you have submitted yourself to the supreme "Judge of all the earth" who does "what is just" (Gen. 18:25). When we do this, we will be able to say with Paul, "How unsearchable are his judgments and how inscrutable his ways!" (Rom. 11:33).

Article 2

But in this the love of God was manifested, that He sent His only begotten Son into the world, that whosoever believeth on Him should not perish, but have everlasting life. "In this was manifested the love of God toward us, because that God sent His only begotten Son into the world, that we might live through Him" (1 John 4:9). "For God so loved the world, that He gave His only begotten Son, that whosoever believeth in Him should not perish, but have everlasting life" (John 3:16).

GOD'S LOVE

The second Christian conviction before we speak about predestination is **the love of God**, which article 2 says **was manifested** in the sending of his Son, quoting 1 John 4:9 and John 3:16. In any relationship, you always have to remember the most basic fact of that relationship: there are two of you! It's not just about *you*. It's not just about the other person knowing you, but

---

[31] *Dutch Annotations* on Romans 3:23. These notes were included in the Synod's approved Bible translation..

[32] *Dutch Annotations* on Romans 6:23.

you knowing him or her. In order for us to have a relationship with God, we have to know God and how he relates to us in predestination.

The apostle John exhorted his hearers, saying, "Beloved, let us love one another" (1 John 4:7), and then again, "Beloved, if God so loved us, we also ought to love one another" (1 John 4:11). In the midst of this John speaks of the cause of our love. We are to love because "love is from God" (1 John 4:7). He has given it to those who have "been born of God" and who now "[know] God" (1 John 4:7). Then he states the ultimate cause: "God is love" (1 John 4:8). D. A. Carson distinguishes five senses of love in the Scriptures.[33] On the basis of this kind of exegetical work, Christian theologians have made distinctions in God's love.[34]

God's Love Of Himself

John speaks of "the love *of* God" (1 John 4:9). He's not speaking of God as the object of our love, but of God as the subject who loves: *God's* love.[35] This love exists internally, naturally, and necessarily in God and is later manifested voluntarily from God externally in the sending of his Son. This love "is at the heart of the entire missionary enterprise," which begins with God.[36] We know God's love because he has manifested it in the sending of his Son to the world in his birth, life, death, resurrection, and ascension. Since God is the perfection of all Being, this means his love exists prior to its historical manifestation and certainly before our experience of it. We get a glimpse of its essence in 1 John 4:9–10 when we read of God and his only Son.

As God *he* exists eternally and self-sufficiently as *them*—Father, Son—both mentioned here—and Holy Spirit. What God was doing in

---

[33] On the five senses of "love," see D. A. Carson, *The Difficult Doctrine of the Love of God* (Wheaton, IL: Crossway Books, 2000), 16–24. See also Geerhardus Vos, "The Scriptural Doctrine of the Love of God," in *Redemptive History and Biblical Interpretation: The Shorter Writings of Geerhardus Vos* (Phillipsburg, NJ: P&R, 1980), 425–57.

[34] See Richard A. Muller, "amor Dei," in *Dictionary of Latin and Greek Theological Terms: Drawn Principally from Protestant Scholastic Theology*, 2nd ed. (Grand Rapids, MI: Baker Academic, 2017), 23.

[35] On the subjective genitive, see Daniel B. Wallace, *Greek Grammar beyond the Basics: An Exegetical Syntax of the New Testament* (Grand Rapids, MI: Zondervan, 1996), 113–16.

[36] Hoekema, "The Missionary Focus of the Canons of Dort," 212.

eternity before creation was existing in love within the relationships be-tween Father, Son, and Holy Spirit. Our love for our parents had a begin-ning. Our love for our friends had an inception point. What John is talking about, though, is love that has always been—better yet, that just *is*. He al-ways has been, and he always has been satisfied with himself. In other words, he did not need anything beyond himself.

In John 17:22–23, Jesus prays to the Father for the unity of his church. At the end of verse 23 we read the purpose: "so that the world may know that you sent me and loved them *even as you loved me*." Was this just the love of the Father for Jesus while he was on earth? That love was manifest-ed in his baptism: "This is my beloved Son" (Matt. 3:17). The Father's love for his Son goes back further. In John 17:24 Jesus prays that his people "may be with me where I am, to see my glory that you have given me *because you loved me before the foundation of the world*." Finally, in John 17:26 Jesus says, "I made known to them your name, and I will continue to make it known, that *the love with which you have loved me* may be in them, and I in them." This means that God's love of himself as Trinity is an eternal self-sufficient love. The later English Presbyterian pastor, Thomas Manton (1620–1677), said,

> God's love is as ancient as himself, there was no time when God did not think of us, and love us. We are wont to prize an ancient friend; the ancientest friend we have is God, who loved us not only before we were lovely, but be-fore we were at all. He thought of us before ever we could have a thought of him.[37]

This means that God's love of himself as Trinity is a perfect love. Therefore it is the paradigm for our love according to 1 John 4. God's love of himself as Trinity is an intimate love of Father for his only Son in the fellowship of the Holy Spirit.[38] The eternal Son is the first object of the whole of the Father's love.[39] Owen said that the Son "is in the bosom of the Father—in the eternal embraces of his love."[40] Manton expressed

---

[37] Thomas Manton, "Sermons upon the Seventeenth Chapter of St. John," in *The Works of Thomas Manton* (repr., Birmingham, AL: Solid Ground Christian Books, 2008), 11:80.

[38] See Manton, "Sermons upon the Seventeenth Chapter of St. John," in *Works*, 11:74ff.

[39] John Owen, "Christologia," in *Works*, 1:144.

[40] Owen, "Christologia," in *Works*, 1:144.

God's love in terms of infinity. As an infinite love it is unbounded by time: the Father "taketh an infinite contentment in Christ, before hill or mountain were brought forth."[41] As infinite, it's also unbounded by earthly conceptions: "God's love is like himself, infinite; it is not to be measured by the affection of a carnal parent. Yet he gave up Christ. Love goeth to the utmost; had he a greater gift, he would have given it. How could he show us love more than in giving such a gift as Christ?"[42]

God's Love of the World

The eternal, internal, self-sufficient love among the persons of the Holy Trinity (*ad intra*) is then "made manifest among us" in God's sending of "his only Son into the world" (*ad extra*).

What does it mean that God's love was manifested "into the world"? The Greek word κόσμος (*kosmos*), "world," is used in many different ways in John's writings.[43] First, it speaks of the created world (John 1:3, 10 [2x]; 17:5, 24; 21:25). Coupled with God's attributes this means that there is a love of God for his creation in general.[44] As Psalm 104 says of the creation, "may the LORD rejoice in his works" (Ps. 104:31). Psalm 136 says the Lord "gives food to all flesh, for his steadfast love"—that is, his faithfulness to his covenant promises—"endures forever" (v. 25). Second, it speaks of the world of humanity (e.g., John 1:10, 29; 4:42; 6:33, 51; 1 John 2:2; 3:1) as well as the world of humanity in its lost condition (e.g., John 3:16, 17 [3x], 19; 4:42; 1 John 4:14). This world needs a Savior because it hates Jesus (John 7:7) and his disciples (John 15:18–19; 1 John 3:13, 17). This means that while humanity justly deserves condemnation because of its sins, there is a special love of God for sinners in particular. "For God so loved the world"

---

41 Manton, "Sermons upon the Seventeenth Chapter of St. John," in *Works*, 11:74.

42 Manton, "Sermons upon the Seventeenth Chapter of St. John," in *Works*, 11:75.

43 The following threefold distinction is also found in Benedict Pictet (1655–1724), *Christian Theology*, trans. Frederick Reyroux (Philadelphia: Presbyterian Board of Publication, 1845), 84–86. See also the excellent summary in Mark Jones, *Antinomianism: Reformed Theology's Unwelcome Guest?* (Phillipsburg, NJ: P&R, 2013), 83–87.

44 Vos says the Old Testament uses love in an absolute sense toward his people while his more general "goodness" is toward all. Vos, "The Scriptural Doctrine of the Love of God," 440; cf. 442.

(John 3:16).[45] Commenting on John 3:16, Geerhardus Vos said, "If the Son of God was filled with tender compassion for every lost human soul, and grieved even over those whose confirmed unbelief precluded all further hope of salvation, it is plain that there must be in God something corresponding to this."[46] Jesus was the Word and Son of the Father made flesh to declare the Father to us (John 1:1–18).

God loves the world of his creation, God loves the world of fallen humanity, but most specially, God loves his peculiar people whom he takes out of the world: "In this is love, not that we have loved God but that he loved *us* and sent his Son to be the propitiation for *our* sins" (1 John 4:10). Just as Adam's sin brought spiritual and eternal death, 1 John 4:9 says Jesus' sacrifice brings us life "spiritually and eternally."[47]

As J. I. Packer explained, "God loves all in some ways...he loves some in all ways."[48] The fundamental difference is that those who enjoy God's general love as Creator outside of Jesus Christ also have the wrath of God as Judge upon them, while those who enjoy God's love as Father have his wrath removed in Christ.[49] In the words of our forefathers, God has an eternal love of benevolence to elect us, a love of beneficence to redeem us, and a love of complacency to reward us. Why does God love us? Because he decided to love us.

> My heart owns none before Thee,
> For Thy rich grace I thirst;
> This knowing, if I love Thee,
> Thou must have loved me first.[50]

---

[45] This love for creation and humanity is not sufficiently expressed by Reformed believers today out of fear of sounding "Arminian." For an example of a commentary that says too little on article 2, see Feenstra, *Unspeakable Comfort*, 25–26.

[46] Vos, "The Scriptural Doctrine of the Love of God," 443.

[47] *Dutch Annotations* on 1 John 4:9.

[48] J. I. Packer, "The Love of God: Universal and Particular," in *Still Sovereign*, ed. Thomas Schreiner and Bruce Ware (Grand Rapids, MI: Baker, 2000), 283–84.

[49] Vos, "The Scriptural Doctrine of the Love of God," 445–46.

[50] From the hymn "'Tis Not That I Did Choose Thee," in *Psalter Hymnal* (Grand Rapids, MI: CRC, 1976), #385:2.

Article 3

And that men may be brought to believe, God mercifully sends the messengers of these most joyful tidings to whom He will and at what time He pleaseth; by whose ministry men are called to repentance and faith in Christ crucified. "How then shall they call on Him in whom they have not believed? and how shall they believe in Him of whom they have not heard? and how shall they hear without a preacher? And how shall they preach, except they be sent?" (Rom. 10:14–15).

GOD'S MERCY

We are sinners. But God is love. Expressing these two truths and how we are brought into fellowship together, Jesus once said, "No one can come to me unless the Father who sent me draws him" (John 6:44). How does the Father "draw" sinful people to Jesus Christ? That's the third Christian conviction: preaching. Article 3 teaches that God ordains the *end* of our salvation as well as the *means* of our salvation: "the Apostle declares the means whereby Faith in Christ is obtained. Namely, by the preaching of the Gospel, preached by them that are lawfully sent for this purpose."[51] Peter speaks of preaching as the means of our salvation: "Since you have been born again, not of perishable seed but of imperishable, through the living and abiding word of God… And this word is the good news that was preached to you" (1 Pet. 1:23; 1:25).[52] Article 3 quotes from another Scripture—Romans 10—one of the great passages on preaching in the Word of God.

In Romans 9–11 Paul is explaining why Israel does not all believe Jesus is the Messiah. Chapter 9 deals with this from the vantage point of predestination, while in chapter 10 he's dealing with it from the vantage point of the preaching of the gospel. And you can see his progression very easily in verses 14–15: call, believe, hear, preach, and sent. It all culminates in the famous words of verse 17: "So faith comes from hearing, and hearing through the word of Christ." John Calvin said it like this: "Preaching…is not something done haphazardly, neither do men come of their own

---

[51] *Dutch Annotations* on Romans 10:14–15.

[52] On the Word's relationship to regeneration, see Herman Bavinck, *Saved by Grace: The Holy Spirit's Work in Calling and Regeneration*, trans. Nelson D. Kloosterman, ed. J. Mark Beach (Grand Rapids, MI: Reformation Heritage Books, 2008).

selves…but God himself visits us and comes to us."[53] Article 1 says that God is just. Article 2 says that God is love. Now article 3 says that God is merciful.

His Mercy in *Why* He Sends

The world is disillusioned spiritually by the fog of sin, blinded by the darkness of sin, and lies under the just condemnation of God for its sin. That's the bad news. The good news is that "everyone who calls on the name of the Lord will be saved" (Rom. 10:13). Verses 14–17 go on to explain how those who have not believed in Christ—because they have never heard of Christ—because a preacher of Christ has not been sent—call upon Christ to receive Christ and all his benefits.

In the context of predestination, the eternal God has from eternity past ordained the eternal *end* of all things. He also ordained the *means* by which those predestined to the end of glory get to that goal of glory. Preaching is that means. This is why article 3 says, **And that *people* (*homines*) may be brought to believe**. Notice it's not just preaching about God in general. It is the preaching of Jesus Christ that is the means of obtaining eternal salvation. Article 3 says, **by whose ministry *people* (*homines*) are called to repentance and faith in Christ crucified**.

Look at that in Romans 10: "How then will they call on Him *in whom* they have not believed? How will they believe in Him *whom* they have not heard?" (v. 14 NASB).[54] When Paul says, "in him *whom* they have not heard," he's saying preaching the gospel is the very voice of Christ! "So faith comes from hearing, and hearing through the word of *Christ*" (v. 17), meaning, not the word about Christ but Christ's word! As the 1566 *Second Helvetic Confession* expressed it, "Wherefore when this Word of God is

---

[53] John Calvin, *Sermons on the Epistle to the Ephesians*, trans. Arthur Golding (1577; repr., Edinburgh: Banner of Truth, 1987), 202.

[54] On the grammatical clause in which the pronoun οὗ is in the genitive case plus the verb ἤκουσαν (ἀκούω) means, see C. E. B. Cranfield, *A Critical and Exegetical Commentary on the Epistle to the Romans*, 2 vols. (1979; repr., London: T&T Clark, 2004), 2:534; Leon Morris, *The Epistle to the Romans* (Grand Rapids, MI: Eerdmans, 1988), 389–90; John Murray, *The Epistle to the Romans*, New International Commentary on the New Testament (1959; repr., Grand Rapids, MI: Eerdmans, 1968), 58–59.

now preached in the church by preachers lawfully called, we believe that the very Word of God is preached, and received of the faithful."[55]

As C. H. Spurgeon once said, "The sermon which does not lead to Christ, or of which Jesus Christ is not the top and the bottom, is a sort of sermon that will make the devils in hell laugh, but might make the angels of God weep."[56] Why does God send preachers? To mercifully bring us to Jesus.

His Mercy in *Whom* He Sends

In his mercy God has ordained that we need to hear the preaching of the gospel of his Son in order for us to come to faith in his Son. But in order for sinners to hear, there must be a voice: "And how are they to hear without someone preaching?" (Rom. 10:14). As Paul asks rhetorically in 1 Corinthians 12: "Are all apostles? Are all prophets? Are all teachers?" (v. 29). No, for only God can set one apart and send that one out. Paul says, "And how are they to preach unless they are sent?" (Rom. 10:15). He then cites the prophet Isaiah's words, "How beautiful are the feet of those who preach the good news!" (Rom. 10:15; cf. Isa. 52:7). All of this is summarized in our article: **God mercifully sends the messengers of these most joyful tidings**.

Practically speaking, this means for you that you need to stop, meditate, and stand in awe at the mercy of God that he mercifully chose you from eternity, that he mercifully looked upon you in your lostness, and that he mercifully sent you a preacher. Behold the mercy of God!

His Mercy in *Where* He Sends

We need to know that God's mercy is a sovereign mercy. It's also a merciful sovereignty. He not only determines who is saved from eternity and how they are saved through preaching of the gospel but also in that he sends the

---

[55] James T. Dennison Jr., ed., *Reformed Confessions of the 16th and 17th Centuries in English Translation: Volume 2, 1552–1566* (Grand Rapids, MI: Reformation Heritage Books, 2010), 811.

[56] Charles H. Spurgeon, *Metropolitan Tabernacle Pulpit* (Pasadena, TX: Pilgrim, 1972), 25:634.

preachers of this gospel **to whom** (*quos*) **He will and at what time** (*quando*) **He pleaseth**.

Romans 10 assumes a world that needs to believe in Christ but that has not heard of Christ (v. 14). God determines to whom and when to send his Word. Acts 16:6–10 illustrates this so poignantly. Luke speaks about the Holy Spirit as the sovereign Spirit of preaching. The Holy Spirit leads whom he wants, to whom he wants, when he wants, and where he wants. He also leads where *not* to preach.[57]

Paul, Silas, and Timothy were traveling through Asia Minor, where we see the sovereign Spirit in action. How did they get there? Back in Acts 13:1–3 we learn that while fasting and worshipping, the prophets and teachers of the church in Antioch were told by the Holy Spirit, "Set apart for me Barnabas and Saul for the work to which I have called them" (v. 2). It was the Holy Spirit's sovereign choice to call Paul and Barnabas for the task of preaching. Notice where they tried to go but where the Holy Spirit led them to go. First, Acts 16:6 says that they were going "through the region of Phrygia and Galatia" because they were "forbidden by the Holy Spirit to speak the word in Asia." They were trying to go north toward the Black Sea

---

[57] In his comments upon this text, John Calvin asked the difficult question, "Why did the Lord forbid Paul to speak in Asia, and did not allow him to come into Bithynia?" His answer was to say that instead of rooting this in one people group being better than or more worthy than another people group, we should root it in God's sovereign wisdom:

> Therefore there is nothing better than to leave God the freedom and power to deem those, whom He pleases, worthy of His grace, or deprive them of it. And certainly since His eternal election is of grace, so must the calling, which flows from it, be considered of grace, and it is not founded on men, since it owes nothing to anyone. Accordingly let us realize that the Gospel comes forth to us from the one fountain of pure grace. However God does not lack a legitimate reason why He offers His Gospel to certain ones, but passes others by; but I maintain that the reason is hidden in His secret purpose. In the meantime let believers know that they have been called gratuitously when others have been neglected, so that they may not ascribe to themselves what belongs to the mercy of God alone.

John Calvin, *The Acts of the Apostles, Volume II*, trans. John W. Fraser, ed. David W. Torrance and Thomas F. Torrance, Calvin's New Testament Commentaries, 12 vols. (1966; repr., Grand Rapids, MI: Eerdmans, 1973), 7:69.

but were led through the center of Asia Minor. Second, Acts 16:7 says that when "they had come up to Mysia," which is the northwest corner of Asia Minor, "they attempted to go into Bithynia, but the Spirit of Jesus did not allow them." They were still trying to get up into the northern territories, going clockwise around Asia Minor. They were being led in between the region of Asia in the south and Bithynia in the north through a desolate region with no major cities.[58]

Why would the Holy Spirit actually forbid the gospel from being preached to particular people? Notice that in verse 9 Paul sees a vision of a man in Macedonia, and in verse 10 they leave for Macedonia. Were the Macedonians more worthy and deserving of the gospel than the Asians or Bithynians? Did God love Macedonia more? God forbid. It was the secret will of God why Paul, Silas, and Timothy were forbidden to preach in Asia and Bithynia, while it was the revealed will of God to preach in Macedonia. By preaching in Macedonia the gospel came to Lydia; the Philippian jailer; Thessalonica, one of Paul's great ministerial joys; the Bereans, the studious believers; Athens, with the great debate on Mars Hill; and Corinth. God is merciful.

Article 4

The wrath of God abideth upon those who believe not this gospel. But such as receive it, and embrace Jesus the Savior by a true and living faith, are by Him delivered from the wrath of God and from destruction, and have the gift of eternal life conferred upon them.

FAITH

To our sinful world, God in his love sent his Son. The world lies under the curse of sin. In his mercy he sends preachers of the good news of Jesus. But Scripture and experience show that some believe while others do not. Article 4 confesses the fourth Christian conviction: the necessity of faith.

There are two responses to Jesus' call in John 3: "Whoever believes in him is not condemned"—that is, is justified—"but whoever does not

---

[58] The *Dutch Annotations* on Acts 16:6–7 said, "The Holy Ghost prescribed the Apostles what order they should hold in travelling and preaching the word to one people first, and to another after."

believe is condemned already."[59] Why? "Because he has not believed in the name of the only Son of God... Whoever believes in the Son has eternal life; whoever does not obey the Son shall not see life, but the wrath of God remains on him" (John 3:18, 36). These texts are expressed in article 4: **The wrath of God abideth upon those who believe not this gospel. But such as receive it, and embrace Jesus the Savior by a true and living faith, are by Him delivered from the wrath of God and from destruction, and have the gift of eternal life conferred upon them.**

Again, after Jesus fed the five thousand (men, not including women and children), the entire crowd left him except for his twelve disciples, and one of them was Judas (John 6)! Remember what Jesus said in John 10 to the Pharisees: "you do not believe because you are not among my sheep" (v. 26). Remember what Paul struggled with so personally in Romans 9: God made promises to Abraham that his descendants were the Lord's people, yet not all of them believed.

What is Faith?

The essence of faith is found in Jesus' words in John 3 when he speaks of believing "in him." This is to put all your confidence, all your hope, and all your trust in Jesus. That's faith in its essence. It's putting everything that you are in Jesus and not in yourself. That's why our forefathers spoke with a varied vocabulary of faith here in article 4: **believe** (*credunt*), **receive** (*recipiunt*), **embrace** (*servatorem*), and **true and living faith** (*vera ac viva fide*).[60] That's also why our forefathers also spoke of **true and living faith** as including knowledge (*notitia*), assent (*assensus*), and trust (*fiducia*).[61] This is so

---

[59] On the language of not being condemned in John's Gospel as equivalent to Paul's "justification," see D. A. Carson, *The Gospel according to John* (Grand Rapids, MI: Eerdmans, 1991), 256.

[60] The Westminster Confession of Faith (1647) defines saving faith as "receiving and resting on Him (Jesus) and His righteousness by faith" (11.1, 2; cf. 14:2).

[61] Muller, "fides," in *Dictionary of Latin and Greek Theological Terms*, 120–21. Feenstra only recognizes two aspects of faith: "sure knowledge" and "firm confidence" based on Heidelberg Catechism, Q&A 21. *Unspeakable Comfort*, 30. But this is a misreading of the Catechism, which defines true faith as "not only a sure knowledge, where I hold for truth all that God has revealed to us in His Word, but also a hearty trust." In fact, the Latin edition of the Catechism speaks of the three aspects reference by Muller above: *Est non tantum **notitia**, qua firmiter **assentior** omnibus, quae Deus nobis in Verbo suo patefecit, sed etiam certa **fiducia**. De Nederlandse beli-*

important because all too often we can think of faith as just some mental gymnastics you do or just some ethereal connection to some ethereal thing called God or Jesus. "Accept," "embrace," and "receive" should evoke that faith is personal. When I put my faith in Jesus, this means that I receive him and all that he is for myself. This is no theological Christianese, but what John says earlier in John 1:11–12: "He came to his own, and his own people did not receive him. But to all who did receive him, who believed in his name…" That's faith. I know this is a theology book, but I have to ask the personal question: Does that describe your relationship to Jesus? Do you receive and embrace all he is for yourself?

Why is Faith Necessary?

Most simply, faith is necessary because as we see in John 3, with it we will not perish (v. 16), we will have eternal life (v. 16), and we will be saved (v. 17). On the other hand, faith is necessary because without it we will perish (v. 16), we will be condemned (v. 18), and, in fact, the wrath of God is already upon us (v. 36). Faith in Jesus is necessary because it's how we as members of "the world" of sinners in opposition to God receive the remedy for our sinful condition, for our sinful actions, and for our impending condemnation. Faith is so important because "without [it] it is impossible to please [God]" (Heb. 11:6).

What are the Blessings of Faith?

I've already alluded to this, but when Jesus speaks of believing "in him" (John 3:16) and "in the Son" (John 3:36), he is speaking of the blessings of faith. The blessing—singular—is Jesus himself. The blessings—many—are what Jesus gives to us. In John 3 Jesus speaks of the blessing of eternal life in contrast to eternal condemnation and wrath.

This means that through the means of faith we are delivered from something to something: from condemnation, wrath, and destruction to eternal life. When we receive and embrace, Jesus he delivers us from the wrath of God. As Paul says, "Since, therefore, we have now been justified by his blood, much more shall we be saved by him from the wrath of God"

---

jdenisgeschriften, ed. J. N. Bakhuizen van den Brink, 2nd ed. (Amsterdam: Ton Bolland, 1976), 162.

(Rom. 5:9). When we receive and embrace Jesus, he delivers us to eternal life. As Paul says, "For the wages of sin is death"—meaning eternal death or condemnation—"but the free gift of God is eternal life in Christ Jesus our Lord" (Rom. 6:23). As the hymn says:

> Pardon for sin and a peace that endureth
> Thine own dear presence to cheer and to guide;
> Strength for today and bright hope for tomorrow,
> Blessings all mine, with ten thousand beside![62]

Article 5

The cause or guilt of this unbelief, as well as of all other sins, is no wise in God, but in man himself; whereas faith in Jesus Christ and salvation through Him is the free gift of God, as it is written: "For by grace are ye saved through faith; and that not of yourselves: it is the gift of God" (Eph. 2:8). "For unto you it is given in the behalf of Christ, not only to believe on Him," etc. (Phil. 1:29).

The fifth Christian conviction is that faith is a gift of God. If faith is receiving and embracing Jesus and so necessary that apart from it we will perish everlastingly, the question is, where does this faith come from? John answers this question at the beginning of his Gospel where he says, "To all who did receive him, who believed in his name, he gave the right to become children of God" (John 1:12). He explains this further by saying what happened prior to their believing: "who were born [past tense], not of blood nor of the will of the flesh nor of the will of man, but of God" (John 1:13). And what does it mean to be "born of God"? That's Jesus' teaching in John 3:6. To be born again is also to be born from above, that is, to be given new birth by God himself. So those whom God gave new birth to are those who believe in Jesus.

The Cause of Unbelief

The natural implication of John 1 and 3 is that unbelief has its cause and fault in sinful humanity: **The cause or guilt of this unbelief, as well as of**

---

[62] From the hymn "Great Is Thy Faithfulness."

all other sins, is no wise (*neutiquam*; not at all) **in God, but in man him-self**. It cannot be in God or else he cannot be God: "God is light, and in him is no darkness at all" (1 John 1:5). As James says, "Let no one say when he is tempted, 'I am being tempted by God,' for God cannot be tempted with evil, and he himself tempts no one" (James 1:13). It must be in us, who were born dead in trespasses and sins (Eph. 2:1–3). Let me illustrate. In our natural state we are like an untrained dog—wild, out of control, acting on instinct and according to its dispositions and nature. You don't need to tell an untrained dog to run away; it does that anyway. This is what we are like apart from the Lord's working in us, to "train" us to place faith in Jesus.

The Cause of Faith

On the other hand, faith's cause is not in us but in God himself: **faith in Jesus Christ and salvation through Him is the free gift of God**. Only God makes alive: "But God" (Eph. 2:4)! One of the passages article 5 cites is Ephesians 2:8. In the context of verses 8–9 we read: "For by grace you have been saved through faith. And this is not your own doing; it is the gift of God, not a result of works, so that no one may boast." Some point to the grammar and say "it" is not faith, but salvation in general. Technically, this is correct. But "it" or "this" can also be taken as generally referring to the entirety of our salvation because "faith" and "works" are pitted against each other throughout Scripture. The *Dutch Annotations* brought it out like this: while "this grace of God in Christ is received by us, and applied to us," it is "not of you that ye believe; for otherwise the Apostle should say one thing twice, and not only salvation itself, but faith also is a gift of God."

Even if Ephesians 2:8–9 were inconclusive, we still have Philippians 1:29, which article 5 also cites. Paul says, "For it has been *granted* to you that for the sake of Christ you should not only believe in him but also suffer for his sake." Notice that. Paul takes for granted that God grants faith, which is the lesser gift; the greater gift is that we suffer for Jesus.

If anyone says, "This is just a *Reformed* reading of these texts," it's im-portant to note that the Synod of Dort was reading them along with the ancient church in this way. Canon 5 of the Council of Orange (529) said:

If any one says that just as the increase, so also the beginning of faith (*initium fidei*), and the very feeling of belief by which we believe on Him who justifies the "impious" man, and come to the Regeneration of sacred Bap-tism, is not by the gift of grace (*i.e.*, by the inspiration of the Holy Spirit

70

correcting our will [*corrigentem voluntatem nostram*] from infidelity to faith, from impiety to piety), but is implanted in us by nature, he is proved an adversary to the doctrines of the Apostle [quoting Phil. 1:6, Phil. 1:29, and Eph. 2:8].[63]

Another clear text that states the relationship between God's grace and faith is Acts 13:48, where Luke records the result of Paul and Barnabas's preaching in Antioch in Pisidia: "And as many as were appointed to eternal life believed."

One of the issues article 5 highlights, which will be mentioned again throughout the canons, is that God's sovereignty and human responsibility are not contradictory. As one writer said,

It is misleading—indeed, wholly false and untenable—to contend that Dort defended divine sovereignty while the Arminians defended human responsibility. Both Dort and the Arminians held to divine sovereignty and human responsibility. But two different and contradict theologies were involved.[64]

If faith is caused by God, is unbelief equally caused by him, too? Think of it like this: lined up behind the defense's table is a group of criminals, none of whom are penitent. Then the judge announces that all who are penitent will be pardoned. No one budges, so the judge asks defendant #1 to stand up. He then humbles him with an array of arguments and evidence, leading him to become penitent. This does not make the judge the cause of the impenitence of the other ones, though.[65]

Article 6

That some receive the gift of faith from God and others do not receive it proceeds from God's eternal decree, for "known unto God are all His works from the beginning of the world" (Acts 15:18). "Who worketh all things after the counsel of His own will" (Eph. 1:11). According to which decree, He graciously softens the hearts of the elect, however obstinate, and inclines them to believe, while He leaves the non-elect in His just judgment to their own wickedness and obduracy. And herein is especially displayed the profound, the merciful, and at the same time the righteous

---

[63] Woods, *Canons of the Second Council of Orange*, 39.

[64] Klooster, "The Doctrinal Deliverances of Dort," in De Jong, *Crisis in the Reformed Churches*, 52.

[65] I've adapted this illustration from *1980 Acts of Synod*, 520.

discrimination between men, equally involved in ruin; or that decree of election and reprobation revealed in the Word of God, which though men of perverse, impure and unstable minds wrest to their own destruction, yet to holy and pious souls affords unspeakable consolation.

The sixth and final common conviction is the connection between faith and predestination.

The Eternal Source of Faith

As a gift, faith comes from God. Some are given this gift; others are not. Why? The answer finds its ultimate answer in God himself, who is the eternal source of faith. In Ephesians 1 Paul blesses God because he has blessed us with every blessing (v. 3), described under the headings of the blessing of predestination (vv. 4–6), the blessing of Jesus Christ's redeeming work (vv. 7–12), and the blessing of the sealing work of the Holy Spirit in our lives now that guarantees our salvation in eternity (vv. 13–14). Not only is God blessed for choosing us in Christ before the foundation of the world (v. 4) and predestining us in love (v. 5), but he did so "according to the purpose of his will" (v. 5). God's eternal choice of us was not arbitrary, chance, or random, but was in accord with his intentional will. Again in verse 11 we read that in Christ we have obtained an inheritance. That's speaking of our coming into possession by faith of Christ and all his benefits. And how did we come to obtain this? Verse 11 continues: "having been [past tense] predestined according to the purpose of him who works all things according to the counsel of his will." This was one of those verses that virtually jumped off the page in my life when I was wrestling with truth and faith. Not only does Paul say that we came into possession of Christ because we were predestined to obtain Christ, but that the God who predestined us to faith also works out everything according to his will. "All that God does in time, that he determined from everlasting so to do."[66] Do you see what Paul is saying here? *Everything* happens according to the will of God, whether his will positively ordains it or passively permits it. Your faith in Christ is one of those positively purposed things!

---

[66] *Dutch Annotations*, Acts 15:18. Paraeus called this "an undoubted Rule" of divinity. "Epitome of Arminianisme," 820.

What does this mean for us? It means that we need to magnify God even more because salvation from eternity and unto eternity is merely and purely of his grace. This means we need to stand still and ponder the fact that from eternity past—if we can ever speak of such a thing in such a way!—God the Father decided to love me, to choose me out from a mass of damnation, and predestined me to believe in him. Me, me of all people! And so we sing,

> 'Tis not that I did choose Thee,
> For Lord, that could not be;
> This heart would still refuse Thee,
> Hadst Thou not chosen me.
> Thou from the sin that stained me
> Hast cleansed and set me free;
> Of old Thou hast ordained me,
> That I should live to Thee.[67]

The Temporal Softening unto Faith

Let me anticipate a common objection or a misunderstanding of this. "If God's will is involved in everything, including faith, there's no need to worry about any of this because there's nothing you can do about it anyway." The answer is that the God of eternal predestining is also the God of temporal softening. The God who chooses us apart from our faith enables us to come to him in faith.

How does God as the eternal source of faith lead to the temporal faith of sinners? Remember Acts 13:48 mentioned above? Paul is preaching the gospel to Gentiles when we read, "As many as were appointed to eternal life believed." Do you see the connection? "But how, practically speaking, did this eternal appointing lead to believing in time?" That's where Acts 16 comes into play. As Paul preached the gospel to Lydia, we read this: "The Lord opened her heart to pay attention to what was said by Paul" (Acts 16:14). The same God who predestined that she would believe opened her heart to believe. This is why article 6 says so wonderfully, **According to which decree, He graciously softens the hearts of the elect,**

---

[67] From the hymn "'Tis Not That I Did Choose Thee."

however obstinate, and inclines them to believe. God graciously *softens* our stone-hard hearts and *inclines* them to believe in his Son. This is what is going on behind the scenes, so to speak, when we heard the Word and believed. God who requires faith as the necessary means of receiving the blessings of his Son is the same God who gives that faith. Isn't this a wonderful assurance to us who have believed? Isn't this a wonderful promise to us for the hard hearted we know? Isn't this a wonderful encouragement to pray to the God who is able and willing to do such a thing? We've all heard pious and well-meaning brothers and sisters say predestination is like a cold shower on Christian enthusiasm, that it's like a dry sponge that soaks up all spiritual zeal, that it's too intellectual, too lifeless, too philosophical, and too sterile of a doctrine! But it's a truth given to us in Scripture, therefore we are to adore God for it, be comforted by it, and be inspired by it to pray for and desire the salvation of the lost.

On the other hand, God's gracious gift to some demonstrates **His just judgment** by leav[ing] **the non-elect...to their own wickedness and obduracy** [hardness of heart]." There's no injustice with God. All humanity is sinful and under the curse. Everyone is born with a hard heart. Therefore God's **righteous discrimination between** *people* (*hominum*) is between those **equally involved in ruin**. This is beyond us. It is **profound** in his mercy and justice. But it's a revealed truth for us to stand in awe of. Some whom the article says are **of perverse, impure and unstable minds** will **wrest** [distort] this teaching **to their own destruction, yet to holy and pious souls** it **affords unspeakable consolation.**

Article 7

Election is the unchangeable purpose of God, whereby, before the foundation of the world, He hath out of mere grace, according to the sovereign good pleasure of His own will, chosen, from the whole human race, which had fallen through their own fault from their primitive state of rectitude into sin and destruction, a certain number of persons to redemption in Christ, whom He from eternity appointed the Mediator and Head of the elect, and the foundation of salvation. This elect number, though by nature neither better nor more deserving than others, but with them involved in one common misery, God hath decreed to give to Christ, to be saved by Him, and effectually to call and draw them to His communion by His Word and Spirit, to bestow upon them true faith, justification and sanctification; and having powerfully preserved them in the fellowship of His Son, finally, to glorify them for the demonstration of His mercy and for the praise of

His glorious grace, as it is written: "According as He hath chosen us in Him before the foundation of the world, that we should be holy and without blame before Him in love: having predestinated us unto the adoption of children by Jesus Christ to Himself, according to the good pleasure of His will, to the praise of the glory of His grace, wherein He hath made us accepted in the beloved" (Eph. 1:4–6). And elsewhere: "Whom He did predestinate, them He also called: and whom He called, them He also justified: and whom He justified them He also glorified" (Rom. 8:30).

ELECTION DEFINED

With the basic biblical teachings of articles 1–6 laid out as a canvas, we're finally ready to paint on God's predestinating work in articles 7–14. One of the reasons this is so important to highlight is that it keeps us from overfocusing on predestination. The Belgic Confession of Faith (1561) had one short article on predestination that says God "delivers and preserves from this perdition [of Adam's fall] all whom He in His eternal and unchangeable counsel of mere goodness has elected in Christ Jesus our Lord, without any respect to their works" while "leaving others in the fall and perdition wherein they have involved themselves" (art. 16).[68] As Andreas Beck writes, "Indeed there is little if anything at all in this article of the *Belgic Confession* that would be specific to the Reformed tradition."[69] According to Gomarus, it was Arminius who made a mountain out of a molehill, overemphasizing predestination in the controversy over his theology.[70] Yet even Reformed theologians can make this mistake, calling predestination "the beating heart" of the canons.[71] Another reason is the catholic context of predestination. In the words of Willem van Asselt, "Dordt did not invent the doctrine of predestination and the opposition against it is not new either…[they] did not have the intention to be original or introduce something new into the

---

[68] Dennison, *Reformed Confessions of the 16th and 17th Centuries*, 2:433–34.

[69] Beck, "Reformed Confessions and Scholasticism," 29.

[70] Goudriaan, "Justification by Faith and the Early Arminian Controversy," 160.

[71] Wim Verboom, "The Christology in the *Heidelberg Catechism* and in the *Canones of Dordt*," in *Strangers and Pilgrims on Earth: Essays in Honor of Abraham van de Beek*, ed. E. Van der Borght and P. van Geest, Studies in Reformed Theology 22 (Leiden: Brill, 2012), 118. See also Herman Hoeksema, *Predestination: The Heart of the Gospel* (Grand Rapids, MI: Radio Committee of the First Protestant Reformed Church, 1949). Available online at https://www.prca.org/articles/predestination/index.html.

Christian tradition—original are only the heretics."[72] The biblical truth of God's eternal predestination to salvation passed down through the ages reveals to us the glorious grace of our triune God. Here in article 7 we are finally give the Reformed definition.[73]

It is Unchangeable

What makes the doctrine of election so glorious? **Election is the *un-changeable* purpose of God**. Nowhere in any biblical passage do we ever get any idea that what God planned, either God himself has changed or can be changed by us. God's eternal plans are always described as certain, fixed, and immovable—"the unchangeable character of [God's] purpose" (Heb. 6:17–18). We'll see in the rejection of errors how the followers of Arminius taught that there were various kinds of election, including a revocable kind.[74] Scripture does speak of God "changing," but this is accommodated language. What this highlights for us practically is that it's so easy for us to judge God on the basis of our experience. Dad would make promises, Dad would break promises; God is a Father, therefore he, too, changes. It's easy for us to see people in church and then not and to think that somehow they were genuinely saved but then lost that salvation. Election is glorious because it is unchangeable.

It is Eternal

What makes the doctrine of election so glorious? *It is eternal.*[75] **Election is the unchangeable purpose of God, whereby, *before* the foundation of the world.** This language comes right from Ephesians 1:4. Scripture reveals to us that before anything was, there was only God. Before he actually made anything, he had a plan. Since he is eternal, so are his plans. His eternal plan for us was a gracious plan, saving us according to "his own purpose and grace, which he gave us in Christ Jesus *before the ages began*" (πρὸ

---

[72] Van Asselt, "No Dordt without Scholasticism," 204–5, 206.

[73] See how this definition was the foundation in *Synopsis Purioris Theologiae/Synopsis of a Purer Theology: Volume 2*, ed. Henk van den Belt, trans. Riemer A. Faber (Leiden: Brill, 2016), 31.

[74] See rejection of errors 2 in chapter 2 below.

[75] *Synopsis Purioris Theologiae: Volume 2*, 31.

χρόνων αἰωνίων; 2 Tim. 1:9). This is why Paul praises God for this, saying, "For who has known the mind of the Lord, or who has been his counselor? Or who has given a gift to him that he might be repaid?" (Rom. 11:34–35).

This is not only glorious, but it should be inspiring to you and me. Have you come to realize that the eternal and glorious God had a plan *for you* in particular from all of eternity and for all of eternity?

It is Gracious

What makes the doctrine of election so glorious? In his unchangeable pur-pose before the foundation of the world **out of mere *grace*, according to the sovereign** (*liberrimum*; free) **good pleasure of His own will, cho-sen…in Christ…** Paul says that at the heart of our praise to God the Fa-ther is his love for us. His love is an eternal love "as he chose us in him before the foundation of the world" (Eph. 1:4). His love for us is the cause of his predestining us (Eph. 1:5). His eternal love for us was that we would know his love in time, as his predestining love was "for adoption to himself as sons through Jesus Christ" (Eph. 1:5). And his love for us was rooted in his prior love for his Son, "the Beloved" (Eph. 1:6).

This eternal grace was initiated, executed, and purposed in God him-self, and not in us. "*He* chose us" (Eph. 1:4), "*he* predestined" us (Eph. 1:5), and this was "according to the purpose of *his* will" (Eph. 1:5). That word "purpose" (εὐδοκία; *eudokia*) can also be translated as "pleasure," or "good pleasure" (NIV, NKJV, respectively) or "kind intention" (NASB).[76] The cause of election is God's love. It is not arbitrary or capricious, but rooted in a deep love for us. As Moses revealed to the Israelites in Deuteronomy 7, it was not because they were more in number or greater than anyone else that he chose them, but it was merely because the Lord loved them!

So why did God elect one person and not another? More personally, why did God choose you and not another? God "chose us in [Christ] be-fore the foundation of the world." Then we read why: "*that* we should be holy and blameless before him" (Eph. 1:4). In other words, it was not because we *were* holy and blameless. Again, we read that "in love [the Fa-ther] predestined us *for* adoption to himself as sons through Jesus Christ, according to the purpose of his will, to the praise of his glorious grace"

---

[76] εὐδοκία, ας, ἡ in *A Greek-English Lexicon of the New Testament*, 319.

(Eph. 1:4–6). His predestining us made us sons; we were not predestined because he saw us becoming sons. Have you ever heard a preacher use the illustration of a parade, where God, as it were, was in the broadcast booth watching the entire parade; from that vantage point he could see all humanity pass before him, believing or not, and then he reacts to this with his choice. Ephesians 1 says otherwise, that it was according to the riches of grace in God before time began that he chose you, not because of your faith in time.

The graciousness of God's electing work is particularly glorious when we realize that he chose "us" *as sinners*. We were chosen **from the whole human race, which had fallen through their own fault from their primitive state of rectitude** (*integritate*; innocence) **into sin and destruction** not because we were **by nature neither better nor more deserving than others, but with them involved in one common misery.**

Because he chose *us* of all people, we sing at the top of our lungs from the bottom of our hearts, "O to grace how great a debtor, daily I'm constrained to be!" Why did God choose you and not another? It was *not* because of you!

This is so important for us, because it keeps grace gracious. Therefore, we are humbled to the core, not being puffed up because we were better. Grace is gracious.

Let me pause and anticipate a concern you may have. You may be thinking, "This sounds arbitrary." But here's the answer to that. If it were arbitrary, it would be for no reason. Like a bunch of ping pong balls in a lottery machine, one just comes up out of chance, luck, or odds. If all we said about election was that it was based on nothing *in us*, then yes, it would be arbitrary. You would be like one of billions and billions of white Ping-Pong balls with absolutely nothing to distinguish you. But election is not arbitrary, as it is based on something *in God*—but something that lies hidden from us. He gives it purpose and reason. Instead of what is in us, God elects on what is in him: grace and love. The simplicity of Scripture demands this.

Another concern is that this makes God the author of sin. This first point of doctrine, though, began with Adam's fall into sin. Article 5 asserted that **the cause or guilt of this unbelief, as well as of all other sins, is no wise** (*neutiquam*; not at all) **in God, but in man himself.** Now article 7 says God elects **from the whole human race, which had fallen through their** own fault from their primitive state of rectitude (*integritate*; innocence) into sin and destruction and that this elect number, though by nature neither better nor more deserving than others, but with them involved in one common misery. "But if God ordains everything, didn't he ordain that Adam would sin?" While some particular Reformed theologians spoke in simplistic, even harsh tones, by the time of the synod Reformed theologians such as Theodore Beza endorsed the medieval doctrine of divine permission. One of the delegates to the synod, Gisbertus Voetius,[77] used the fine distinctions of the theological tool kit of his day to say that "God does not have a positive act of will in relation to sin and the fall, although He *positively wills His not having a positive act of will towards sin.*"[78] Elsewhere he cited Aquinas, who said, "God therefore neither wills evil to be done, nor wills it not to be done, but wills to permit evil to be done; and this is a good."[79] In simple terms, God wills some things effectively while others things he abstains from permissively. We'll see more of this below in relation to article 15.

Notice with me several passages of Scripture. First, we read in Romans 9:11 of God's word to Rebekah about her twins, Jacob and Esau: "though they were not yet born and had done nothing either good or bad—in order that God's purpose of election might continue, not because of works but because of him who calls." Election is based not in our works but in God's grace.

Second, in 2 Timothy 1:9 we read this: "who saved us and called us to a holy calling, *not because of* [οὐ κατὰ, or, "not according to"] our works but *because of* [κατὰ, or, "according to"] his own purpose and grace, which he gave us in Christ Jesus before the ages began." Election is not on the basis of our purposing to do so much but because God purposed grace for us.

---

[77] Variously spelled Gisberti Voetii, Gijsbertus Voetius, Gisbertus Voetius.

[78] Cited in Beck, "Reformed Confessions and Scholasticism," 21. Emphasis added. See Aza Goudriaan, *Reformed Orthodoxy and Philosophy, 1625–1750. Gisbertus Voetius, Petrus van Mastricht, and Anthonius Driessen,* Brill's Series in Church History 26 (Leiden: Brill, 2006), 188–92; Andreas J. Beck, "'Expositio reverentialis': Gisbertus Voetius's (1589–1676) Relationship with John Calvin," *Church History and Religious Culture* 91, nos. 1–2 (2011): 121–33.

[79] Thomas Aquinas, *St. Thomas Aquinas: Summa Theologica*, trans. Fathers of the English Dominican Province (1948; repr., Notre Dame, IN: Christian Classics, 1981), I, Q. 19, art. 9 (p. 111).

It is Definite

What makes the doctrine of election so glorious? In his unchangeable, eternal, and gracious purpose God chose **from the whole human race...a** *certain number* **of persons to redemption in Christ**. The doxology of Ephesians 1 is that "*we*" bless God because he has blessed "*us*" (Eph. 1:4). This is not an indefinite mass or class of people, but real people like you and me. Augustine said the "number [of the predestined] is so certain that one can neither be added to them nor taken away...neither to be increased nor diminished."[80]

Why is this so important to debate over? If predestination were indefinite and impersonal, we would ever be in doubt as to our participation in it. On the contrary, because it is definitely of particular persons, John Calvin said Paul's intention in Ephesians 1 was "to rouse [our] hearts to gratitude, to set [us] all on flame, to occupy and fill [us] with this thought.... No doctrine is more useful...[to] stir us up to give thanks."[81]

It is Christ Centered

Another aspect article 7 points out that makes the doctrine of election so glorious is that we were chosen **in Christ**.[82] This is one of the areas we need to grow in appreciation for. We can so often speak abstractly of "predestination," forgetting that this doctrine is Christ centered. In Ephesians 1, before he even says a word about predestination Paul roots everything in Jesus Christ. How so? We bless "the God and Father *of our Lord Jesus Christ*" (v. 3); God has "blessed us *in Christ* with every spiritual blessing" (v. 3); God chose us "*in him*," that is, Jesus Christ (v. 4); God "blessed us *in the Beloved*" (v. 6). "In Christ" doesn't mean that Christ's foreseen merit was the basis of our then being chosen in him, as the Remonstrants taught, but that "even before [we] are fully united with Christ through faith, there is some

---

[80] Augustine, "On Rebuke and Grace," 39 in *Nicene and Post-Nicene Fathers: First Series*, ed. Philip Schaff (1887; repr., Peabody, MA: Hendrickson, fourth printing 2004), 5:487, 488.

[81] John Calvin, *The Epistles of Paul the Apostle to the Galatians, Ephesians, Philippians and Colossians,* trans. T. H. L. Parker, ed. David W. Torrance and Thomas F. Torrance, Calvin's New Testament Commentaries 11 (1965; repr., Grand Rapids, MI: Eerdmans, 1972), 123, 126.

[82] *Synopsis Purioris Theologiae: Volume 2*, 39.

specific connection and mutual relationship between him, as the head, and the elect, as the members destined for and given to him."[83] Paul also told Timothy that God "saved us and called us to a holy calling, not because of our works but because of his own purpose and grace, which he gave us *in Christ Jesus* [ἐν Χριστῷ Ἰησοῦ] before the ages began" (2 Tim. 1:9).

Article 7 summarizes what it means to have been chosen **in Christ** saying **God hath decreed to give to Christ, to be saved by Him, and effectually to call and draw them to His communion by His Word and Spirit.** How? The article goes on: **to bestow upon them true faith, justification and sanctification; and having powerfully preserved them in the fellowship of His Son, finally, to glorify them.**

> We have heard the joyful sound: Jesus saves! Jesus saves!
> Spread the tidings all around: Jesus saves! Jesus saves!
> Sing, ye islands of the sea! Echo back, ye ocean caves!
> Earth shall keep her jubilee; Jesus saves! Jesus saves![84]

Our Lord can do all this because God **from eternity appointed** [him] **the Mediator and Head of the elect, and the foundation of salvation.** This paragraph makes the comment of Wim Verboom perplexing: "At a certain point, the CD turns the spotlight away from the work of Christ and illuminates the eternal decree of God."[85] This whole section of article 7 is that Christ is mediator, head, and foundation and that God gave the elect to Christ, incorporated them into Christ, and saves them through Christ. Nothing can be more Christological than this!

This Christological focus brings up one of the internal disagreements at the synod between Franciscus Gomarus and Matthias Martinius. Gomarus said Christ was the foundation of the elect (*fundamentum electorum*), not the foundation of election (*fundamentum electionis*); what this meant for Gomarus was that Christ was the one who executed the eternal decree of election in time but was not election's author. Martinius, on the other hand, believed Ephesians 1 taught that Christ was both the executor and author

---

[83] *Synopsis Purioris Theologiae: Volume 2*, 41.

[84] From the hymn "We Have Heard the Joyful Sound."

[85] Verboom, "The Christology in the *Heidelberg Catechism* and in the *Canones of Dordt*," in *Strangers and Pilgrims on Earth*, 120. For a critique of Verboom's work on the Canons of Dort, see van Asselt, "No Dordt without Scholasticism," 203–10.

of election. One of the problems was that this issue had come up in Theodore Beza's debate with the Lutheran Jacob Andreae. Andreae charged Beza with reducing Christ from being the foundation of election (*fundamentum electionis*) to being merely the foundation and executor of the elect (*fundamentum electorum*). Beza actually responded that Christ was both, first in the counsel of the Trinity and second by his Incarnation.[86] The problem was that by the time of the synod, Andreae's language had been taken over by the Remonstrants. The issue Gomarus had with saying Christ is the foundation of election (*fundamentum electionis*) was that it could be used to say there was no eternal decree but only that at the cross did election begin. This, in fact, is what Arminius had done in his fundamental redefining of election, calling election "the decree of God by which He from eternity has determined to justify believers in Christ, and to receive them to life eternal, to the praise of His glorious grace."[87]

This redefined election because in mainstream Reformed thought, the decree of election *preceded* the decree to send Christ to make atonement for sin; Arminius reversed this order. He said, "Predestination rests not merely on the death, but also on the merit of the death of Christ: and therefore Christ has not died for the predestinated, but those are predestinated for whom Christ has died, though not all."[88] He used the distinction Gomarus and Martinius debated to say: "For, if Christ be the foundation of the execution of election only, then election itself has already been made, in the decree of God preceding its real execution, without respect to Christ.... But the Scripture puts Christ as the foundation, not of the execution only, but also of the making of election itself."[89]

This debate got so tense and fiery that Gomarus challenged Martinius to a duel! The synod concluded discussion and ended with prayer only to have Gomarus immediately reissue his challenge.[90] It goes to show that the-

---

[86] See W. Robert Godfrey, "Reformed Thought on the Extent of the Atonement to 1618," *Westminster Theological Journal* 37, no. 2 (Winter 1975): 141.

[87] "Modest Examination of a Pamphlet, Which That Very Learned Divine, Dr. William Perkins, Published Some Years Ago, on the Mode and Order of Predestination, and on the Amplitude of Divine Grace," in *The Works of James Arminius: Volume 3*, 293.

[88] "Modest Examination," in *The Works of James Arminius: Volume 3*, 325.

[89] "Modest Examination," in *The Works of James Arminius: Volume 3*, 303.

[90] John Hales, *Golden Remains of the Ever Memorable Mr. John Hales of Eton College* (London, 1659), 72–73.

se were mere men. In the end the synod crafted this statement that both men could affirm to say: **Before the foundation of the world** [God] **hath...chosen, from the whole human race...a certain number of persons to redemption in Christ**. This was biblical language right from Ephesians 1. Again, the article says God chose **in Christ, whom He from eternity appointed the Mediator and Head of the elect,** *and the foundation of salvation*. This language satisfied Gomarus. Then it speaks in a way that satisfied Martinius: **God hath decreed** *to give to Christ, to be saved by Him,* **and effectually to call and draw them effectively to His communion by His Word and Spirit.**

In practical terms, this means that Jesus Christ is like the mirror of our election. If the knowledge of God's good pleasure and powerful love before the foundation of the world still leaves you in doubt, then the only remedy is to gaze upon Christ, as in a mirror. Look at him, and you will see reflected back yourself, being renewed in his image and chosen to be so.

What a doctrine! It reveals the glory of our wonderful God! As it does, it leads us to respond in praise and in holiness: "that we should be holy and blameless before him" (Eph. 1:4). This is no hyper-Calvinism or fatalism that says, "God will do what God will do, therefore it doesn't matter." He did what he did in eternity and has made that real in your life *so that* your life would matter! He "chose us," that is, he called us out (ἐξελέξατο; *exelexato*) of the mass of sinners deserving punishment. And having called us out from eternity past, in time we become his "sons through Jesus Christ" by adoption (Eph. 1:5).

When we meditate on his glory we burst forth in praise: "Blessed be the God and Father of our Lord Jesus Christ" (Eph. 1:3) and "to the praise of his glorious grace" (Eph. 1:6)! When we meditate on his glory, we respond in seeking to be holy. We were chosen for this. Out of the mass of sinners deserving punishment we were called forth "that we should be holy and blameless before him" (Eph. 1:4). What a God! What a life he has called us to![91]

---

[91] In the notes on Ephesians 1:4–6, the *Dutch Annotations* virtually show how the points in article 7 flow directly from the biblical text: "God chose us in Christ, *before the foundation of the world* [*Dutch Annotations* "from everlasting"], so that we should be holy and blameless before him with love; he predestined us [*Dutch Annotations* "from eternity"] whom he adopted as his children through Jesus Christ, in himself, according to the good pleasure of his will [*Dutch Annotations* "not for any merit or worthiness of ours but only according to his undeserved favor, grace and pleas-

Article 8

There are not various decrees of election, but one and the same decree respecting all those who shall be saved, both under the Old and New Testament; since the Scripture declares the good pleasure, purpose and counsel of the divine will to be one, according to which He hath chosen us from eternity, both to grace and glory, to salvation and the way of salvation, which He hath ordained that we should walk therein.

ELECTION ACROSS THE TESTAMENTS

God chose *us*—new covenant Christians. But what about those who went before us? We'll see in the rejections of errors that there are not various decrees of election but one.[92] This means the God who chose Abraham and Israel is the same God who chose us. His choosing some to salvation, then, is the same choosing that leads to salvation today. In other words, article 8 expresses how God's electing grace in the Old Testament relates to his electing grace in the New.

Unity of the Will of God

In Ephesians 1 (again) Paul says in verse 4 that "he chose [ἐξελέξατο] us in [Christ] before the foundation of the world" and in verses 4–5 that "in love he predestined [προορίσας] us." Some might say that this speaks of *us*, meaning, Christians in the new covenant and not believers in the old. But notice that Paul speaks very simply—if I can say that when speaking of election and predestination!—of "the purpose of his will" (τὴν εὐδοκίαν τοῦ θελήματος αὐτοῦ) in verse 5, and "the mystery of his will" (τὸ μυστήριον τοῦ θελήματος αὐτοῦ) in verse 9, and again of "his purpose" (τὴν εὐδοκίαν αὐτοῦ) in verse 9, and again of being "predestined [προορισθέντες] according to [God's] purpose" (πρόθεσιν), which is the same as "the counsel of his will" (τὴν βουλὴν τοῦ θελήματος αὐτοῦ), in verse 11.

This is why article 8 says **this are not various** (*multiplex*; many kinds) **decrees of election**, meaning, it is not complex, but simple and solitary.

---

ure"], to the praise of his glorious grace, by which he freely made us pleasing to himself in his beloved." *Dutch Annotations* on Ephesians 1:4–6.

[92] See rejection of errors 2 in chapter 2 below.

The simplicity is found in Scripture defining **the good pleasure** (*beneplacitum*), **purpose** (*propositium*), **and counsel** (*consilium*) **of the divine will to be one**. This may not sound like it has any benefit to you that you should spend brain cells on it. Here's the benefit: God doesn't change his mind about you! Every single soul he set his love upon from eternity past and chose to share in his glory for eternity, whether they were before Christ came or after, he will find and bring into his fellowship. God's purpose for you is one.

Unity of the Testaments

Speaking of all those under both testaments, we read of **one and the same decree respecting all those who shall be saved, both under the Old and New Testament**. Eternal election has a close connection to the history of God's covenantal dealings with his people. There's unity of **all those who shall be saved** while there's the diversity of **the Old and New Testament**. This leads us back to Deuteronomy 7.

As Israel was preparing to enter the Promised Land and to conquer the Lord's enemies in it (vv. 1–5), the Lord stopped them and reminded them of who they were. They were about to triumph, but the Lord wanted to remind them that it was *he* who triumphed over them in grace first. He first states their identity: "For you are a people holy to the LORD your God" (v. 6). Then he explains how they became this: "The LORD your God has chosen you to be a people for his treasured possession, out of all the peoples who are on the face of the earth" (v. 6). Talk about confidence building! Yet the Lord did not want them to be puffed up, but to know the reason for his choosing them and not those they were going in to conquer:

> It was not because you were more in number than any other people that the LORD set his love on you and chose you, for you were the fewest of all peoples, but it is because the LORD loves you and is keeping the oath that he swore to your fathers, that the LORD has brought you out with a mighty hand and redeemed you from the house of slavery, from the hand of Pharaoh king of Egypt. (Deut. 7:7–8)

Israel was elected according to the love of God. Sound familiar? Again, Ephesians 1:4–5 says God "chose us in [Christ] before the foundation of the world...in love he predestined us." And when the Lord states that Israel was "a people holy to the LORD your God" (Deut. 7:6), this is what Paul says of us: "He chose us in him before the foundation of the world, that we should be holy and blameless before him" (Eph. 1:4); this is what Peter says of us: "But you are a chosen race, a royal priesthood, a holy nation, a people for his own possession" (1 Pet. 2:9).

So because of God's one eternal purpose of election and predestination, all those saved before the coming of Christ and all those saved after the coming of Christ are one. The one God has one purpose and one people. I don't know about you, but coming from a broken family background, this gives me identity and significance. I belong to a spiritual family that spans the ages! Whether you come from the same kind of background or not, you know the effects of a fallen world upon your relationships. You, too, belong to the church of Old Testament and New Testament believers. You sit at the same family banquet with Abraham, with Moses, with David, with Peter, with Paul, and with all the saints. The ancient hymn *Te Deum* in part says it like this:

> We praise thee, O God: we acknowledge thee to be the
> Lord.
> All the earth doth worship thee: the Father everlasting.
> Heaven and earth are full of the Majesty: of thy glory.
> The glorious company of the Apostles: praise thee.
> The goodly fellowship of the Prophets: praise thee.
> The noble army of Martyrs: praise thee.
> The holy Church throughout all the world: doth
> acknowledge thee.[93]

Unity of the Benefits

Another way we see this unity of God's eternal, electing will throughout both testaments is in the *unity of the benefits* of election. Notice again article 8; it says the **good pleasure, purpose and counsel of the divine will...hath chosen us from eternity, both to grace and glory, to salvation and the**

---

[93] Book of Common Prayer, 6–7.

way of salvation, which He hath ordained that we should walk therein.

This is so important for your assurance and confidence before God. When God elected his people, he elected them **both to grace and glory**; that means, both to receive grace in this life and to experience it fully in the life to come. When God elected his people, he elected them **both…to salvation and the way of salvation, which He hath ordained that we should walk therein**; that means, he not only elected us to receive Christ for our justification but also to live a life of sanctification that leads to glorification.[94] This is why Deuteronomy 7, after it proclaims the wonder of the Lord's electing grace, goes on to say, "You shall therefore be careful to do the commandment and the statutes and the rules that I command you today" (v. 11). The three tenses of our salvation are that we have been saved, we are being saved, and we will be saved.

Now, hear me loud and clear: our obedience cannot be said to be necessary for our justification, as it is impossible for dead sinners to hear and obey God. Yet obedience is necessary for the justified believer as **the way of salvation**. The canons are using "salvation" in its broad sense. The article is not speaking of justification. Justification is not the whole of salvation; salvation encompasses justification and sanctification, and ultimately glorification. Obedience, then, is the heartfelt response to the grace of God by children of God who are on their way to eternal fellowship with God.

Article 9

This election was not founded upon foreseen faith, and the obedience of faith, holiness, or any other good quality or disposition in man, as the prerequisite, cause or condition on which it depended; but men are chosen to faith and to the obedience of faith, holiness, etc.; therefore election is

---

[94] This is exactly what the Westminster Larger Catechism, Q&A 32, says:

> Q. How is the grace of God manifested in the second covenant?
>
> A. The grace of God is manifested in the second covenant, in that he freely provideth and offereth to sinners a Mediator, and life and salvation by him; and requiring faith as the condition to interest them in him, promiseth and giveth his Holy Spirit to all his elect, to work in them that faith, with all other saving graces; and to enable them unto all holy obedience, as the evidence of the truth of their faith and thankfulness to God, and as the way which he hath appointed them to salvation.

the fountain of every saving good, from which proceeds faith, holiness, and the other gifts of salvation, and finally eternal life itself, as its fruits and effects, according to that of the apostle: "He hath chosen us [not because we were but] that we should be holy, and without blame, before Him in love" (Eph. 1:4).

Article 9 explains the Augustinian interpretation of Ephesians 1:4 that God **hath chosen us [not because we were but] that we should be holy, and without blame, before Him in love.**

NOT CHOSEN BECAUSE OF FAITH

The article begins by referring back to the definition of election in article 7—**This election**—explaining that it **was not founded upon foreseen faith, and the obedience of faith, holiness, or any other good quality or disposition in** *the person* (*homine*), **as the prerequisite, cause or condition on which it depended.**

In other words, there was nothing in sinful human beings or nothing done by them that led God to choose them. In the first few centuries of theology, Christian theologians had to counter Stoic fatalism and Gnostic/Manichean dualism in which the world was divided into the good and the evil. In response, Greek theologians emphasized free will and God's foreknowledge.[95] For example, in the context of speaking of the judgment of the devil and evil spirits, Justin Martyr (ca. 100–165) said:

For the reason why God has delayed to do this, is His regard for the human race. For He foreknows that some are to be saved by repentance, some even that are perhaps not yet born. In the beginning He made the human race with the power of thought and of choosing the truth and doing right, so that all men are without excuse before God; for they have been born rational and contemplative.[96]

In Augustine's earlier writings on predestination he followed this doctrine that God elected or condemned based on his foreknowledge of man's belief or unbelief. Eventually he came to see the inadequacy of fore-

---

[95] See Sinnema, "The Issue of Reprobation at the Synod of Dort," 8–9.

[96] Justin Martyr, *First Apology*, 1.28 in *Ante-Nicene Fathers: Volume 1*, ed. Alexander Roberts and James Donaldson (1885; repr., Peabody, MA: Hendrickson, fourth printing 2004), 172.

knowledge as a means of interpreting Romans 9.[97] Down through the ages this became the standard interpretation. Peter Lombard passed down approvingly Augustine's mature statement: "And so God elected whom he willed by a freely given mercy, not because they would be faithful in the future, but so that they might be faithful; and he gave grace to them not because they were faithful, but that they might become so."[98]

Article 9, therefore, is consistent Augustinianism as exemplified in the Second Council of Orange (529), which said, for example, "God loves us for what we shall be by His gift, not for what we are by our own merit" (canon 12).[99] As mentioned before, at the heart of this teaching is that sinners are justified in the sight of God only through faith alone in Jesus Christ alone. To say anything in you—however little—was the reason God looked down and chose you is to turn justification into a matter of personal works.

CHOSEN FOR FAITH

But, on the contrary, God's purpose of election was **to faith and to the obedience of faith, holiness, etc.** This means that **election is the fountain of every saving good, from which proceeds faith, holiness, and the other gifts of salvation, and finally eternal life itself, as its fruits and effects**. The Remonstrants taught that faith, holiness, and perseverance led *to* predestination and that they did not flow *from* predestination. In the words of Paraeus, this necessarily meant that "God must be robbed of the full glory of our salvation, man must be puffed up with pride, our Christian comfort in life and death must be undermined, free justification and the assurance of salvation must be denied."[100] One practical area this impacts is how we view and live out our sanctification. You can't sit back and be inactive all the while you claim to be reveling in the grace of election. God chooses in grace, sinners, so that sinners will more and more be changed in thought, word, and deed by grace to his glory.

---

[97] On Augustine, see Sinnema, "The Issue of Reprobation at the Synod of Dort," 9–14.

[98] Peter Lombard, *The Sentences, Book 1: The Mystery of the Trinity*, trans. Giulio Silano, Mediaeval Sources in Translation 42 (Toronto: Pontifical Institute of Mediaeval Studies, 2007), 41.2.7 (p. 228). On Peter Lombard, see Sinnema, "The Issue of Reprobation at the Synod of Dort," 21–23.

[99] Woods, *Canons of the Second Council of Orange*, 40–41.

[100] Paraeus, "Epitome of Arminianisme," 818. See also p. 824.

Article 10

The good pleasure of God is the sole cause of this gracious election, which doth not consist herein, that out of all possible qualities and actions of men God has chosen some as a condition of salvation; but that He was pleased out of the common mass of sinners to adopt some certain persons as a peculiar people to Himself, as it is written, "For the children being not yet born, neither having done any good or evil," etc., it was said (namely to Rebecca): "The elder shall serve the younger. As it is written, Jacob have I loved, but Esau have I hated" (Rom. 9:11–13). "And as many as were ordained to eternal life believed" (Acts 13:48).

Article 10 goes on to express that **the good pleasure of God is the sole cause of this gracious election.** Dort followed the medieval consensus in saying this. In replying to the objection "there can be no other reason for predestination than the foreknowledge of merits. Therefore it must be the cause or reason of predestination," Thomas Aquinas said, "Predestination has its foundation in the goodness of God."[101] In his good pleasure God did not choose **out of all possible qualities and actions of** *people* (*humanas*) **God...as a condition of salvation;** instead **He was pleased out of the common mass of sinners to adopt some certain persons** (*personas*) **as a peculiar people to Himself.** God did not choose faceless possibilities but persons.

The biblical proof texts offered are Romans 9:11–13 and Acts 13:48. In Romans 9 Paul is making the argument that election is gracious, saying, **For the children being not yet born, neither having done any good or evil**. It wasn't a matter of merit or even demerit that God chose Jacob and not Esau. On the phrase **neither having done any good or evil**, the *Dutch Annotations* say it means

> whereby they could be differentiated one from the other. For otherwise they were already conceived in sin, and alive in their mothers womb when this divine answer happened concerning them: so that God looked not upon faith in them, seeing true believers cannot be said to be like to unbelievers, forasmuch as they being sanctified by the Spirit of God, are better than unbelievers.[102]

---

[101] Aquinas, *Summa Theologica*, I, Q. 23, art. 5 (p. 129). On Thomas, see Sinnema, "The Issue of Reprobation at the Synod of Dort," 25–28.

[102] *Dutch Annotations* on Romans 9:11.

We see this also in Acts 13:48, cited above, **as many as were ordained to eternal life believed,** not the other way around.

Article 11

And as God Himself is most wise, unchangeable, omniscient and omnipotent, so the election made by Him can neither be interrupted nor changed, recalled or annulled; neither can the elect be cast away, nor their number diminished.

Isaiah 40–55 makes up what is known as "the book of comfort." After chronicling Judah's sins in chapters 1–39, the prophet offers comfort to them as they go off into captivity in Babylon. And in the midst of this comfort to exiled Israelites, the Lord speaks of his glory over the idols of Babylon in chapters 46–47. The key is in 46:9–10. Because God is God and there is no other, his decrees and purposes cannot be annulled, changed, or revoked. This text illustrates for us what article 11 is getting at: the relationship between God's character and God's actions and works. The theologians at Dort applied the classic doctrine of the simplicity of God to predestination. *Simplicitas* means that God is different from everything else because he is not composed of different parts like creatures are. We have two "parts," bodies *and* souls, for example. God simply *is*.[103] He is not composed of his "attributes" as if they were a bunch of different qualities that he has or that he adds to who he really is from outside himself; they are who he is.[104] He's not 50 percent love and 50 percent just. He *is* love; He *is* just. In other words, what we believe about God has implications for what we believe about God's saving work in our lives. Voetius called him *Deus simplicissimus est essentia*, "God is the most simple essence." Therefore because he *is*, he does not change and we therefore can rely on him.[105]

---

[103] See the *Thirty-Nine Articles of Religion* (1563), art. 1; *Westminster Confession* (1647), ch. 2.1.

[104] For example, this was emphasized by William of Ockham. See Sinnema, "The Issue of Reprobation at the Synod of Dort," 30–31.

[105] Gisberti Voetii, *Selectarum Disputationum Theologicarum: Pars Prima* (Utrecht: Joannem à Waesberge 1648), 245.

GOD'S CHARACTER

The Lord calls upon his people in Isaiah 46:3 to listen to him because as he says in verse 4, "I am he." He is the Great I AM of Exodus 3; he is the God of Israel; he is the God of the universe. And what a God he is. Notice the personal pronouns and verbs in verse 4: "*I* will carry you. *I* have made, and *I* will bear; *I* will carry and *[I]* will save." Is there any other God like this? No! That's what he goes on to say in verse 5: "To whom will you liken me and make me equal, and compare me, that we may be alike?" They are about to be invaded, defeated, and carried off to Babylon to the east, away from the presence of God in the Promised Land and Holy Place. Yet there is none like him. In fact, all the other "gods" are in fact just the works of men's hands. Notice the irony in verses 6–7: "Those who lavish gold from the purse, and weigh out silver in the scales, hire a goldsmith, and he makes it into a god; then they fall down and worship!" They find the gold, they weigh the gold, and they form the gold; but then worship it. How ridiculous! Again we read: "They lift it to their shoulders, they carry it, they set it in its place, and it stands there; it cannot move from its place. If one cries to it, it does not answer or save him from his trouble." So much for these "gods."

The Lord then calls upon his people to remember this in exile in verses 8–9. Then he says this at the end of verse 9 and following: "For I am God, and there is no other; I am God, and there is none like me, declaring the end from the beginning and from ancient times things not yet done, saying, 'My counsel shall stand, and I will accomplish all my purpose'" (vv. 9–10). What is God like? We see God's eternal existence here. We see God's eternal wisdom here. We see God's unchangeable purpose here. We see God's eternal power here. Hence article 11 says **as God Himself is most wise, unchangeable, omniscient and omnipotent…**

One of the things that should strike us as we think about predestination and Christians' responses to it is that they forget their God. If we would just remember what Scripture says about God's character, a lot of our debates would go away!

GOD'S CHOICE

Because of who God is, according to the Lord himself in Isaiah 46, his choices, decrees, plans, and works in eternity are settled: "My counsel shall stand, and I will accomplish all my purpose" (v. 10). Is God perfectly wise? Then his choice of us and as many as he has chosen from eternity cannot be confused. Is God unchangeable? Is God all-knowing? Is God almighty? Then **the election made by Him can neither be interrupted nor changed, recalled or annulled; neither can the elect be cast away, nor their number diminished**.

YOUR COMFORT

What does this mean for us? To know God's character is the most comforting thing you can imagine in this life. The reason is that to know who he is as unchangeable means he's unchangeable toward you too. In other words, why is election so important, so practical for us as Reformed Christians? It's not to win an argument. It's not to figure God out. It's not to show off how smart we are. Election is so important and so practical to us because it gives us assurance that God is for us. It gives us confidence that God is on our side and that we are his people. It gives us comfort when we are tempted. It gives us comfort when we don't feel saved. It gives us comfort when our lives are a mess and it feels there is no meaning or purpose. Take this away and there's no reason to live!

Article 12

The elect in due time, though in various degrees and in different measures, attain the assurance of this their eternal and unchangeable election, not by inquisitively prying into the secret and deep things of God, but by observing in themselves, with a spiritual joy and holy pleasure, the infallible fruits of election pointed out in the Word of God—such as a true faith in Christ, filial fear, a godly sorrow for sin, a hungering and thirsting after righteousness, etc.

PASTORAL PROBLEMS CAUSED BY ELECTION

Articles 12–13 now deal with the practical issue of assurance. Imagine living life unsure who your parents are. Imagine living life unsure of whether you have a place to sleep tonight. Imagine living life unsure of where your next meal is coming from. Imagine living life unsure whether your next step will plunge you into a wormhole that takes you through the known universe and plants your feet firmly on an exoplanet outside our solar system! That would not be a life you'd want to live. Now imagine living life unsure of your eternal state. Even more so, this would be a life unworthy of living.

Once we begin to talk about predestination according to Scripture and understand that it is the eternal source of our coming to faith in Jesus, we will inevitably ask, "Am I elect?" This is the question of assurance. In the sixteenth century the Roman Catholic Council of Trent declared that believers who said they could know they were elect were guilty of rash presumption: "No one, moreover, so long as he is in this mortal life, ought so far to presume as regards the secret mystery of divine predestination, as to determine for certain that he is assuredly in the number of the predestinate."[106]

Then in the seventeenth century the theologians known as the Arminians said something similar: "There is in this life no fruit and no consciousness of the unchangeable election to glory, nor any certainty, except that which depends on a changeable and uncertain condition."[107] There is only thing we can be certain of as believers—uncertainty.

Our Standing in Relationship to God

The first part of the answer to the question, "Am I elect?" is that the Word of God says that our standing in relationship to God as believers in Jesus Christ is secure. To ask the question is not to question your faith and salvation, and behind that, your election. It is not intended to cause despair or fear. There is such a group called **the elect** that God has loved from eternity unchangeably, and if you believe in his Son Jesus, you are secure.

In 2 Peter 1, Peter writes not only as a "servant" but also as an "apostle of Jesus Christ" (v. 1). Then he identifies the recipients of this letter: "To those who have obtained a faith of equal standing with ours by the righteousness of our God and Savior Jesus Christ" (v. 1). These are astonishing words! They are astonishing because Peter once refused to eat with Gentile Christians for fear of losing his street cred with Jewish Christians. Because of that Paul says in Galatians 2 that he had to confront Peter face-to-face because Peter was denying the good news with his actions that

---

[106] Session 6, January 13, 1547. *The Canons and Decrees of the Sacred and Oecumenical Council of Trent*, trans. J. Waterworth, (London: C. Dolman, 1848), 39–40.

[107] See rejection of errors 7 below.

spoke louder than his words, saying Jewish Christians were a higher sort of Christian than Gentile Christians. These are astonishing words because they say to us that all who call upon Jesus' name by faith have a faith that is the same as that of the apostles themselves!

Further, God has "called us to his own glory and excellence" (v. 3), and therefore we have "escaped from the corruption that is in the world because of sinful desire" (v. 4). Then in verse 9, while he is exhorting and warning, he says that we have been "cleansed from…former sins." Because of all this Peter gives his "therefore": "be all the more diligent to confirm your calling and election" (v. 10). Did you hear that? We have a calling, and we have been elected. All we do is "*confirm*" it.

The Stages in Our Relationship with God

While in principal our standing with God is secure, each of us as believers needs to recognize practically the stages in our relationship with God. We all experience differently our standing before almighty God our heavenly Father. The objective reality of our standing with God is different than our subjective experience of it. The object of our faith is totally secure, but our grasping that object may or may not feel so secure at every moment. This is why article 12 says **the elect in due time, though in various degrees and in different measures, attain the assurance of this their eternal and unchangeable election**.

We need to grow. That's what 2 Peter 1:5–7 is all about. We are all at different places in our spiritual maturity. Some of us are spiritual grandparents. Some of us are spiritual parents. Some of us are spiritual twenty- and thirty-somethings. Some of us are spiritual adolescents. Some of us are spiritual babies. All the "qualities" Peter speaks about in verses 5–7 need to be "increasing" in us, and if they are, "they keep you from being ineffective or unfruitful in the knowledge of our Lord Jesus Christ" (1 Pet. 1:8). We can be stagnant or dynamic in our growth in relationship to God. Notice that Peter uses another illustration of this in verse 9. True believers can even "lack[…] these qualities" and therefore be spiritually "nearsighted" so that it is as if they are "blind, having forgotten that he was cleansed from his former sins."

Practically this means you shouldn't compare yourself to others, because God is at work in them differently. Your growth may not be equal to another's growth. Growth occurs individually **in various degrees and in**

different measures because we all have a different "measure of faith" (Rom. 12:3; cf. CD 5.9) and we each exercise that faith in different degrees at different times in life.

The Signs of Our Relationship with God

So how may I know I am growing in maturity and thus growing in assurance? We need to know the signs of our relationship with God. Stating this negatively, we need to know that assurance is **not** found **by inquisitively prying into the secret and deep things of God**. Assurance is not a matter of speculation, but revelation, meaning, we are not to look for a sign from God that he elected us but are to look into his Word.

What does the Word of God say are outward signs that he has chosen us? Article 12 is so helpful: believers are to **observ[e] in themselves, with a spiritual joy and holy pleasure, the infallible fruits of election pointed out in the Word of God—such as a true faith in Christ, filial fear, a godly sorrow for sin, a hungering and thirsting after righteousness, etc.** Peter says by the "divine power" of Jesus Christ "he has granted to us his precious and very great promises" (2 Pet. 1:3–4). Later in the canons we are told the same thing in a different way, that "this assurance does not derive from some private revelation beyond or outside the Word, but from faith in the promises of God which he has very plentifully revealed in his Word for our comfort" (5.10).

Those promises include those mentioned here in this chapter: we "have obtained a faith of equal standing…by the righteousness of our God and Savior Jesus Christ" (2 Pet. 1:1). It's interesting that article 12 mentions first **true faith in Christ**. The faith that apprehends Christ for justification is the first sign of our relationship with God.

The next signs relate to our sanctification. **Filial**, meaning childlike, **fear** of God. This means reverence as a child for a father. We are God's children and reverently listen to him and follow his leading.

The next is **a godly sorrow for sin**. We are grieved that we have grieved our Father by our disobedience and rebelliousness against his laws for us.

The final fruit or sign mentioned in the canon is **a hungering and thirsting after righteousness**. That's right from Jesus in Matthew 5. And you see that expressed in our passage: "For this very reason, make every effort to supplement your faith with virtue, and virtue with knowledge, and

knowledge with self-control, and self-control with steadfastness, and steadfastness with godliness, and godliness with brotherly affection, and brotherly affection with love" (2 Pet. 1:5–7).

How contrary are Peter's words to the popular caricature that if you
believe in election then you will have no incentive for faith, repentance, and
holiness? That's been the charge ever since the days of the apostle Paul.
"Why not do evil that good may come?—as some people slanderously
charge us with saying" (Rom. 3:8). "Are we to continue in sin that grace
may abound?" (Rom. 6:1). The doctrine of election's effects in the child of
God do not include carnal assurance. Be aware of this temptation in your
own life. Carnal assurance leads to carelessness, not carefulness. Carnal assurance leads to complacency, not zealotry. True, spiritual (that is, Spirit-
created) assurance, on the contrary, gives us even greater cause for godliness. Assurance leads to humility. Assurance leads to adoration of God's
infinite mercy. Assurance leads to a desire for purity in thoughts, words,
and deeds. Assurance leads to heartfelt love of the Savior, his people, and
the lost world.

Can I be sure I am chosen? The great English hymn writer John
Newton (1725–1807) once asked that question in one of his songs, saying,

> 'Tis a point I long to know,
> Oft it causes anxious thought,
> Do I love the Lord or no?
> Am I his, or am I not?
>
> If I love, why am I thus?
> Why this dull and lifeless frame?
> Hardly, sure, can they be worse,
> Who have never heard his name!
>
> Could my heart so hard remain,
> Prayer a task and burden prove,
> Every trifle give me pain,
> If I knew a Savior's love?
>
> When I turn my eyes within,
> All is dark and, vain and wild,
> Filled with unbelief and sin,
> Can I deem myself a child?

If I pray, or hear, or read,
Sin is mixed with all I do;
You who love the Lord indeed,
Tell me, is it thus with you?

Does this sound like you? Know from the Word of God that your standing with him is like standing on a huge rock in the ocean. Your footing is totally secure because the rock is secure. It's how you feel about standing on a rock in the ocean and how those waves keep hitting against it and splashing you that is unstable. But the longer you stand on it, the more you see that the rock isn't moving, that the waves cannot sweep you away, and that the splashing water and mist cannot harm you. Be assured!

Article 13

The sense and certainty of this election afford to the children of God additional matter for daily humiliation before Him, for adoring the depth of His mercies, for cleansing themselves, and rendering grateful returns of ardent love to Him, who first manifested so great love towards them. The consideration of this doctrine of election is so far from encouraging remissness in the observance of the divine commands or from sinking men in carnal security, that these, in the just judgment of God, are the usual effects of rash presumption or of idle and wanton trifling with the grace of election in those who refuse to walk in the ways of the elect.

For so many young Reformed people, the knowledge and assurance that God has elected them in his grace leads to what has been called the "cage phase." Cage phase Calvinists are the ones who are always arguing about doctrine or are living so freely in reaction to their legalistic past that they are like rabid dogs that need to be put in a cage until they calm down. The apostle Paul stands as a ready example to us of what true assurance looks like and what it does not look like.

The Results of Carnal Assurance

Article 13 says **the sense and certainty of this election...is so far from encouraging**. Our forefathers wanted to distance the true biblical doctrine from what was masquerading as the truth. What is our doctrine **so far from**?

First, from **encouraging remissness in the observance of the divine commands**. Second, **from sinking men in carnal security**. Where do these attitudes and actions (or lack thereof) come from? Notice what article 13 goes on to say: **these, in the just judgment of God, are the usual effects of rash presumption or of idle and wanton trifling with the grace of election in those who refuse to walk in the ways of the elect**. This is an exhortation and warning to us. We need to seriously examine ourselves.

Let me briefly go back to the two results of carnal assurance. First, a carnal assurance leads to carelessness, not carefulness. But Paul's example blows these out of the water. In Romans 6 he asks should he continue sinning that grace would continue increasing? His answer was absolutely not. Second, a carnal assurance leads to complacency, not zealotry. In Romans 7, in the midst of all he says about his struggles in the Christian life, he says he delighted in the law of God.

The Results of Spiritual Assurance

The sense and certainty of this election afford to the children of God additional matter for godliness. It's not just that we find a few good reasons to do a few good little things—no—it says that because of our assurance of being elect we have the greatest cause for godliness. In what ways?

First, when the Holy Spirit grants us more and more assurance of our election, it leads us to **daily humiliation before Him** (*coram Deo*).

Second, when the Holy Spirit grants us more and more assurance of our election, it leads us into **adoring the depth** (*abyssum*) **of His mercies**.

Third, when the Holy Spirit grants us more and more assurance of our election, it leads us to **cleansing [our]selves**.

Fourth, when the Holy Spirit grants us more and more assurance of our election, it leads us to **rendering grateful returns of ardent love to Him, who first manifested so great love towards** us.

Carnal assurance versus spiritual assurance. Carelessness versus carefulness. The canons give no quarter to the "cage phase" Calvinist. Al Martin once said it like this:

> The expression, a proud Calvinist, is a misnomer. If a Calvinist is a man who has seen God as He is high and lifted up, enthroned, then he is a man who has been brought to

brokenness before that throne as was Isaiah…. If your understanding of Calvinistic thinking has led you to the place where you can, as it were, boast in your liberty and use it as an occasion for licence, then you have never become a biblical Calvinist. God makes Calvinists today the same way he made them in Isaiah's day.[108]

Article 14

As the doctrine of divine election by the most wise counsel of God was declared by the prophets, by Christ Himself, and by the apostles, and is clearly revealed in the Scriptures, both of the Old and New Testament, so it is still to be published in due time and place in the Church of God, for which it was peculiarly designed, provided it be done with reverence, in the spirit of discretion and piety, for the glory of God's most holy Name, and for enlivening and comforting His people, without vainly attempting to investigate the secret ways of the Most High. "For I have not shunned to declare unto you all the counsel of God" (Acts 20:27); "O the depth of the riches both of the wisdom and knowledge of God! how unsearchable are His judgments, and His ways past finding out! For who hath known the mind of the Lord? or who hath been His counsellor?" (Rom. 11:33–34); "For I say, through the grace given unto me, to every man that is among you, not to think of himself more highly than he ought to think; but to think soberly, according as God hath dealt to every man the measure of faith" (Rom. 12:3); "Wherein God, willing more abundantly to shew unto the heirs of promise the immutability of His counsel, confirmed it by an oath: that by two immutable things, in which it was impossible for God to lie, we might have a strong consolation, who have fled for refuge to lay hold upon the hope set before us" (Heb. 6:17–18).

PREACHING PREDESTINATION

From at least the fifth century, Augustine recounted in his letters that some said, "'The definition of predestination is opposed to the advantage of preaching,' as if, indeed, it were opposed to the preaching of the apostle!"[109]

---

[108] Al Martin, "The Practical Implications of Calvinism," BannerofTruth.org, https://banneroftruth.org/us/resources/articles/2002/the-practical-implications-of-calvinism (accessed May 9, 2018).

[109] Augustine, "On the Gift of Perseverance," ch. 34, in *Nicene and Post-Nicene Fathers: First Series*, Vol. 5 (1887; repr., Peabody, MA: Hendrickson, fourth printing 2004), 539.

And who wants an obstacle? In his 1559 *Institutes of the Christian Religion*, John Calvin had to go out of his way to state that preachers should no less preach on the deity of the Son, the deity of the Holy Spirit, or the creation of the universe than on predestination.[110]

Should we even talk or preach about predestination? Because predestination is a biblical doctrine, the answer is a resounding "Yes!" You see, without predestination you would have no Bible. Abram was chosen out of Ur of the Chaldeans (Gen. 12). Israel was chosen out of all the nations of the earth (Deut. 4:37; 7:6–8; Ps. 105:6). A new Israelite remnant was chosen after their exile (Isa. 41:8–9; 42:1; 43:1–7; 44:1–2; 45:4). Jesus taught predestination (e.g., Matt. 11:25–27; 13:11–16; Mark 4:11–12; John 6:37, 66; 10:26–30). The apostles taught predestination (Rom. 8:28–39; ch. 9–11; Eph. 1; Phil. 1:6; 2:13; 1 Pet. 2:5–10). In the words of article 14: **As the doctrine of divine election by the most wise counsel of God was declared by the prophets, by Christ Himself, and by the apostles, and is clearly revealed in the Scriptures, both of the Old and New Testament.**

Since predestination is a biblical doctrine, we must talk about it. The question is how? Before the assembled members of synod, Joseph Hall preached a sermon in which he described "two sorts of Theology, the popular and that of the schools." What distinguished these two were that

> the former seems to regard the foundation of religion, the latter is form and external ornaments: the former the things which ought to be known, the latter the things which may be known. The understanding of the former makes a man a Christian, of the latter a disputer: or, if you please, the former makes a Theologian, the latter adorns one.[111]

Why the need for Hall to press this home? Because at the time of the synod, the Remonstrants accused Reformed theologians and pastors of serious errors in their teaching. We get a glimpse of these some of these accusations in the conclusion to the canons. Remonstrant preachers were saying

---

[110] John Calvin, *Institutes of the Christian Religion*, ed. John T. McNeill, trans. Ford Lewis Battles, 2 vols. (Philadelphia: Westminster, 1960), 2:925 (3.21.4). See also the 1541 French edition: *Institutes of the Christian Religion*, trans. Robert White (Edinburgh: The Banner of Truth Trust, 2014), 465.

[111] Milton, *The British Delegation and the Synod of Dort*, 129 (3/6).

the Reformed doctrine of predestination "by its very nature and tendency draws the minds of people away from all godliness and religion, is an opiate of the flesh and the devil, and is a stronghold of Satan where he lies in wait for all people, wounds most of them, and fatally pierces many of them with the arrows of both despair and self-assurance." It also "makes people carnally self-assured, since it persuades them that nothing endangers the salvation of the chosen, no matter how they live." In response, the synod

> urges all fellow ministers in the gospel of Christ to deal with this teaching in a godly and reverent manner, in the academic institutions as well as in the churches; to do so, both in their speaking and writing, with a view to the glory of God's name, holiness of life, and the comfort of anxious souls; to think and also speak with Scripture according to the analogy of faith; and, finally, to refrain from all those ways of speaking which go beyond the bounds set for us by the genuine sense of the Holy Scriptures and which could give impertinent sophists a just occasion to scoff at the teaching of the Reformed churches or even to bring false accusations against it.[112]

In article 14 we find the ground rules for preaching predestination **in due time and place in the Church of God**.[113] In fact, **it was peculiarly designed** to be preached.

With Reverence

Article 14 says this doctrine **was peculiarly designed** to be preached **provided it be done with reverence**. How much more reverently could Paul talk of predestination than Romans 9:20–21: "But who are you, O man, to answer back to God? Will what is molded say to its molder, 'Why have you made me like this?' Has the potter no right over the clay, to make out of the same lump one vessel for honorable use and another for dishonorable use?"

---

[112] From the Conclusion to the Canons.

[113] See Daniel R. Hyde, "Handling a High Mystery: The Westminster Confession on Preaching Predestination," *Puritan Reformed Journal* 2, no. 2 (June 2010): 235–58; *Synopsis Purioris Theologiae: Volume 2*, 23.

This was the pinnacle in the progression of Paul's argument in Romans 9. The argument began because of the unbelief of the ancient covenant people, his fellow Jews (Rom. 9:1–5). The first objection he addresses was whether God's promise to Israel had failed (Rom 9:6). But Paul says that ever since God began his promises to the patriarchs, there was a distinction between those "descended from Israel" and those who truly "belong to Israel" (Rom. 9:6), between those who are merely Abraham's outoutward children of the flesh and those who truly are children because they are his offspring of the promise (Rom. 9:7–8). Paul starts in history and then works his way back into eternity: "though they were not yet born and had done nothing either good or bad—in order that God's purpose of election might continue, not because of works but because of him who calls" (Rom. 9:11).

The next objection is whether God is unjust because he chooses one and not another. Paul answer is, "By no means!" (Rom. 9:14). He doesn't speculate but simply quotes Scripture (Rom. 9:15–17), concluding that God "has mercy on whomever he wills, and he hardens whomever he wills" (Rom. 9:18).

But if this is true, then "why does he still find fault? For who can resist his will?" (Rom. 9:19). Do you hear the objection? It's that predestination makes us robots since there's nothing we can do about it. Paul doesn't offer a philosophical response sorting out this conundrum. He asserts that God is God and we are not; he is the Creator and we are creatures; he is a potter and we are mere clay! (Rom. 9:20–21).

Because predestination is a topic shrouded in mystery as well as much misunderstanding, we should talk of it reverently as Paul did **without vainly attempting to investigate the secret ways of the Most High.** In the words of Hall's sermon again, "shall we dare to measure the depths of the divine law with the diminutive standard of our intellect? shall we trample on things, which even the Angels gaze on with awe?"[114]

Did you know that even the apostle Peter wrote about some of Paul's teaching being difficult? Second Peter 3:16 says, "There are some things in them that are hard to understand, which the ignorant and unstable twist to their own destruction, as they do the other Scriptures." We can see those twists (*streblousin*) in the three objections of Romans 9. Notice how Paul ends this entire section of Romans 9–11 by saying, "Oh, the depth of the

---

[114] Milton, *The British Delegation and the Synod of Dort*, 130 (3/6).

riches and wisdom and knowledge of God! How unsearchable are his judgments and how inscrutable his ways!" (Rom. 11:33). In commenting on this passage, John Calvin (1509–1564) said that when we discuss God's eternal counsel "we must always restrain both our language and manner of thinking, so that when we have spoken soberly and within the limits of the Word of God, our argument may finally end in an expression of astonishment."[115] He said elsewhere that "we should not investigate what the Lord has left hidden in secret, that we should not neglect what he has brought into the open."[116] In the words of Deuteronomy 29:29, "The secret things belong to the LORD our God, but the things that are revealed belong to us and to our children forever, that we may do all the words of this law."[117]

With all this warning about not prying, wouldn't it be better to avoid predestination altogether? David Paraeus said to this: "As it is then unlawfull curiositie, to search into the mysteries of Predestination, not revealed in the Gospel; so it is damnable ingratitude to deny, or suppresse what God hath revealed concerning Predestination in the Gospel."[118]

With Discernment/Wisdom

Election **was peculiarly designed** to be preached **provided it be done…in the spirit of discretion and piety**. This means we must talk about predestination with discernment and discrimination. When Paul penned Romans 9 he was writing to a Christian congregation made up of Jews and Gentiles in distinction from unbelieving Jews and Gentiles. Believing Jews were those who are of the promise while unbelieving Jews were

---

[115] John Calvin, *The Epistles of Paul the Apostle to the Romans and to the Thessalonians*, trans. Ross Mackenzie, ed. David W. Torrance and Thomas F. Torrance, Calvin's New Testament Commentaries 8 (Grand Rapids, MI: Eerdmans, 1961), 259.

[116] Calvin, *Institutes*, 3.21.4; cf. "A Treatise on the Eternal Predestination of God," in *Calvin's Calvinism: Treatise on the Eternal Predestination of God & the Secret Providence of God*, trans. Henry Cole (1856; repr., Grand Rapids, MI: Reformed Free Publishing Association, 1987), 144–50.

[117] Cf. John Calvin, *Commentaries on the Last Four Books of Moses Arranged in the Form of a Harmony: Volume 1*, trans. Charles William Bingham, Calvin's Commentaries 2 (1852–1855; repr., Grand Rapids, MI: Baker Books House, 1996), 410–12; Matthew Poole, *A Commentary on the Holy Bible, Volume I: Genesis–Job* (Peabody, MA: Hendrickson, 2008), 394–95.

[118] Paraeus, "Epitome of Arminianisme," 823.

those merely of the flesh (Rom. 9:3, 6–8). Paul used another illustration of this when he said among the Jews there were those who were among the vast sand of ethnic Israel while there were also those who were a small gathered remnant (Rom. 9:27).

Discernment and wisdom also means it is taught **in due time and place**. When you talk and preach about predestination, you must ever keep in mind those you are talking with. There are all kinds of hearers. Are you talking to unbelievers? If so, are they hard hearted and scoffing at the doctrine, or do you discern the working of the Holy Spirit in genuinely questioning? Are you talking to a congregation of professing believers? If so, some may be strong in faith and be able to plumb the depths and scale the heights of such a doctrine while others may be weak in faith and the very mention of predestination will cause doubts and worries. Are you talking to adults, with all the distinctions above, or are there also children in the audience? And while you are talking to such a congregation, keep in mind that there are those who genuinely believe, whether strongly or weakly, and that there may also be those who are pretending to believe as hypocrites.

For God's Glory

We must also talk of predestination in such a way that it is done **for the glory of God's most holy Name**. "God has failed." "God is unjust." "God makes us robots." Paul's point in Romans 9 is that predestination solves these objections because it is ultimately for God's glory, not our intellectual satisfaction. "Who are you, O man?" (Rom. 9:20). God is God! You are not! "Has the potter no right?" (Rom. 9:21). Absolutely he does! He glorifies himself in his pottery, making "one vessel for honorable use and another for dishonorable use" (Rom. 9:21). Paul's ultimate point is that God glorifies himself in his works: "What if God, desiring to show his wrath and to make known his power, has endured with much patience vessels of wrath prepared for destruction, in order to make known the riches of his glory for vessels of mercy, which he has prepared beforehand *for glory*" (Rom. 9:22–23). God glorifies himself by allowing us to share in his glory!

When you talk or preach about predestination, are you doing so to bring him praise? "Blessed be the God and Father of our Lord Jesus Christ, who has blessed us in Christ with every spiritual blessing in the heavenly places, even as he chose us in him before the foundation of the world"

(Eph. 1:3–4). When you talk or preach about predestination, are you doing so to magnify his grace? "To the praise of his glorious grace" (Eph. 1:6). In fact, Paul repeats this doxology two more times in Ephesians 1:12 and 1:14 because God has poured out his extravagant grace upon his people. It's not just for a mysterious doctrine that he give him glory, but it's because this doctrine is all about the love of God the Father who loves us so much that he gave us his Son and gave us to his Son from eternity! When you talk or preach about predestination, can your words be "translated" to say this: "For from him and through him and to him are all things. To him be glory forever. Amen" (Rom. 11:36)?

For Our Comfort

Finally, we must talk of predestination in such a way that it is for **enlivening and comforting His people**. What comfort does all that Romans 9 says have for you, the world, and me? After starting with recorded redemptive history in the Old Testament, then tracing backward into eternity, Paul ends up placing the gospel right in our laps, in our own personal history: "even us whom he has called, not from the Jews only but also from the Gentiles?" (Rom. 9:24). Don't accuse God of lying. Don't accuse God of injustice. Don't accuse God of making robots. Believe!

But the objection people had and still have is that when we talk of predestination, it is only beneficial for those whom God "calls." When you talk of predestination, it should always lead to the gospel: Do you want to know that you have been called into God's kingdom because he predestined you for that glory? Then believe in Jesus! When we do and when we talk this way, there is the experience of the joy of knowing that while we and others once were "not my people," God now calls us "my people" and "sons of the living God" (Rom. 9:25–26). When you believe you will know the joy of being one who was described as "not beloved" but who is now called by God "beloved" (v. 25). As Martin Luther once wrote:

Follow the order of the Epistle to the Romans. Worry first about Christ and the gospel, that you may recognize your sins and his grace, and then fight your sin, as Paul teaches from the first to the eighth chapters. Then, when you come under the cross and suffering in the eighth chapters, this will teach you of foreknowledge in chapters 9, 10, and 11, and how comforting it is.[119]

Yes, we should talk about predestination. We should talk about it in a way that leads sinners to Jesus Christ, which brings God eternal glory and brings them eternal comfort.

WHY EVANGELIZE IF GOD PREDESTINES?

This leads to a brief aside: Why evangelize if God predestines? From the outset we have to realize it's not as if some Christians believe in sovereignty and therefore don't believe in missions and evangelism, while others do because they believe in human responsibility. As J. I. Packer so simply explained many years ago, all Christians believe in the sovereignty of God because all Christians pray, all Christians thank God for saving them, and all Christians pray that the Lord would save their lost loved ones. The problem is that some Christians either do not realize this, have not thought through what they believe, or have certain presuppositions about man and God that makes their theology different than their practice of prayer.

Former professor of theology at Calvin Theological Seminary Anthony Hoekema says this article of the Canons of Dort "teaches the indispensability of missions."[120] He goes on to say:

> We could therefore say that the main focus of the Canons is on the *Missio Dei* (the mission of God): God's redemption of the cosmos through the saving work of Jesus Christ applied to the hearts of his people by the Holy Spirit.[121]

So why specifically do we believe in missions and evangelism?

First, God commands us to do so. Since we are to live our lives not wondering about God's secret will for our lives or the lives of others but according to his revealed will as found in his Word, we are to be passionate

---

[119] *The Solid Declaration*, XI, 33, in *The Book of Concord: The Confessions of the Evangelical Lutheran Church*, ed. Robert Kolb and Timothy J. Wengert, trans. Charles Arand, Eric Gritsch, Robert Kolb, William Russell, James Schaff, Jane Strohl, and Timothy J., Wengert (Minneapolis, MN: Fortress, 2000), 646. See also Pronk, *Expository Sermons on the Canons of Dort*, 19.

[120] Hoekema, "The Missionary Focus of the Canons of Dort," 212.

[121] Hoekema, "The Missionary Focus of the Canons of Dort," 210–11.

about our preachers preaching the gospel to the lost. We are also as believers to be ever ready to give an answer for our hope (1 Pet. 3:15).

Second, we are to evangelize because without the gospel no one would be saved. As we saw in 1.3, preaching is the necessary means by which God brings the dead to life. Notice how Titus 1:2–3 links God's sovereign and eternal plan of salvation with election. He promised salvation "before the ages began and at the proper time manifested in his word through the preaching with which I have been entrusted."

Third, we are called to love our neighbors. And what greater love can we show them than to care for their eternal situation with God? Thus we are to love our neighbors with an urgency.

Fourth, God genuinely offers salvation and spiritual rest to all who hear the gospel. In 2 Corinthians 5:19–20 Paul says that God himself pleads with sinners to be reconciled to him!

Fifth, the sovereignty of God in salvation is our only hope of any success in evangelism. He has promised his Word will not return void (Isa. 55). Therefore we should be bold, but also patient with the lost. As well, we need to be prayerful in our evangelism. As one pastor has said:

Predestination gives the church a great incentive to preach the gospel everywhere. She knows that God's Word will not return to him void; that God will gather in his chosen ones from every tribe and tongue and people and nations.[122]

Article 15

What peculiarly tends to illustrate and recommend to us the eternal and unmerited grace of election, is the express testimony of sacred Scripture that not all, but some only are elected, while others are passed by in the eternal decree; whom God, out of His sovereign, most just, irreprehensible and unchangeable good pleasure, hath decreed to leave in the common misery into which they have wilfully plunged themselves, and not to bestow upon them saving faith and the grace of conversion; but permitting them in His just judgment to follow their own ways, at last for the declaration of His justice, to condemn and perish them forever, not only on account of their unbelief, but also for all their other sins. And this is the decree of reprobation which by no means makes God the author of sin (the very thought of which is blasphemy), but declares Him to be an awful, irreprehensible, and righteous Judge and avenger thereof.

---

[122] Henry Petersen, *The Canons of Dort* (Grand Rapids, MI: Baker, 1968), 23.

REPROBATION DEFINED

After laying out the canvas of basic biblical teachings in articles 1–6 and then applying the paint of predestination in terms of election to salvation in articles 7–14, the canons then go on to add more concerning "the negative or dark-side of Calvinist predestination,"[123] or reprobation in articles 15–17. Notice why article 15 says this is even brought up: **what peculiarly tends to illustrate and recommend to us the eternal and unmerited grace of election, is the express testimony of sacred Scripture that not all, but some only are elected**. It's mentioned because it adds further clarity to our gracious election in Christ. As we approach it, the phrase John Calvin to describe it is appropriate: *decretum horribile*.[124] It means the "awe-full decree." Let's be filled with awe and humility.

Our triune God in his amazing grace has elected some of fallen humanity to salvation. So the question legitimately comes up: What of the rest of those not elected? As we approach with humility, it's important to keep perspective. Sinnema said, "There is no single Calvinist view of reprobation. The diversity among 'orthodox' Calvinist theologians on a number of points was significant, although the differences did not go so deep as to create division."[125] For example, it's popularly said that Reformed theology confesses what is known as "double predestination." John Piper calls himself a "seven point Calvinist" because he says the co-called five points "point[...] toward two additional 'Calvinistic' truths that follow from them: double predestination and the best-of-all-possible worlds."[126] Double predestination, though, is neither distinctly Reformed nor even agreed upon as to what one means by it. There is a long history of development of Augustine's thought that led men such as Isidore of Seville (ca. 560–636) to speak of a "double predestination" (*gemina predestinatio*) and Thomas Bradwardine (ca. 1300–1349) to speak of a "twofold predestination" (*duplex predestina-*

---

[123] Sinnema, "The Issue of Reprobation at the Synod of Dort," 1.

[124] Calvin, *Institutes* 3.23.7.

[125] Sinnema, "The Issue of Reprobation at the Synod of Dort," 3. "To speak of the 'Calvinist' view of reprobation in this period is much too imprecise, for there was no single Calvinist position." Ibid., 52.

[126] https://www.desiringgod.org/articles/what-does-piper-mean-when-he-says-hes-a-seven-point-calvinist (accessed on May 15, 2018).

tio).[127] Further, saying predestination has two "sides" is not to say they're equal in every respect: election to salvation and reprobation to condemnation. Even those like Gottschalk (803–869) who spoke of God predestining to life and "equally" (*pariter*) predestining to death still viewed them unequally. Soon after Dort, Antonius Walaeus would say that "predestination is used correctly to refer to both reprobation and election, not as indicating categories that are synonymous in every respect, but only as analogous."[128] As we'll see, God "actively" predestined some to life graciously apart from their works while those not elected he "passively" left in their sins and because they deserved death, he then actively decreed their ultimate condemnation because of their sin. Seán Hughes sums up the doctrine of Dort, saying, "It seems to make no sense to describe such a position as 'the Calvinist doctrine of double predestination.'"[129] This debate continued right up to the synod and continues to this day.

Is it Biblical?

Scripture is the foundation upon which our faith stands. This is the reason why those who deny the doctrine of reprobation do so: they don't think it's in Scripture.[130] One theologian even called it "an antiquated piece of rationalistic theology."[131] At the Synod of Dort, the various delegations reported their views with written statements. On the issue of reprobation a list of propositions and supporting Scripture texts were given to show the biblical nature of reprobation.[132] Let me survey several biblical passages to show that it is.

---

[127] On the development of the doctrine of reprobation in the patristic and medieval periods, see Sinnema, "The Issue of Reprobation at the Synod of Dort," 8–51.

[128] *Synopsis Purioris Theologiae: Volume 2*, 25.

[129] Hughes, "The Problem of 'Calvinism,'" 243.

[130] Harry Boer in *DeKoster vs. Boer: Debate; A Debate Originally Given at the Request of the Men's Christian Fellowship of the 3rd Christian Reformed Church of Kalamazoo, Michigan, March 7, 1979* (Blue Island, IL: Paracletos, 1979), 11, 16–19. In response to Boer, see W. Robert Godfrey, "Reprobation—the Critics and the Canons," *Outlook* 26, no. 9 (September 1976): 2–5. For a fuller reply, see *1980 Acts of Synod*, 486–558.

[131] Harry R. Boer, *The Doctrine of Reprobation in the Christian Reformed Church* (Grand Rapids, MI: Eerdmans, 1983), viii.

[132] For the full list, see *1980 Acts of Synod*, 534–35.

First, when Jesus gave his bread of life discourse, he said, "Whoever comes to me shall not hunger, and whoever believes in me shall never thirst" (John 6:35). Yet, he also said to the crowds: "You have seen me and yet do not believe" (John 6:36). Why didn't they believe? "All that the Father gives me will come to me, and whoever comes to me I will never cast out" (John 6:37). Do you understand what Jesus said? To those hard-hearted people Jesus explicitly said to them that the Father gave to Christ some to be saved and not others. In other words, some were chosen while others were left in their hard-heartedness, unable to come to Christ. Jesus went on to speak of Judas in particular in John 10:26.

Second, most likely the most famous passage is in Romans 9, where Paul contrasted the figures of Jacob and Esau affirming that God loved Jacob while Esau was hated; Jacob was chosen while Esau was not. These brothers stood as examples of what is true of all humanity.

Third, in 1 Thessalonians 5:9 Paul comforted believers living in dark times: "For God has not destined us for wrath, but to obtain salvation through our Lord Jesus Christ." There are those who are comfortable in their own safety saying, "There is peace and safety" (1 Thess. 5:3), who are also described as children of the night and the darkness (1 Thess. 5:5), and who are said to be asleep in the days in which we live (1 Thess. 5:6, 7). These were destined for wrath; but we believers have not been.

Fourth, in 1 Peter 2:4, Peter said that we came to Christ, that is, we believed in him. In contrast, he said in verse 7 that some do not believe, citing Psalm 118, which says like a stone Jesus was rejected by the builders. And as verse 8 cited Isaiah 8, Jesus is a stone that causes people to stumble and a rock that causes offense to them. Then Peter said, "They stumble because they disobey the word"—this is the word of the gospel back in 1:23–25—"as they were destined to do."

Finally, in Jude 4 we learn that false teachers were a part of the plan of God to affect the church: "For certain people have crept in unnoticed who long ago were designated for this condemnation."[133]

---

[133] On Jude 4, see Daniel R. Hyde, *Content Yet Contending: Jude* (Welwyn Garden City, UK: EP Books, 2017).

Is it Merely Logical?

So is this doctrine biblical? Yes, just a simple reading of Scripture shows that not only are some chosen to salvation in God's eternal purpose, but some are not. Article 15 says **the express testimony of sacred Scripture is that not all, but some only are elected.** Those Scripture passages that teach God's election of a particular people unto salvation also teach God's nonelection of others. This is not merely a logical deduction,[134] but as Cornelis Venema states, "Unless words no longer have an identifiable meaning, any Scriptural passage which teaches God's election of a particular people unto salvation, teaches equally God's non-election of others."[135]

Is it Ethical?

Remember what I said at the beginning? We have to approach this subject humbly. None of us deserve grace. When that begins to sink in, you can understand what reprobation is all about. It **peculiarly tends to illustrate and recommend to us the eternal and unmerited grace of election.** We know why election is gracious, but why is God just toward those who have **not** been **elected** or **passed by in the eternal decree?** The answer the article gives is that **out of** [God's] **sovereign, most just, irreprehensible and unchangeable good pleasure** he **decreed to leave in the common misery** (*in communi miseria*) **into which they have wilfully plunged themselves.** This takes us back to article 1. It's also how Augustine spoke. He said humanity was a *massa peccati* (mass of sin), *massa perditionis* (mass of perdition), and *massa damnata* (mass of damnation). So the language article 15 uses for this nonelection is **passed by** (*præteritos*), **to leave** (*relinquere*)/**permitting** (*relictos*; having been left), and **not to bestow** (*nec...donare*)...**saving faith and the grace of conversion.** This was entirely just.

Sinnema shows that the delegates at the synod debated at least six different views of reprobation.[136] The solution that was adopted was that of the late medieval church and its helpful distinction between negative and positive reprobation developed by Nicholas of Lyra and later popularized

---

[134] *DeKoster vs. Boer*, 14–15.

[135] Venema, *But for the Grace of God*, 28.

[136] Sinnema, "The Issue of Reprobation at the Synod of Dort," 136–40.

by Etienne Brulefer.[137] God's will is the cause of negative reprobation or "preterition" (*praeteritio*), in which he passed over the nonelect. Human sin is the cause of positive reprobation or "condemnation" (*damnatio*), in which the subsequent condemnation of the nonelect left in their sins are delivered to punishment. This means "there is no positive divine act concerning human sin, whereas positive reprobation presupposed human sin."[138] Those whom God passed by in preterition he **permitt**[ed] **them in His just judgment to follow their own ways, at last for the declaration of His justice, to condemn and punish them forever, not only on account of their unbelief, but also for all their other sins**.

Consistent with Belgic Confession article 16, the canons do not teach "double predestination" in which election and reprobation are precisely parallel.[139] God positively chooses certain people in grace and prepares glory for them. We speak of election actively and directly. On the other hand, we speak of God passively and indirectly withholding grace in his passing by others. Only then do we speak of him actively giving those in sin the condemnation they deserve.[140] In the conclusion to the canons we read that the Remonstrants "wish[ed] to persuade the public...that in the same manner in which the election is the fountain and the cause of faith and good works, reprobation is the cause of unbelief and impiety." This had also been attributed as a "false and erroneous doctrine of the Calvinists" in 1592 in the *Saxon Visitation Articles*, which rejected "that God created the greater

---

[137] See *Synopsis Purioris Theologiae*, disputation 24 on predestination where this distinction is approved and that negative reprobation presupposed the common sin of humanity while positive reprobation in God's foreknowledge presupposed particular sins. *Synopsis Purioris Theologiae: Volume 2*, 50–65. Disputation 11 on providence argues that human freedom is not destroyed but established because sin is under God's providence in the sense that he willingly does not prevent them without approving them in his divine permission. Ibid., 2:276–81.

[138] Beck, "Reformed Confessions and Scholasticism," 32.

[139] Beck, "Reformed Confessions and Scholasticism," 29. In this way Dort moderated the stricter view of Calvin, for example. See Donald W. Sinnema, "Calvin and the Canons of Dordt (1619)," *Church History and Religious Culture* 91, nos. 1–2 (2011): 89–92.

[140] For comparisons and contrasts of various theologians' ways of speaking of election and reprobation, see J. V. Fesko, *Diversity within the Reformed Tradition: Supra- and Infralapsarianism in Calvin, Dort, and Westminster* (Greenville, SC: Reformed Academic, 2001); John Murray, "Calvin, Dort, and Westminster: A Comparative Study," in De Jong, *Crisis in the Reformed Churches*, 150–60.

part of mankind for eternal damnation."[141] The synod went on to say "many other things of the same kind which the Reformed Churches not only do not acknowledge, but even detest with their whole soul."

Article 15 ends by saying **the decree of reprobation...by no means makes God the author of sin (the very thought of which is blasphemy), but declares Him to be an awful, irreprehensible, and righteous Judge and avenger thereof.** This is consistent with the Second Council of Orange (529), which said in its concluding definition of faith, "But that any are by the Divine power predestined to evil, we not only do not believe, but if there are any who would believe such an evil doctrine, we altogether detest them and anathematize them."[142]

Article 16

Those who do not yet experience a lively faith in Christ, an assured confidence of soul, peace of conscience, an earnest endeavor after filial obedience, and glorying in God through Christ, efficaciously wrought in them, and do nevertheless persist in the use of the means which God hath appointed for working these graces in us, ought not to be alarmed at the mention of reprobation, nor to rank themselves among the reprobate, but diligently to persevere in the use of means, and with ardent desires devoutly and humbly to wait for a season of richer grace. Much less cause have they to be terrified by the doctrine of reprobation, who, though they seriously desire to be turned to God, to please Him only, and to be delivered from the body of death, cannot yet reach that measure of holiness and faith to which they aspire; since a merciful God has promised that He will not quench the smoking flax nor break the bruised reed. But this doctrine is justly terrible to those, who, regardless of God and of the Savior Jesus Christ, have wholly given themselves up to the cares of the world and the pleasures of the flesh, so long as they are not seriously converted to God.

PASTORAL PROBLEMS CAUSED BY REPROBATION

Article 16 takes up the practical problem of reprobation. The detractors of reprobation say that it is debilitating to the Christian life.[143] Think about the Disney story Winnie the Pooh. If you are anything like Eeyore, you are al-

---

[141] Schaff, *Creeds*, 3:189

[142] Woods, *Canons of the Second Council of Orange*, 47.

[143] *DeKoster vs. Boer*, 19–23.

ways down, you are always thinking about life as a glass half-full. It's easy for us to take a doctrine like reprobation and begin to think that because there is a glass half-empty, that all I get in this life is emptiness. It's important to read articles 15 and 16 together. Article 16 describes three categories of people who hear this doctrine of reprobation and have a difficult time.

First, there are believers struggling with assurance **who do not yet experience a lively faith in Christ, an assured confidence of soul, peace of conscience, an earnest endeavor after filial obedience, and glorying in God through Christ**. Note, though, that they don't just throw their hands up and say, "God is sovereign, after all!" In their struggles they **nevertheless persist in the use of the means which God hath appointed for working these graces in us**. The pastoral advice of the article is that these **ought not to be alarmed at the mention of reprobation, nor to rank themselves among the reprobate, but diligently to persevere in the use of means, and with ardent desires devoutly and humbly to wait for a season of richer grace**.

Is this you? Don't be afraid of reprobation. Continue using the means of the Word and sacraments (cf. 5.14).

Second, there are believers struggling with ongoing sin who have **much less cause...to be terrified by the doctrine of reprobation** since **they seriously desire to be turned to God, to please Him only, and to be delivered from the body of death** [but] **cannot yet reach that measure of holiness and faith to which they aspire**.

Are you beset by some sin that is keeping you from a stronger relationship with Christ? Is there some sin in your life you desire to move past into a new phase of holiness? You should not be afraid. Again, the article says these have **much less cause...to be terrified by the doctrine of reprobation**. The reason is a beautiful gospel passage from Isaiah 42:3: **a merciful God has promised that He will not quench the smoking flax nor break the bruised reed**.

Believers can be weak. When they are, our powerful God does not snuff out the faintly burning wick of their faith or snap them in two like a stick that is already bent a little; instead, "he shall bear with the infirmities of poor sinners, and will refresh their dejected or wounded consciences, and comfort them with the promise of the forgiveness of their sins."[144]

---

[144] *Dutch Annotations* on Isaiah 42:3.

Finally, there *is* a category of hearer that needs to be worried when this doctrine is mentioned. It's **justly terrible** to them. It's not believers who need to be terrified but **those, who, regardless of God and of the Savior Jesus Christ, have wholly given themselves up to the cares of the world and the pleasures of the flesh, so long as they are not seriously converted to God.**

If this is you, reprobation should be fearful; but its mention is also the opportunity to repent and believe in Jesus Christ. Turn away; be converted; know assurance.

You see, this doctrine is full of awe. It should make us stand in awe at the judgments and purposes of God. It should make us full of wonder that in his plan, he chose us who believe in his Son.

Article 17

Since we are to judge of the will of God from His Word which testifies that the children of believers are holy, not by nature, but in virtue of the covenant of grace, in which they, together with the parents, are comprehended, godly parents have no reason to doubt of the election and salvation of their children whom it pleaseth God to call out of this life in their infancy.

ELECTION, REPROBATION, & THE DEATH OF INFANTS

A second practical problem is how reprobation relates to infants who die. This was a huge issue in the seventeenth century. Around this time in France the recorded mortality rate was between 15 to 30 percent of babies born *alive*. Of those who lived between one and five years, another 18 percent died.[145] This is still a huge issue. Miscarriage is the most common type of pregnancy loss. According to the American College of Obstetricians and Gynecologists (ACOG), anywhere from 10 to 25 percent of all clinically recognized pregnancies will end in miscarriage.[146]

---

[145] Lawrence Stone, *The Family, Sex and Marriage in England 1500–1800* (1977; rev. ed., Harmondsworth, UK: Penguin, 1985), 54–58.

[146] "Miscarriage," American Pregnancy Association, last updated December 5, 2017, http://www.americanpregnancy.org/pregnancycomplications/miscarriage.html. See my lecture, "Ministering after Miscarriages" (audio file, 42:11), https://www.sermonaudio.com/sermoninfo.asp?SID=28111739547.

This practical issue also involved a theological issue. In 1608 an anonymous tract accused Arminius of teaching that "original sin will condemn no man. In every nation, all infants who die without actual sins are saved."[147] Arminius then responded in a writing he wrote just before his death in 1609, accusing some Reformed men of teaching that "all the infants of those who are strangers from the covenant are damned; and of the offspring of those parents who are in the covenant, some infants that die are damned, while others are saved."[148] The 1610 *Remonstrance* rejected the belief that God "determined to let others, the young as well as the old; indeed even some children of covenant members, and those baptized in the name of Christ, dying in childhood, remain in the curse through his righteous judgment, to the declaration of his righteousness."[149] The *Counter-Remonstrance* said "children of the covenant so long as they do not in their conduct manifest the contrary [are God's elect children]...believing parents, when their children die in infancy, have no reason to doubt the salvation of these their children."[150] At the Synod of Dort, the Remonstrants continued their assault, saying no children of believers dying "before the use of reason will perish" and no one was to be considered reprobate "before they have committed any actual sins in their own persons."[151]

The caricature is that those who believe in reprobation believe **many children of the faithful are torn, guiltless, from their mothers' breasts, and tyrannically plunged into hell so that neither baptism nor the prayers of the Church at their baptism can at all profit them** (CD, conclusion).[152] John Calvin first penned this blasphemous caricature but not because he affirmed it; rather he was putting these words on the lips of Se-

---

[147] James Arminius, "The Apology or Defence against Thirty-One Theological Articles," in *The Works of James Arminius: Volume 2,* trans. James Nichols (1828; repr., Grand Rapids, MI: Baker Books, 1999), 10.

[148] Arminius, "The Apology or Defence," 2:14.

[149] Cited in W. Robert Godfrey, "Election and Covenant: The Synod of Dort and Children Dying in Infancy" (unpublished), 3.

[150] "The Opinions of the Remonstrants," appendix H in De Jong, *Crisis in the Reformed Churches,* 224.

[151] Cited in Godfrey, "Election and Covenant," 4, 5.

[152] B. B. Warfield traces this language to John Calvin in his debate with Sebastian Catellio. "The Development of the Doctrine of Infant Salvation," in *Studies in Theology: The Works of Benjamin B. Warfield,* 10 vols. (1932; repr., Grand Rapids, MI: Baker Book House, 2000), 9:435n78.

bastian Castellio who was using them as a caricature.[153] For many of us who have experienced the loss of a child or who know someone who has, this is very difficult and personal experientially, let alone theologically. Ultimately, this is another area in which Reformed theology seeks to comfort.

This issue of predestination's relationship to the death of children led to a tract war in which the Remonstrants used the emotional issue of infant mortality to appeal to the people.[154] One tract called upon grieving parents to ask for comfort from their orthodox preachers who believed things such as: "1. By the power of God's decree there are people who from their mother's womb have truly been delivered up to death and damnation.... 4. God drags infants to ruin, and he has not chosen them. 5. Indeed, he hates them, rejects them, and curses them."[155]

The churches had to get involved. The Provincial Synod of Gelderland in 1618 discussed several propositions, including,

> That among those condemned are innumerable children of believers, who, having died in their infancy, without having committed any sin, have been snatched from their mother's breasts and cruelly cast into hellish fire, in such way that neither the blood of Christ nor their baptism nor any prayer to the Lord can be of any use to them.

The synod made clear this was *not* the teaching of the Reformed church and that any teaching such should be reported "in order to be purged, or confess his sin by conviction."[156]

The Remonstrants' position was stated in two propositions at the Synod of Dort in session 31, December 13, 1618:

> All the children of believers are sanctified in Christ, so that none of them who leave this life before the use of reason will perish. By no means, however, are to be considered

---

[153] Donald W. Sinnema, "Are the Canons of Dordt a True Reflection of Calvin's View of Predestination?," *In die Skriflig* 52, no. 2 (2018): a2347, p. 9, https://doi.org/10.4102/ids.v52i2.2347.

[154] Erik A. de Boer, "'O, Ye Women, Think of Thy Innocent Children, When They Die Young!' The Canons of Dordt (First Head, Article Seventeen) between Polemic and Pastoral Theology," in Goudriaan and van Lieburg, *Revisiting the Synod of Dordt*, 271–74.

[155] Cited in de Boer, "'O, Ye Women,'" 272.

[156] Cited in de Boer, "'O, Ye Women,'" 272.

among the number of the reprobate certain of believers who leave this life in infancy before they have committed any actual sin in their own person, so that neither the holy bath of baptism nor the prayers of the church for them in any way be profitable for their salvation.

No children of believers who have been baptised in the name of the Father, the Son and the Holy Spirit, living in the state of infancy, are reckoned among the reprobate by an absolute decree.[157]

There were various responses at the synod. During the debate and discussion of the drafts of the canons, John Jacob Breitinger, chairman of the Swiss delegates, said, "We need to take particularly into account the viciousness wherewith the Remonstrants make the orthodox doctrine of Predestination hated by expectant women. Truly, there is hardly anything (according to experience) that can touch the parents, especially the female gender, more painfully—in both respects—than when they listen to discussions about the salvation or reprobation of their little one," and therefore an article needed to be included "as it will not only comfort the doubt of believing parents regarding their children but also the viciousness of their opponents."[158]

Children of Believers

So how does the doctrine of reprobation relate to this struggle? Back in 1611 the Contra-Remonstrants wrote in their conference with the Remonstrants at The Hague,

That we regard as God's children not only the adults who believe in Christ and who walk piously according to the gospel, but also the children of the covenant, as long as their actions do not demonstrate to the contrary; and that therefore believing parents have no reason to doubt the salvation of their children when these die in their infancy.[159]

---

[157] Cited in de Boer, "'O, Ye Women,'" 276.

[158] Cited in de Boer, "'O, Ye Women,'" 282.

[159] Cited in de Boer, "'O, Ye Women,'" 269.

Why would they speak this way? The Scriptures teach us as believers that our children are *covenant* children. The Lord made his covenant with Abraham *and* his children (Gen. 17:7). When David found out his child died, he ceased weeping and fasting and arose in confidence that while his son would not come back to him, one day David would see him (2 Sam. 12:23). Where? In the presence of God. David prayed as a covenant member that when he was in his mother's womb it was the Lord who was forming him and who knew him (Ps. 139). The prophet Isaiah described the Messianic age to come as in which covenant children would be taught by the Lord and have great peace (Isa. 54:13). Jeremiah's call from the womb evidenced that God can regenerate in utero (Jer. 1:5).

Moving into the New Testament, we see that nothing changes. Jesus and the apostles inherit this outlook on children and never say anything to abolish or revoke it. Jesus said to such children belonged his kingdom and therefore of such belong as well (Matt. 19:14; Mark 10:16; Luke 18:16). On Pentecost Peter said God's promise was to those who believed and their children (Acts 2:39). The children of at least one believing parent are holy (1 Cor. 7:14) not because they are sinless but because they belong to God's set-apart people. Galatians 1:15, like Jeremiah 1:5, shows that God is able to call and set apart in the womb. Paul addressed children in Ephesians 6:1 as they would have been present with the covenant community when this letter was read.[160] Finally, during the debate at the synod on this article the British delegation wished for Revelation 20:12 and 21:27 to be included. These might seem like odd insertions to us, but they believed they teach that little ones are in the book of life (Rev. 20:12) and in the New Jerusalem (Rev. 21:27).[161]

So how did this covenant theology, mixed with the practical issue of Christian comfort at the loss of a little one, and the theological issue of election come together? There were various ways of responding to this issue at the synod. Some said nothing: the Palatinate, Hesse, Geneva, Emden, and the letter of David Paraeus (foreign delegates); Gelderland, North Holland,

---

[160] On the covenant theology of this text, see Daniel R. Hyde, *The Nursery of the Holy Spirit: Welcoming Children in Worship* (Eugene, OR: Wipf & Stock, 2014).

[161] On why this means we should baptize infants of professing Christians, see Daniel R. Hyde, *Jesus Loves the Little Children: Why We Baptize Children* (2006; Grandville, MI: Reformed Fellowship, second printing 2012). For the list of verses cited here, see de Boer, "'O, Ye Women,'" 277.

Zeeland, Friesland, Groningen, and the Walloon churches (Dutch delegates).

The British rejected the Remonstrant idea that there was no election of children before the use of reason. In fact, in a brilliant theological move, they said if as the Remonstrants taught, election was based on foreseen faith, then infants could not be saved! This was the least pastoral of all positions![162] The Swiss stated it positively:

> Infants of the faithful, since God by virtue of the covenant of grace is their God, and since Paul calls holy those children of at least one faithful parent, and since the Lord of heaven proclaims that such children are the heirs of the heavenly kingdom, if they should die in infancy before the years of discretion, we hope the best for them. We do not doubt that the angels, those ministers and most beloved spirits of that tender age, to whom God always exhibits his face, were especially sent forth for them and most promptly perform in their service.[163]

The delegates from Nassau-Wetteravia said:

> Although it is true that God has the right to condemn children because of original sin, nevertheless Christian parents ought not to doubt concerning the salvation of their children, for the promise is given to them and their children.[164]

According to Cornelis Venema,

> None [of the delegations' statements] is more forthright than that of the Bremen delegates."[165] In their judgment they said "children of believers only...who die before the age of doctrinal understanding are loved by God and are

---

[162] *Acta Synodi* (1610), part 2, p. 10.

[163] *Acta Synodi Nationalis...Dordrechti habitae Anno MDCXVII et MDCXIX* (Dordrecht, 1620), part 2, p. 40. Cited in Godfrey, "Election and Covenant," 6.

[164] *Acta Synodi*, part 2, p. 44. Cited in de Boer, "'O, Ye Women,'" 278. See also Godfrey, "Election and Covenant," 6.

[165] Cornelis P. Venema, "The Election and Salvation of the Children of Believers Who Die in Infancy: A Study of Article I/17 of the Canons of Dort," *Mid-America Journal of Theology* 17 (2006): 68.

saved by the same good pleasure of God on account of Christ, through Christ, and in Christ as an adult.[166]

Of children of believers versus other children of nonbelievers, the Dutch professors Johannes Polyander, Anthonius Thysius, and Antonius Walaeus said:

> There is a great difference between those infants born to parents in the covenant and those not born in the covenant...children of believers dying in infancy ought to be reckoned elect since they are graciously taken away by God from this life before they have violated the conditions of the covenant...children of unbelievers born outside the church of God, ought to be left to the judgment of God.[167]

Professor Franciscus Gomarus wrote his own statement:

> We piously believe that the infants of true believers, covenanted to God through Christ are also elect, if they die before the use of reason.... But if they should attain the use of reason, we recognize only those to be elect who believe in Christ.[168]

De Boer summarizes that there was "almost complete unanimity" on this issue:

1. Because of original sin, God would be in the right to condemn all children.

2. There is election and reprobation among children who die in infancy before the age of reason.

3. Because of God's covenant promises, children of believers are in the covenant and sanctified in Christ and therefore are to be regarded as elect and in heaven by their parents.

The one difference was whether the children of unbelievers are reckoned among the reprobate (Drenthe) or left to the judgment of God (Dutch profs.).[169]

---

[166] *Acta Synodi*, part 2, p. 63. Cited in Godfrey, "Election and Covenant," 7.

[167] *Acta Synodi*, part 3, p. 10–11. Cited in Godfrey, "Election and Covenant," 7.

[168] *Acta Synodi*, part 3, p. 24. Cited in de Boer, "'O, Ye Women,'" 278. See also Godfrey, "Election and Covenant," 7.

[169] De Boer, "'O, Ye Women,'" 281.

Because article 17 does not follow the logic of articles 15 and 16 with a reference to Romans 9:6 as the Heidelberg theologians desired, de Boer says that "canon seventeen offers more than reassurance. This is a doctrinal response to a religious question with pastoral sensitivity."[170]

Unbaptized Children of Believers?

What of unbaptized children of believers? Notice article 17 says our children *are* covenant children. Baptism is the sign of their adoption into God's family. John Calvin once wrote a letter to a brother whose son died in infancy before he was able to have him baptized. Because of that, others were telling him his child was condemned. No doubt this was a reference to Roman Catholic people in this man's life. To this, Calvin tenderly wrote him, saying, "For though baptism be the seal of our adoption, yet we are enrolled in the book of life, both by the gratuitous goodness of God, and by his promise to that effect." In other words, God's promise about our children determines reality, not the sign of that promise. The sign assures, to be sure, but it does not determine. This is why he went on to say, "If their salvation is assured by the promise, and the foundation of which it rests is sufficiently solid of itself, we must not conclude that all the children who die without baptism go to perdition."[171]

Children of Unbelievers

Does this mean all human life that dies in its infancy is in heaven? Whereas Scripture is explicit about the children of believers, it and the canons is silent about the rest. Great men have personally believed that all infants dying are saved, such as C.H. Spurgeon,[172] Charles Hodge,[173] and B.B. Warfield.[174]

---

[170] De Boer, "'O, Ye Women,'" 289.

[171] John Calvin, "To a Gentleman of Provence," in *Selected Works of John Calvin: Tracts & Letters*, ed. Jules Bonnet, trans. Marcus Robert Gilchrist, 7 vols. (Grand Rapids, MI: Baker Book House, 1983), 6:71–74.

[172] C. H. Spurgeon, "Misrepresentations of True Calvinism Cleared Away," https://www.spurgeongems.org/vols7-9/chs002.pdf (accessed May 9, 2018).

[173] Charles Hodge, *Systematic Theology* (repr., Grand Rapids, MI: Eerdmans, 1995), 2:211–12.

[174] Warfield, "The Development of the Doctrine of Infant Salvation," 9:411–44.

So what *do* we say about aborted life, miscarried life, or precious children of nonbelievers who die tragically before their life can even get going? We say that God is a good, gracious, and just God and that he will do what is right. We can trust him.[175]

Infants Versus the Age of Reason

"But what about older children who die and didn't yet believe?" This article doesn't speak of older children, but only of infants. In the aforementioned words of Gomarus, the theology behind article 17 is that "infants of true believers...are elect, if they die before the use of reason." So before a covenant child reaches the age of reason (an undefined age), we judge on the basis of the Word that they are elect should they die. On the other hand, once they reach an age where they have "the use of reason," should they die we can only say what Scripture says: "only those [are...] elect who believe in Christ."[176]

Believers' Comfort

Based on the foregoing wrestling with the biblical material, article 17 says **godly parents** (*pii parentes*; pious parents) **have no reason to doubt of the election and salvation of their children whom it pleaseth God to call out of this life in their infancy.** Other translations say *ought not* to doubt (*dubitare non debent*). You may be thinking, "But what does that say to me in my grief?" This is a figure of speech known as a litotes. A litotes is a rhetorical understatement by using a negative to assert a positive. When Paul said to the crowd after he was arrested, "I am a Jew, from Tarsus in Cilicia, a citizen of *no obscure city*" (Acts 21:39), he was saying he was a citizen of a *major city*. When Luke says in Acts 27:20, "When neither sun nor stars appeared for many days, and *no small tempest* lay on us, all hope of our being saved was at last abandoned," he was saying that there was a *huge tempest*. I

---

[175] This is the basic approach of R. C. Sproul, who says the status of children of believers who die in infancy is addressed in Scripture while that of children of unbelievers is not. Although, Sproul speaks of the children of believers being saved by "special provisions of God's mercy" and not in reference to God's covenant herein canon 1.17. *Surprised by Suffering* (Wheaton, IL: Tyndale House, 1988), 187–88.

[176] *Acta Synodi*, part 3, p. 24. As cited in de Boer, "'O, Ye Women,'" 278. See also See also Godfrey, "Election and Covenant," 7.

mention this because some people read this and say, "Well, the canons aren't really saying anything," No! They're saying everything with rhetorical effect! **Godly parents** *have no reason to doubt* means godly parents are to be confident![177] As one commentator said, "When God-fearing parents cry over their precious gifts they could only briefly enjoy having, they may look up together and remind one another: Our children were fruits early ripe for heaven. And with this they can comfort one another."[178]

Because this article expresses seventeenth-century Reformed doctrine differently than the opinions of twentieth-century thinking, some have problems with it. For example, Herman Hoeksema (1886–1965) said:

> This article leaves much to be desired as far as clarity and sharpness of definition are concerned; and it cannot be denied that in the form in which it is here cast it really cannot be considered an item for a confession. In a confession the church expresses what it believes concerning the truth of God revealed in the Scriptures. And it can hardly be said that the church here does that.[179]

"But doesn't the Bible say, 'All who call on the name of the Lord shall be saved'? My child couldn't believe." Your child was a covenant child, and therefore you ought not to doubt the election and salvation of your child because God is sovereign and able to save them apart from their exercising true faith. To this, some of our forefathers said the Holy Spirit put the habit or principle of faith in them just like they had the habit or principle of original sin before actually sinning. After all, we read of Jeremiah (Jer. 1:5) and Paul (Gal. 1:15) being set apart for God from the womb as well as John the Baptist leaping with joy at the news of Mary's pregnancy (Luke 1:41).

---

[177] N. H. Gootjes, "Can Parents Be Sure? Background and Meaning of Canons of Dort I, 17 (1)," *Clarion: The Canadian Reformed Magazine* 44, no. 20 (October 6, 1995): 465n5; Venema, "The Election and Salvation of the Children of Believers Who Die in Infancy," 83.

[178] M. Meijering cited in Venema, "The Election and Salvation of the Children of Believers Who Die in Infancy," 83.

[179] Herman Hoeksema, *Believers and Their Seed*, trans. Homer C. Hoeksema (1971; repr., Grand Rapids, MI: Reformed Free Publishing Association, 1977), 149.

Article 18

To those who murmur at the free grace of election and just severity of reprobation, we answer with the apostle: "Nay but, O man, who art thou that repliest against God?" (Rom. 9:20), and quote the language of our Savior: "Is it not lawful for Me to do what I will with Mine own?" (Matt. 20:15). And therefore with holy adoration of these mysteries, we exclaim in the words of the apostle: "O the depth of the riches both of the wisdom and knowledge of God! how unsearchable are His judgments, and His ways past finding out! For who hath known the mind of the Lord? or who hath been His counsellor? Or who hath first given to Him, and it shall be recompensed unto him again? For of Him, and through Him, and to Him, are all things: to whom be glory for ever. Amen" (Rom. 11:33–36).

CONCLUSION: MAN'S RESPONSE TO GOD'S REVELATION

We finally come to the conclusion. There is a twofold response to the doctrine of election and reprobation: **those who murmur at the free grace of election and just severity of reprobation** and **we** who embrace it.

In the end, what both the doctrines of election and reprobation teach us is that we have a totally sovereign but also totally good God. In his sovereign purpose and goodness he sent his eternal Son to become just like us, without sin. Jesus knows what it is to grieve. When you grieve at your own loss or at the loss of another, know that Scripture speaks clearly that children of believers belong to Christ. Because they belong to Christ, he will sort out how to save them. In the end, he will be glorified for his justice but especially his grace, love, and mercy.

This is why we say with the apostle Paul, **"Nay but, O man, who art thou that repliest against God?" (Rom. 9:20)**. This is why we say with Jesus, **"Is it not lawful for Me to do what I will with Mine own?" (Matt. 20:15)**. Commenting on Romans 9:20, the *Dutch Annotations* said, "A frail man ought not to dispute against God, as being too mean [low] and unfit to judge of God's doings," and again, "it is unseemly for a man to ask God a reason of his actions, seeing God is his Creator, and he his workmanship or Creature."[180] This is why we conclude all talk of predestination as Paul did in Romans 11 **with holy adoration of these mysteries.**

---

[180] *Dutch Annotations* on Romans 9:20.

On Romans 11:33–36, the *Dutch Annotations* offer a brilliant set of explanatory notes that we'll end these eighteen articles on predestination with:

> **"Oh, the depths"**—which are "the exceeding great mystery of spiritual wisdom."
>
> **"of the riches both of the wisdom and the knowledge of God!"**—which is "in God himself, by which he wisely disposes and orders all things."
>
> **"How unsearchable are his judgments, and his ways beyond tracing out!"**—which are "the ways and courses which he takes in the disposing and ordering of men's election and reprobation."
>
> **"For who has known the mind of the Lord? Or who has been his counselor?"**—"who should have given him counsel, and on whom he should bring about salvation for his own greatest honor...no man but himself according to his infinite wisdom."
>
> **"Or who has first given to God, that God should repay him?"**—"God is not indebted to give any man any recompense, and therefore salvation is given by him not of mercy but of grace."
>
> **"For from him"**—"as the first cause, which orders and disposes all things according to his wise counsel."
>
> **"and through him"**—"as who works all things that are necessary to man's salvation, and powerfully execute that which is ordained, according to his wise counsel."
>
> **"and to him"**—"as to the utmost end, to whose glory all things must tend and be brought."
>
> **"are all things"**—"not only which concern the creation, preservation, and governing of all creatures, but especially which concern the salvation of men, which here is principally treated of."
>
> **"To him be the glory forever! Amen!"**[181]

---

[181] *Dutch Annotations* on Romans 11:33–36.

II:
WHAT WE REJECT
REJECTION OF ERRORS 1-9

THE CANONS of Dort begin with eighteen positive articles on predestination before turning to nine rejections of errors. This pattern of assertion and denials helpfully elucidates what is believed as well as what is outside the bounds of that belief. At the beginning of these rejections is this heading: **The true doctrine concerning election and reprobation having been explained, the Synod rejects the errors of those who teach.** Let's briefly look at each.

Rejection of Errors 1

That the will of God to save those who would believe and would persevere in faith and in the obedience of faith, is the whole and entire decree of election unto salvation, and that nothing else concerning this decree has been revealed in God's Word.

For these deceive the simple and plainly contradict the Scriptures which declare that God will not only save those who will believe, but that He has also from eternity chosen certain particular persons to whom above others He in time will grant both faith in Christ and perseverance, as it is written: "I have manifested Thy Name unto the men which Thou gavest Me out of the world" (John 17:6). "And as many as were ordained to eternal life believed" (Acts 13:48). And: "According as He hath chosen us in Him before the foundation of the world, that we should be holy and without blame before Him in love" (Eph. 1:4).

Alluding to the original 1610 *Remonstrance*, the first rejection begins *that the will of God to save those who would believe and would persevere in faith and in the obedience of faith*. By itself, this is not objectionable; the issue was that according to the Remonstrants this *is the whole and entire decree of election unto salvation, and that nothing else concerning this decree has been revealed in God's Word*.

This view is rejected for two reasons: first, for a pastoral reason: **these deceive the simple**. Second, for a biblical reason: **these…plainly contradict the Scriptures which declare that God will not only save those who will believe as the rejection began** (cf. art. 2), **but that He has also from eternity chosen certain particular persons to whom above others He in time will grant both faith in Christ and perseverance** (cf. art. 7). The Remonstrant doctrine was contrary to this gracious election by making it merely a decree about the things to be done for salvation. A summary of Scripture passages that teach this is then offered.

First, Jesus' words in John 17:6: **"I have manifested Thy Name unto the men which Thou gavest Me out of the world."** As the *Dutch Annotations* would go on to say, God chose these men "not only to be faithful Apostles and witnesses, but also to save them" and also those "out of the common heap of mankind…by thine eternal election."[1]

Second, a text we've seen before from the pen of Luke: **"And as many as were ordained to eternal life believed"** (Acts 13:48). This text connected Lydia's faith and those with her to God's eternal purpose.

Finally, another text we've seen from Paul in Ephesians 1:4 where he says of believers in Ephesus: **"According as He hath chosen us in Him before the foundation of the world, that we should be holy and without blame before Him in love."**

Rejection of Errors 2

That there are various kinds of election of God unto eternal life: the one general and indefinite, the other particular and definite; and that the latter in turn is either incomplete, revocable, nondecisive and conditional, or complete, irrevocable, decisive and absolute. Likewise: that there is one election unto faith and another unto salvation, so that election can be unto justifying faith without being a decisive election unto salvation.

---

[1] *Dutch Annotations* on John 17:6.

> For this is a fancy of men's minds, invented regardless of the Scriptures, whereby the doctrine of election is corrupted, and this golden chain of our salvation is broken: "Moreover whom He did predestinate, them He also called: and whom He called, them He also justified: and whom He justified, them He also glorified" (Rom. 8:30).

Rejection 2 relates to article 7, which explained the unchangeable nature of election. This is in contrast to Remonstrant teaching concerning an *incomplete, revocable, nondecisive and conditional* election. It also relates to article 8, which spoke of there being one kind of election, not many. The Remonstrants followed Arminius himself in saying God had an antecedent will (*voluntas antecedens*) before he foresaw anyone exercising faith in which he willed everyone to be saved. He also had a consequent will (*voluntas consequens*) after he foresaw those who would exercise faith. These he then willed to elect on the basis of their foreseen faith.[2] Rejection 2 cites Remonstrant views of *various kinds of election of God unto eternal life: the one general and indefinite, the other particular and definite; and that the latter in turn is either incomplete, revocable, nondecisive and conditional, or complete, irrevocable, decisive and absolute.* They also spoke of *one election unto faith and another unto salvation, so that election can be unto justifying faith without being a decisive election unto salvation.* The end result of teaching that there were different kinds of election, and because of that, different decrees and wills of God, is that we end up being confused in all the complexity and unsure whether we are saved or not. They said—and people still say today—that you can be elected to faith, only to lose your faith, and therefore not be elected to salvation.

What do we say to this? Rejection 2 goes on to call this *humani cerebri commentum, a fancy* (or, "fiction") *of people's minds* that is *invented regardless of* ("apart from") *the Scriptures* (*extra Scripturas*) and therefore *the doctrine of election is corrupted, and this golden chain of our salvation* (*auream salutis catenum*) *is broken.* This golden chain is found in Romans 8:29–30: *"Moreover whom He did predestinate, them He also called: and whom He called, them He also justified: and whom He justified, them He also glorified."* Concerning this **golden chain**, Cornelis Venema

---

[2] See "Examination of Dr. Perkins's Pamphlet on Predestination," in *The Works of James Arminius: Volume 3*, 429–30. On this, see *Synopsis Purioris Theologiae: Volume 2*, 31–33.

said, "Salvation does not hang upon the thin thread of their own initiative and perseverance, but upon the solid chain of God's electing purpose in Christ."[3]

Rejection of Errors 3

That the good pleasure and purpose of God, of which Scripture makes mention in the doctrine of election, does not consist in this, that God chose certain persons rather than others, but in this, that He chose out of all possible conditions (among which are also the works of the law), or out of the whole order of things, the act of faith which from its very nature is undeserving, as well as its incomplete obedience, as a condition of salvation, and that He would graciously consider this in itself as a complete obedience and count it worthy of the reward of eternal life.

For by this injurious error the pleasure of God and the merits of Christ are made of none effect, and men are drawn away by useless questions from the truth of gracious justification and from the simplicity of Scripture, and this declaration of the apostle is charged as untrue: "Who hath saved us, and called us with an holy calling, not according to our works, but according to His own purpose and grace, which was given us in Christ Jesus before the world began" (2 Tim. 1:9).

The third error we reject relates back to article 10 and our teaching that election is of persons, not probabilities. The Remonstrants taught *that the good pleasure and purpose of God...does not consist in this, that God chose certain persons rather than others.* They rejected personal election. Instead, they taught God chose *out of all possible conditions (among which are also the works of the law), or out of the whole order of things, the act of faith which from its very nature is undeserving, as well as its incomplete obedience, as a condition of salvation.* In other words, God in his foreknowledge of what would happen purposed that certain conditions would fulfill what was necessary for salvation. Notice how the rejection speaks of *the act of faith which from its very nature is undeserving.* This was a key Protestant doctrine as exemplified in Heidelberg Catechism, Q&A 61:

Q. Why do you say that you are righteous by faith only?

---

[3] Venema, "The Election and Salvation of the Children of Believers Who Die in Infancy," 58.

A. Not that I am acceptable to God on account of the worthiness of my faith, but because only the satisfaction, righteousness, and holiness of Christ are my righteousness before God; and I can receive the same and make it my own in no other way than by faith only.[4]

It is also exemplified in Belgic Confession, article 22, which says of justification by faith alone: "However, to speak more clearly, we do not mean that faith itself justifies us, for it is only an instruction with which we embrace Christ our righteousness."[5]

In saying, therefore, that election means God *would graciously consider* [faith and incomplete obedience] *in itself as a complete obedience and count it worthy of the reward of eternal life* is to obliterate the doctrine of justification by faith alone, which Gomarus saw so clearly in his debates with Arminius as well as Sibrandus Lubbertus with Arminius's follower Petrus Bertius.[6]

This is why the rejection goes on to say **by this injurious error the pleasure of God and the merits of Christ are made of none effect, and** *people* (*homines*) **are drawn away by useless questions from the truth of gracious justification and from the simplicity of Scripture**. To say this also makes **this declaration of the apostle** [to be] **charged as untrue: "Who hath saved us, and called us with an holy calling, not according to our works, but according to His own purpose and grace, which was given us in Christ Jesus before the world began" (2 Tim. 1:9).**

When the apostle says **"not according to our works"** (οὐ κατὰ τὰ ἔργα ἡμῶν), he means not "as a precedent or foreseen cause [that] should merit this calling, or have moved God thereunto."[7]

---

4 Dennison, *Reformed Confessions of the 16th and 17th Centuries*, 2:783.

5 Dennison, *Reformed Confessions of the 16th and 17th Centuries*, 2:437.

6 See also Paraeus, "Epitome of Arminianisme," 822. See again Goudriaan, "Justification by Faith and the Early Arminian Controversy," 155–78.

7 *Dutch Annotations* on 2 Timothy 1:9. The *Annotations* also offer the insightful comment that "this grace was not actually given us from everlasting, but in time, where we are actually called; but it is so said, because this actual giving comes to pass according to that eternal purpose of God, which is so sure, as if it were already accomplished."

Rejection of Errors 4

That in the election unto faith this condition is beforehand demanded, namely, that man should use the light of nature aright, be pious, humble, meek, and fit for eternal life, as if on these things election were in any way dependent.

For this savors of the teaching of Pelagius, and is opposed to the doctrine of the apostle, when he writes: "Among whom also we all had our conversation in times past in the lusts of our flesh, fulfilling the desires of the flesh and of the mind; and were by nature the children of wrath, even as others. But God, who is rich in mercy, for His great love wherewith He loved us, even when we were dead in sins, hath quickened us together with Christ, (by grace ye are saved;) and hath raised us up together, and made us sit together in heavenly places in Christ Jesus: that in the ages to come He might show the exceeding riches of His grace in His kindness toward us through Christ Jesus. For by grace are ye saved through faith; and that not of yourselves: it is the gift of God: not of works, lest any man should boast" (Eph. 2:3–9).

Rejection 4 relates back to article 9, which said election was **not founded upon foreseen faith, and the obedience of faith, holiness, or any other good quality or disposition**. One of those "good qualities" mentioned by the Remonstrants is found in this rejection: *in the election unto faith this condition is beforehand demanded, namely, that man should use the light of nature aright, be pious, humble, meek, and fit for eternal life, as if on these things election were in any way dependent.* *The light of nature* (*lumine naturae*) was a synonymous term for reason, which God implanted in Adam by nature as his creature, enabling him to understand the revelation of God in creation and natural law.[8] In other words, the Remonstrant use of this was another way of compromising our free justification by grace alone through faith alone since election was seen as being based on our ability to use our reason to align ourselves with God.

---

[8] "Lumen naturae," in Muller, *Dictionary of Latin and Greek Theological Terms*, 206. For a helpful work in understanding early seventeenth-century natural law (*lex naturalis*)/light of nature (*lumen naturae*) distinctions, see particularly theses 1–5 in Franciscus Junius, *The Mosaic Polity*, trans. Todd M. Rester, ed. Andrew M. McGinnis, Sources in Early Modern Economics, Ethics, and Law (Grand Rapids, MI: Christian's Library, 2015), 37–49. On this natural reason in relation to natural theology, see David Haines, "Natural Theology in Reformed Orthodoxy," in *Philosophy and the Christian: The Quest for Wisdom in the Light of Christ*, ed. Joseph Minich (Lincoln, NE: Davenant, 2018), 250–91.

In response the synod for the first time invoked the name of Pelagius: **For this savors**[9] **of the teaching of Pelagius**. This was the first of eight references to Pelagius/Pelagianism in the canons.[10] In other words, if it walks like a duck and quacks like a duck, it's a duck! As such, the doctrine rejected **is opposed to the doctrine of the apostle**, illustrated in a lengthy quotation from Ephesians 2:3–9.

Rejection of Errors 5

That the incomplete and non-decisive election of particular persons to salvation occurred because of a foreseen faith, conversion, holiness, godliness, which either began or continued for some time; but that the complete and decisive election occurred because of foreseen perseverance unto the end in faith, conversion, holiness and godliness; and that this is the gracious and evangelical worthiness for the sake of which he who is chosen is more worthy than he who is not chosen; and that therefore faith, the obedience of faith, holiness, godliness and perseverance are not fruits of the unchangeable election unto glory, but are conditions, which, being required beforehand, were foreseen as being met by those who will be fully elected, and are causes without which the unchangeable election to glory does not occur.

This is repugnant to the entire Scripture which constantly inculcates this and similar declarations: Election is not out of works, but of Him that calleth. "That the purpose of God according to election might stand, not of works, but of Him that calleth" (Rom. 9:11). "And as many as were ordained to eternal life believed" (Acts 13:48). "He hath chosen us in Him before the foundation of the world, that we should be holy" (Eph. 1:4). "Ye have not chosen Me, but I have chosen you" (John 15:16). "But if it be of works, then is it no more grace" (Rom. 11:6). "Herein is love, not that we loved God, but that He loved us, and sent His Son" (1 John 4:10).

Rejection 5 is the lengthiest of the rejections. It relates back to article 8 and rejection 2, which spoke of there being one kind of election, not many. It relates back to article 9, which said election was not based on foreseen qualities. The Remonstrants made the distinction between *general and indefinite* election and *particular and definite* election and that this *latter* kind was *either incomplete, revocable, nondecisive and conditional, or complete, irrevocable, decisive and absolute* (RE 2).

---

[9] The phrase used is *Pelagium enim sapiunt. Sapiunt* is from *sapio,* "taste, savor."

[10] See also 2.RE 3; 2.RE 6; 3/4.2; 3/4.10; 3/4.RE 7; 3/4.RE 9; 5.RE 2.

Rejection 5 first mentions *incomplete and non-decisive election of particular persons to salvation.* The Remonstrants taught that this *occurred because of a foreseen faith, conversion, holiness, godliness, which either began or continued for some time.* Rejection 5 then mentions *complete and decisive election,* which the Remonstrants taught, *occurred because of foreseen perseverance unto the end in faith, conversion, holiness and godliness.* This goes back to rejection 2, in which there is *one election unto faith and another unto salvation.*

Rejection 5 continues to quote the Remonstrant doctrine that was the sum of the above: *and that this is the gracious and evangelical worthiness for the sake of which he who is chosen is more worthy than he who is not chosen* because of what God foresees them accomplishing by faith and obedience. Because of this *faith, the obedience of faith, holiness, godliness and perseverance are not fruits of the unchangeable election unto glory* as we confessed in article 9 *but are conditions, which, being required beforehand, were foreseen as being met by those who will be fully elected, and are causes without which the unchangeable election to glory does not occur.*

It almost goes without saying that we find much that is objectionable here. Rejection 5 states it simply: **This is repugnant to the entire Scripture which constantly inculcates this and similar declarations: Election is not out of works, but of Him that calleth.** Then it goes on to cite several passages from the New Testament.

First, Romans 9:11: **"That the purpose of God according to election might stand, not of works, but of Him that calleth."** The importance of this saying was expressed by the *Dutch Annotations*: "Therefore it is not of faith, for that is not in God that calls, but in the man that is called."[11]

The second and third texts we've seen already: **"And as many as were ordained to eternal life believed"** (Acts 13:48), not the other way around, and, **"He hath chosen us in Him before the foundation of the world, that we should be holy"** (Eph. 1:4), not because we were.

The fourth text is Jesus' statement to his disciples in John 15:16: **"Ye have not chosen Me, but I have chosen you."** Again, even the choosing of the first disciples was not because of their choice, but Jesus.

---

[11] *Dutch Annotations* on Romans 9:11–12.

Fifth, Paul's aphorism in Romans 11:6: **"But if it be of works, then is it no more grace."** Again, in the words of the *Dutch Annotations*, "Grace excludes all debt, merit or worthiness, and cannot consist therewith; for grace is in no wise grace, if it be not every way grace."[12]

Finally, the beloved apostles' words: **"Herein is love, not that we loved God, but that He loved us, and sent His Son"** (1 John 4:10). These teach us not "that by our love we should have stirred up God to love us again."[13]

Rejection of Errors 6

That not every election unto salvation is unchangeable, but that some of the elect, any decree of God notwithstanding, can yet perish and do indeed perish.

By which gross error they make God to be changeable, and destroy the comfort which the godly obtain out of the firmness of their election, and contradict the Holy Scripture which teaches that the elect cannot be led astray: "Insomuch that, if it were possible, they shall deceive the very elect" (Matt. 24:24); that Christ does not lose those whom the Father gave Him: "And this is the Father's will which hath sent Me, that of all which He hath given Me I should lose nothing" (John 6:39); and that God hath also glorified those whom He foreordained, called and justified: "Moreover whom He did predestinate, them He also called: and whom He called, them He also justified: and whom He justified, them He also glorified" (Rom. 8:30).

Rejection 6 takes us back to article 11 and predestination to salvation being unchangeable. The Remonstrants taught *that not every election unto salvation is unchangeable, but that some of the elect, any decree of God notwithstanding, can yet perish and do indeed perish.* This latter clause will be explained in greater detail in the fifth point of doctrine below, but for now we'll focus on the former part of the sentence.

The synod said in response that first and foremost **by which gross error they make God to be changeable.** As someone once said, all theological error goes back to the doctrine of God. Second, the Remonstrants **destroy the comfort which the godly obtain out of the firmness of their election.** There is a pastoral issue on the line here: Are Christians to live in confidence and ever-greater assurance or live in fear? Finally, the

---

[12] *Dutch Annotations* on Romans 11:6.

[13] *Dutch Annotations* on 1 John 4:10.

synod said the Remonstrants **contradict the Holy Scripture which teaches**, then citing three passages.

First, Matthew 24:24 teaches **that the elect cannot be led astray,** which the *Dutch Annotations* explained is true "not in respect of the will or power of the elect in themselves; but in respect of the immutability of God's decree concerning them, and of his powerful keeping of them against seduction, according to his promised, of which he cannot repent."[14]

Second, John 6:39 teaches **that Christ does not lose those whom the Father gave Him: "And this is the Father's will which hath sent Me, that of all which He hath given Me I should lose nothing." "*I*"** shows the power of Jesus. "Should lose nothing" is the same phrase Jesus used when he said to his disciples: "Gather up the leftover fragments, that *nothing may be lost*" (John 6:12). His power is expressed by "los[ing] nothing *of all*" the Father gave him, which is personal: "of them" (ἐξ αὐτοῦ). Just previous in verse 37 Jesus spoke of "all that the Father gives me" as a definable group of people who come one by one to the Son; now in verse 39 he says out of that group he will lose not even one!

Third, Romans 8:30 from the golden chain we saw in rejection 2: **that God hath also glorified those whom He foreordained, called and justified: "Moreover whom He did predestinate, them He also called: and whom He called, them He also justified: and whom He justified, them He also glorified."** In complete contrast to the Remonstrant doctrine, this chain extends from eternity past into eternity future. In context of Romans 8, Paul said that we have been justified—past tense (v. 1); that we are being sanctified through suffering—present tense (vv. 17–25); and that we will be glorified—future tense (vv. 18–25). But in the golden chain he says **whom He did predestinate** (προώρισεν; past tense) **them He also called** (ἐκάλεσεν; past tense) **and whom He called** (ἐκάλεσεν; past tense) **them He also justified** (ἐδικαίωσεν; past tense) **and whom He justified** (ἐδικαίωσεν; past tense) **them He also glorified** (ἐδόξασεν; past tense). Why does Paul say everything in the chain is past tense, even our future glorification? He does this to speak of the certainty the believer has that all

---

[14] *Dutch Annotations* on Matthew 24:24.

his or her sufferings are a part of God's plan now and in the future—so certain, in fact, that it's as if you've already been glorified.[15]

Rejection of Errors 7

That there is in this life no fruit and no consciousness of the unchangeable election to glory, nor any certainty, except that which depends on a changeable and uncertain condition.

For not only is it absurd to speak of an uncertain certainty, but also contrary to the experience of the saints, who by virtue of the consciousness of their election rejoice with the apostle and praise this favor of God; who according to Christ's admonition rejoice with His disciples that their names are written in heaven, "but rather rejoice, because your names are written in heaven" (Luke 10:20); who also place the consciousness of their election over against the fiery darts of the devil, asking: "Who shall lay any thing to the charge of God's elect?" (Rom. 8:33).

Rejection 7 applies what we saw in articles 12–13 and the possibility of the attainment of assurance in this life. On the contrary, Dort was responding to those who taught *that there is in this life no fruit and no consciousness of the unchangeable election to glory, nor any certainty, except that which depends on a changeable and uncertain condition.* This confession of uncertainty was the natural consequence of Remonstrant teaching in which there were various kinds of election based on future conditionals and hypotheticals.

This is why the synod strongly said **not only is it absurd to speak of an uncertain certainty** (*certitudinem incertam*). It *is* absurd to speak this way, but that's not the only reason we as orthodox churches object. It goes against Christian experience: but [it is] **also contrary to the experience of the saints, who by virtue of the consciousness of their election rejoice with the apostle and praise this favor of God**. Think of the opening of Paul's letter to the Ephesians: "Blessed be the God and Father of our Lord Jesus Christ, who has blessed us in Christ with every spiritual blessing in the heavenly places" (1:3), in particular the grace of predestination (1:4–5).

---

15 See the discussion in Thomas R. Schreiner, *Romans*, Baker Exegetical Commentary on the New Testament (Grand Rapids, MI: Baker Books, 1998), 454–55; Colin G. Kruse, *Paul's Letter to the Romans*, The Pillar New Testament Commentary (Grand Rapids, MI: Eerdmans, 2012), 357–58.

The certainty of election is exemplified in two texts listed by the synod. First, Jesus' words in Luke 10:20: **who according to Christ's admonition rejoice with His disciples that their names are written in heaven, "but rather rejoice, because your names are written in heaven" (Luke 10:20)**. Rejoice is the command, not be uncertain. The second example of certainty comes from the pen of the apostle Paul in Romans 8:33: **who also place the consciousness of their election over against the fiery darts of the devil, asking: "Who shall lay any thing to the charge of God's elect?"** Note that by the very fact of being charged a believer is conscious of being one of **God's elect**.

Rejection of Errors 8

That God, simply by virtue of His righteous will, did not decide either to leave anyone in the fall of Adam and in the common state of sin and condemnation, or to pass anyone by in the communication of grace which is necessary for faith and conversion.

For this is firmly decreed: "Therefore hath He mercy on whom He will have mercy, and whom He will He hardeneth" (Rom. 9:18). And also this: "It is given unto you to know the mysteries of the kingdom of heaven, but to them it is not given" (Matt. 13:11). Likewise: "I thank Thee, O Father, Lord of heaven and earth, because Thou hast hid these things from the wise and prudent, and hast revealed them unto babes. Even so, Father: for so it seemed good in Thy sight" (Matt. 11:25–26).

Rejection 8 refers back to article 1 and Adam's fall, article 5 and the cause of mankind's sin and unbelief being in man alone, article 6 on faith being given according to God's plan, and finally article 15, the main article on reprobation. In fact, this is the only rejection of errors that refers to the Remonstrants' doctrine of reprobation. As we saw in connection with article 15, Sinnema summarized Dort's response as offering a "mild rejection" of the Remonstrant view, leaving many areas unanswered and to the mystery of God.[16]

The particular view the synod rejected was *that God, simply by virtue of His righteous will, did not decide either to leave anyone in the fall of Adam and in the common state of sin and condemnation, or to pass anyone by in the communication of grace which is necessary for*

---

[16] Sinnema, "The Issue of Reprobation at the Synod of Dort," 448.

faith and conversion. This takes us back to our discussion of how the divines at Dort appropriated the medieval catholic consensus interpretation of the earlier and stricter view of Augustine. The medieval distinction was between *negative reprobation,* in which God left/passed by those not chosen to salvation, and *positive reprobation,* in which God then gave over to punishment. God's will in negative reprobation was not in any way conditioned on his foreknowledge of the merits or demerits of sinners.

For support, the synod cited several passages, saying, **for this is firmly decreed**, then listing three passages.

First, Romans 9:18 says, **"Therefore hath He mercy on whom He will have mercy, and whom He will He hardeneth."** According to the *Dutch Annotations*, this means God "takes not away the hardness of heart which they have of themselves, but gives them up to the same." That's a careful way of stating the negative and positive aspects of reprobation: he decreed not to remove their hard hearts but to leave them in their hardness, and he decreed to ultimately give them over to that hardness. Concerning the language of "wills" in Romans 9:18, the *Annotations* went on to say it

> is not taken for a will that should have no reason of its actions. For the will of God is a rule of all righteousness (Deut. 32:4) and is never separated from his wisdom and righteousness, albeit that the reasons thereof are not revealed to us, or are above our understanding (Rom. 11:33, 34). Wherewith also we must always hold ourselves content.[17]

In other words, this is a mystery to us; be content with the mystery.

The second text cited is Matthew 13:11 where Jesus says to his disciples: **"It is given unto you to know the mysteries of the kingdom of heaven, but to them it is not given."** In other words, Jesus teaches us that those who are given to know the kingdom are so "by God, of grace, according to his good pleasure," while those to whom God has not given this knowledge (notice the negative language) Jesus says "the Gospel is hid to them that are lost."[18]

The third and final text is again from Jesus' lips in Matthew 11:25–26: **"I thank Thee, O Father, Lord of heaven and earth, because Thou**

---

[17] *Dutch Annotations* on Romans 9:18.

[18] *Dutch Annotations* on Matthew 13:11.

hast hid [again, notice the negative] **these things from the wise and prudent,"** which the *Dutch Annotations* took to mean, 'according to the flesh,' **"and have revealed them to little children,"** again, which the *Annotations* took to mean, 'children in understanding or little esteemed,' **"yes, Father, because that was your pleasure."**[19]

Rejection of Errors 9

That the reason why God sends the gospel to one people rather than to another is not merely and solely the good pleasure of God, but rather the fact that one people is better and worthier than another to whom the gospel is not communicated.

For this Moses denies, addressing the people of Israel as follows: "Behold, the heaven and the heaven of heavens is the LORD's thy God, the earth also, with all that therein is. Only the LORD had a delight in thy fathers to love them, and He chose their seed after them, even you above all people, as it is this day" (Deut. 10:14–15). And Christ said: "Woe unto thee, Chorazin! woe unto thee, Bethsaida! for if the mighty works, which were done in you, had been done in Tyre and Sidon, they would have repented long ago in sackcloth and ashes" (Matt. 11:21).

The final rejection related to the grace of predestination reflects what we've already seen in article 3 concerning God's mercy in sending preachers to bring sinners to faith and article 7 concerning the "definition" of election being rooted in the good pleasure of God.

The error rejected is *that the reason (causam; cause) why God sends the gospel to one people rather than to another is not merely and solely the good pleasure of God, but rather the fact that one people is better and worthier than another to whom the gospel is not communicated.* One people group rather than another people group is sent the gospel on the basis of God's foreseeing their faith. In other words, the gospel is God's response to those who distinguish themselves as worthier than others as opposed to finding its basis in God's good pleasure that causes people to believe.

The synodically cited texts to prove that election is based solely in the good pleasure of God come from the Old and New Testaments.

First, before citing Deuteronomy 10:14–15, the rejection says, **for this Moses denies:**

---

[19] *Dutch Annotations* on Matthew 11:25–26.

> Behold, the heaven and the heaven of heavens is the
> LORD's thy God, the earth also, with all that therein
> is. Only the LORD had a delight in thy fathers to love
> them, and He chose their seed after them, even you
> above all people, as it is this day. (Deut. 10:14–15)

The generation of pastors and theologians at Dort understood this
text to teach election based solely in the good pleasure of God because all
creatures are equal before him, he did not need any of them, and he is free
to choose or not chose any as he desires:

> There was no cause of the election of Israel, and of their
> fathers, but the mere good will and pleasure, and free grace
> of God; for all his creatures in regard of creation, were
> equally nigh unto him; he stood not in need of any, and it
> was free for him to leave Israel and their fathers in their
> sinful state and condition, as well as other nations; and to
> choose, and show mercy to whom, and to what people he
> pleased.[20]

Especially instructive is the second cited text by the synod from the
words of our Lord in Matthew 11:21: **"Woe unto thee, Chorazin! woe
unto thee, Bethsaida! for if the mighty works, which were done in
you, had been done in Tyre and Sidon, they would have repented
long ago in sackcloth and ashes."** Jesus' **mighty works** were done in
Chorazin and Bethsaida but, in fact, Tyre and Sidon were *better and worthier*; yet Jesus was sent to the former and not the latter. The gospel *isn't*
sent because of human worthiness. Because of this, J. Gresham Machen
made the applicable statement, "Never have we any right to assume that
any man or group of men that we can name is outside of God's plan for
salvation."[21]

---

[20] *Dutch Annotations* on Deuteronomy 10:14–15.

[21] J. Gresham Machen, *The Christian View of Man* (Edinburgh: The Banner of Truth
Trust, 1984), 82.

THE GRACE OF SATISFACTION

III:
WHAT WE CONFESS
ARTICLES 1-9

THE REMONSTRANT DOCTRINE

THE ORIGINAL *Remonstrance* of 1610 transitioned from eternal predestination in its first article to the historical work of Jesus Christ in its second article: "That in agreement with this [doctrine of predestination] Jesus Christ the Savior of the world *died for all people and every person (omnibus et singulis hominibus mortuus est)*."[1] David Paraeus told the Synod of Dort this was "ambiguous."[2] In other words, we shouldn't be disagreeable toward it as it's noncontroversial apart from explanation. Scripture simply speaks this way. Jesus is called "the Savior of the world," which comes from the Samaritans' confession of Jesus in John 4:42 (cf. 1 John 4:14). Even the language of "died for all people and every person" is not controversial. Even as Arminius himself said concerning universal texts of Scripture, "All the controversy therefore lies in the interpretation."[3] The Heidelberg Catechism, in question and answer 37 on the meaning of "suffered" in the Apostles' Creed, said Christ "bore ('sustained'; *sustinuisse*), in body and soul, the wrath of God against the sin of the whole human race" (*peccatum universi generis humani*).[4]

---

[1] Emphasis added. See appendix 1 for this reference to the *Remonstrance* and those to follow.

[2] Paraeus, "Epitome of Arminianisme," 826.

[3] Arminius, "The Apology or Defence," 2:10.

[4] Dennison, *Reformed Confessions of the 16th and 17th Centuries*, 2:778; van den Brink, ed. *De Nederlandse belijdenisgeschriften*, 170. See Paraeus's exposition of this Q&A in

The proof texts it offered included Isaiah 53:12, "he bore the sin of many," and 1 John 2:2, "He is the propitiation for our sins, and not for ours only but also for the sins of the whole world." At the synod, the Remonstrants wrote up a further list of their opinions and continued using this language:

> 1. The price of redemption which Christ offered to God the Father is not only in itself and by itself sufficient for the redemption of the whole human race but has also been paid *for all men and for every man...*

> 2. Christ has, by the merit of his death, so reconciled God the Father to *the whole human race...*

> 3. Though Christ has merited reconciliation with God and remission of sins *for all men and for every man...*[5]

THE ISSUE

The issue with Remonstrant article 2 was twofold. First, connecting these basic biblical affirmations with the clause "*so that* he merited reconciliation and forgiveness of sins for all through the death of the cross." This is where Paraeus said the Remonstrants began to be "equivocall and false."[6] Why? That word "merited" (*promeritus*) meant Christ accomplished and acquired reconciliation and forgiveness.[7] If "for all" merely meant that "the greatnesse of the merit of Christ's death [was] sufficient to all men for reconcilliation," it would be fine.[8] But this leads to the second problem with the Remonstrant article: "yet so that no one actually enjoys this forgiveness of sins except the believer." Again, at the synod the Remonstrants argued:

> 4. Though Christ has merited reconciliation with God and remission of sins for all men and for every man, *yet no one,*

---

the context of Arminian attempts to appropriate it into their system. "Epitome of Arminianisme," 830–31.

[5] "The Opinions of the Remonstrants," appendix H in De Jong, *Crisis in the Reformed Churches*, 224. Emphasis added.

[6] Paraeus, "Epitome of Arminianisme," 826.

[7] "Promeritum," in Thomas Holyoak, *A Large Dictionary: In Three Parts* (London: Printed by W. Rawlins for G. Sawbridge, et al., 1677), n.p.

[8] Paraeus, "Epitome of Arminianisme," 826.

according to the pact of the new and gracious covenant, *becomes a true partaker* of the benefits obtained by the death of Christ *in any other way than by faith*; nor are sins forgiven to sinning men *before they actually and truly believe in Christ.*[9]

In other words, the *Remonstrance* says Jesus accomplished reconciliation for every human being on the cross, but this reconciliation would not actually be applied to any particular person. As the third and fourth points of doctrine in the chapters below will make clearer, the application of redemption was up to the sinner's use of free choice; it was not a benefit of either election or the cross.[10]

This issue still exists among evangelicals who reject the Reformed vision of grace. One popular anti-Calvinist is George Bryson in his comments on 1 Timothy 2:

> Notice that Paul says the Christ, the only Mediator, mediated for all. That is, if as every Calvinist would agree, Christ did His mediating work on the cross, then it follows that what He did on the cross (i.e., die a substitutionary death for our sins) He did for all sinners. Notice also that this teaching about our Lord's mediating work, which paid the ransom for all, is mentioned immediately after Paul tells us about God's desire to save all men. How could God's intentions toward all sinners be stated more clearly? How could the Calvinist not see this?... The gospel is indeed good news for the lost. Not some of the lost, but all of the lost. The fact that some of the lost refuse to believe the good news and thereby forfeit the benefit and blessing which could otherwise be theirs is for that reason all the more tragic.[11]

While there is much agreeable in this statement, there's also not much nuance. To say, "Jesus did everything; now you need to cooperate and make it your own," is not very good news.

---

[9] "The Opinions of the Remonstrants," appendix H in De Jong, *Crisis in the Reformed Churches*, 225.

[10] As cited in "The *Remonstrance* of 1610," appendix C in De Jong, *Crisis in the Reformed Churches*, 208.

[11] George Bryson, *The Five Points of Calvinism: Weighed and Found Wanting* (Costa Mesa, CA: Word for Today, 1996), 92.

HISTORICAL BACKGROUND

As with our discussion of predestination above, the issue of Christ's satisfaction at the Synod of Dort was another episode in a centuries-old tradition.[12]

Augustine

From as far back as Augustine, the issues of relating the universality and particularity of Christ's death have been discussed. In *Tractate 48.4* on John 10:22–42, Augustine commented on Jesus' dialogue with the leadership of the Jews about his being the Messiah:

> Jesus answered them, I tell you, and you believe not: the works that I do in my Father's name, they bear witness of me: but you believe not; because you are not of my sheep. You have already learned above (in Lecture XLV.) who the sheep are: be ye sheep. They are sheep through believing, sheep in following the Shepherd, sheep in not despising their Redeemer, sheep in entering by the door, sheep in going out and finding pasture, sheep in the enjoyment of eternal life. What did He mean, then, in saying to them, You are not of my sheep? *That He saw them predestined to everlasting destruction, not won to eternal life by the price of His own blood.*[13]

Augustine connects faith and unbelief with Jesus' death: some are won by his blood while others are not.

In one of his later writings, *On Rebuke and Grace*, Augustine commented on Jesus' "high priestly prayer" in John 17: "Those, therefore, are understood to be given to Christ who are ordained to eternal life. These are they who are predestined and called according to the purpose, of whom not one perishes."[14] Notice the eternal ordination of some to eternal life, given to the incarnate Son, who are then called; in other words, those elected are infallibly brought to eternal life by the Son.

---

[12] On this history, see Davenant, *A Dissertation on the Death of Christ*, 2:317–39.

[13] *Nicene and Post-Nicene Fathers [NPNF]: First Series*, ed. Philip Schaff (1888; repr., Peabody, MA: Hendrickson, 2004), 7:267. Emphasis added.

[14] *NPNF: First Series*, 5:480.

In *Homily 1.8* on 1 John 1:1–2:11, Augustine commented on 1 John 2:2, "He is the propitiation for our sins, and not for ours only but also for the sins of the whole world." In the context of the Donatists who severed themselves from the church, Augustine commented on John's including himself with the church, not saying "you" by "we" have an advocate (1 John 2:1), not saying "your" sins but "our" sins (1 John 2:2). Schism, he said, was the result of men saying "we" are righteous and not that together we have Christ, who is the Righteous One. Those who have divided themselves from the church were like those Jesus warned against who say, "'Look, here is the Christ!' or 'There he is!'" (Matt. 24:23). Augustine then commented that they "show Him in a part *who bought the whole and possesses the whole*." When John went on to say, "Not for ours only but also for the sins of the whole world (1 John 2:2)," Augustine said:

> We have found *the Church in all nations*. Behold, Christ "is the propitiation for our sins; not ours only, but also the sins of the whole world." Behold, you have *the Church throughout the whole world*; do not follow false justifiers who in truth are cutters off. Be in that mountain which has filled *the whole earth*: because "Christ is the propitiation for our sins; not only ours, but also the sins of the whole world," *which He has bought with His blood.*[15]

Augustine interprets the universal language of "whole world" meaning the church in every place, not every single person. He also speaks particularly in this comment saying Christ purchased the church with his blood.

Another "all" text Augustine interpreted was 1 Timothy 2:4: "who desires all people to be saved." Augustine confesses the experiential difficulty of this phrase since "it would seem that what God wills is not done, man's will interfering with, and hindering the will of God. When we ask the reason why all men are not saved, the ordinary answer is: 'Because men themselves are not willing.'" On the contrary, Augustine pointed out infants for whom "it is not in their power either to will or not to will."[16] He went on to discuss God's will of predestination in Romans 9, then came back to 1 Timothy 2:

---

[15] *NPNF: First Series*, 7:465. Emphasis added.

[16] St. Augustine, *The Enchiridion on Faith, Hope, and Love*, trans. J. F. Shaw, ed. Henry Paolucci (Chicago: Regnery Gateway, 1961), 97 (p. 111).

When we hear and read in Scripture that He "will have all men to be saved," although we know well that all men are not saved, we are not on that account to restrict the omnipotence of God, but are rather to understand the Scripture...as meaning that no man is saved unless God wills his salvation: not that there is no man whose salvation He does not will, but that no man is saved apart from His will; and that, therefore, we should pray Him to will our salvation, because if He will it, it must necessarily be accomplished.[17]

God's will is determinative for Augustine. He wills the salvation for all, but not all are saved except by his will. He then added,

We are to understand by "all men," the human race in all its varieties of rank and circumstances—kings, subjects; noble, plebeian, high, low, learned, and unlearned; the sound in body, the feeble, the clever, the dull, the foolish, the rich, the poor, and those of middling circumstances; males, females, infants, boys, youths; young, middle-aged, and old men; of every tongue, of every fashion, of all arts, of all professions, with all the innumerable differences of will and conscience, and whatever else there is that makes a distinction among men. For which of all these classes is there out of which God does not will that men should be saved in all nations through His only-begotten Son, our Lord, and therefore does save them; for the Omnipotent cannot will in vain, whatsoever He may will.[18]

As with his comments on 1 John 2:2, Augustine speaks of God willing the salvation of the church in all nations. And just like Jesus said of the Pharisees, "You tithe...every herb" (Luke 11:42), Augustine said, "For the Pharisees did not tithe what belonged to others, nor all the herbs of all the inhabitants of other lands. As, then, in this place we must understand by 'every herb,' every kind of herb, so...may understand by 'all men,' every sort of men."[19] And while Augustine asserted exegetical freedom—"we may

---

[17] Augustine, *The Enchiridion*, 103 (pp. 119–20).

[18] Augustine, *The Enchiridion*, 103 (pp. 120–21). On Augustine's interpretation that "God wills all men to be saved" means "the elect," see also "On Rebuke and Grace," 44 (5:489).

[19] Augustine, *The Enchiridion*, 103 (p. 121).

interpret it in any other way we please"—this boundary marker had to be kept: "so long as we are not compelled to believe that the omnipotent God has willed anything to be done which was not done."[20] Even if there are differences in exegesis, there cannot be posited a contradictory or fallible will in God.

Several contemporaries of Augustine spoke to this issue as well.

Jerome

Jerome commented on Jesus' statement that "the Son of Man came…to give his life as a ransom for many" (Matt. 20:28), by emphasizing the saving benefit of Jesus' death only for believers: "he did not say 'to give his life as a redemption' for all, but 'for many,' that is for those who wanted to believe."[21]

John Chrysostom

John Chrysostom asked why the angel told Joseph that Jesus would save "*His people*, and not add the Gentiles also?" He answered: "For to him who listens with understanding he darkly signified the Gentiles too. For *His people* are not the Jews only, but also all that draw nigh and receive the knowledge that is from Him."[22]

Ambrose

Ambrose of Milan also spoke in universal and particular ways of Christ's death: "If Christ died for all, yet he suffered particularly (*specialiter*) for us, because he suffered for the church."[23]

---

[20] Augustine, *The Enchiridion*, 103 (pp. 121–22).

[21] Jerome, *Commentary on Matthew*, trans. Thomas P. Scheck, Fathers of the Church: A New Translation (Washington, DC: Catholic University of America Press, 2008), 117:229.

[22] *The Homilies of S. John Chrysostom Archbishop of Constantinople on the Gospel of St. Matthew: Part I, Homilies I–XXV*, trans. Frederic Field (London: Walter Smith, 1885), 55.

[23] *Expositio Evangelii Secundum Lucam*, 6.25; cited in Gatiss, *For Us and for Our Salvation*, 60.

Prosper of Aquitaine

"The most definitive spokesman for this point of view in the early period of the Church" was Augustine's contemporary and theological successor, Prosper of Aquitaine.[24] Prosper sought to defend Augustine after his death from various charges and objections by Pelagians and Semi-Pelagians. One was that "the Saviour was not crucified for the redemption of the entire world." In response, Prosper said:

> Though it is right to say that the Saviour was crucified for the redemption of the entire world, because He truly took our human nature and because all men were lost in the first man, yet it may also be said that He was crucified only for those who were to profit by His death.[25]

Notice that while Prosper doesn't use "sufficiency/efficiency" language, following Augustine there is a sense in which we can speak of the universality and another sense in which we can speak of the particularity. Prosper locates the universality in the Fall of all humanity and subsequent Incarnation of the Son in that humanity. He then locates the particularity with reference to those who would benefit from the death of Christ.

In another defense, he takes up the objection that "our Lord Jesus Christ did not suffer for the salvation and redemption of all men." Again, he speaks of both aspects of Christ's death:

> Considering, then, on the one hand the greatness and value of the price paid for us, and on the other hand the common lot of the whole human race, one must say that the blood of Christ is the redemption of the entire world. But they who pass through this world without coming to the faith and without having been reborn in baptism, remain untouched by the redemption. Accordingly, since our Lord in very truth took upon Himself the one nature and condition which is common to all men, it is right to say that all

---

[24] Godfrey, "Reformed Thought on the Extent of the Atonement to 1618," 136.

[25] "Answers to the Objections of the Gauls," in *Prosper of Aquitaine: Defense of St. Augustine,* trans. P. De Letter, Ancient Christian Writers 32 (New York: Newman, 1963), 149–50.

have been redeemed, and that nevertheless not all are actually liberated from the slavery of sin.[26]

This time Prosper speaks of "the greatness and value of the price paid," which we'll see below in the canons. Because of this value and because of our common fallen humanity, Jesus redeems the world; yet, Prosper again locates the particularity in those with faith who are "actually liberated."

Remigius of Rheims

John Davenant showed that "there was some difference at least in the mode of speaking among the Doctors of that age," by discussing Remigius of Rheims (437–533). In his comments on Romans 8:32, "He who did not spare his own Son but gave him up for us all," Remigius spoke particularly: "for us all, that is, for those who are predestined to eternal life." On 1 Timothy 2:6, "Who gave himself as a ransom for all," he said, "Understand, for the elect." Then he spoke universally. On Hebrews 2:9, which says Jesus "taste[d] death for everyone," Davenant wrote, "Some Doctors understand this absolutely, that it means for all for whom he tasted it, that is, for the elect, who are predestined to eternal life. But others understand it generally, that He tasted death for all, believing and unbelieving, saying, He died indeed for all though all will not be saved."[27]

Gregory the Great

Davenant also mentioned Gregory the Great (540–604), who said in *Homily 2* on Ezekiel 1:1 both that Christ is the "Redeemer of mankind, and the Redeemer of all," and that "the Author of life handed himself over, even to death for the life of the elect."[28]

---

[26] "Answers to the Vincentian Articles," in *Prosper of Aquitaine: Defense of St. Augustine*, 164.

[27] Quoted in Davenant, *Dissertation*, 2:332.

[28] Quoted in Davenant, *Dissertation*, 2:332. Cf. Gatiss, *For Us and for Our Salvation*, 61.

Haimo/Haymo of Halberstadt

Another is Haimo/Haymo of Halberstadt (d. 853), of whom Davenant said "determines nothing certain on either side."[29] On 2 Corinthians 5, Haimo said, "Christ came into the world, being born without sin; though innocent He died for all those who are predestinated to life. And as Prosper says, and John Chrysostom, and other Doctors, although all do not believe, He did his part, dying for all.... Through Christ [God] reconciled to himself the world, that is, all those who were predestinated."[30] Davenant concluded his survey with these important words, which we'll see in our look at the Canons of Dort:

> When they [the ancients] **restrict** the death of Christ to the predestinate, [they] do <u>not</u> do it <u>absolutely</u>; but in <u>consideration of the saving effect</u> which, by means of faith, it brings to them alone: and on the other hand, when they **extend** this death of Christ to all, they <u>do not extend to all that special will of God</u> in calling them according to his own purpose, in giving them faith, and effectually working in certain individuals according to his own counsel and operation, that they may reap the benefit of the death of Christ. Therefore they so understand the universality of redemption that they did not subvert the secret counsel of predestination, in which thing they differed widely from the Pelagians and Semipelagians. They also understood redemption in such a restricted sense, that at the same time they acknowledged that it pertained to all men individually under the condition of faith.[31]

Gottschalk

There was a period of contentious debate about this subject during the time of Gottschalk, who spoke much more rigidly and simplistically.[32] He said

---

[29] Davenant, *Dissertation*, 2:332.

[30] Quoted in Davenant, *Dissertation*, 2:332–33.

[31] Davenant, *Dissertation*, 2:333. Emphasis added.

[32] On Gottschalk, see Victor Genke, introduction to *Gottschalk and a Medieval Predestination Controversy*, 7–63; D. E. Nineham, "Gottschalk of Orbais: Reactionary or Precursor of the Reformation?" *Journal of Ecclesiastical History* 40 (1989): 1–18.

things like, "Our omnipotent God…willed to be the Savior of none of the perpetually reprobate, the redeemer of none, the glorifier of none."[33] To say that Christ "suffered in general for the salvation and redemption of all, that is, of both the elect and reprobate, contradicts God the Father himself."[34] Those described in 2 Peter 2:1 as "denying the Master who bought them" were "bought" merely "by the sacrament of baptism" and not by the cross, death, and blood of Jesus.[35] Here Gottschalk hints at what we might call a more "covenantal" sense of redemption in which those outwardly in the church via baptism are described as the redeemed people of God. One of the interesting notes about Gottschalk is the connection between his "extreme" view of double predestination and the intentional death of Christ and Gottschalk's own life: he was a zealous preacher and missionary. For his views he was tried in an ecclesiastical court, condemned, beaten, and imprisoned under Hincmar of Reims (806–882).

Despite this, "Gottschalk's views were generally supported by prominent contemporary theologians."[36] In fact, one writer says, "the best respected theologians of the period tended to support Gottschalk's theories, while those who opposed him were either not noted by their contemporaries as theologians…or else where held in positive disregard."[37]

Lupus of Ferrieres/Remigius of Lyons

Two of these supporters of Gottschalk were Lupus of Ferrieres (805–862), who approvingly cited the aforementioned words of Jerome,[38] and Remigius of Lyons (d. 875). Remigius followed Augustine on 1 Timothy 2:4: "God does not will all men to be saved, but only those who are saved…Christ did not come to save all, or to suffer for all, but only on behalf of those who

---

[33] "Reply to Rabanus Maurus," 9, in *Gottschalk and a Medieval Predestination Controversy*, 67.

[34] "Tome to Giselmar," 2 in *Gottschalk and a Medieval Predestination Controversy*, 69.

[35] "Tome to Giselmar," 3 in *Gottschalk and a Medieval Predestination Controversy*, 69–70.

[36] Gatiss, *For Us and for Our Salvation*, 64.

[37] T. R. Roberts, "A Translation and Critical Edition of Ratramnus of Corbie's *De Predestinatione Dei*" (PhD diss., University of Missouri–Columbia, 1977), 11–12. Cited in Gatiss, *For Us and for Our Salvation*, 64.

[38] See Gatiss, *For Us and for Our Salvation*, 64.

are saved by the mystery of his suffering."[39] Remigius, in fact, spoke against Hincmar's writings, saying:

> We would wish that nothing should be spoken or defined confusedly and inconsiderately on this subject; since it has its own depth and difficulty, which should be diligently searched out from the truth of the Holy Scriptures and the authority of the orthodox Fathers, and not determined by our own presumption. [40]

John Davenant made a summary conclusion from this episode in the history of doctrine that still applies:

> Two things are to be observed: One is that Remigius and the council of Valence, although they did not approve the sentiment of those who extended the death of Christ to all men individually, yet they have not confined it to the predestinate alone. The other is, That in this difference of opinions, those ancient Fathers cultivated the peace of the church, and did not interrupt it in order to accuse each other of heresy.[41]

Peter Lombard

With the rise of theological schools during the medieval period, theology took on a more precise discussion. Oftentimes, the caricature goes, theologians had nothing better to do than debate how many angels could dance on the head of a pin. These "Schoolmen," as they're known, "were fruitful artificers of disputes, yet were unwilling to renew this subject. To them it seemed sufficient to teach that Christ died for all sufficiently, for the predestinated effectually." Davenant illustrated this unanimity, saying, "Since no one could deny, no handle was given for using the saw of contention."[42] This language of "sufficiency/efficiency" was codified in the magisterial work of Peter Lombard who said, "Christ...offered himself on the altar of the cross not to the devil, but to the triune God, and he did so for all with

---

[39] Cited in Gatiss, *For Us and for Our Salvation*, 64–65.

[40] Quoted in Davenant, *Dissertation*, 2:334.

[41] Quoted in Davenant, *Dissertation*, 2:336.

[42] Davenant, *Dissertation*, 2:336.

regard to the sufficiency of the price, but only for the elect with regard to the efficacy, because he brought about salvation only for the predestined."[43] So solid was Peter Lombard's popular distinction that Thomas Aquinas merely passed it on.[44]

Glossa Ordinaria

The medieval period also saw the development of a running commentary on Scripture with quotations of those who had commented before called the *Glossa Ordinaria*. One comment on the aforementioned Matthew 20:28 was "for man, not for all, but for those who were predestined to life."[45]

In a "limited" sense, then, we can say with Theodore Beza that the effectiveness of Jesus' death to the elect was "the consent of the orthodox church against the Pelagians" (*ex orthodoxo adversus Pelagianos Ecclesiae consensus*).[46] It would seem, then, that the statement by Raymond Blacketer that the above was merely "a trajectory of thought in the Christian tradition" and "a minority position" is too conservative.[47] More than being a minority, the basic building blocks of what was adopted at Dort were mainstream commentaries on the biblical passages passed down through the ages.

THE MOST DIFFICULT DOCTRINE OF DORT

Despite this historical pedigree, the second point of doctrine was and still is the most controversial and difficult doctrinal point of Dort.[48]

---

[43] Peter Lombard, *The Sentences, Book 3: On the Incarnation of the Word*, 4 vols. (Toronto: Pontifical Institute of Medieval Studies, 2008), 20.5.1 (p. 86).

[44] On Aquinas, see Lee Gatiss, "Grace Tasted Death for All: Thomas Aquinas on Hebrews 2.9," *Tyndale Bulletin* 62, no. 2 (2012): 217–37; Raymond A. Blacketer, "Definite Atonement in Historical Perspective," in *The Glory of the Atonement, Biblical, Historical & Practical Perspectives: Essays in Honor of Roger Nicole* (Downers Grove, IL: IVP Academic, 2004), 311–13.

[45] Cited in Blacketer, "Definite Atonement in Historical Perspective," 308.

[46] Cited in Godfrey, "Reformed Thought on the Extent of the Atonement to 1618," 143.

[47] Blacketer, "Definite Atonement in Historical Perspective," 313.

[48] I wish to thank my friend Michael Lynch, whose PhD studies on John Davenant and issues related to Dort have greatly enriched my understanding.

The Difficulty of Language

This doctrine is difficult because language can be difficult. Think about labels. Those who won the debate in the seventeenth century (righty so, I believe) got to call themselves "orthodox." What's a quick way to label an opponent, corner them, and ostracize them? Call them followers of a man: "Arminians." In tit for tat, those like me are called followers of a mere man: "Calvinists." Bring this forward and today we speak flippantly of Arminians and Calvinists and even of "*the* five points of Calvinism."[49] Modern terminology oversimplifies historical complexities.[50]

If I could travel back just before the synod to the Dutch city of Heusden and ask its new pastor and future delegate to the synod Gisbertus Voetius, "Domine Voetius, what does it mean to be *Reformed?*" he might've said, "To believe the *thirty-seven* articles of the Belgic Confession and the *one hundred twenty-nine* questions and answers of the Heidelberg Catechism, of course!" As I mentioned earlier, authentic "Calvinism" back then was *136-point Calvinism!* After the synod, though, a "Form of Subscription" was adopted for ministers, professors, schoolteachers, elders, and deacons to declare "sincerely and in good conscience before the Lord...that we heartily believe and are persuaded that all the" doctrines of the Belgic Confession, Heidelberg Catechism, *and* Canons of Dort "do fully agree with the Word of God."[51] The churches I serve still require this. I'm a 259-point Calvinist. What's interesting is how this form describes the canons: "the explanation of *some points* of the aforesaid doctrine made by the National Synod of Dordrecht."

Another difficulty is, what's really being debated? Popularly, we speak of "limited atonement." The problem is that except for consistent univer-

---

[49] See comments in the introduction above.

[50] The so-called TULIP acronym has been traced to a 1905 address by a Dr. McAfee of Brooklyn, New York, before the Presbyterian Union of Newark, New Jersey. *The Outlook*, June 21, 1913, 394–95. See also Richard A. Muller, "Was Calvin a Calvinist? Or, Did Calvin (or Anyone Else in the Early Modern Era) Plant the 'TULIP'?" As found at: https://www.calvin.edu/meeter/Was%20Calvin%20a%20Calvinist-12-26-09.pdf (accessed August 13, 2017).

[51] See W. Robert Godfrey, "Subscription in the Dutch Reformed Tradition," in *The Practice of Confessional Subscription*, ed. David W. Hall (Oak Ridge, TN: Covenant Foundation, 2001), 67–75.

salists, who believe everyone enters heaven, even the Remonstrants limited the saving efficacy of Christ's death. We saw that in their second point above: "Jesus Christ the Savior of the world died for all men and for every man, so that he merited reconciliation and forgiveness of sins for all through the death of the cross." Sounds *unlimited*, right? Not so fast: "…yet so that *no one actually enjoys* this forgiveness of sins *except the believer*."[52] What of the word "atonement"? What does this mean? It was William Tyndale's attempt to popularize the language of "propitiation" and "satisfaction," which is really what was being debated at Dort.[53] When the synod wrote its canons, their title for the second point was "Concerning the Death of Christ and the Redemption of Humanity through It" (*De Morte Christi et Hominum per eam Redemptione*). In other words, what is the relation of what Jesus did in his death to purchasing ("redeeming") those in slavery to sin? Thus "limited atonement" has limited usefulness.

The Difficulty of Remonstrant Doctrine

This doctrine is difficult because the Remonstrants' doctrine was difficult and full of complexity. Seventeenth-century "Arminianism" wasn't as simple as it's been made out to be today: "Christ died for everyone." The general contour of Remonstrant thinking in 1610 was stated in more detail at the 1611 conference in The Hague (*Collatio Hagiensis*): Jesus "impetrated [*impetraverit*] reconciliation and forgiveness of sin for all human beings."[54] They used a common distinction between "impetration" and "application" or as we now speak, redemption accomplished and applied. But since impetration could mean actually acquiring, meriting, obtaining, or procuring redemption as well as potentially doing the same,[55] this distinction was blurred.

---

[52] "The *Remonstrance* of 1610," appendix C in De Jong, *Crisis in the Reformed Churches*, 208. Emphasis added.

[53] Gatiss, *For Us and for Our Salvation*, 14. On Tyndale, see David Daniell, *The Bible in English: Its History and Influence* (New Haven, CT: Yale University Press, 2003), 133–59.

[54] Petrus Bertius, *Scripta Adversaria Collationis Hagiensis* (Lugduni Batavorum, 1615), 123.

[55] David Paraeus said that *impetrare* ("impetrate") could be substituted for seven different words. *Acta Synodi Nationalis…Dordrechti* (Lugduni Batavorum, 1620), 215; Paraeus, "Epitome of Arminianisme," 828.

In the years leading to the synod, Remonstrant theologians developed their system further. We get a glimpse in the "rejection of errors" after each positive doctrinal point in the canons where the Remonstrant writings are quoted. Here's a summary:

- Jesus died for no particular individual, therefore it is possible that redemption accomplished is not applied to anyone. (RE 1)

- Jesus' death did not establish a new covenant of grace, but only the mere right for the Father to enter into a covenant with humanity. (RE 2)

- Jesus did not merit for anyone the faith by which his satisfaction is effectively applied to salvation, but only acquired for the Father the authority to impose conditions that depend on the free choice of humanity. (RE 3)

- The new covenant of grace is not that we are justified through faith that accepts Christ's merit, but that God no longer demands perfect obedience to the law and instead counts faith and imperfect obedience as if it were perfect obedience. (RE 4)

- All people have been received into a status of reconciliation, thus no one is condemned on account of original sin. (RE 5)

- While God wished to bestow equally on all people the benefits of redemption accomplished, its application does not depend on his gift of faith but on their own free choice to apply grace to themselves. (RE 6)

- Jesus did not die for those God loved and elected since such people do not need his death being already elect. (RE 7)

Again, this is not the simple "Arminianism" we hear of today.

The Difficulty of Intra-Reformed Debate

One final difficulty is that among Reformed thinkers at Dort, there were strong disagreements over how to express the relation between

Christ's death and our redemption.[56] It would be somewhat overstated, then, to say that in the lead-up to the synod "there was a general Reformed consensus on the death of Christ. There were differences and ambiguities of expression to be sure, but the issue was not a matter of controversy with the Reformed community."[57]

After the synod, Voetius would write that as to the question of "whether Christ died for all and every man"—that was the Remonstrant phrase we saw above—"that is, did he merit anything as the surety for all and every man by his satisfaction and obedience...*the orthodox...do not speak in one manner.*"[58] Notice that. There were *several* opinions about how Jesus' death related to the "all" passages of Scripture, and these were within the bounds of Reformed orthodoxy. There were three basic positions represented at Dort revolving around whether and/or how to appropriate the ancient distinction between the sufficiency and efficiency of Christ's death mentioned above. In a somewhat inconsistent statement from what he said above, Godfrey stated:

> Despite general agreement the Reformed fathers had expressed themselves rather differently on the doctrine of the atonement. Most had used the traditional distinction between sufficiency and efficiency in writing about this doctrine; while some, like Beza, Piscator, and Ames had felt that greater theological clarity and precision was possible without it. This discrepancy would have to be faced by the Synod and resolved.[59]

Patristic and medieval theologians affirmed a sense in which the death of Christ was unlimited and a sense in which it was limited. That debate and distinction continued in the days leading to Dort.

First, some spoke of Christ's death and merit as simply efficient on behalf of the elect. The Genevan, North Holland, Overijssel, and Emden delegations thought this ancient distinction was unhelpful despite its pedi-

---

[56] "The sharpest disagreement," in fact. Godfrey, "Reformed Thought on the Extent of the Atonement to 1618," 133.

[57] Godfrey, "Reformed Thought on the Extent of the Atonement to 1618," 150.

[58] See Gijsbertus Voetius, *Selectae Disputationes Theologicae*, 5 vols. (Utrecht: Johannes à Waesberge, 1648–1669), 2:238–55. Emphasis added.

[59] Godfrey, "Reformed Thought on the Extent of the Atonement to 1618," 170.

gree and use among reformers such as Martin Luther, John Calvin, and Peter Martyr Vermigli.

Second, a minority such as the British theologians, John Davenant and Samuel Ward, disagreed with their own delegation. Along with the Bremen theologian, Matthias Martinius, they agreed with the first group that the death of Christ was savingly efficient for the elect alone, but wanted to say more about the sufficiency side of things. His death was not merely valuable and sufficient in a potential way to pay the price for the sins of every human; it was ordained by God to pay that price while its application was conditioned on faith and repentance (which were purchased efficaciously for the elect). Michael Lynch summarizes John Davenant's description of Christ's death having a twofold goal: it was *ordained* as a universal remedy for sin for all sinners who repent and believe and it *obtained* salvation effectually to be applied to the elect alone.[60] In the words of Samuel Ward, in distinction from God's special grace toward the elect there was also a *general* grace of redemption to the world, which prior to faith and repentance were redeemable (*redimibilitas*) and reconcilable (*reconciliabilitas*).[61] On the other side of this internal disagreement, Bishop Carleton wrote: "We are playing with words."[62] Davenant didn't think so. He was so convinced that he told his fellow delegation "he would rather have his right hand cut off, than recall or alter any thing."[63]

This is the view known as hypothetical universalism (not to be confused with later Amyraldianism).[64] The British delegates to the synod said it like this: Christ "died for all, that all and every one by means of faith might obtain remission of sins, and eternal life by virtue of that ransom. But Christ so died for the elect, that by the merit of his death in special manner...they might infallibly obtain both faith and eternal life."[65] Samuel Ward

---

[60] Michael Lynch, "Confessional Orthodoxy and Hypothetical Universalism: Another Look at the Westminster Confession of Faith," *Beyond Calvin*, 133–34.

[61] Milton, *The British Delegation and the Synod of Dort*, 201–2 (5/4).

[62] Milton, *The British Delegation and the Synod of Dort*, 202 (5/4).

[63] Milton, *The British Delegation and the Synod of Dort*, 202 (5/4). On Davenant's view vis-à-vis the Westminster Confession of Faith, see Lynch, "Confessional Orthodoxy and Hypothetical Universalism," *Beyond Calvin*, 127–48.

[64] On "Amyraldianism," see Brian G. Armstrong, *Calvinism and the Amyraut Heresy: Protestant Scholasticism and Humanism in Seventeenth-Century France* (1969; repr., Eugene, OR: Wipf & Stock, 2004).

[65] Cited in Gatiss, *For Us and for Our Salvation*, 90.

would write to James Ussher, "Some of us were held by some half remonstrants, for extending the oblation made to the Father to all; and for holding sundry effects thereof offered *serio*, and some really communicated to the reprobate."[66] This charge of being "half remonstrant" shows that it didn't take Twitter for theological discussion to devolve into name-calling.[67] Before you decry the British delegates as sounding Arminian as some do,[68] even the Genevan delegates to the synod, examples of the first group, "did not perceive that hypothetical universalism, as the British had formulated it…represented a grave threat to the unity of the church."[69] King James's directions to his delegates were to write in a way that reflected the ancient councils against the Pelagians and Semi-Pelagians, without using new phraseology, consistent with the Reformed confessions, and with as little offense to the Lutherans.[70] In fact, as Lynch says on the basis of his research: "Some of the strongest criticism of universal impetation [that Christ actually obtained redemption for all] can be found among some hypothetical universalists."[71]

The third view, it seems to me, is not so much a distinct view, but more of a hermeneutical lens to bring both sides together, using the distinction. The Canons of Dort are therefore a consensus—dare I say, *compromise*—document.[72] By using a modified form of the sufficiency/efficiency

---

[66] Cited in Jonathan D. Moore, "James Ussher's Influence on the Synod of Dort," in Goudriaan and van Lieburg, *Revisiting the Synod of Dordt*, 175.

[67] See Margo Todd, "Justifying God: The Calvinisms of the British Delegation to the Synod of Dort," *Archiv für Reformationsgeschichte* 96 (2005): 274.

[68] Hoeksema says, "There were those at the Synod who, to put it mildly, were doctrinally sympathetic with the Arminians. The theologians from Bremen are notorious in this connection…on the second article of the Arminians…the Bremen theologians were in some cases as Arminian as the Remonstrants themselves." He even says, "One of the British delegates later became an avowed Arminian," referring to Samuel Ward. *The Voice of Our Fathers*, 23. For a meticulous reading of primary sources that responds to this defunct historiographical reading of Ward, see Todd, "Justifying God," 272–89.

[69] Fornerod, "'The Canons of the Synod Had Shot Off the Advocate's Head,'" 211.

[70] Milton, *The British Delegation and the Synod of Dort*, 212 (5/13).

[71] Lynch, "Confessional Orthodoxy and Hypothetical Universalism," *Beyond Calvin*, 136.

[72] "Out of the Synod's debate, however, emerged a balanced compromise statement of the Reformed doctrine of the extent of the atonement which accommodated the considerable varieties of thought on that subject within the international Reformed

distinction, it set up two boundary markers for the Reformed:[73] (1) Christ's death has infinite and intrinsic value and therefore is sufficient to save the whole world (CD 2.3) and (2) Christ's death is efficacious for the elect alone (CD 2.8). These boundaries actually allowed considerable room for different varieties of Reformed orthodoxy to peacefully co-exist. This allows for more "Genevan" types for whom #1 was a "mere sufficiency" while #2 was their emphasis. This allows for more "British" types who also affirmed these points as well as an "ordained sufficiency" that the canons do not condemn or even speak to. Lynch, again, helpfully summarizes Davenant's logic:

> The gospel offer, which ministers are called to proclaim, must indiscriminately include this proposition: God is, according to his divine justice and on account of the person and work of Jesus Christ, able to forgive any person of their sins. For this proposition to be true, it then must be the case that God in Christ made a remedy for every person such that God is able to fulfill the antecedent condition proclaimed in the gospel—viz., that God is able to forgive the sins of any person. In order to claim that God in Christ made a remedy sufficient for every person, we must affirm that God intended that Christ make a remedy for every person.[74]

Yet these boundaries left many questions unanswered, allowing the various delegations to go to their home countries as a united front, but also free to fill in the gaps in their own distinctive ways.[75] One writer reflected on it like this:

> Yet, in the Synod of Dort, there were many able advocates for the doctrine that *Christ died for all*, in the only sense in which it is contended for now, by that part of the Calvinis-

---

community." Godfrey, "Reformed Thought on the Extent of the Atonement to 1618," 171.

[73] See Stephen Strehle, "The Extent of the Atonement and the Synod of Dort," *Westminster Theological Journal* 51, no. 1 (Spring 1989): 1–23.

[74] Lynch, "Confessional Orthodoxy and Hypothetical Universalism," *Beyond Calvin*, 134–35. Empahsis added.

[75] G. Michael Thomas, *The Extent of the Atonement: A Dilemma for Reformed Theology from Calvin to the Consensus (1536–1675)* (Carlisle, UK: Paternoster, 1997), 133.

tic school who plead for a *general propitiation*. The delegates from England, *Hesse* and *Bremen*, were explicit in their declaration to this effect. But all were not of the same mind; and, therefore, though they agreed upon a *form of words*, under which every man might take shelter, still it wears the appearance of a compromise, and is not sufficiently definite to satisfy the rigid inquirer.[76]

Some of these unanswered questions were the links between the infinite sufficiency of Christ's death and indiscriminate preaching, between infinite sufficiency and the nonelect, and between sufficiency itself and efficiency. For example, on the relationship between the infinite sufficiency of Jesus' death and the nonelect Geerhardus Vos, in exegetically defending Romans 5:12–21 against those who see in them "a reference to God's saving purpose to every individual, and not merely to the world collectively," concluded, "It must be granted…some sort of reference of the atonement to every man may be affirmed." While "the Bible gives us no right to say that Christ in His atoning work acted as the legal substitute of every individual human being…certainly neither does it require us to assert that for the non-elect the atonement is void of all benefit or significance." One such benefit was "the continued existence of the race in spite of sin." Another was "the offer of the gospel illumines the entire earthly existence of every one to whom it comes by the hope that he may find himself through faith one of the actual heirs of redemption."[77]

COMMENTARY

Just as in the first point of doctrine, the second point does not get to the heart of the issue until it first expresses basic biblical truths that are the common inheritance of all Christians. It does this in articles 1–7. After these articles there are two more articles that define this particular doctrine. In all this discussion, though, I don't want you to miss the big picture. John Davenant said it like this:

---

[76] James Richards, *Lectures on Mental Philosophy and Theology* (New York: M. W. Dodd, 1846), 306. Italics in original.

[77] Vos, "The Scriptural Doctrine of the Love of God," 449, 450, 451.

Hence it comes to pass that from too much altercation on the points, *For whom did Christ die, and for whom did He not die? Little is thought by mankind individually of applying to ourselves the death of Christ, by a true and lively faith, for the salvation of our own souls.*[78]

Article 1

God is not only supremely merciful, but also supremely just. And His justice requires (as He hath revealed Himself in His Word), that our sins committed against His infinite majesty should be punished, not only with temporal, but with eternal punishment, both in body and soul; which we cannot escape unless satisfaction be made to the justice of God.

"The main thing is keeping the main thing the main thing." I heard this once when I was a young Christian, and it's stuck with me ever since. When we deal with the question of the death of Jesus Christ, this is so important. The main thing is what did Jesus do and for whom did he do it. The canons get us there by first expressing the basic biblical truth that because God is just and we are sinners, there is need for his justice to be satisfied in order for us to be reconciled to him.

THE NECESSITY OF SATISFACTION

As we saw in 1.11, God is simple. This means he *is* a God of infinite mercy and infinite justice: **God is not only supremely merciful, but also supremely just**. His mercy and justice are limitless. We so often hear "God is love" as a one-sided slogan. Yet Scripture says the Lord is not only "merciful and gracious, slow to anger, and abounding in steadfast love and faithfulness, keeping steadfast love for thousands, forgiving iniquity and transgression and sin" but he is also the one "who will by no means clear the guilty" (Ex. 34:6–7). It's not that he's more of some attributes than others or some attributes at some times and others at other times. In other words, God *cannot* accept you "just as you are," to use another popular slogan. He cannot cease to be either merciful or just. Both will be expressed. Anselm expressed God's simplicity in the eleventh century in a prayer. He

---

[78] Davenant, *Dissertation*, 2:317. Emphasis added.

asked, "What are You, Lord, what are You; what shall my heart understand You to be?" He went on to express who God was as expressed in his attributes: "You are, assuredly, life, You are wisdom, You are truth, You are goodness, You are blessedness, You are eternity, and You are every true good." He then made this confession: "These are many things, and my limited understanding cannot see them all in one single glance so as to delight in all at once." This led to a question: "How then, Lord, are You all these things?" He asked whether this meant God was a composite being: "Are they parts of You, or rather, is each one of these wholly what You are?" But Anselm confessed the simplicity of God:

> For whatever is made up of parts is not absolutely one, but in a sense many and other from itself, and it can be broken up either actually or by the mind—all of which things are foreign to You, than whom nothing better can be thought. Therefore there are no parts in You, Lord; neither are You many, but You are so much one and the same with Yourself that in nothing are You dissimilar with Yourself. Indeed You are unity itself not divisible by any mind. Life and wisdom and the other [attributes], then, are not parts of You, but all are one and each one of them is wholly what You are and what all the others are. Since, then, neither You nor Your eternity which You are have parts, no part of You or of Your eternity is anywhere or at any time, but You exist as a whole everywhere and Your eternity exists as a whole always.[79]

Because he is infinitely just, each and every one of our sins must be punished: **His justice requires (as He hath revealed Himself in His Word), that our sins committed against His infinite majesty should be punished** (*puniantur*)**, not only with temporal, but with eternal punishment** (*poenis*)**, both in body and soul**. His mercy cannot just nullify his justice. We hear that threat in the Garden: "In the day that you eat of [the tree of the knowledge of good and evil] you shall surely die" (Gen. 2:17). We hear that threat in the New Testament: "The wages of sin is death, but the free gift of God is eternal life in Christ Jesus our Lord" (Rom. 6:23).

---

[79] *Anselm of Canterbury: The Major Works*, ed. Brian Davies and G. R. Evans, Oxford World's Classics (Oxford: Oxford University Press, 1998), 98.

So how do sinners under the just judgment of God because of their sins experience his mercy? **We cannot escape** [punishment] **unless satisfaction be made to the justice of God** (*satisfiat*). Notice that. Satisfaction is making amends for sin, which reveals and upholds both God's justice and mercy. The only way we can escape God's infinitely just punishment is by satisfying his justice. When his justice is satisfied, mercy can be poured out on us. This is the issue in point two of the canons, not a generic, undefined "atonement."[80] There are two ways of making this satisfaction: either by a combination of Christ's works to satisfy for eternal punishment and our own to satisfy for temporal punishments, according to some in the medieval period, or solely by Jesus Christ and his works.[81]

The necessity of satisfying the justice of God is implied and expressed in several ways in 2 Corinthians 5, for example. Note verse 18 where Paul says it was "God, who through Christ reconciled us to himself." Reconciliation means to bring two opposing, warring sides together in peace. On the one side there is us. As verse 19 says, we have many "trespasses." We have gone beyond the bounds of God's law. We have seen his sign up, giving us a boundary, but we have thumbed our noses to him and kept going. So on the other side there is God. Because of our trespasses, we have violated his laws, therefore, have come under his judgment and punishment.

Another way the necessity of satisfying the justice of God is seen in verse 21. Paul is speaking of justification and says that we become "the righteousness of God." God's righteousness is his upright, perfect keeping of his own law and standard. He is a judge who takes no bribes. He is a judge who cannot be fooled. He is a judge who does not make mistakes. He is a judge who never lets sentiment or public opinion sway him.

So when the article says **we cannot escape** [punishment] **unless satisfaction be made to the justice of God**, we have a truth that is so necessary to know but is not often taught in today's church. We hear so much about God's love: "God loves you and has a wonderful plan for your life"; "God loves you and so do we"; "Love wins." But where is the justice of God? Where is salvation seen as God's infinite justice being satisfied so that his infinite mercy may be lavished upon us?

---

[80] See "satisfactio vicaria," in Muller, *Dictionary of Latin and Greek Theological Terms*, 120, 273.

[81] "Satisfactio," in Muller, *Dictionary of Latin and Greek Theological Terms*, 320–21.

Article 2

Since therefore we are unable to make that satisfaction in our own persons or to deliver ourselves from the wrath of God, He hath been pleased in His infinite mercy to give His only begotten Son, for our surety, who was made sin, and became a curse for us and in our stead, that He might make satisfaction to divine justice on our behalf.

THE NATURE OF SATISFACTION

How can an infinitely just God be reconciled to a people who deserve an infinite punishment? The Roman Catholic Church says we contribute toward this satisfaction through faith, obedience, and participation in the sacraments such as penance or reconciliation, which require some form of payment afterward. Think of John Tetzel's famous slogan that enraged Martin Luther: "When a coin in the coffer rings, a soul from purgatory springs." But can our coins really satisfy? The Orthodox Church says we grow more and more like the divine in this life through mystical union through their liturgy and sacraments until one day we are united to the divine. But how, since God is just? This is why our article says we can't do this work: **Since therefore we are unable to make that satisfaction** (*satisfacere*) **in our own persons or to deliver** (*liberare*) **ourselves from the wrath of God.** Since we cannot contribute to satisfaction and thereby deliver ourselves from God's just anger, what hope is there for us? It is found here in the very nature of what satisfaction is.

First, the nature of satisfaction is that it is God who initiates and accomplishes it. Look again at 2 Corinthians 5 and who is doing the action. In verse 14 we read of "the love *of Christ*," that is, not merely Paul's love for Christ but Christ's own love for sinners.[82] In verse 18 Paul says, "All this is from *God, who* through Christ reconciled us *to himself* and *gave* us the ministry of reconciliation," and then again in verse 19, "that is, in Christ *God* was reconciling the world to himself...and *entrusting to* us the message of reconciliation." Verse 20 amazingly says that it is "God" who is "making *his* appeal through us." What a God! What good news! Article 2 is one of the most succinct summaries of the gospel in all the confessional literature of the sixteenth and seventeenth centuries: **He hath been pleased in His**

---

[82] On the subjective genitive, see Wallace, *Greek Grammar beyond the Basics*, 113–16.

infinite mercy (*immensa misericordia*; boundless mercy) **to give His only begotten Son, for our surety** (*sponsorem*; guarantee), **who was made sin, and became a curse for us and in our stead, that He might make satisfaction** (*satisfaceret*) **to divine justice on our behalf.** As one hymn asks:

> Can holiness and wisdom join,
> With truth, with justice, and with grace,
> To make eternal blessings mine,
> And sin, with all its guilt erase?

The author answers:

> O love! beyond conception great,
> That form'd the vast, stupendous plan!
> Where all divine perfections meet
> To reconcile rebellious man!

God's perfections of justice and mercy, in particular, meet:

> There wisdom shines in fullest blaze,
> And justice all her rights maintains!
> Astonish'd angels stoop to gaze,
> While mercy o'er the guilty reigns.

> Yes, mercy reigns, and justice too—
> In Christ harmoniously they meet:
> He paid to justice all her due,
> And now he fills the mercy-seat.[83]

Second, the nature of satisfaction is that God has provided his Son as a vicarious or substitutionary sacrifice. God is infinitely just. He must punish with an infinite punishment all our sins. We cannot escape because we cannot make satisfaction to that kind of justice. Therefore Christ stands in our place and takes upon himself the infinite justice of God for us. Look at 2 Corinthians 5:14 where Paul says of "the love of Christ" that "one has died *for* all" and again in verse 15 that "he died *for* all" and "for *their sake* died and was raised."

---

[83] From the hymn "Infinite Grace! And Can It Be."

Third, the nature of satisfaction is that God has provided this vicarious sacrifice in a great exchange. Is there any more beautiful gospel promise in all the Scriptures than 2 Corinthians 5:21? "For our sake he made him to be sin who knew no sin, so that in him we might become the righteousness of God." That means: "For our sake" the righteous God "made" his Son Jesus Christ "to be sin who knew no sin, so that in" Jesus Christ "we might become the righteousness of God." Paul says God himself has provided for you a vicarious sacrifice in your place so that there would be a great exchange between God's justice on your sins and Christ's righteousness to your benefit. This is why article 2 says Jesus **who was made sin, and became a curse for us** (*pro nobis*) **and in our stead** (*vice nostra*).

Why is this so important? Why bicker among believers? Paul says in 2 Corinthians 5 that God himself has provided for you a vicarious sacrifice in your place so that there would be a great exchange between God's justice on your sins and Christ's righteousness to your benefit. When the Remonstrants said that Christ died for our sake and for our benefit but not in our place personally, meaning, he did not actually satisfy the justice of God and merit salvation for anyone in particular,[84] they took away the glory of Christ's substitution.[85] The Remonstrant error is that "for our sake" means "for our (potential) sake" but not "in our place." It also takes away the comfort of our salvation, expressed in some of our great hymnody. P. P. Bliss celebrated this substitutionary satisfaction like this:

> Bearing shame and scoffing rude,
> In my place condemned he stood,
> Sealed my pardon with his blood;
> Hallelujah! What a Savior!

> Guilty, helpless, lost were we;
> Blameless Lamb of God was he,
> Sacrificed to set us free:
> Hallelujah, what a Savior![86]

This is why Horatius Bonar once wrote:

---

[84] See rejection of errors 1 and 3 below.

[85] See J. van Genderen and W. H. Velema, *Concise Reformed Dogmatics*, trans. Gerrit Bilkes and Ed M. van der Maas (Phillipsburg, NJ: P&R, 2008), 526.

[86] From the hymn "'Man of Sorrows,' What a Name."

On merit not my own I stand;
On doings which I have not done,
Merit beyond what I can claim,
Doings more perfect than my own.

Upon a life I have not lived,
Upon a death I did not die;
Another's life, another's death,
I stake my whole eternity.

Jesus, O Son of God, I build
On what Thy cross has done for me;
There both my death and life I read,
My guilt, my pardon there I see.[87]

Article 3

The death of the Son of God is the only and most perfect sacrifice and satisfaction for sin, and is of infinite worth and value, abundantly sufficient to expiate the sins of the whole world.

"Behold, the Lamb of God, who takes away the sin of the world!" (John 1:29). This is one of those gospel texts that we all need to have emblazoned in our minds and upon our hearts. It contains the sweet honey, the inner marrow, and the rich fatness of the gospel. It brings peace to our consciences, joy to our hearts, and praise to our lips. After more than a thousand years of the Day of Atonement, Passover, daily morning and evening sacrifices, and freely offered sacrifices, the final Old Testament prophet (Matt. 11:13), John the Baptizer, proclaims that what the shadow of all those sacrificial lambs pointed forward to had come.[88] Jesus is the once-for-all sacrifice for the sin. Jesus is the Savior of this world that God long ago created, against whom this world has committed its sin (Heb. 7:27;

---

[87] Horatius Bonar, "Christ for Us," in *Communion Hymns* (London: James Nisbet, 1881), 73.

[88] On the tabernacle, priesthood, and sacrificial system, see Daniel R. Hyde, *God in Our Midst: The Tabernacle and Our Relationship with God* (Orlando, FL: Reformation Trust, 2012).

9:12, 26; 10:10). He is *the* Lamb of God. Jesus is the answer to every ethnicity's struggle with sin.

Such a statement is also a classic place to consider the sufficiency of Jesus Christ's sacrifice.[89] We move from the doctrine of God in articles 1–2 to Christology in articles 3 and following. Some say that the mere mention of texts such as John 1:29 or John 3:16 defeat Reformed theology, as if to say, "You see, Jesus died for everyone." One book even has an image of a scale, with "John Calvin" on the high side and "John 3:16" weighing down the other.[90] But as we've seen already, this is overly simplistic. Unless one believes in universally effectual salvation, "everyone" limits the effectiveness of Jesus' death.[91] We have to ask, in what sense does Jesus take away the sins of the world? Thus texts like John 1:29 have been understood throughout the history of the church to express the unlimitedness and vastness of the sufficiency of Jesus' satisfaction of God's infinite justice on the cross.

THE INFINITE VALUE OF THE SATISFACTION

When John said the Lamb of God takes away the sin of the world, at a minimum he proclaimed the infinite value of Jesus' satisfaction. This value or worth is expressed in that part of John's proclamation: "the sin of the world." What do you notice about this phrase that's important? John speaks of "sin" in the singular, doesn't he? Why? He's speaking of the collective sin and guilt of "the world" of humanity that stands opposed to its Creator beginning with Adam's first sin. He's not speaking here of just the Jews' *sins*, just the Greeks' *sins*, or just the Romans' *sins*. He's speaking of "the sin," meaning that guilty state under which our entire race finds itself whether you're a Jew or a Gentile, slave or free, male or female, rich or poor, black or white, and everything in between! Because he's speaking of the collective state of sin, this helps us understand that he's speaking of the

---

[89] Feenstra misstates the issue of sufficiency and efficiency when he states that "the only and entirely complete sacrifice and satisfaction for sins" equals efficiency and "more than sufficient to atone for the sins of the whole world" equals sufficiency. *Unspeakable Comfort*, 77.

[90] See the cover of Bryson, *The Five Points of Calvinism*.

[91] Carson, See *The Difficult Doctrine of the Love of God*, 73–79.

infinite value of Christ's satisfaction of the justice of God toward that sinful state.[92]

The Canons of Dort state it like this: **The death of the Son of God is the only and most perfect sacrifice and satisfaction** (*satisfactio*) **for sin, and is of infinite worth and value, abundantly sufficient to expiate** (*expianda*) **the sins of the whole world**. Contra the Roman Catholic Church, there is no other satisfaction for sins than **the only and most perfect sacrifice and satisfaction for sin** offered by Jesus. In biblical texts such as Hebrews 7:27, 9:12, 9:26, 9:28, 10:10, and 10:14 we read of the "once for all" sacrifice of Christ.

Infinite worth; infinite…value; abundantly sufficient; the whole world. What wonderful statements to sinners like you and me who think, "Can his satisfaction reach all the way down to me? Can his satisfaction reach all the way over here to me?" We think like children when we think of blood. After you get cut, blood comes out, and if your body is working as it's supposed to, the blood clots and dries up. You and I need to think of Jesus' blood on the cross differently. It's like his blood is ever pumping, ever flowing, but never drying. That's how infinite the value of his satisfaction is for us in our ongoing sins!

This is why this sufficiency has been expressed in "millions of worlds" language. The medieval theologian Thomas Aquinas said the death of Christ "is sufficient to redeem and save all as well as if there were infinite worlds."[93] Even those Reformed theologians who affirmed that Jesus' death was for the elect, period, and considered the sufficiency/efficiency distinction unhelpful at best, spoke this way. William Perkins said, "The price is in itself sufficient to redeem everyone without exception from his sins, albeit there were a thousand worlds of men."[94] John Owen said, "If there were a thousand worlds, the gospel of Christ might, upon this ground, be preached to them all, there being enough in Christ for the salvation of them all, if so

---

[92] For the background and meaning, see the discussion in Carson, *The Gospel according to John*, 148–51.

[93] Thomas Aquinas, *Opera Omnia*, 34 vols. (Paris: Ludovicus Vives, 1871), 32:168.

[94] William Perkins, "A Christian and Plain Treatise of the Manner and Order of Predestination, and of the Largeness of God's Grace," trans. Francis Cacot and Thomas Tuke, in *The Workes of that Famous and Worthy Minister of Christ in the University of Cambridge M. William Perkins*, 3 vols. (London: John Kegatt, 1631), 2:609 col. 1.

be they will derive virtue from him by touching him in faith."[95] No matter how many worlds there might have been, Jesus' death is sufficient for them all.

SOME BIBLICAL COMMENTS

When article 3 says Jesus' death is **abundantly sufficient to expiate the sins of the whole world**, it's alluding to texts such as John 1:29 and 3:16. Let me comment on a few of these "all" and "world" texts.

John 3:16 is the most popular text brought up in this discussion. Notice the purpose of God sending his Son in both verses 16 and 17 is explained with two purpose clauses: "*that* whoever believes in him should…have eternal life" (v. 16) and "*in order that* the world might be saved through him" (v. 17). As we've seen, "world" has a wide range of meaning in John's Gospel and writings. Here it has the sense of the "world" of darkness and unbelief (cf. 1:10). God loved this world despite its hatred of him. Even further, it has the sense of God's love extending not only to the Jews, but the entire "world," that is, Gentiles (cf. John 4:42; 11:51–52; 12:32; Rev. 5:9).[96] John 3:16, therefore, is not an "atonement text," per se, but a text that points out that God's love is so immense, that any sinner who believes shall be saved. In other words, it expresses the sufficiency of Christ.

1 John 2:1–2 says the nature of "propitiation" is to turn away God's wrath. If this text means every human, then it means the wrath of almighty God is no longer against anyone. When John says, "And not for ours only but…the whole world," he's speaking of the world as he spoke in John 3:16–17. In other words, this is a general statement that Jesus propitiates God's wrath for sinful Jews and Gentiles (the world).

1 Timothy 2:4–6 is not in the context of the satisfaction of Christ, but on prayer in public worship. Paul commands prayer for "all people." His concern is for "all sorts and conditions of men," to use the language of the Book of Common Prayer.[97] The evidence is that he specifies prayer for

---

[95] Owen, "Salus Electorum, Sanguis Jesu; or, The Death of Death in the Death of Christ," in *Works*, 10:297.

[96] On John 3:16 the *Dutch Annotations* said God's love was "not only the Jews, but also the Gentiles, scattered throughout the whole world."

[97] "A Collect or Prayer for All Conditions of Men," in Book of Common Prayer, 42.

government officials—prayer for them so that we can continue praying for everyone else! God does desire the salvation of "all people," as he is not only concerned with Jews, but Gentiles; the rich and poor; white and black; aristocrats and workers; men, and women; and so forth. There are distinctions we can make in speaking of God's "will/desire" so that while it's true for every human person, yet God also reveals himself as particularly and savingly willing the salvation of those whom he calls his "elect."[98]

Article 4

This death derives its infinite value and dignity from these considerations because the person who submitted to it was not only really man and perfectly holy, but also the only begotten Son of God, of the same eternal and infinite essence with the Father and the Holy Spirit, which qualifications were necessary to constitute Him a Savior for us; and because it was attended with a sense of the wrath and curse of God due to us for sin.

THE INFINITE VALUE OF THE SAVIOR

What made Jesus' satisfaction of infinite value? John said the "Lamb of God" offered himself, and he is of infinite value. The Lamb of John 1:29 is the same Person described earlier as the eternal Word, who is both God and in relation to God (John 1:1–2, 18), the one through whom all things came to be in the beginning (John 1:3, 10), and the one full of glory, grace, and truth (John 1:14, 17). The infinite value of Jesus' satisfaction is rooted in his infinite divinity. Article 3 above didn't say "the death of Christ," but when it speaks of **this death**, it speaks of it as being of **the only begotten Son of God**, echoing Paul's language that God's own blood obtained a church for himself (Acts 20:28).

It's also rooted in his being really human like you and me: "And the Word became flesh and dwelt among us" (John 1:14). He was "made like

---

[98] See the comments by Augustine above on the meaning of Paul's words being not one nation or a few of a particular class but all classes of men. This view of 1 Timothy 2 was echoed by John Calvin, *The Second Epistle of Paul the Apostle to the Corinthians and the Epistles to Timothy, Titus, and Philemon*, trans. T. A. Smail, ed. David W. Torrance and Thomas F. Torrance, Calvin's Commentaries, 12 vols. (Grand Rapids, MI: Eerdmans, 1964), 10:208–9.

his brothers in every respect" (Heb. 2:17), "shar[ing] in flesh and blood" with us (Heb. 2:14). He is flesh and blood like you and me. He was born, he was nursed, he ate, he drank, he slept, he walked, he talked, and did everything you and I do. Yet he was unlike you and me. He was perfectly human: "in every respect...tempted as we are, yet without sin" (Heb. 4:15). Because he did not sin, the infinite value of Jesus' satisfaction is rooted in his being perfectly holy. As the book of Hebrews says, he is the kind of perfect priest we need: "holy, innocent, unstained, separated from sinners" (Heb. 7:26).

The Person of the divine Son who took to himself a true and perfect human nature, in the Incarnation, offered himself up as an infinitely valuable sacrifice and satisfaction.[99] Antonius Thysius said, "From his human nature came the payment, while from his divine nature came the quantity and quality—obviously the infinitude—and the value or dignity of the paid price."[100] Because on the cross hung helpless he through whom all things were made, we, finite sinners, have hope for acceptance with almighty God, singing:

> Well might the sun in darkness hide,
> And shut his glories in,
> When Christ, the mighty Maker, died
> For man the creature's sin.[101]

The way in which the canons connect Christology to soteriology in this article is truly astounding. It also makes comments like those of Wim Verboom perplexing. Verboom compares and contrasts the respective emphases of the Heidelberg Catechism and Canons of Dort, but ends up pitting them against one another. He states first that "in the *Canones* it is not so much a matter of *how* the salvation of God for men has been achieved, as *for whom* this salvation has been achieved. And, in connection with this, it shows in *what manner* humans share in that salvation."[102] This leads him to state, "Whereas the HC gives Christology a central place, in the CD that has

---

[99] On the two natures in the one Person of Christ, see Daniel R. Hyde, *God with Us: Knowing the Mystery of Who Jesus Is* (Grand Rapids, MI: Reformation Heritage Books, 2007).

[100] *Synopsis Purioris Theologiae: Volume 2*, 185.

[101] From the hymn "Alas! And Did My Savior Bleed."

[102] Verboom, "The Christology in the *Heidelberg Catechism* and in the *Canones of Dordt*," in *Strangers and Pilgrims on Earth*, 120. Emphasis in original.

changed....In the CD Christology becomes a means of election in God's hands in order to realize his aims....In short, the Christology of the HC has been absorbed in the doctrine of predestination."[103] What Verboom misses is that the same Dutch professors and pastors who signed onto the Canons of Dort also signed the Form of Subscription that included the Heidelberg Catechism and Belgic Confession. They did not see these documents or the doctrines they espoused as contradictory in any way. Further, although Verboom does take into account the differing historical and theological contexts of these confessional documents, he still presses his point to separate Heidelberg from Dort.[104] The canons were the fruit of yet another generation of theological precision as well as application into specific issues they had to face. One of these most important contextual issues is the fact that the synod *responded* to the five points of the Remonstrants. The Remonstrants set the agenda for the debate; the synod merely replied and did not meet to lay out an entire systematic theology on the matter.

THE INFINITE VALUE OF THE SUFFERING

Jesus Christ, the God-man, is "the Lamb of God," that is, he is the "Lamb" sent by God in mercy to be the remedy for our sinful condition as a human race. But how does he provide this remedy? John 1:29 says that as this sacrificial "Lamb," he "takes away the sin of the world." Because God's justice is infinite, the suffering of this divine-human "Lamb of God" was also of infinite value. Not only does his **death derive**[...] **its infinite value and dignity from** being the God-man, but also **because it was attended with a sense of the wrath and curse of God due to us for sin**. To "take[...] away the sin of the world," this Lamb had to experience God's anger and curse on the cross. Jesus didn't just die. Jesus suffered the wrath of God against the sin of the whole human race and experienced the curse of God upon that sin. He even cried out, "My God, my God, why have you forsaken me?" (Matt. 27:46).[105] After the synod, Andreas Rivetus said Jesus

---

[103] Verboom, "The Christology in the *Heidelberg Catechism* and in the *Canones of Dordt*," in *Strangers and Pilgrims on Earth*, 121.

[104] Verboom, "The Christology in the *Heidelberg Catechism* and in the *Canones of Dordt*," in *Strangers and Pilgrims on Earth*, 121–23.

[105] On the connection between this idea and what the Apostles' Creed calls Jesus' "descent into hell, see Daniel R. Hyde, *In Defense of the Descent: A Response to Contem-*

died not only a natural death, but in some sense also a supernatural death. He was separated from God in terms of willing what is pleasant, though not in terms of willing what is righteous. To be sure, he was not separated from his Godhead as far as the union in Person is concerned, but the divine power in him hid itself for the time being, so that in his great need there was no display of divine power, and there was no manifestation of majesty.[106]

In his poem "La Corona"—the crown—Puritan poet John Donne spoke of the suffering of the God-man in these terms:

Measuring self-life's infinity to span,
Nay to an inch. Lo! where condemned He
Bears His own cross, with pain, yet by and by
When it bears him, He must bear more and die.

The cross bore Christ, but Christ bore the curse, the judgment, the punishment, the wrath of God. As we sing on Good Friday:

O noblest Brow and dearest,
In other days the world
All feared when Thou appearedst;
What shame is on Thee hurled!
How art Thou pale with anguish,
With sore abuse and scorn!
How does that visage languish,
Which once was bright as morn![107]

God's punishment was not partial, but entire. There was nothing more the Son had to suffer; there still is nothing more he has to suffer. Back to article 3, Christ's death is **abundantly sufficient to expiate the sins of the whole world**. English translators get stuck using the language of "atonement," which is not specific.[108] The writers of the canons, though,

---

porary Critics, Explorations in Reformed Confessional Theology (Grand Rapids, MI: Reformation Heritage Books, 2010).

[106] *Synopsis Purioris Theologiae: Volume 2,* 135, 137.

[107] From the hymn "O Sacred Head, Now Wounded."

[108] See the 1986 and 2011 translations of the Christian Reformed Church.

used the specific word *expianda*, "expiate." Satisfaction, we saw, is a payment of debts; expiation, on the other hand, is the purgation of those debts.[109]

Let me give an illustration. If a fire captain enters a burning building, he experiences the full danger and heat of that fire, whether he rescues one or a hundred people.[110] Jesus suffered all there is to suffer on the cross when he came to rescue us. There was no limit to that suffering. If he came to save one person or every person on a million worlds, what he suffered was sufficient. What does this doctrine mean for you?

First, I don't know where you are with Jesus, but this means that there is no special kind of sinner that is outside the sufficiency of his suffering. What have you done? It doesn't matter. Jesus suffered the infinite wrath of God. No particular sin can exclude you. Repent and believe. Behold the Lamb.

Second, for the child of God, this means that Jesus' sufficient suffering of the infinite justice and wrath of God continues to flow out to us. It is the ever-flowing, life-giving stream to our souls. We can never get enough of Christ. We can never outlive his infinite sacrifice. We can never outsin his infinite sacrifice. We can never outrun his infinite sacrifice. Be assured. Be encouraged. Behold the Lamb.

Article 5

Moreover, the promise of the gospel is, that whosoever believeth in Christ crucified, shall not perish, but have everlasting life. This promise, together with the command to repent and believe, ought to be declared and published to all nations, and to all persons promiscuously and without distinction, to whom God out of His good pleasure sends the gospel.

CAN WE PREACH TO ALL PEOPLE?

Several years ago the popular anti-Calvinist writer Dave Hunt summarized many evangelical Christians' opinions when he said that Calvinists "bring the gospel to the world not *because* of their Calvinism, but only *in spite* of

---

[109] "Expiatio," in Muller, *Dictionary of Latin and Greek Theological Terms*, 116.
[110] Pronk, *Expository Sermons*, 126.

it."[111] The logic goes that since we believe in eternal and unconditional election, since we believe that Christ's satisfaction of God's justice on the cross is only effective for some, and since we believe that all humanity is so dead in sin that they can do nothing of their own will to save themselves, then no matter what, some will be saved and others not. So according to Hunt, in spite of all this, if you're a Calvinist your desire to bring the gospel to the world is inconsistent.

Anti-Calvinists such as today's evangelicals and the old Remonstrants have been saying this for centuries. But saying it's so doesn't make it so. I want to testify here that Hunt's opinion is not true. *Because* I believe with the Synod of Dort that Jesus laid down his life effectively for a particular people, I preach the gospel and want to see it preached everywhere! In the words of the nineteenth-century theologian of Utrecht, Jan Jacob van Oosterzee, "No unhappy confusion of ideas between the doctrine of predestination and that of reconciliation may be allowed to detract aught from the freshness and kindliness of the proclamation of the Gospel."[112]

Article 5 of the second point of doctrine was an article originally drafted by the British delegation and says we bring the gospel to the ends of the earth *because* of our theology. As Hoekema said, it is "a kind of *Magna Carta* for missions."[113] Articles 3–4 said Jesus' death was sufficient to satisfy for the sins of a thousand, million, or infinite worlds. Article 5 deliberately uses **moreover** (*caeterum*), which is not as strong as "therefore" (*ergo*). This means it's not explaining the precise relationship between Jesus' sufficiency and preaching to allow for the different ways of expression that one can see among Reformed theologians.[114] One expression was that of the delegates from Hesse:

> The conviction that the value of the death of Christ is so great that it is sufficient to reconcile every man to God, though there should be more than a thousand worlds, is the reason why the gospel can be preached to all without

---

[111] Dave Hunt, *What Love Is This? Calvinism's Misrepresentation of God* (Sisters, OR: Loyal, 2002), 29.

[112] J. J. van Oosterzee, *Christian Dogmatics: A Text Book for Academical Instruction and Private Study*, trans. John Watson Watson and Maurice J. Evans (1870; 5th ed., London: Hodder and Stoughton, 1891), 604.

[113] Hoekema, "The Missionary Focus of the Canons of Dort," 214.

[114] Gatiss, *For Us and for Our Salvation*, 81.

distinction, to elect and reprobate alike, why all must be bidden to believe in Christ, and why unbelievers are justly condemned on account of their unbelief.[115]

But what Article 5 does clearly say is that if your view of "limited atonement" limits your evangelistic outlook, you don't understand the historic Reformed view. John Davenant said:

> This is one thing I should wish to be observed, That our orthodox Doctors so explained the doctrines of election and reprobation, that the decree concerning the chusing of certain individual persons to the infallible obtaining of eternal life, and passing by others, might not infringe the universality of the redemption accomplished by the death of Christ.[116]

Far from limiting preachers and all believers in evangelizing and witnessing, this doctrine frees us to sow the seed of the gospel freely (Matt. 13). Why? Because we know that God knows whom he has elected, whom Christ died for, and in whom the Holy Spirit will powerfully work. Listen to the echo of Jesus' command to his apostles in Matthew 28:19 and Mark 16:15 here in article 5: **this promise...ought to be declared and published to all nations**. The language of preaching **to all nations, and to all persons promiscuously and without distinction** is drawn from texts such as 2 Corinthians 5 where Paul said he sought to "persuade others" (5:11), to proclaim "if anyone is in Christ, he is a new creation" (5:17), and to "implore you on behalf of Christ, be reconciled to God" (5:20) because he was compelled by "the love of Christ" who "died for all" (5:14) and that "in Christ God was reconciling the world to himself...God making his appeal through us" (5:19–20).[117]

---

[115] Cited in Hoekema, "The Missionary Focus of the Canons of Dort," 214.

[116] Davenant, *Dissertation*, 2:339.

[117] On Calvin's exegesis of such "all" texts, see Michael A. G. Haykin and C. Jeffrey Robinson Sr., *To the Ends of the Earth: Calvin's Missional Vision and Legacy* (Wheaton, IL: Crossway, 2014), 31–51. On pages 53–63 there is also a great discussion of Calvin's doctrine that God uses means including our need to pray and be zealous.

A Universal Promise

Can we preach to all people? Yes. Jesus has a universal authority: "All authority in heaven and on earth has been given to me" (Matt. 28:18). He issues a universal command in verses 19–20, which we'll come to in a moment. Then he makes a universal promise: "And behold, I am with you always, to the end of the age" (Matt. 28:20). This promise of his presence is joined to the church's universal task to baptize and teach the nations. Article 5 speaks narrowly of **the promise of the gospel** and cites John 3:16, "whosoever believes in [Christ crucified] should not perish but have eternal life." In Matthew 28, Jesus speaks in the broadest terms of baptizing and teaching everything he has commanded.

He does this in fulfillment of Scripture. God made the world in order that through Adam's obedience all who would come from him would be blessed to live in everlasting fellowship with the Creator. But Adam sinned. Because he did, the Lord intervened with promises that one day he would bless and save the world. To Abram he said, "In you all the families of the earth shall be blessed" (Gen. 12:3). The Psalms of Israel celebrated this future promise in poetic prayers and songs: "All the ends of the earth shall remember and turn to the LORD, and all the families of the nations shall worship before you" (Ps. 22:27). The prophets longed for that day to come: "It shall come to pass in the latter days that the mountain of the house of the LORD shall be established as the highest of the mountains, and shall be lifted up above the hills; and all the nations shall flow to it" (Isa. 2:2); "For from the rising of the sun to its setting my name will be great among the nations, and in every place incense will be offered to my name, and a pure offering. For my name will be great among the nations, says the LORD of hosts" (Mal. 1:11).

"But look at world evangelism. Where are the Calvinists?" Do you mean the Reformed church of Geneva sending missionaries to Brazil in the 1550s? Do you mean John Eliot (1604–1690) of Massachusetts, who went every other week to preach to and catechize the children of Native Americans beginning in 1646? Do you mean the English Parliament that created the "Society for the Propagation of the Gospel in New England" in the seventeenth century? Do you mean the Synod of Dort that began a missionary school? Do you mean David and John Brainerd, who preached to the Housatonic people in the mid-1700s? Do you mean William Carey, the father of modern missions, who founded what came to be called the London Missionary Society? Do you mean Robert Moffat (1795–1883) and David Livingstone (1813–1873), who gave themselves to South and Central Africa? Do you mean Robert Morrison (1782–1834), who translated the Bible into Chinese by 1818? The list goes on! "Far from being a hindrance to missions [our doctrine] is a powerful incentive for missions. The missionary knows that his work is not in vain, since God applies the Word to the hearts of the hearers by the efficacious working of his Holy Spirit."[118]

A Universal Command

Can we preach to all people? Yes, because we also have *a universal command.* "Go therefore and make disciples of all nations, baptizing them in the name of the Father and of the Son and of the Holy Spirit, teaching them to observe all that I have commanded you" (Matt. 28:19–20). At the synod, though, the Remonstrants caricatured the Reformed position, saying:

> Only those are obliged to believe that Christ died for them for whom Christ has died. The reprobates, however, as they are called, for whom Christ has not died, are not obligated to such faith, nor can they be justly condemned on account of the contrary refusal to believe this. In fact, if there should be such reprobates, they would be obliged to believe that Christ has not died for them.[119]

More recently this caricature has been expressed by Calvary Chapel anti-Calvinist George Bryson like this:

> From a thoroughly Calvinistic perspective…just as no amount of preaching will *help* the unelect, no failure of Christians to reach out to the elect will *hinder* them from coming to Christ. Thus, while the Gospel is to be proclaimed, it is difficult to see why we should be all that concerned—Calvinistically speaking. After all, according to Calvinism, the elect will be saved, period. The unelect will be damned period.[120]

---

[118] Hoekema, "The Missionary Focus of the Canons of Dort," 215.

[119] "The Opinions of the Remonstrants," appendix H in De Jong, *Crisis in the Reformed Churches,* 225.

[120] Bryson, *The Five Points of Calvinism,* 55. Emphasis in original.

In contrast, here is how the Calvinist and father of modern missions, William Carey, opened his famous work on the obligation of Christians to spread the gospel:

> As our blessed Lord has required us to pray that his king-dom may come, and his will be done on earth as it is in heaven, it becomes us not only to express our desires of that event by words, but to use every lawful method to spread the knowledge of his name.[121]

It seems the anti-Calvinist likes to deal in caricature rather than reali-ty. It is precisely because there is an elect number known only to God, pre-cisely because Christ died effectually for them, and precisely because the Holy Spirit uses the means of preaching to bring them to faith that we preach. Our doctrine is no disincentive, it *is* the incentive! The same Paul who quoted God himself, "I will have mercy on whom I have mercy, and I will have compassion on whom I have compassion" (Rom. 9:15), and said, "But who are you, O man, to answer back to God? Will what is molded say to its molder, 'Why have you made me like this?'" (Rom. 9:20), also said,

> How then will they call on him in whom they have not be-lieved? And how are they to believe in him of whom they have never heard? And how are they to hear without someone preaching? And how are they to preach unless they are sent? [...] So faith comes from hearing, and hear-ing through the word of Christ (Rom. 10:14–15, 17).

God has promised us he will save when we obey his command and preach!

We have a command to go, to baptize, and to teach (Matt. 28:19–20). We have a **command** to issue to all: **repent and believe**, and this **ought to be declared and published to all nations, and to all persons promis-cuously** (*promiscue*) **and without distinction** (*indiscriminatim*; indiscriminate-ly)**, to whom God out of His good pleasure sends the gospel.**

I don't want you to miss this, but the canon just said in God's love for the entire human race, he sends the gospel. The phrase above **good pleasure** is the Latin *beneplacito.* As before in 1.2, when our forefathers read the Bible they saw it speak of God's love for everything outside him in

---

[121] William Carey, *An Enquiry into the Obligations of Christians, to Use Means for the Con-version of the Heathens* (Leicester, UK: Ann Ireland, 1792).

three senses: toward all creation, toward all humanity in general, and toward his elect.[122] The word above was chosen deliberately to express love that was "more than" just toward creation but "less than" toward the elect.

This good pleasure of God in sending the gospel to whom he wills is seen in Matthew 28. It's also in Jesus' words that "this gospel of the kingdom will be proclaimed throughout the whole world as a testimony to all nations" (Matt. 24:14). It's in Jesus' postresurrection teaching on the road to Emmaus: "that repentance for the forgiveness of sins should be proclaimed in his name to all nations" (Luke 24:47). It's in Jesus' words just before his ascension: "and you will be my witnesses in Jerusalem and in all Judea and Samaria, and to the end of the earth" (Acts 1:8). It's in Paul's words about "the hope of the gospel…which has been proclaimed in all creation under heaven" (Col. 1:23) and "we have received grace and apostleship to bring about the obedience of faith for the sake of his name among all the nations" (Rom. 1:5). Paul's practice and Dort's decision is completely contrary to men like Homer Hoeksema, who interpreted article 5 to say "the canons here teach a particular promise, for the elect alone."[123] He said "whosoever will" was "an element in the preaching [that] serves to identify the elect" and therefore "preaching must always be addressed to faith, must single out the believers, and must proclaim that the promise of everlasting like is for all those, and for those only, who believe in Christ crucified."[124] Contrast Hoeksema with the British delegates to the synod: "As far as the manner [in which men are to be called to participate in the sacrifice of Christ] is concerned, there is no man who cannot be earnestly called to participate in the forgiveness of sins and everlasting life obtained through the death of Christ."[125] Contrast Hoeksema with John Calvin on John 3:16:

> The true looking of faith, I say, is placing Christ before one's eyes and beholding in Him the heart of God poured out in love…. For men are not easily convinced that God loves them; and so, to remove all doubt, He has expressly stated that we are so very dear to God that for our sakes He did not spare even His only begotten Son…. God's love for His only begotten Son is a measure of how pre-

---

[122] See "amor Dei," in Muller, *Dictionary of Latin and Greek Theological Terms*, 23.

[123] Hoeksema, *The Voice of Our Fathers*, 358.

[124] Hoeksema, *The Voice of Our Fathers*, 356, 357.

[125] Cited in Hoekema, "The Missionary Focus of the Canons of Dort," 213–14.

cious our salvation was to Him, that He willed that the death of the Only Begotten Himself should be its price.... He has used a general term [whoever], both to invite indiscriminately all to share in life and to cut off every excuse from unbelievers.... He...is favorable to the whole world when He calls all without exception to the faith of Christ.... Moreover, let us remember that although life is promised generally to all who believe in Christ, faith is not common to all. Christ is open to all and displayed to all, but God opens the eyes only of the elect that they may seek Him by faith.[126]

And again, on Romans 5:18, "As one trespass led to condemnation for all men, so one act of righteousness leads to justification and life for all men," Calvin said: "Paul makes grace common to all men, not because it in fact extends to all, but because it is offered to all. Although Christ suffered for the sins of the world, and is offered by the goodness of God without distinction to all men, yet not all receive Him."[127]

It's important to recognize that up to this point in the canons the sufficiency of Christ's death is asserted as is the imperative to preach Christ to all. The connection between these two is left unanswered.[128]

Can we preach to all people? Some say we can't because it's inconsistent with our theology. But Jesus says we must! So let's start praying for the lost. Let's start witnessing to them. Let's continue preaching the good news.

Article 6

And whereas many who are called by the gospel do not repent nor believe in Christ, but perish in unbelief, this is not owing to any defect or insufficiency in the sacrifice offered by Christ upon the cross, but is wholly to be imputed to themselves.

---

[126] John Calvin, *The Gospel according to St. John 1–10*, trans. T. H. L. Parker, ed. David W. Torrance and Thomas F. Torrance, Calvin's Commentaries, 12 vols. (Grand Rapids, MI: Eerdmans, 1959), 4:74, 75.

[127] John Calvin, *The Epistles of Paul the Apostle to the Romans and to the Thessalonians*, trans. Ross Mackenzie, ed. David W. Torrance and Thomas F. Torrance, Calvin's Commentaries, 12 vols. (Grand Rapids, MI: Eerdmans, 1961), 4:117–118.

[128] For Samuel Ward's reconciliation, see Todd, "Justifying God," 279–80, 286–87.

Picking up on article 5 and the announcement of the gospel promise to **whosoever believeth** among **all nations** and **all persons**, article 6 begins **whereas**. It goes on to reiterate a point we saw in the first point of doctrine that human beings are responsible for their sins and unbelief, God is not (cf. 1.4, 5, 15). Now human responsibility is particularly applied to the topic of the cross.

The harsh reality is **many who are called by the gospel do not repent nor believe in Christ, but perish in unbelief.** Before he went to the cross, Jesus spoke to his disciples this parable: "The kingdom of heaven may be compared to a king who gave a wedding feast for his son" (Matt. 22:2). The invitations went out; then the king "sent his servants to call those who were invited to the wedding feast, but they would not come" (Matt. 22:3). Then the king "sent other servants" to announce to those invited, "See, I have prepared my dinner, my oxen and my fat calves have been slaughtered, and everything is ready. Come to the wedding feast" (Matt. 22:4). Sadly, "they paid no attention," with some going back to their farms, some going back to their business (Matt. 22:5), while others did even worse: they "seized [the king's] servants, treated them shamefully, and killed them" (Matt. 22:6). This led the king to retaliate (Matt. 22:7). Then he sent his servants back out: "to the main roads and invite to the wedding feast as many as you find" (Matt. 22:8–9). They "gathered all whom they found, both bad and good. So the wedding hall was filled with guests" (Matt. 22:10). When the king entered and saw the guests, he noticed "a man who had no wedding garment" (Matt. 22:11). When he asked, "Friend, how did you get in here without a wedding garment?" the man was speechless, leading the king to have him bound and cast out (Matt. 22:12–13). Then Jesus concluded: "For many are called, but few are chosen" (Matt. 22:14).

The reason those who are called do not all repent and believe is *not owing* **to any defect or insufficiency in the sacrifice offered by Christ upon the cross.** We've already seen that Jesus' death is **the only and most perfect sacrifice and satisfaction for sin, and is of infinite worth and value, abundantly sufficient to expiate the sins of the whole world** (2.3). Instead, the reason many who are called perish in unbelief is **wholly to be imputed to themselves.** The fault lies not at the feet of the Savior, but of the sinner.

Article 7

But as many as truly believe, and are delivered and saved from sin and destruction through the death of Christ, are indebted for this benefit solely to the grace of God, given them in Christ from everlasting, and not to any merit of their own.

In article 7 we have the final common Christian conviction. In it we're reminded of another truth from the first point of doctrine: faith is the gift of God (cf. 1.5, 6, 7). God is responsible for our faith while we are responsible for unbelief as we saw in article 6. Like article 6, article 7 opens with the word *autem*, **but**. In contrast to the unbeliever in article 6 we read here **as many as truly believe, and are delivered and saved from sin and destruction through the death of Christ, are indebted for this benefit solely to the grace of God, given them in Christ from everlasting, and not to any merit of their own.**

Notice the connection between the appropriation of redemption by those who **truly believe** (*vere credunt*) and the accomplishment of redemption for those who believe who are **delivered and saved from sin and destruction through the death of Christ**. Both, according to the article as it reflects Ephesians 2:8–9, **are indebted for this benefit solely to the grace of God**. This **benefit**, in fact, was **given them in Christ from everlasting**, pointing us back to the first point of doctrine. This language of **benefit…given…from everlasting** comes right from the apostle Paul when he sought to encourage Timothy "do not be ashamed of the testimony about our Lord, nor of me his prisoner" (2 Tim. 1:8). The way he did this was to remind Timothy that God "saved us and called us to a holy calling, *not because of our works*" (οὐ κατὰ τὰ ἔργα ἡμῶν). We didn't earn it and God didn't owe it. "But" (ἀλλὰ), the apostle goes on to say, "*because of his own purpose and grace*" (κατὰ ἰδίαν πρόθεσιν καὶ χάριν). Paul contrasts the basis by which (οὐ κατὰ…κατὰ), on which (τὰ ἔργα…πρόθεσιν καὶ χάριν), and from which (ἡμῶν…ἰδίαν) God gave us salvation from all eternity: "which he gave us in Christ Jesus before the ages began" (2 Tim. 1:9).

In our exploration of the common Christian convictions about Jesus Christ's death and its relation to the accomplishment of and application of our redemption, the canons so far help us keep the main thing the main thing by emphasizing that God is just, we with all humanity are sinful, we need God's justice to be satisfied through punishment, and that God has showed his mercy by sending his Son to do this very thing.

Article 8

For this was the sovereign counsel, and most gracious will and purpose of God the Father, that the quickening and saving efficacy of the most precious death of His Son should extend to all the elect, for bestowing upon them alone the gift of justifying faith, thereby to bring them infallibly to salvation: that is, it was the will of God, that Christ by the blood of the cross, whereby He confirmed the new covenant, should effectually redeem out of every people, tribe, nation, and language, all those, and those only, who were from eternity chosen to salvation and given to Him by the Father; that He should confer upon them faith, which together with all the other saving gifts of the Holy Spirit, He purchased for them by His death; should purge them from all sin, both original and actual, whether committed before or after believing; and having faithfully preserved them even to the end, should at last bring them free from every spot and blemish to the enjoyment of glory in His own presence forever.

CHRIST'S SATISFACTION DEFINED

With article 8 we move from the common doctrines to the definitional statement of the controversy at hand.[129]

What Did the Father Intend on the Cross?

"'All' means all and that's all 'all' means." Have you heard that line before? It's become a truism for so many of our evangelical brothers and sisters as they talk about Jesus' death. It makes them sound so biblical and so compassionate while the Calvinists coldheartedly cling to their confessions like Charlton Heston to his guns "with these cold, dead hands." How do we talk about it?

As I've already mentioned, the phrase "limited atonement" is not used by the Canons of Dort. It's not helpful because when we think in crass quantitative terms we make it sound like Jesus' death gathered as many sinners as possible with the available blood he spilled but then he ran out.[130] In

---

[129] See *Synopsis Purioris Theologiae: Volume 2*, 197.

[130] Gatiss, *For Us and for Our Salvation*, 11–12.

point of fact, all evangelical Christians limit the effectiveness of Christ's sacrifice in some way, whether you say his death is effectual for those whom God elected and whom the Holy Spirit actually brings to salvation or whether you say Christ died for all sins of all people but only those who believe benefit from it. One of the things we on the Reformed side tend to say is this: "Calvinists limit extent; Arminians limit efficacy."[131] I think this is an overly simplified reading of the issue at hand. In reading the canons closely, the issue is that the orthodox Reformed understood Christ's death as acquiring *both* reconciliation and its application for a definite number of people; in contrast, the Remonstrants saw Christ's death acquiring reconciliation *only* but not its application, which was left to the will of man to perform. In other words, we both limit the extent of Christ's death; the difference is that we limit it according to God's will while Arminians limit it according to man's.

One Reformed response to this classic Remonstrant scheme of "limited atonement" is to question how can it be said that Jesus died for all the sins of everyone if the sin of unbelief keeps one out of salvation? This is the "universalist dilemma" according to John Owen. Either *Christ died for all the sins of all men* or *all the sins of some men* or *some sins of all men*. This last option no one would affirm as it means all have some sins to answer for before God and thus no one will be saved. The second option is Owen's version of the Reformed position in which Christ died effectually for some who will all be saved (but does not speak of any universal sufficiency). The first option is the classic Remonstrant position that many evangelicals are unaware of where they got their view. If Jesus died for all the sins of all people, then all are saved. But the Remonstrant says not all believe and so are not saved. Owen's question is this: Is unbelief a sin or not? If it's not a sin, why would an unbeliever be punished for it? If it is a sin, then Christ died for it because he died for all sins. If it is a sin, why does this sin hinder an unbeliever more than his or her other sins? If Jesus did not die for the sin of unbelief, then did he not die for all the sins of all people.[132] Before Owen, David Paraeus

---

[131] My friend Matthew Barrett says it like this: "It is essential to observe that while the Calvinist may limit the *extent* of the atonement…the Arminian limits the efficacy." *The Grace of Godliness*, 53.

[132] Owen, "The Death of Death in the Death of Christ," in *Works*, 10:173–74. Gatiss makes the helpful comment that although today Owen's work "is often considered *the* book on limited atonement, his voice is just one of a number of Reformed voices in this debate and not everyone within that tradition would agree

saw this dilemma at the time of the synod. If, as the Remonstrants said, Jesus impetrated or accomplished redemption for all, and "all" means believers, then why are we arguing? But if this means for every human being, how so? If Jesus did so in terms of the sufficiency of his merit, then, again, we have nothing to argue about. But if he did so in terms of the efficacy of his merit being applied to every human being, then comes the dilemma. Did Jesus accomplish efficacious redemption for all absolutely regardless of faith? "Of course not, you have to believe," someone will say. But then how can it be said Jesus purchased redemption for everyone if everyone isn't saved? But if they said Jesus purchased efficacious redemption under the condition of faith for all, but some do not have faith, then how can he be said to have purchased redemption for them? Paraeus concluded by saying it's all just one big contradiction: "He hath impetrated for all, He hath not impetrated for many."[133]

This brings us to the real issue about what Christ's death accomplished and to whom it is applied. Louis Berkhof stated it like this: "Did the Father in sending Christ, and did Christ in coming into the world, to make atonement for sin, *do this with the design or for the purpose of saving only the elect or all men?* That is the question, and that is the only question."[134] In one sense, yes, this is the issue contra Arminianism. Yet as we've seen, it's more complex than our more modern way of turning everything into an either/or choice. The issue is really the efficacy (effectiveness) of the death of Jesus. What did God the Father intend his Son to do on the cross? Did he intend that Jesus would only make salvation possible, or did he intend it to actually satisfy the justice of God for the elect who will come to share in this sacrifice by faith? In other words, did God intend that Jesus' death would be effectual for some, or was it intended for all? The extent of the saving bene-

---

with Owen on every detail of how he defends this doctrine." *For Us and for Our Salvation*, 18n6. In fact, Owen himself said of this work: "I was desired and pressed to handle the things of that discourse *in the most popular way* they were capable of, and *in the best accommodation to vulgar capacities*; so that it is no wonder, if some expressions therein may be found to want some grains of accurateness (though they have not one dram the less of truth) in a scholastical balance." Owen, "Of the Death Christ," in *Works*, 10:435.

[133] Paraeus, "Epitome of Arminianisme," 828, 829.

[134] Louis Berkhof, *Systematic Theology* (1941; 4th rev. ed., Grand Rapids, MI: Eerdmans, 1994), 394. Emphasis added.

fits of his cross, then, are rooted in the intent of the Father to send him in the first place.

In the lengthiest article in this section on Christ's redemption, article 8 addresses this. It's long and complex, so let me restate it in outline form:

I. Summary definition of the Reformed position:
For this was the sovereign counsel, and most gracious will and purpose of God the Father,

[Link between redemption accomplished and applied]
that the quickening and saving efficacy of the most precious death of His Son should extend to all the elect, for bestowing upon them alone the gift of justifying faith, thereby to bring them infallibly to salvation:

II. Lengthier definition of the Reformed position:
that is, it was the will of God,

[Lengthier description of the link between redemption accomplished and applied]:
that Christ by the blood of the cross, whereby He confirmed the new covenant, should effectually redeem out of every people, tribe, nation, and language, all those, and those only, who were from eternity chosen to salvation and given to Him by the Father;

that He should confer upon them faith, which together with all the other saving gifts of the Holy Spirit, He purchased (*aquisivit*) for them by His death;

should purge them from all sin, both original and actual, whether committed before or after believing;

and having faithfully preserved them even to the end, should at last bring them free from every spot and blemish to the enjoyment of glory in His own presence forever.

God Has a Will

This article is a nuanced version of the sufficiency/efficiency distinction as it puts an emphasis on the **counsel**, **will**, and **purpose** of God and not merely on the sufficiency of Jesus' death.[135] This means that when we speak about what God *intended*, we're speaking about his *will*. The triune God has

---

[135] Gatiss, *For Us and for Our Salvation*, 82–83.

a plan and purpose for all things. He "works all things according to the counsel of his will" (Eph. 1:11). In John 6, Jesus says, "I have come down from heaven, *not to do my own will but the will of him who sent me*" (John 6:38). As the Son of God in human flesh, our Lord Jesus Christ voluntarily humbled himself to do not his own will but the Father's. And you see this again in verse 39, where Jesus speaks of "the will of him who sent me," and again in verse 40, "for this is the will of my Father."

Why is this so important? Think about the last time you spoke with a believer who kept talking about Jesus making salvation possible for everyone by his death. This view comes off as believing that what Jesus did had no plan behind it from God. Yes, Jesus was sent down, died, but his death was in no sense for anyone in particular. Because of that, everyone has a chance to believe, everyone has a chance to make Jesus their own, and everyone can use their own will to make salvation a reality in their lives. The point is that Jesus says God has a will—a definite, determined, well-thought-out plan not only for the world as a whole but for each and every sinner whom he brings into his kingdom.

The Father Communicated this Will to the Son

Jesus also says in John 6 that the Father communicated this will to the Son. Not only does Jesus say the Father has a plan now, but that this plan was planned out in eternity and then passed on to Jesus. "All that the Father gives me will come to me" (v. 37). As article 8 says, **it was the will of God, that Christ by the blood of the cross...should effectually redeem...all those, and those only, who were from eternity chosen to salvation and given to Him by the Father.** To use Jesus' words, "I have come down from heaven" to do "the will of him who sent me" (John 6:38). Then he says, "the will of him who sent me" was that he "should lose nothing of all that he has given me" (John 6:39).

What's going on here that's so important for us? In theological terms, some of our forefathers called what Jesus is describing the covenant of redemption. It's not the term that's important but the content that is. What is that content? First, that in "eternity past"—if we can even speak that way!—there was a deliberate and personal plan between the persons of the Holy Trinity to organize and orchestrate redemption. There was not one will of the Father, another of the Son, and another of the Holy Spirit for redemption, with each doing what they wanted. Second, that plan was about persons. The article repeatedly speaks of **the elect, them,** and **those.** That's the wonder of all our doctrines of grace. That God—*God!*—thought of me, loved me, and planned human history to rescue me! As we sing:

> I find, I walk, I love; but O the whole
> Of love is but my answer, Lord, to Thee!
> For Thou wert long beforehand with my soul;
> Always, always Thou lovedest me.[136]

The Son Executed this Will

Finally, Jesus says here that as the Son he executed this will of God. All that was planned from eternity past concerning the Son of God becoming man and going to the cross and all that was planned to redeem sinners, Jesus actually did. God didn't plan one thing and Jesus executed another. He did what was planned.

Listen to Jesus again: "For I have come down from heaven, not to do my own will but the will of him who sent me" (John 6:38). Jesus came to do the will of God in that eternal conversation; and he did it on the cross! Call this "limited atonement" if you must; I will call it Jesus doing exactly what God planned! In other words, I said "limited atonement" is unhelpful and misleading because what really matters is not the quantity of the saved, but what God in his sovereign purpose intended for Christ on the cross.

Think of it like this: Think of a light, without any kind of cover or shade, that's turned on. What happens to the light? It is dispersed everywhere, isn't it? So we've seen with Jesus' death on the cross. It is infinitely sufficient to satisfy the infinite justice of God for a million worlds. All that Jesus needed to do, he did; there is no more he would need to do to save even one more sinner. Now, back to that light. Once you put on some sort of a cap or cover, you can focus all that light in a particular direction, like a flashlight. Jesus' death is that ever-spreading light that is then intentionally pointed toward certain people. The redemption God's Son, your Lord Jesus Christ, actually accomplished he also particularly applies to persons whom the Bible calls "the elect": **the quickening and saving efficacy of the most precious death of His Son should extend to all the elect, for be-**

---

[136] From the hymn "I Sought the Lord, and Afterward I Knew."

stowing upon them alone the gift of justifying faith, thereby to bring them infallibly to salvation.

That's the big picture theologically. "But how do I know if the will of God in eternity that was communicated from the Father to the Son and that the Son did was done for me?" If "all" doesn't mean "all," how can I be sure? This is why Jesus brings his message home to us. He doesn't only speak of eternity, he speaks to you personally and says: "For this is the will of my Father, that everyone who looks on the Son and believes in him should have eternal life, and I will raise him up on the last day" (John 6:40). Do you believe in Jesus? Then be assured that he came to execute that eternal plan of God, which means in that eternal plan, the Father spoke your name to the Son, and the Son agreed to come down *for you*! Amazing, isn't it?

Whereas earlier articles have dealt with the sufficiency of Christ's death, now the connection is made between **the sovereign counsel, and most gracious will and purpose of God the Father** and the efficiency of Christ's death: **that the quickening and saving efficacy of the most precious death of His Son should extend to all the elect, for bestowing upon them alone the gift of justifying faith, thereby to bring them infallibly to salvation.** The death of Jesus is not only about impetration but application of redemption. As the article says, Jesus **purchased for** [his elect] **by His death** all the gifts of the Holy Spirit from faith to perseverance.

As the above shows, the sufficiency/efficiency distinction was nuanced at Dort to say Christ's death is sufficient for all but effectively applied to the elect. Gatiss mentions how this was crafted in such a way that all the delegates could affirm, including those such as the British delegation. God willed **that Christ...should effectually** (*efficaciter*) **redeem...all those, and those only, who were from eternity chosen to salvation.** Technically, this does not deny a love of God for the nonelect at least in some sense, a general sense in which Christ is Redeemer of the world, nor did it deny a "complex-intention" view in which Christ died for the elect while also making the nonelect "redeemable."[137]

---

[137] Gatiss, *For Us and for Our Salvation*, 91.

Article 9

This purpose proceeding from everlasting love towards the elect has from the beginning of the world to this day been powerfully accomplished, and will henceforward still continue to be accomplished, notwithstanding all the ineffectual opposition of the gates of hell, so that the elect in due time may be gathered together into one, and that there never may be wanting a church composed of believers, the foundation of which is laid in the blood of Christ, which may steadfastly love and faithfully serve Him as their Savior, who as a bridegroom for His bride, laid down His life for them upon the cross, and which may celebrate His praises here and through all eternity.

ELABORATION ON CHRIST'S SATISFACTION

For Whom Did Christ Die?

"For you were slain, and by your blood you ransomed people for God from every tribe and language and people and nation, and you have made them a kingdom and priests to our God, and they shall reign on the earth" (Rev. 5:9–10). What a song! What a Savior! Jesus Christ is the object of our praise because we were the objects of his passion. He gave himself for us, and so we give ourselves for him. We should go on singing this song to this Savior for this reason forever and ever. And we will. Yet in this age there is controversy. Not all Christians believe that Jesus died intentionally and efficaciously for his people alone. How does a song answer this theological vexing question?

The Biblical Descriptions

I want you to notice two things described in Revelation 5:9–10 that are described by many other biblical passages as well.

First, *the Bible describes Jesus Christ as actually dying to accomplish every aspect of our salvation.* The heavenly choirs praise the Lamb. In their praise we see the connection between what Christ did—"For you were slain…you ransomed people for God"—and what it has accomplished—"you have made them a kingdom and priests to our God"—and what it will accomplish in the future—"they shall reign on the earth." The eternal song is not just that Jesus died. It was not just to make redemption a hypothetical for all who will or a potential for every single man, woman, and child. In other words, this song does not say Jesus died unintentionally. No, notice that the reason for praise is that that "you ransomed people for God." He actually paid the price to set the captives free, to release the prisoners. Again we sing, "And you have made them a kingdom and priests to our God." Jesus' death definitely did something!

- There are many, many more descriptions just like this one. For example, Jesus Christ's death is described in the following ways throughout Scripture:

- As accomplishing the definite plan and purpose of God by coming down from the eternal realm of heaven to manifest grace (Acts 2:23; Gal. 1:4; 2 Tim 1:9–10; 1 Peter 1:1–2);

- As accomplishing all that is necessary for our complete salvation so that already we are blessed in him with every spiritual blessing (Eph. 1:3);

- As accomplishing the obedience God required for us (Rom. 5:19);

- As accomplishing expiation, that is, the removing and sending away from the face of God our sins (Heb. 1:3; 9:14; 10:10, 14);

- As accomplishing propitiation, that is, the turning away of the justice and wrath of God toward us (Rom. 3:25);

- As accomplishing reconciliation, that is, the bringing together of God and us into a relationship of peace and love (Rom. 5:10);

- As accomplishing redemption, that is, leading us out of Egypt (Matt. 20:28; Rom. 3:24–25; 1 Cor. 1:30; Gal. 3:13; Col. 1:13–14; Heb. 9:12; 1 Pet. 1:18–19);

- As accomplishing faith for us: we "have obtained a faith of equal standing with ours by the righteousness of our God and Savior Jesus Christ" (2 Pet. 1:1);

- As accomplishing sanctification by giving himself for the purpose of redeeming us from lawlessness and purifying us as a people for his own possession who are zealous for good works (Titus 2:14);

- As accomplishing glorification by giving himself in love for his bride so that he might sanctify her in this life and so that he might present her without spot or wrinkle or any such thing, holy and without blemish, in the splendor of eternity (Eph. 5:25–27). As Gatiss helpfully points out, Ephesians 1:4 says we were predestined to be holy and blameless while Ephesians 5:25–27 says through the cross Jesus makes us holy and blameless. In other words, "The cross achieved what predestination planned."[138]

The second way *the Bible describes Jesus Christ is actually dying in the place of particular people.* Let me illustrate. It's hard for us to make the connection between what happened decades ago on D-day on Normandy Beach. How did those guys so long ago actually die in my place? But when someone in our lives actually steps in front of a car, comes between us and a bullet, or enters a fire to rescue us, it's personal and it's powerful, isn't it? That's what Jesus did. He is not an abstract person who died for an abstract, faceless mass of people he never knew. No, he personally died for each and every one of those he loved from before the foundation of the world.

We hear this in the heartfelt cries of heaven praising the Savior who actually "ransomed people for God," but notice how particular this ransom was for particular people as the song goes on to say "from every tribe and language and people and nation." The prepositional phrase "from every" (ἐκ πάσης) should be applied to each of the four nouns in the genitive case. The Lamb redeemed "*out of* every tribe (φυλῆς) and *out of* every language (γλώσσης) and *out of* every people (λαοῦ) and *out of* every nation" (ἔθνους). He gave his life effectually for those, and not the others. Even more, the song celebrates this with the pronouns: "you have made *them* a kingdom and priests to our God, and *they* shall reign on the earth." Greg Beale comments: "This is not a redemption of all peoples without exception, but of all without distinction (people *from* all races)."[139]

Again, there are many, many more descriptions just like this one as there were with the first. Listen to the following Scriptures and how they describe Jesus dying effectually for a particular people:

Jesus did not just make salvation a possibility for all, but those he saves he effectually saves: "the Son of Man came to seek and to save

---

[138] Gatiss, *For Us and for Our Salvation*, 30.

[139] G. K. Beale, *The Book of Revelation: A Commentary on the Greek Text* (Grand Rapids, MI: Eerdmans, 1999), 359.

the lost" (Luke 19:10); "if while we were enemies we were reconciled to God by the death of his Son, much more, now that we are reconciled, shall we be saved by his life" (Rom. 5:10); "For our sake he made him to be sin who knew no sin, so that in him we might become the righteousness of God" (2 Cor. 5:21); "who gave himself for our sins to deliver us from the present evil age, according to the will of our God and Father" (Gal. 1:4); "In him we have redemption through his blood, the forgiveness of our trespasses" (Eph. 1:7).

Jesus laid down his life for his people: "And you shall call his name Jesus, for he will save his people from their sins" (Matt. 1:21). The aforementioned defender of Gottschalk, Remigius, is cited by Thomas Aquinas as interpreting this verse to mean: "He saves indeed not the unbelieving, but His people; that is, He saves those that believe on Him, not so much from visible as from invisible enemies; that is, from their sins, not by fighting with arms, but by remitting their sins."[140]

"Blessed be the Lord God of Israel, for he has visited and redeemed his people" (Luke 1:68). Bede said of this verse: "But he says, *His people*, not that when He came He found them His own, but that by visiting He made them so."[141]

"I have been crucified with Christ. It is no longer I who live, but Christ who lives in me. And the life I now live in the flesh I live by faith in the Son of God, who loved me and gave himself for me" (Gal. 2:20).

Jesus laid down his life for his sheep: "I am the good shepherd. The good shepherd lays down his life for the sheep...I am the good shepherd. I know my own and my own know me, just as the Father knows me and I know the Father; and I lay down my life for the sheep" (John 10:11, 14–15).

Jesus gave his life for many: "The Son of Man came not to be served but to serve, and to give his life as a ransom for many" (Matt. 20:28).

---

[140] Thomas Aquinas, *Catena Aurea: Commentary on the Four Gospels Collected out of the Works of the Fathers*, St. Matthew: Volume I, Part I (Oxford: John Henry Parker, 1841), 51.

[141] Thomas Aquinas, *Catena Aurea: Commentary on the Four Gospels Collected out of the Works of the Fathers*, St. Luke: Volume III, Part I (Oxford: John Henry Parker, 1843), 54.

Origin said the "many" Jesus mentions in this verse are "they...who believed on Him."[142]

"This is my blood of the covenant, which is poured out for many for the forgiveness of sins" (Matt. 26:28). Of these "many" Remigius said, "And it is to be noted, that He says not, For a few, nor, For all, but, *For many*; because He came not to redeem a single nation, but many out of all nations."[143]

Jesus laid down his life for his church: "Pay careful attention to yourselves and to all the flock, in which the Holy Spirit has made you overseers, to care for the church of God, which he obtained with his own blood" (Acts 20:28); "Husbands, love your wives, as Christ loved the church and gave himself up for her, that he might sanctify her, having cleansed her by the washing of water with the word, so that he might present the church to himself in splendor, without spot or wrinkle or any such thing, that she might be holy and without blemish" (Eph. 5:25–27). "As Christ loved the church." This reminds us of the analogy that just as a husband does not love all women equally with the same kind of love, so too with Jesus and his church in contrast to Jesus and all human beings.

Jesus laid down his life for his elect: "He who did not spare his own Son but gave him up for us all, how will he not also with him graciously give us all things? Who shall bring any charge against God's elect? It is God who justifies. Who is to condemn? Christ Jesus is the one who died— more than that, who was raised—who is at the right hand of God, who indeed is interceding for us. Who shall separate us from the love of Christ?" (Rom. 8:32–35).

Jesus prays for his people: "I am praying for them. I am not praying for the world but for those whom you have given me, for they are yours" (John 17:9). Augustine asked, "if He speaks of the disciples only...what glory is to be known to twelve or eleven men? But if by the men which were given to Him out of the world, He means all those who should believe in Him afterwards, this is without doubt the glory wherewith the

---

142 Thomas Aquinas, *Catena Aurea: Commentary on the Four Gospels Collected out of the Works of the Fathers*, St. Matthew: Volume I, Part II (Oxford: John Henry Parker, 1841), 697.

143 Thomas Aquinas, *Catena Aurea: Commentary on the Four Gospels Collected out of the Works of the Fathers*, St. Matthew: Volume I, Part III (Oxford: John Henry Parker, 1842), 895.

Son glorifies the Father."[144] He then said "by the world He means those who live according to the lust of the world, and have not the lot to be chosen by grace out of the world, as those had for whom He prayed…It was because the Father had given Him them, that they did not belong to the world. Nor yet had the Father, in giving them to the Son, lost what He had given."[145]

Jesus saves those the Father gives him: "All that the Father gives me will come to me, and whoever comes to me I will never cast out. For I have come down from heaven, not to do my own will but the will of him who sent me. And this is the will of him who sent me, that I should lose nothing of all that he has given me, but raise it up on the last day" (John 6:37–39). Just before this Jesus said the crowds who ate his miraculous bread did not believe (John 3:36). Augustine commented: "But, because ye have seen Me, and believed not, I have not therefore lost the people God."[146] Bede said on verse 37: "*All*, He saith, absolutely, to shew the fullness of the number who should believe. These are they which the Father gives the Son, when, by His secret inspiration, He makes them believe in the Son."[147] On the link between these verses, Augustine said, "They there who by God's unerring providence are foreknown, and predestined, called, justified, glorified, even before their new birth, or before they are born at all, are already the sons of God, and cannot possibly perish; they are they who truly come to Christ."[148]

All this shows us is that Jesus' death was a substitution. If he died in the place of all people, then all people will be saved. If he was substituted for some, then those will be saved. This substitution was motivated by love. As a husband, Jesus has a special love for his wife that he has for no other woman. If he loved all women equally, his wife would be nothing special.

---

[144] Thomas Aquinas, *Catena Aurea: Commentary on the Four Gospels Collected out of the Works of the Fathers*, St. John: Volume IV, Part II (Oxford: John Henry Parker, 1845), 528.

[145] Aquinas, *Catena Aurea*, St. John: Volume IV, Part II, 531.

[146] Thomas Aquinas, *Catena Aurea: Commentary on the Four Gospels Collected out of the Works of the Fathers*, St. John: Volume IV, Part I (Oxford: John Henry Parker, 1845), 230.

[147] Aquinas, *Catena Aurea*, St. John: Volume IV, Part I, 230.

[148] Aquinas, *Catena Aurea*, St. John: Volume IV, Part I, 232.

The "Biblical" Objection

"Wait a minute! What about all the 'all' passages in the Bible that say Jesus died for all?" There are several passages, but what I want to say is that the "all" type of passages must be read with *all* their context in mind as well as with *all* the rest of Scripture. As I mentioned before, "all" doesn't always mean all and that's not all "all" means! Sometimes all means what it means here in Revelation 5:9 when all kinds of people are being described as being redeemed. Other times it means all nations—the Jews along with the Gentiles. Along with all the particularity of the particular passages I've just mentioned you can see that the best reading of Scripture is that Jesus gave himhimself a ransom for many kinds of people, Jews and Gentiles, "from every tribe and language and people and nation."

The Biblical Benefits

So why does all this matter? I want to conclude by offering three *biblical benefits* to affirming the intentional and effectual satisfaction of God's justice by Jesus Christ on the cross.

First, it gives us assurance and confidence that our Savior has been for us from eternity, on the cross, and into eternity. That assurance and confidence can say, "Worthy are you to take the scroll and to open its seals, for you were slain" *for me*, "and by your blood you ransomed" *me* "for God from" *this* "tribe and" *this* "language and" *this* "people and" *this* "nation, and you have made" *me* "a kingdom and" *a* "priest[…] to our God, and [*I*] shall reign on the earth" (Rev. 5:9–10).

Second, it gives us reason to worship. He actually and personally died for me to actually and powerfully accomplish my redemption from the slavery of sin and the kingdom of Satan.

Third, it gives us reason to preach, evangelize, and bear witness in the world. If Jesus Christ actually, personally, and powerfully died for some *out of* every tribe and *out of* every language and *out of* every people and *out of* every nation, then that means there are particular people in every tribe, every language, every people, and every nation that must come to repentance and faith.

What a song being sung in heaven even now. Let's make it our song here on earth! The affirmative articles in the second point of the Canons of Dort end with these words in article 9:

This purpose proceeding from everlasting love towards the elect has from the beginning of the world to this day been powerfully accomplished, and will henceforward still continue to be accomplished, notwithstanding all the ineffectual opposition of the gates of hell, so that the elect in due time may be gathered together into one, and that there never may be wanting a church composed of believers, the foundation of which is laid in the blood of Christ, which may steadfastly love and faithfully serve Him as their Savior, who as a bridegroom for His bride, laid down His life for them upon the cross, and which may celebrate His praises here and through all eternity.

The tribes, languages, peoples, and nations are right outside on our doorstep. What are we waiting for? Jesus' death is sufficient for an infinite number of worlds of sinners; tell them, knowing God will effectually apply it by his mighty grace.

IV:

WHAT WE REJECT

REJECTION OF ERRORS 1-7

HAVING SET forth the orthodox teaching, the synod again went on to reject several errors on the issue of the satisfaction of Jesus Christ. Let's look at these briefly.

Rejection of Errors 1

That God the Father has ordained His Son to the death of the cross without a certain and definite decree to save any, so that the necessity, profitableness and worth of what Christ merited by His death might have existed, and might remain in all its parts complete, perfect and intact, even if the merited redemption had never in fact been applied to any person.

For this doctrine tends to the despising of the wisdom of the Father and of the merits of Jesus Christ, and is contrary to Scripture. For thus saith our Savior: "I lay down My life for the sheep, and I know them" (John 10:15, 27). And the prophet Isaiah saith concerning the Savior: "When thou shalt make His soul an offering for sin, He shall see His seed, He shall prolong his days, and the pleasure of the LORD shall prosper in his hand" (Is. 53:10). Finally, this contradicts the article of faith according to which we believe the catholic Christian church.

The first rejection is against any idea *that God the Father has ordained His Son to the death of the cross without a certain and definite decree to save any.* The conclusion to this kind of thinking is this: if Jesus died for no particular individual, then it is possible that redemption accomplished is not applied to anyone. In the words of the rejection: *so that the necessity, profitableness and worth of what Christ merited by His death might have existed, and might remain in all its parts complete, perfect and intact, even if the merited redemption had never in fact been applied to any person.* One Remonstrant, Nicholaas Grevinchovius (d. 1632), said it like this: "I acknowledge in God indeed a constant and perpetual desire of applying to all men individually the good obtained; but I deny that the application itself was destined by the certain counsel and will of God for any man but him that believeth." Notice that God desires to apply Christ's death to everyone, but to no one in particular. Therefore he could go on to say,

> That there was not any absolute promise or will of God concerning the effectual redemption of any individual persons, but that God willed or did not will the application of the death of Christ to all men individually not absolutely but conditionally; He willed it to all if they had faith; he did not will it if they disbelieved and therefore, although Christ laid down his life, it was possible nevertheless that his death might not be applied to any.[1]

Read that line again: "it was possible that [Jesus] might be defrauded of his promised seed." At least Grevinchovius was honest about his belief.

Dort considered **this doctrine** to be a **despising of the wisdom of the Father and of the merits of Jesus Christ**. In other words, why send the Son if his work would have no guarantee of accomplishing anything? Also, this was considered to be **contrary to Scripture**. Where in Scripture do we read of God the Father giving his Son for actual individuals? In John 10 Jesus said, **"I lay down My life for the sheep"** (v. 15). This is a definite group. Unless one thinks it sounds impersonal, Jesus goes on to speak of them with personal pronouns: **"and I know them"** (αὐτά; v. 27). Jesus has sheep, and he knows who they are. In the great Servant Song of Isaiah 53 we read: **"When thou shalt make His soul an offering for sin, He shall see *His seed*, He shall prolong his days, and the pleasure of the LORD shall prosper in his hand"** (v. 10). Not only does the Servant have a seed or offspring, the intentionality of this text comes out in the parallel language that the Servant shall offer himself just as he shall see his offspring.

---

[1] Quoted in Davenant, *Dissertation*, 2:516, 524–25.

At the end of this rejection the synod also said **this contradicts the article of faith according to which we believe the catholic Christian church**. The catholicity of the Reformation is expressed in the ancient Apostles' Creed where it is confessed, "I believe the holy catholic Church." We cannot make this confession if God has not always loved a people from all eternity (point of doctrine one) for whom Jesus came and definitely purchased from sin (point of doctrine two).[2]

Rejection of Errors 2

That it was not the purpose of the death of Christ that He should confirm the new covenant of grace through His blood, but only that He should acquire for the Father the mere right to establish with man such a covenant as He might please, whether of grace or of works.

For this is repugnant to Scripture which teaches that Christ has become the Surety and Mediator of a better, that is, the new covenant, and that a testament is of force where death has occurred. "By so much was Jesus made a surety of a better testament" (Heb. 7:22); "And for this cause He is the Mediator of the new testament, that by means of death, for the redemption of the transgressions that were under the first testament, they which are called might receive the promise of eternal inheritance"; "For a testament is of force after men are dead: otherwise it is of no strength at all while the testator liveth" (Heb. 9:15, 17).

The second rejection also deals with the issue of Jesus actually accomplishing something by his death and not merely acquiring something hypothetical. The Remonstrants taught *that it was not the purpose of the death of Christ that He should confirm the new covenant of grace through His blood*. Instead, they taught that he died *only that He should acquire for the Father the mere right to establish with man such a covenant as He might please, whether of grace or of works*. Along with rejection 1, this meant that God could potentially never establish a covenant of grace with anyone, therefore never giving his Son a people for whom to be Mediator. Even more, this meant that God could reenter into a covenant of works with humanity like he did with Adam in the Garden; and we know how that turned out! In the background to this rejection, as with most of

---

[2] On this, see Belgic Confession of Faith, art. 27 and Heidelberg Catechism, Q&A 54.

the canons, is the developing doctrine of the intra-Trinitarian covenant be-tween Father, Son, and Holy Spirit in which predestination, redemption, and application are all linked.[3]

Like rejection 1, the synod said of this error: **this is repugnant to Scripture**, especially pointing out the teaching of the death of Christ as priest in the Epistle to the Hebrews. **Christ has become the Surety** (*sponsorem*; sponsor, guarantee) **and Mediator of a better, that is, the new covenant** according to Hebrews 7:22 and 9:15. The verb in 7:22 that Jesus "has become" (γέγονεν) is perfect active indicative, meaning in this context, Jesus became and continues to be **Surety and Mediator of…the new covenant**. In 9:15 the author uses the present tense of "to be" (ἐστίν) to say this is what he is.

According to Hebrews 9:17 **a testament is of force where death has occurred**. In other words, because Jesus died and is alive, the old cov-enant is ended and a new has been inaugurated.

Rejection of Errors 3

That Christ by His satisfaction merited neither salvation itself for anyone, nor faith, whereby this satisfaction of Christ unto salvation is effectually appropriated; but that He merited for the Father only the authority or the perfect will to deal again with man, and to prescribe new conditions as He might desire, obedience to which, however, depended on the free will of man, so that it therefore might have come to pass that either none or all should fulfill these conditions.

For these adjudge too contemptuously of the death of Christ, do in no wise acknowledge the most important fruit or benefit thereby gained, and bring again out of hell the Pelagian error.

The next rejection continued on the same **issue** *that Christ by His satisfaction merited* (*meruisse*) *neither salvation itself for anyone, nor faith, whereby this satisfaction of Christ unto salvation is effectually appropriated*. In other words, there is no one in particular for whom Jesus accomplished redemption or the faith to apply redemption. Instead, the Remonstrants taught that Jesus *merited* (*acquisivisse*; acquired) *for the Fa-*

---

[3] On this, see Richard A. Muller, "Toward the *Pactum Salutis*: Locating the Origins of a Concept," *Mid-America Journal of Theology* 18 (2007): 11–65.

ther only the authority or the perfect will to deal again with man, and to prescribe new conditions as He might desire, obedience to which, however, depended on the free will of man (*libero hominis arbitrio*). This vision of the cross is that it removed all the obstacles in the way so that God is able to set up a scenario in which he can forgive sinners. But notice the result of this teaching: *so that it therefore might have come to pass that either none or all should fulfill these conditions.* Everything is contingent and dependent on the exercise of man's unbounded free will.

The Remonstrants **adjudge too contemptuously of the death of Christ**. How could the death of the Son of God himself accomplish nothing particular for particular people? Those particular things are mentioned next when the rejection says the Remonstrants **do in no wise acknowledge the most important fruit or benefit thereby gained**. The benefit is the application of redemption. Finally, the seriousness of the issue was put in ancient terms: they **bring again out of hell the Pelagian error**—unbounded free will.

Rejection of Errors 4

That the new covenant of grace, which God the Father, through the mediation of the death of Christ, made with man, does not herein consist that we by faith, inasmuch as it accepts the merits of Christ, are justified before God and saved, but in the fact that God having revoked the demand of perfect obedience of faith, regards faith itself and the obedience of faith, although imperfect, as the perfect obedience of the law, and does esteem it worthy of the reward of eternal life through grace.

For these contradict the Scriptures: "Being justified freely by His grace through the redemption that is in Christ Jesus: whom God hath set forth to be a propitiation through faith in His blood" (Rom. 3:24–25). And these proclaim, as did the wicked Socinus, a new and strange justification of man before God against the consensus of the whole church.

The fourth rejection continues the discussion of *the new covenant of grace, which God the Father, through the mediation of the death of Christ, made with man, does not herein consist that we by faith, inasmuch as it accepts the merits of Christ, are justified before God and saved.* This was what the Reformation was all about: justification before God on the basis of Christ's merits received by faith. Gomarus's perception into the result of Arminius's error had come to fruition. Instead, the Remonstrant position was *but in the fact that God having revoked the de-*

mand of perfect obedience of faith, regards faith itself and the obedience of faith, although imperfect, as the perfect obedience of the law, and does esteem it worthy of the reward of eternal life through grace. Remember the Remonstrants taught that Christ's death opened the way for God to enter into a covenant with humanity either as a covenant of grace or of works (rejection 2) and that Christ's death allowed God to set up new conditions of salvation (rejection 3). What they taught was a lessened covenant of works in which the necessity of perfect obedience to a holy God was substituted with faith and imperfect obedience. Instead of crediting to our account Christ's perfect righteousness received through faith, faith itself and imperfect obedience were counted as if they were the perfect obedience God required. There is no good news in this system.

In contrast, the Synod of Dort reminded its readers that this **contradict[s] the Scriptures** in clear passages like Romans 3:24–25: **"Being justified freely by His grace through the redemption that is in Christ Jesus: whom God hath set forth to be a propitiation through faith in His blood."** Justification is a free act of God's grace. Its basis is Christ's work of redemption alone. Its means is faith alone in the blood of Christ. The *Dutch Annotations* offered a pristine explanation of the Reformed doctrine of justification from this text utilizing the categories of causation:

> From hence forward the Apostle describes all the causes, and properties of the justification of faith, which is revealed to us in the Gospel. The supreme cause therefore is the undeserved grace of God, the moving and meritorious cause, is the reconciliation and redemption made by Christ; the means whereby that is imputed to us, is faith in Christ's blood; the end is the showing forth of God's righteousness and the forgiveness of sins.[4]

The Dortian fathers called the Remonstrant denial of this for what it was: **these proclaim, as did the wicked Socinus, a new and strange justification of man before God against the consensus of the whole church.** Remonstrantism/Arminianism was understood to be just a newfangled way of introducing Socinianism into the church. Socinianism taught that in the old covenant God required obedience to the law but now he requires faith. Because all that was needed was sincere faith and obedience,

---

[4] *Dutch Annotations* on Romans 3:24–25.

Jesus was the supreme example of godliness; but that's all he could be. He did not die in the place of anyone since all anyone had to do was trust and obey.[5]

Rejection of Errors 5

That all men have been accepted unto the state of reconciliation and unto the grace of the covenant, so that no one is worthy of condemnation on account of original sin, and that no one shall be condemned because of it, but that all are free from the guilt of original sin.

For this opinion is repugnant to Scripture which teaches that we are by nature children of wrath (Eph. 2:3).

Rejection 5 deals with another aspect of Remonstrant covenant theology. Because they failed to make distinctions in how Jesus' death was sufficient for all and efficacious for some, they taught *all people (homines) have been accepted unto the state of reconciliation and unto the grace of the covenant.* Remember how they said in the original 1610 *Remonstrance* that Jesus dies for everyone in precisely the same way. One way at least some Remonstrants applied that language was to say everyone is received into a status of reconciliation and the covenant of grace. Because of this *no one is worthy of condemnation on account of original sin, and that no one shall be condemned because of it, but that all are free from the guilt of original sin.* We find this in Arminius himself who said Jesus not only wiped away original sin and obtained for every man reconciliation and redemption, but that no one is condemned by original sin, "because God has assumed the whole human race into the grace of reconciliation, and has entered into a covenant of grace with Adam and his whole posterity in him."[6] One consequence of this Remonstrant teaching relates back to canon 1.17, which we saw spoke of the salvation of infants of believers while being silent on the issue of infants of unbelievers. The Remonstrant teaching cited here in rejection 5 would mean all infants, even those born to unbelieving parents, who die are *accepted unto the state of reconciliation and*

---

[5] See "Reformed Thought on the Extent of the Atonement to 1618," 144–45.

[6] *Examen Libelli Perkinsiani de Praedestinationis Ordine et Modo*, in *Opera Theologicia* (Leiden: Godefridus Basson, 1629), 745; *Apologia…Arminii adversus Articulos*, in *Opera Theologica*, 153, 154.

unto the grace of the covenant. Why? *All people* would include infants. Even more, original sin condemns no one.

The issue with **this opinion** is that it **is repugnant to Scripture which teaches that we are by nature children of wrath,** citing Ephesians 2:3. The meaning of this text is that "from our birth, or, even from our mother's womb…[we are] subject to the wrath of God by reason of sin, in which we were born" (Eph. 2:3).[7]

Rejection of Errors 6

The use of the difference between meriting and appropriating, to the end that they may instill into the minds of the imprudent and inexperienced this teaching that God, as far as He is concerned, has been minded of applying to all equally the benefits gained by the death of Christ; but that, while some obtain the pardon of sin and eternal life, and others do not, this difference depends on their own free will, which joins itself to the grace that is offered without exception, and that it is not dependent on the special gift of mercy, which powerfully works in them, that they rather than others should appropriate unto themselves this grace.

For these, while they feign that they present this distinction in a sound sense, seek to instill into the people the destructive poison of the Pelagian errors.

Some Remonstrants, though, did make fine theological distinctions about the death of Jesus. One of the most important was *between meriting and appropriating* (*impetrationis et applicationis*). We've seen this already, and it corresponds to what we call redemption accomplished and applied. The Remonstrants used this distinction *to the end that they may instill into the minds of the imprudent and inexperienced this teaching that God, as far as He is concerned, has been minded of applying to all equally the benefits gained by the death of Christ.* While the Reformed taught that by his death Jesus purchased both redemption accomplished and applied, the Remonstrants severed this relationship and taught that Jesus only purchased redemption accomplished. What about redemption applied? *While some obtain the pardon of sin and eternal life, and others do not, this difference depends on their own free will, which joins itself to the grace that is offered without exception.* Again, free will was key for the Remonstrants. A person's free will determined whether or not redemp-

---

[7] *Dutch Annotations* on Ephesians 2:3.

tion applied would be theirs. It was *not dependent on the special gift of mercy, which powerfully works in them, that they rather than others should appropriate unto themselves this grace.*

In response, the synod allowed for an orthodox understanding of this distinction between impetration and application: **while they feign** (pretend) **that they present this distinction in a sound sense** [the Remonstrants] **seek to instill into the people** *the destructive poison of the Pelagian errors (perniciosum Pelagianismi venenum)*. Again, free will was the determinative factor.

Rejection of Errors 7

That Christ neither could die, needed to die, nor did die for those whom God loved in the highest degree and elected to eternal life, and did not die for these, since these do not need the death of Christ.

For they contradict the apostle, who declares: "the Son of God, who loved me, and gave Himself for me" (Gal. 2:20). Likewise: "Who shall lay any thing to the charge of God's elect? It is God that justifieth. Who is he that condemneth? It is Christ that died" (Rom. 8:33–34), namely, for them; and the Savior who says: "I lay down My life for the sheep" (John 10:15). And: "This is My commandment, That ye love one another, as I have loved you. Greater love hath no man than this, that a man lay down his life for his friends" (John 15:12–13).

The final rejection on this second point should sound shocking to our sensibilities if we hold dear the Word of God: *that Christ neither could die, needed to die, nor did die for those whom God loved in the highest degree and elected to eternal life, and did not die for these, since these do not need the death of Christ.* Jesus couldn't nor didn't die for those God loved and elected since already-elect people do not need his death. After the synod, Episcopius wrote a Confession in 1621 that said, "Those who are predestined unto Life, have no need of any such Expiation."[8]

This was in direct **contradict**[ion] to **the apostle** and **the Savior**. One of Paul's most memorable saying is **"the Son of God, who loved me,**

---

[8] Simon Episcopius, *The Confession or Declaration of the…Remonstrants* (London, 1676), 136–37. Cited in Gatiss, *For Us and for Our Salvation*, 88. On this, see *Synopsis Purioris Theologiae: Volume 2*, 105–7, 203–5.

and gave Himself for me" (Gal. 2:20). He did die for elect people. Again, in one of Paul's more rhetorically comforting sayings he said, "Who shall lay any thing to the charge of God's elect? It is God that justifieth. Who is he that condemneth? It is Christ that died" (Rom. 8:33–34). Note the connection between God's choosing and Christ's dying. Jesus says it like this: "I lay down My life for the sheep" (John 10:15) and "This is My commandment, That ye love one another, as I have loved you. Greater love hath no man than this, that a man lay down his life for his friends" (John 15:12–13). Jesus not only could and would die, he had to die for elect sinners to bring them to saving faith in himself.

THE GRACE OF REGENERATION

V:

WHAT WE CONFESS

ARTICLES 1-17

THE REMONSTRANT DOCTRINE

ONE OF THE issues with the narrative that "TULIP" accurately summa-rizes what happened at the Synod of Dort is the first letter, "T." The Re-formed asserted "total depravity" because the Remonstrants didn't believe humanity was that bad, right? Going back to the original *Remonstrance* of 1610, we read the following in article 3 on the doctrine of man's will:

> That man does not have saving faith of himself nor by the power of his own free will, since he in the state of apostasy and sin can not of and through himself think, will or do any good which is truly good (such as is especially saving faith); but that it is necessary that he be regenerated by God, in Christ, through his Holy Spirit, and renewed in understanding, affections or will, and all powers, in order that he may rightly understand, meditate upon, will, and perform that which is truly good, according to the word of Christ, John 15:5: "Without me ye can do nothing."[1]

Every human is in a state of unbelief and sin therefore cannot think, will, or do any saving good including faith. This is why we must be born again. What's wrong with this? Nothing. Paraeus said it "needs not much

---

[1] As cited in "The *Remonstrance* of 1610," appendix C in De Jong, *Crisis in the Reformed Churches*, 208.

examination: if wee follow the naturall sense of the words" that are "consentaneous [in agreement with] Holy Writ."[2] In fact, as we'll see below, it sounds similar to the actual canons themselves in article 3. Maybe the Reformed taught the big "T" version of total depravity and the Remonstrants taught the little "t" version? Something's off in popular conceptions of Dort. Because of the third Remonstrant point, the canons confess two articles of common Christian convictions on sin then give a definition of sin in article 3.

You may have noticed as well that the canons have a third *and* fourth point of doctrine. The reason for this is that the third Remonstrant article wasn't the issue, nor was the first part of article 4:

> That this grace of God [mentioned in article 3 that enables to saving good] is the commencement, progression, and completion of all good, also in so far that regenerate man cannot, apart from this prevenient or assisting, awakening, consequent and cooperating grace, think, will or do the good or resist any temptations to evil; so that all good works or activities which can be conceived must be ascribed to the grace of God in Christ.[3]

Some of the synod delegates even noticed this as the articles of the *Remonstrance* sounded more orthodox than the doctrine the Remonstrants defended in their writings.[4]

THE ISSUE

What was the issue? "There is poyson in the taile," to use the image of Paraeus;[5] meaning, it's the second part of article 4: "But with respect to the mode of this grace, it is not irresistible, since it is written concerning many that they have resisted the Holy Spirit. Acts 7 and elsewhere in many places."[6] It was King James who said the Remonstrant articles "were perhaps

---

[2] Paraeus, "Epitome of Arminianisme," 832.

[3] As cited in "The *Remonstrance* of 1610," appendix C in De Jong, *Crisis in the Reformed Churches*, 208–9.

[4] Goudriaan, "The Synod of Dordt on Arminian Anthropology," 85.

[5] Paraeus, "Epitome of Arminianisme," 832.

[6] As cited in "The *Remonstrance* of 1610," appendix C in De Jong, *Crisis in the Reformed Churches*, 208–9.

not greatly to be misliked: but…they were expressed with cunning and art to make a specious shew…the articles served but for a bait to swallow doctrine, which was of more danger than the articles would pretend."[7] A part of that cunning was the phrase "irresistible grace." Paraeus called it "horrid and barbarous" and that "our orthodox men…acknowledge not this barbarous and ambiguous terme."[8] In fact, as we'll see below, there is a sense in which we affirm grace *is* resistible as well as irresistible.

In the words of Richard Muller, it's in the fourth Remonstrant article that "this insistence on prevenient grace is drawn into relation with the synergism of the first two articles."[9] Recall that the *Remonstrance* said God predestines on the basis of foreseen faith (article 1) and Jesus died to impetrate (accomplish) redemption for everyone in the same way but the application of its benefits was left to free will and thus only some receive it (article 2). The emphasis was on the human will. When article 3 mentions faith, it denies that it arises from the power of human free will; but this has to be interpreted in light of article 4 and its insistence on "prevenient grace" (*gratia praeveniens*). This was the grace that "comes before" a human's response to God. The Reformed would agree that God's grace "comes before" sinful man's response. The issue is that the Remonstrants taught that its mode or way of working was to be a resistible grace. In other words, yes God's grace comes before the overall work of conversion and specifically regeneration and even the good works of the converted and regenerated, but, it's only effective when the free will of the sinner cooperates with it; if a person rejects it, it does not work.[10]

This issue in terms of the relationship between sin and the particular work of God's grace in regeneration and the confusion among so many Christians is still among us. Let me illustrate from the words of Chuck Smith again, the founder of the Calvary Chapel movement so prominent where I minister in Southern California. In seeking to define terms and place Calvary Chapel in the ecclesiastical landscape, Smith said in his short

---

[7] Milton, *The British Delegation and the Synod of Dort*, 21n59.

[8] Paraeus, "Epitome of Arminianisme," 832, 833.

[9] Muller, "Arminius and Arminianism," 34–35. On the issues of theological anthropology at Dort, see Goudriaan, "The Synod of Dordt on Arminian Anthropology," 81–106.

[10] On prevenient grace, see Muller, "gratia praeveniens," in *Dictionary of Latin and Greek Theological Terms*, 144.

writing *Calvinism, Arminianism, and the Word of God* the following. Defining Arminianism, Smith said, "Arminius believed that the fall of man was not total, maintaining that there was enough good left in man for him to will to accept Jesus Christ unto salvation."[11] But article 3 of the *Remonstrance* above said that "man does not have saving faith of himself nor by the power of his own free will," and article 4 said all saving good was because of prevenient grace, which is his grace that goes before any human action. Defining Calvinism, Smith said, "The Calvinists believed that man is in absolute bondage to sin and Satan, unable to exercise his own will to trust in Jesus Christ without the help of God."[12] But the Remonstrants would've agreed with this statement too, as we've seen. The point in all this is to say there is so much confusion popularly speaking among Christians, which I believe is rooted in not reading the public confessions of the Reformed churches but instead relying on individual theologians' writings.[13] We'll see this later, but at the time of the synod the delegates made this exhortation:

> Judge of the faith of the Reformed Churches not from the calumnies, which on every side are heaped upon it; nor from the private expressions of a few among ancient and modern teachers, often dishonestly quoted or corrupted and wrested to a meaning quite foreign to their intention; but from the public confessions of the Churches themselves.

HISTORICAL BACKGROUND

Augustine versus Pelagius

We've already mentioned the debate in the Western church between Augustine and Pelagius in terms of the grace of God in predestination. Let me return to that debate as it relates to human nature, sin, and God's grace. J. N. D. Kelly summarized the patristic teaching through the fourth century as "revealing the firm hold which...Christians had on the truth of man's fallen

---

[11] Chuck Smith, *Calvinism, Arminianism, and the Word of God: A Calvary Chapel Perspective* (Costa Mesa, CA: Word for Today, 2005), 7.

[12] Smith, *Calvinism, Arminianism, and the Word of God*, 9.

[13] For example, George Bryson never once cites the Canons of Dort in his polemical work *The Five Points of Calvinism*.

condition and consequent need of divine help…[but also] side by side with it, of a dogged belief in free will and responsibility."[14] If Augustine was the representative of the former, Pelagius was the poster child of the latter.[15]

Pelagius was a popular teacher in Rome from 380 onward but had to flee to North Africa in 409 in view of Alaric's invasion. In North Africa, Pelagius was shocked by the pessimistic view of human nature in Augustine's backyard. Emblematic was Augustine's line in his *Confessions*: "Give what you command, and command what you will" (*da quod iubes et iube quod uis*).[16] Augustine recorded Pelagius's response: "Pelagius…could not bear [these words]; and contradicting somewhat too excitedly, nearly came to a quarrel with him who had mentioned them."[17] In contrast, "the keystone of [Pelagius'] whole system is the idea of unconditional free will and responsibility."[18] This meant that even after the Fall, Pelagius "rejects the idea that man's will has any intrinsic bias in favour of wrong-doing."[19] This also meant "he equally resists the suggestion that there can be any special pressure on man's will to choose the good."[20] Grace was necessary in Pelagius's system, but he radically redefined it as the gift of free will itself with its possibility of not sinning, God's will in the law for what we ought to do, and the example of Christ to counteract the evil customs around us.[21]

For Augustine, original sin means we participate in and are held responsible for Adam's sin. This was also the view of his contemporary Ambrose of Milan:

> For death is alike to all, without difference for the poor, without exception for the rich. And so although through the sin of one alone, yet it passed upon all (Rom.

---

[14] J. N. D. Kelly, *Early Christian Doctrines* (1960; rev. ed., New York: HarperSanFrancisco, 1978), 357.

[15] For a summary of what follows, see Hubertus R. Drobner, *The Fathers of the Church: A Comprehensive Introduction*, trans. Siegrief S. Schatzmann (Peabody, MA: Hendrickson, 2007), 404–9.

[16] Augustine, *Confessions: Books 9–13*, ed. and trans. Carolyn J.-B. Hammond, Loeb Classical Library 27 (Cambridge, MA: Harvard University Press, 2016), 10.29.40

[17] Augustine, "On the Gift of Perseverance," ch. 53, *NPNF: First Series*, 5:547.

[18] Kelly, *Early Christian Doctrines*, 357.

[19] Kelly, *Early Christian Doctrines*, 358.

[20] Kelly, *Early Christian Doctrines*, 359.

[21] Kelly, *Early Christian Doctrines*, 359.

5:12); that we may not refuse to acknowledge Him to be also the Author of death, Whom we do not refuse to acknowledge as the Author of our race; and that, as through one death is ours, so should be also the resurrection; and that we should not refuse the misery, that we may attain to the gift. For, as we read, Christ has come to save that which was lost (Luke 19:10) and to be Lord both of the dead and living (Rom. 14:9). In Adam I fell, in Adam I was cast out of Paradise, in Adam I died; how shall the Lord call me back, except He find me in Adam; guilty as I was in him, so now justified in Christ.[22]

Kelly summarized the situation like this: "Others before Augustine had stressed our solidarity with Adam, but none had depicted so vividly our complicity with him in his evil willing."[23] This means that while God's image in fallen man is not completely lost, it is horribly marred. We no longer have the freedom not to sin and enjoy the good, but our will is enslaved to our sinful nature. In the words of Kelly, "In the strict sense of free choice (*liberum arbitrium*)…man is always free, that is, he can choose freely the course he will pursue; but since his will acts on motives and certain motives may press irresistibly on it, the range of choices which are 'live options' for him is limited by the sort of man he is."[24]

Council of Carthage

Some of these issues were dealt with at the Council of Carthage in 418. Eight canons or theological rules were decided upon, anathematizing the following views, which I'll summarize below:[25]

1. That whoever says Adam was created mortal so that whether or not he sinned he would have died in body not because of sin, but by natural necessity.

---

[22] "On the Death of Satyrus," in *Nicene and Post-Nicene Fathers: Second Series*, Volume 10 (1896; repr., Peabody, MA: Hendrickson, fourth printing 2004), 174–75..

[23] Kelly, *Early Christian Doctrines*, 364.

[24] Kelly, *Early Christian Doctrines*, 367.

[25] For the text, see *Nicene and Post-Nicene Fathers: Second Series*, ed. Philip Schaff and Henry Wace (1900; repr., Peabody, MA: Hendrickson, fourth printing 2004), 14:496–99.

2. That whoever denies that infants should be baptized or says that baptism is for remission of sins although they derive from Adam no original sin, despite what the Catholic Church has always understood about Romans 5:12—that even infants who cannot yet commit sin are baptized for the remission of sins.

3. That whoever says the grace of God that justifies through Christ avails only for the remission of past sins, and not for assistance against sins in the future.4. That whoever says the same grace of God through Christ helps us only in not sinning by opening to our understanding the commandments, so that we may know what to seek, to avoid, and also love to do, but that through it we are not helped so that we are able to do what we know we should do.

5. That whoever says the grace of justification was given to us only that we might be able more readily by grace to perform what we were ordered to do through our free will; although not easily, we could without grace fulfill the divine commandments, although Jesus said, "Without me ye can do nothing."

6. That whoever says, "If we say that we have no sin we deceive ourselves and the truth is not in us," is to be understood as meaning out of humility, we ought to say that we have sin, not because it is really so…despite the apostle going on to say not merely of humility but truly, "If we confess our sins, he is faithful and just to forgive us our sins and to cleanse us from all iniquity."

7. That whoever says, "Forgive us our trespasses" not for themselves, because they have no need, but for other sinners; and whoever says the saints cannot say, "Forgive me my trespasses," but only "Forgive us our trespasses." Yet the apostle James says, "For in many things we offend all"; the Psalm says, "Enter not into judgment with thy servant, O Lord, for in thy sight shall no man living be justified"; Solomon says, "There is no man that sinneth not"; Job says, "He sealeth in the hand of every man, that every man may know his own infirmity"; Daniel says, "We have sinned, we have done iniquity."

8. That whoever says "Forgive us our trespasses" are said by the saints out of humility and not in truth.

Carthage expressed a thoroughly Augustinian view of sin and the necessity and power of grace in the lives of sinners.

Council of Orange

A century later at the Council of Orange in 529, this debate came to its ancient culmination. Knowing what this council said will give us some background to the debate within the Reformed community at the time of the Synod of Dort. Orange's doctrinal position is a list of twenty-five canons and then a conclusion.[26] The first eight canons are rejections of Semi-Pelagian errors that come from the writings of Gennadius of Marseilles (d. 496). Canons 9–25 also reject Semi-Pelagian errors from the writings of Prosper of Aquitaine, who was quoting and summarizing Augustine. The final conclusion comes from Gennadius. The opening Gennadian canons state as follows, with my editorial notes:

> **Canon 1** is an overall rejection of Pelagianism by identifying *the necessity of grace* being that Adam's sin has affected man's body *and* soul; therefore, "the liberty of the soul (*animae libertate*) [did not] remain[...] uninjured."

> **Canon 2** identifies *the necessity of grace* being Adam's sin that has affected all humanity in passing "bodily death, which is the punishment of sin, and...sin also, which is the death of the soul" according to Romans 5:12.

> **Canon 3** identifies *the operation of grace before regeneration preceding every effort* in rejecting the view that grace is conferred as a result of human prayer; instead, prayer proceeds from grace.

> **Canon 4** identifies *the operation of grace before regeneration preceding every effort* in rejecting the view that God awaits our desire to be cleansed from sin; instead, this desire "is put into us by the infusion and operation (*infusionem et operationem*) of the Holy Spirit."

---

[26] On the specific sources of these canons in Augustine, Gennadius, and Prosper, see Hefele, *A History of the Councils: Volume 4*, 155–63; Woods, *Canons of the Second Council of Orange*, 14–49. See Woods for the Latin text with an at times antiquated English rendering.

Canon 5 identifies *the operation of grace before regeneration preceding every effort* in rejecting the view that "the beginning of faith" (*initium fidei*) is not a gift of grace but is implanted in us by nature; instead, the gift of grace is described as "correcting our will (*corrigentem voluntatem nostram*) from infidelity to faith, from impiety to piety."

Canon 6 identifies *the operation of grace before regeneration preceding every effort* in rejecting the view that apart from God's grace he gives us mercy because we believe, will, desire, strive, labor, watch, study, seek, ask, or knock; it also rejects the view that God "puts the help of grace as a supplement to human humility or obedience"; instead, all this proceeds from "the infusion and inspiration (*infusionem et inspirationem*) of the Holy Spirit."

Canon 7 identifies *the operation of grace before regeneration preceding every effort* in rejecting the view that we can rightly think of or choose any good that relates to salvation or assent to the preaching of the gospel through our natural powers; instead, these proceed from "the illumination and inspiration (*illumination et inspiratione*) of the Holy Spirit."

Canon 8 identifies *the operation of grace before regeneration (baptism) preceding every effort* in rejecting the view that some are able to come to the grace of baptism by mercy but others through free choice (*liberum arbitrium*), which we know has been impaired (*vitiatum*) but they say was not weakened (*infirmatum*) enough, enabling man to seek salvation apart from the revelation of God.

The Prosperian canons to follow state the relationship between grace and the human will in the context of the previous anathemas:

Canon 9 identifies *the operation of grace after regeneration (baptism)* in confessing that "the help of God" (*adjutorio Dei*) also called his gift of grace enables us to think rightly, keep ourselves from sin, and do good works.

Canon 10 identifies *the operation of grace after regeneration (baptism)* in confessing that we are to implore "the help of God (*adjutorium Dei*)...that [we] may be able to arrive at a good end, or endure in good works."

Canon 11 identifies *the operation of grace after regeneration (baptism)* in confessing that no one can even make a vow to God had he not received from God the object of his vow.

Canon 12 identifies *the operation of grace before regeneration (baptism) preceding every effort* in confessing that "God loves us for what we shall be by His gift, not for what we are by our own merit."

Canon 13 identifies *the operation of grace in baptism* in confessing that "the restoration of free choice" (*De reparation liberi arbitrii*) that was "weakened" (*infirmatum*) and "lost" (*amissum*) in Adam can only be restored by the one who gave it—Jesus.

Canon 14 identifies *the operation of grace in baptism* in confessing that no miserable person is freed from any misery unless the mercy of God goes before (*praevenitur*).

Canon 15 identifies *the operation of grace in baptism* in confessing that Adam was changed for the worse through his iniquity; but by the grace of God believers are changed for the better.

Canon 16 identifies *the operation of grace after regeneration (baptism)* in confessing that no man may boast of what he has as though it were not a gift.

Canon 17 identifies *the operation of grace after regeneration (baptism)* in confessing that the courage of unbelievers in enduring pain is produced by simple greed, but the courage of Christians by the love of God not by the choice of will (*voluntatis arbitrium*).

Canon 18 identifies *the operation of grace before regeneration (baptism) preceding every effort* in confessing that "grace is not prevented (*praeveniri*; preceded) by any merits" but "grace which is not owed precedes (*praecedit*) to enable [good works] to be done."

Canon 19 identifies *the necessity of grace because of the very condition of being a creature* in confessing that even in the state of integrity, human nature could not preserve itself without the help (*adjuvante*) of its Creator; therefore, if man could not keep salvation without God's help in that state, how does man have the power to be able to restore what he has lost without the grace of God?

Canon 20 identifies *the necessity of grace because of the very condition of being a creature* in confessing that a man can do no good without God. While God does much that is good in a man that the man does not do, a man does nothing good for which God did not give the power to do.

Canon 21 confesses that just as Paul says those who would be justified by the law have fallen from grace in the same way the Pelagians who believe man's natural abilities are God's grace.

Canon 22 confesses that no man has anything of his own but untruth and sin, and if he has any truth or righteousness, it is from the fountain of grace.

Canon 23 confesses that men do their own will not God's will when they do what displeases him; but when they do his will willingly, even that is God's will who has prepared (*praeparatur*) and ordered theirs.

Canon 24 identifies *the operation of grace after regeneration (baptism)* in confessing that the branches on the vine do not give life but receive it.

Canon 25 identifies *the operation of grace after regeneration (baptism)* in confessing that to love God is wholly his gift.

Finally there was a concluding summary of this faith that "we ought by God's mercy both to teach and believe" the following:

1. Through the sin of Adam free choice (*liberum arbitrium*) has been so weakened that we cannot love God as we ought, believe in him, or do good works unless God's grace precedes (*praevenerit*). This was true of the patriarchs before the coming of Christ and is true after of us so that the desire to be baptized comes not from free choice (*libero arbitrio*) but the bounty of Christ.

2. After grace has been received through baptism, all baptized persons by the help and cooperation of Christ (*Christo auxiliante et cooperante*) are able if they desire to labor

faithfully to do all that is necessary to the salvation of their soul. We do not believe that any are foreordained to evil by the power of God.

3. In every good work it is not we who take the initiative (*incipimus*) and then are helped by the mercy of God, but God without any preceding (*praecedentibus*) good works of our own inspires in us both faith and love so that we seek baptism and after baptism to do what is pleasing to him by his help (*adjutorio*).

COMMENTARY

As we turn to the third *and* fourth point of doctrine from the Synod of Dort, we notice its strange enumeration. The reason, again, is that the canons were responding to the five points of the Remonstrants. Their original third point was not disagreeable on its own. It was when it was combined with the fourth point that it became objectionable. This means the outline of the third and fourth points is unique in the canons. The title of this point of doctrine says it's about both humanity's corruption (*de hominis corruptione*) and how humans are converted to God (*conversione ad Deum ejusque modo*). "Conversion" is used as a general concept of being changed from a sinner outside God's fellowship to a child of God in relationship with him. The articles will speak of "regeneration" as a particular aspect of this conversion.

Articles 1–2 open with the common Christian convictions about sin then define sin and the necessity of regeneration as the initial aspect leading to conversion in article 3.

Articles 4–5 return to common Christian convictions about the overall process of conversion before defining it in article 6. Articles 7–17 go on to speak of conversion in general and regeneration in particular.[27] In other words, these articles move from the general (conversion) to the particular (regeneration) work of God's grace in the lives of sinners.

---

[27] This outline is contra Feenstra, who divides this point of doctrine into the total corruption of man (arts. 1–5), the miracle of conversion (arts. 6–12), and the manner of conversion (arts. 13–17). *Unspeakable Comfort*, 97.

Article 1

Man was originally formed after the image of God. His understanding was adorned with a true and saving knowledge of his Creator and of spiritual things; his heart and will were upright; all his affections pure; and the whole man was holy; but revolting from God by the instigation of the devil, and abusing the freedom of his own will, he forfeited these excellent gifts; and on the contrary entailed on himself blindness of mind, horrible darkness, vanity and perverseness of judgment, became wicked, rebellious, and obdurate in heart and will, and impure in his affections.

HUMAN NATURE

"What is man?" This is one of the great rhetorical questions the Word of God answers. Martin Luther King Jr., in his sermon "What Is Man?" said, "Though there is widespread agreement in asking the question, there is fantastic disagreement in answering it."[28] We live in a time when everything is referred to science—there's an experiment or arithmetic that gives an explanation for who we are. This materialistic, atheistic philosophy has led our society to believe that we are here for no ultimate reason, that there is nothing beyond the grave, and that life is all about you. Then we wonder why there are school shootings. We wonder why there is so much corruption in politics. We wonder why we so easily can walk right by or right over the wounded one on the road of life and absolve ourselves of being good Samaritans.

What is man? The Word of God answers that we are both body and soul, made in relation to this world being from the dust as well as made in relation with God having the breath of life breathed into us (Gen. 2). How we understand our creation, fall, and the effects of that fall determine how we understand God's gracious work for us and in us.

Our Creation in the Image of God

In Ephesians 4 the apostle Paul calls believers to be godly. Toward the end of this exhortation he says: "And to be renewed in the spirit of your minds, and to put on the new self, created after the likeness of God in true right-

---

[28] As found at http://mlk-kpp01.stanford.edu/primarydocuments/Vol6/ 11July1954WhatIsMan.pdf (accessed August 9, 2018).

eousness and holiness" (vv. 23–24). We are to become more and more im-age-bearers of God because as he says elsewhere, we are new creatures in Christ: "If anyone is in Christ, he is a new creation" (2 Cor. 5:17). Paul addresses us after the Fall of Adam and after we've become new creatures in the second Adam. To become practically more and more these image-bearers, what must be renewed in us was what originally existed in Adam. Paul's exhortation to re-creation presupposes creation. Let me illustrate. Have you ever seen how an ancient painting, covered in ash, faded out, and scratched almost beyond recognition is restored? You can see what it once looked like first by seeing it as it is now and then after it is brought back. In the same way, we can see what the image of God in Adam was by looking at us before Christ and then seeing what we become after Christ.

Man (*homo*), meaning Adam as the representative human, **was originally formed after the image of God** as article 1 begins echoing the language of Genesis 1:26–27, where we read, "Then God said, 'Let us make man in our image, after our likeness,'" and then again we read, "So God created man in his own image, in the image of God he created him; male and female he created them." This creation is extolled in the Psalms. In Psalm 8 David opens saying, "O LORD, our Lord, how majestic is your name in all the earth! You have set your glory above the heavens" (v. 1). Note the parallel between the Lord's majestic name in the earth and his glory that is above the heavens. That's why he goes on to contemplate: "When I look at your heavens, the work of your fingers, the moon and the stars, which you have set in place, what is man that you are mindful of him, and the son of man that you care for him?" (vv. 3–4). God's glory supersedes the heavens; but he's etched on them with his finger a faint picture for us to see. The majesty of God of just that etching in creation makes David feel small and insignificant. "Yet you have made him a little lower than the heavenly beings and crowned him with glory and honor" (v. 5). God's glory is "above the heavens," yet man is crowned with glory as the image of God. Look at how David goes on to echo the words of Genesis 1:26: "You have given him dominion over the works of your hands; you have put all things under his feet" (v. 6).

What did this image mean for what man was in the Garden? Based on what we are to be in Ephesians 4:24, this meant that Adam was "created after the likeness of God in true righteousness and holiness." Righteousness is conformity to God's law and holiness is moral purity. Turning to Colossians 3:10, you'll see a parallel passage where Paul says we "have put on the new self, which is being renewed in knowledge after the image of its Creator." So righteousness, holiness, and knowledge are the good gifts of God that constitute our souls as remade image-bearers of Jesus Christ and that were what Adam had originally.[29] Thus article 1 says Adam's **understanding was adorned with a true and saving knowledge of his Creator and of spiritual things**—that's Colossians 3:10—**his heart and will were upright** (*justitia*; righteous); **all his affections pure; and** *he was wholly holy* (*totus sanctus fuit*)—that's Ephesians 4:24. This article reflects ancient Christian reflection on the "faculties of the soul": mind, will, and affections.[30] Adam was holy all throughout these aspects that made him human.

What is man? He is body and soul, he is the image of God in creation and to all creation, he is the noble king of creation wearing the crown of God's own glory, and he was made to know God with his mind, serve God with his will, and love God with his affections.

Many years ago a group of chemists sought to figure out the chemical composition of an average human. What they came up with was that we are made up of enough fat to make seven bars of soap, enough iron to make a medium-sized nail, enough sugar to fill a shaker, enough lime to whitewash a chicken coop, enough phosphorus to make 2,200 matches, enough magnesium for a dose of magnesia, enough potassium to explode a toy cannon. At that time they figured out that the average human was worth ninety-nine cents.[31] The Word of God says you are priceless.

Our Degeneration into Sin

In Adam we did not remain on the throne of creation as prince. We see this of course in Genesis 3 and Adam and Eve's, but especially Adam's, **revolting from God by the instigation of the devil** by **the freedom of his own**

---

[29] Goudriaan, "The Synod of Dordt on Arminian Anthropology," 88–89.

[30] On the faculties of the soul, see Muller, "anima," in *Dictionary of Latin and Greek Theological Terms*, 27–29; "facultates animae," ibid., 119; *Post-Reformation Reformed Dogmatics: The Rise and Development of Reformed Orthodoxy, ca. 1520 to ca. 1725*, 4 vols., 2nd ed. (Grand Rapids, MI: Baker Academic, 2003), 1:355–56; Heinrich Heppe, *Reformed Dogmatics*, ed. Ernst Bizer, trans. G. T. Thomson (London: George Allen & Unwin. 1950), 224.

[31] Fosdick, "There Is No Death," in *Successful Christian Living* (New York: Harper & Brothers, 1937), 265–66 as cited in King Jr., "What Is Man?"

will (*libera sua voluntate*).[32] In Ephesians 4 Paul is reflecting on what we call our fallen human condition. Contrast Genesis 1, Psalm 8, and Ephesians 4:23–24 with Ephesians 4:17–22.

According to Paul our minds are filled with "futility" and "darkened in…understanding" because of the Fall (vv. 17, 18). What is this "futility" and "darkened…understanding" about? Knowing the true God. As Paul says elsewhere, "The world did not know God through wisdom" (1 Cor. 1:21). Our lives are "alienated from the life of God" (v. 18). We were made for union and communion with God as his created sons and daughters and friends, but sin alienated us. Why? "Because of the ignorance that is in them" (recall what v. 17 just said) "due to their hardness of heart" (v. 18). The heart is the center of the soul, and it is hard. My boys and I like to whittle sticks into spears. But sometimes after cutting a stick off a tree, I leave it out too long before trying to whittle it. What does you think happens? It gets hardened to the point where you cannot shave off any of it. That's us in our alienation from God! Thus Paul continues to say, "They have become callous and have given themselves up to sensuality, greedy to practice every kind of impurity" (v. 19).

What a contrast from our creation to our degeneration! What is true of us goes all the way back to our first father Adam. By his fall **he forfeited these excellent gifts**. Going all the way to Peter Lombard's *Sentences*, the canons reflect the maxim that "by [Adam's] sin, natural goods became corrupt in man and the goods of grace were taken away."[33] This article reflects the commonly held distinction between humanity in its fourfold state. As it relates to the gifts of God endowed upon the faculties of man's soul, it goes like this:

- *State of innocence*: **gifts received**

- *State of misery*: **gifts lost**

- *State of grace*: **gifts renewed**

- *State of glory*: **gifts perfected**

---

[32] On the devil's instigation, see *Synopsis Purioris Theologiae: Volume 1*, 343–49.

[33] Peter Lombard, *The Sentences, Book 2: On Creation*, trans. Giulio Silano, Mediaeval Sources in Translation 43 (Toronto: Pontifical Institute of Mediaeval Studies, 2008), 25.7.1 (p. 119).

These gifts are related from the state of innocence to that of misery in article 1. In accord with the Second Council of Orange (529), Adam's sin has affected the whole person of the whole human race, body and soul (canon 1). His **understanding** (*in mente*; in mind) originally had **a true and saving knowledge of his Creator and of spiritual things**, but by his sin the gifts of God were removed and in their place his mind was filled with **blindness of mind, horrible darkness, vanity and perverseness of judgment**. His **heart and will** originally were **upright** or had *righteousness* (*justita*), but by his sin the gifts of God were removed and in their place his heart and will became **wicked, rebellious, and obdurate** (*duritiem*; hardness). His **affections** (*affectibus*; deep-rooted desires) originally were **pure**, but by his sin the gifts of God were removed and in their place his affections became **impure**. In other words, God created humanity in Adam like a pure gold coin that shone with a beautiful luster. But them that gold coin fell into the mud and began to be oxidized, stained, and tainted.[34] As we'll see below, it was the relation of the damage of the Fall to the will that was "the most profound contrast" between Remonstrant and orthodox Reformed.[35]

But this is not the end of the story. The answer to the question, "What is man?" begins with creation but doesn't end with degeneration. There is the good news of regeneration and ultimately glorification. That regeneration or renewal comes to sinners like us because of the work of Jesus Christ alone through the operation of the Holy Spirit in our lives. "In Jesus," Paul says, "the truth" is found (Eph. 4:20)—the truth of who you were originally, who you are naturally, and who you can become graciously.

Article 2

Man after the fall begat children in his own likeness. A corrupt stock produced a corrupt offspring. Hence all the posterity of Adam, Christ only excepted, have derived corruption from their original parent, not by imitation, as the Pelagians of old asserted, but by the propagation of a vicious nature.

---

[34] On Adam's creation and Fall as presented here as well as in all the Three Forms of Unity in relation to the later nomenclature of "covenant of works," see J. Mark Beach, "Some Observations about the *Three Forms of Unity* and the Doctrine of the Covenant of Works." *Mid-America Journal of Theology* 21 (2010): 103–19.

[35] Goudriaan, "The Synod of Dordt on Arminian Anthropology," 94.

THE FALL

"How bad is it?" Have you ever asked that question? I can recall my fair share of times getting injured playing basketball, wanting to know how bad off I was. This is a question we need to answer spiritually as well. It's such a central question to ask today in the church. We all know the visible church has a lot of problems. Studies have shown between 60 and 80 percent of American evangelical teens leave the faith within their first year of college.[36] We feel like we're losing influence. The remedy is often to add more exciting programs or spend more on more marketing. These examples offer only surface-level solutions to surface-level problems. What the church really needs to get is that the true problem inside as well as outside is sin. Our lack of understanding about how bad sin is and how bad it has made us plagues us. This is the second common Christian conviction offered by our canons.

Sin's Origin

It's bad because of sin's origin.[37] As article 1 outlined Genesis 1–3, God created Adam and Eve in his image to reflect his glory in creation; but instead they reflected the inglorious image of Satan. **After the fall** article 2 goes on to say **man** (*homo*) or Adam...**begat** (*gave birth to* in more common parlance) **children in his own likeness.** We see this in the narrative of Genesis 5 whereas God made man in his likeness (v. 1; cf. 1:26–27), Adam's descendant Seth was born in the likeness of his father (v. 3). This meant that he, too, was an image-bearer of Satan in sin.[38] Like father, like son. **A corrupt stock produced corrupt offspring.** In scientific terms, just like a father's and mother's DNA is passed on to their children, so too sin was the spiritual DNA Adam and Eve passed on to their children. Thus we speak of "original sin" according to Rivetus "because either it exists in each

---

[36]   https://www.campusrenewal.org/wp-content/uploads/2016/09/Campus-Renewal-Campus-Link-Grant-Proposal.pdf (accessed October 2, 2018).

[37] On original sin, see *Synopsis Purioris Theologiae: Volume 1*, 350–83.

[38] On this idea, see Caspar Olevianus, *A Firm Foundation: An Aid for Interpreting the Heidelberg Catechism*, trans. and ed. Lyle D. Bierma (Grand Rapids, MI: Baker Books, 1995), 51; *An Exposition of the Apostles' Creed*, trans. Lyle D. Bierma, Classic Reformed Theology (Grand Rapids, MI: Reformation Heritage Books, 2009), 68.

and everyone from birth, that is, from the very moment of conception, or because it derives from the first origin, that is, from the first parent."[39]

Why is this so important? Imagine going to your doctor and saying that you aren't feeling well. In treating you, your doctor cannot know what remedy to prescribe until it is known what your problem is and where it is coming from. If you just show up and your doctor prescribes open heart surgery when you only have a sore throat, that's not an effective or wise treatment! In the same way, we cannot know what to do with our sins until we first know their origin.

In Romans 5:12 Paul says "just as sin came into the world through one man"—and we saw this in Genesis 3—"and death through sin, and so death spread to all men because all sinned." "Because all sinned" is the key phrase. Is Paul saying death spreads to us all because we have sinned personally, or is he saying that death spreads to us all because Adam sinned for us? That's the question. Notice how the rest of verses 13–14 help answer this. He goes on to say, "For sin indeed was in the world before the law was given" (Rom. 5:13), meaning, the law at Mount Sinai in Moses' day. Then he adds the theological truth: "but sin is not counted where there is no law" (Rom. 5:13) Without the law declaring what is right and wrong and what the punishment for disobedience is, there is no sin. But there's a problem. There was a law before the Fall with Adam, but after the Fall in the time between Adam and Moses there was no publicly stated law. But look at what Paul says: "Yet death reigned from Adam to Moses, even over those whose sinning was not like the transgression of Adam" (Rom. 5:14). How could death reign over all humanity when all humanity did not sin like Adam? The answer is the origin of our sin: Adam's original sin. And his one sin was that bad that we are all sinners because of it and liable to death.

Sin's Corruption

That one sin affects us not only because our status is "sinner" but also because it infects us with the virus of sin. Notice secondly, *sin's corruption.* Remember, what Adam did as the representative of the whole human race continues to have eternal consequences upon us so many millennia afterward. Article 2 states it like this: **Hence all the posterity of Adam, Christ only excepted, have derived corruption from their original parent, not**

---

[39] *Synopsis Purioris Theologiae: Volume 1,* 357.

by imitation, as the Pelagians of old asserted, but by the propagation of a vicious nature.

That's a big sentence so let me explain. There have only been two sinless men. Adam was created without sin and Jesus was conceived without sin. All the rest of us receive our first parent's sinful DNA as I mentioned. As the intro above also states, this led to a debate in the fourth and fifth centuries between Augustine and Pelagius. Pelagius said everyone is conceived sinless and that we learn to sin **by imitation** as we see the bad examples of our parents, our siblings, and those around us. On the contrary, with Augustine, the church confessed at the Council of Carthage (418) that we are born sinful (canon 2). The Second Council of Orange (529) condemned the view that sin is not passed through Adam to the whole human race contra Romans 5:12 (canon 2).

To put it another way, let me ask you to think about this proverbial question: Are you sinful because you sin or do you sin because you are sinful? What would Pelagius say? He would say we're sinful because we sin. What would Augustine say? He would say we sin because we're sinful. The original sin or **corruption** of Adam is passed down to us **by the propagation of a vicious nature.**

Article 3

Therefore all men are conceived in sin, and by nature children of wrath, incapable of saving good, prone to evil, dead in sin, and in bondage thereto, and without the regenerating grace of the Holy Spirit, they are neither able nor willing to return to God, to reform the depravity of their nature, or to dispose themselves to reformation.

SIN DEFINED

Article 3 goes on to give us the definition of sin and what it means to be a sinner. The sin of Adam is so bad that it has also destroyed our spiritual abilities. In other words, we inherit from him depravity and inability. How bad is it, as I asked above? Article 3 summarizes how bad it is to be a sinner the following plethora of Scripture:

Therefore all *people* (*homines*) are conceived in sin. This is Psalm 51:5. It means even the cutest, most "innocent" looking baby in your family is by nature a viper in a diaper! **Therefore all *people* are...by nature chil-**

dren of wrath. This is Ephesians 2:3. In the movie *Willy Wonka and the Chocolate Factory*, the protagonist Willy Wonka possesses golden geese that lay the delicacy of golden chocolate eggs. The way he determines if they are good or bad eggs is to put them on sort of a magical scale. If they are good, they go down a chute for packaging. But if they are bad, well, to the incinerator they go! We are by nature bad eggs deserving of hellfire. **Therefore all *people* are...incapable of saving good.** This is Romans 3:10–12. Why are we incapable of *saving* good—notice that we're not saying unbelievers cannot do "good" things as we measure them, but nothing good in the eyes of God that would save them. The reason is as Paul says: "None is righteous, no, not one; no one understands; no one seeks for God. All have turned aside; together they have become worthless; no one does good, not even one." **Therefore all *people* are...prone to evil.** This is Romans 7:14–20. The evil I don't want to do, I do; the good I want to do, I don't. Why? Because of the struggle within me in this age between my natural sin nature and my supernatural new nature. **Therefore all *people* are...dead in sin.** This is Ephesians 2:3. What does this mean? Imagine a skeleton lying on the ground with a person hovering over it trying to bring it back to life with chest thrusts and mouth-to-mouth resuscitation. It's a ridiculous image, isn't it? **Therefore all *people* are...in bondage** [to sin]. This is John 8:34. Not only were they Jesus' words but they were also the inspiration for Martin Luther's greatest work, *The Bondage of the Will.*

How bad is it? This bad! So bad, in fact, that the definition in article 3 concludes with this line: **without the regenerating** (*regenerantis*) **grace of the Holy Spirit, they are neither able nor willing to return to God, to reform the depravity of their nature, or to dispose themselves to reformation.** While the overall heading to this point of doctrine concerns our "conversion to God" (*Conversione ad Deum*), article 3 introduces us to regeneration as the initial work of God's grace that leads to the conversion of our lives. This is consistent with the shift in emphasis from the sixteenth to the seventeenth centuries when regeneration went from being used for the whole process of sanctification to the initial giving of life.[40] G. C. Berkouwer described this sixteenth-century use as "relat[ing] the totality of human life to divine grace, and therefore our fathers tried, in their termi-

---

[40] For helpful summaries of this transition, see Henry Beets, *The Reformed Confession Explained* (Grand Rapids, MI: Eerdmans, 1929), 186–88; Berkhof, *Systematic Theology*, 466–68.

nology of faith, rebirth, and new creation to indicate the deep-rootedness and priority of grace, thus to exclude, a la John Calvin, any hint of a meritorious transaction."[41] For example, the 1561 Belgic Confession of Faith says:

> We believe that this true faith, being wrought in man by the hearing of the Word of God and the operation of the Holy Spirit, regenerates him and makes him a new man, causing him to live a new life, and freeing him from the bondage of sin. (Art. 24)[42]

Zacharias Ursinus (1534–1583) described the double benefit accomplished by Jesus Christ as justification and *regeneration* while Calvin spoke of regeneration as the restoration into the image of God, which "does not take place in one moment or one day or one year; but through continual and sometimes even slow advances."[43]

Therefore, article 3's language of **without the regenerating grace of the Holy Spirit** sounds like Jesus' words to Nicodemus (John 3). Apart from the grace of the Holy Spirit, Paul says in Romans 3:10–12, "None is righteous, no, not one." Apart from the grace of the Holy Spirit "no one understands." Understands what? The things of the Spirit of God. Apart from the grace of the Holy Spirit "no one seeks for God." This is the most damning accusation Paul gives! Apart from the grace of the Holy Spirit "all have turned aside; together they have become worthless." Apart from the grace of the Holy Spirit "no one does good, not even one." Apart from the grace of the Holy Spirit "their throat is an open grave; they use their tongues to deceive. The venom of asps is under their lips. Their mouth is full of curses and bitterness. Their feet are swift to shed blood; in their paths are ruin and misery, and the way of peace they have not known." Apart from the grace of the Holy Spirit "there is no fear of God before their eyes." At the Second Council of Orange in 529 it was confessed that that necessity of grace was rooted in our very human condition as created.

---

[41] G. C. Berkouwer, *Faith and Sanctification*, trans. John Vriend, Studies in Dogmatics (1952; Grand Rapids, MI: Eerdmans, fifth printing 1972), 94–95.

[42] Compare one of the sources of the Belgic Confession: the French Confession, which says, "We believe that by this faith we are *regenerated* in newness of life, being by nature subject to sin" (art. 22).

[43] Zacharias Ursinus, *The Commentary of Dr. Zacharias Ursinus on the Heidelberg Catechism*, trans. G. W. Williard (1852; repr., Phillipsburg, NJ: P&R), 466; Calvin, *Institutes*, 3.11.1; 3.3.9.

Even then, human nature could not save itself without the assistance of the Creator. Canon 19 then asked the question: "How without the grace of God will [human nature] have the power of restoring what it has lost?"[44] All of this is vital as it sets up the key difference between the Remonstrant and orthodox Reformed views of the freedom of the will. The Remonstrants believed that even after the Fall, human beings' wills have a freedom of in-difference (*equilibrium*) in which the will is neutral between good and evil and can be persuaded either to one side or the other. For the Reformed, the fallen will still contains freedom of spontaneity, that is, the will is free; the difference is that sin has so affected the will that it is inclined to evil and no saving good. This is why the article states ***without*** **the regenerating (***regenerantis***) grace of the Holy Spirit, they are neither able nor willing to return to God, to reform the depravity of their nature, or to dispose themselves to reformation.**

How bad was it for you before the regenerating grace of the Holy Spirit invaded your life? How bad is it now for the world that is still outside of Jesus Christ? This bad! But the good news is the gracious, miraculous, stupendous power of the Holy Spirit to take lifeless bones and to re-create them, to resurrect them, to renew them, to restore them, and to revive them. Your sin's origin, corruption, and destruction is the problem; the remedy is the Holy Spirit. Cry out for him to give this life to the world! Praise him for giving it to you!

Article 4

There remain, however, in man since the fall, the glimmerings of natural light, whereby he retains some knowledge of God, of natural things, and of the differences between good and evil; and discovers some regard for virtue, good order in society, and for maintaining an orderly external deportment. But so far is this light of nature from being sufficient to bring him to a saving knowledge of God and to true conversion, that he is incapable of using it aright even in things natural and civil. Nay, further, this light, such as it is, man in various ways renders wholly polluted and holds it in unrighteousness, by doing which he becomes inexcusable before God.

As mentioned above, since article 3 of the *Remonstrance* was unobjectionable by itself, the canons' corresponding articles give common Christian

---

[44] Woods, *Canons of the Second Council of Orange*, 37.

convictions (arts. 1–2) and a definition of sin (art. 3), but do not go on to elaborate on the doctrine of sin per se. It's when *Remonstrance* article 3 was read in light of article 4, as Paraeus perceptively saw, that the problems with the Remonstrants' doctrine began to manifest. Thus we return to common Christian convictions about conversion in articles 4–5, which will lead to the more particular discussion of regeneration in the articles to follow.

THE LIGHT OF NATURE

Related to the first three articles above, article 4 affirms that fallen man is still man. The substance or faculties of the mind, will, and affections we were given at creation still exists after the Fall, although the accidents or habits have changed.[45] As it relates to our minds, article 4 says **humanity** (*homine*) still **retains some knowledge of God**. As Paul says,

> For what can be known about God is plain to them, because God has shown it to them. For his invisible attributes, namely, his eternal power and divine nature, have been clearly perceived, ever since the creation of the world, in the things that have been made. (Rom. 1:19–20)

Humanity still **retains some knowledge of...natural things**. Humanity still **retains some knowledge of...the differences between good and evil**. "They know God's righteous decree that those who practice such things deserve to die" (Rom. 1:32). Because of this, article 4 even says fallen and unregenerate humanity **discovers some regard for virtue, good order in society, and for maintaining an orderly external deportment**. The "Gentiles, who did not have the law [in the form of the Ten Commandments in stone] by nature do what the law requires...show that the work of the law is written on their hearts" (Rom. 2:14, 15). Antonius Thysius said of man under the state of sin "in affairs that concern the natural and civic life, in affairs subject to the senses and reason, and which concern external discipline and corporal justice...remnants and tiny sparks [of goodness] sur-

---

[45] On how the divines at Dort formulated this, see Goudriaan, "The Synod of Dordt on Arminian Anthropology," 88–89. For Calvin's view, see A. N. S. Lane, "Did Calvin Believe in Freewill?" *Vox Evangelica* 12 (1981): 81–83.

vive."[46] In other words, man still has natural intellectual abilities in earthly matters though even these are damaged by the Fall.

The source of these things **in** *people* (*homine*) **since the fall** are **the glimmerings of natural light**. As we saw in 1.RE 4, this **natural light** (*lumen naturae*) was the reason God implanted in Adam by nature as his creature, enabling him to understand the revelation of God in creation and natural law.[47] This "natural law" (*lex naturalis*), according to Franciscus Junius (1545–1602), was "entirely present in created things according to the image of God."[48] Pre-Fall humanity in Adam was able to live rightly according to it using natural light. Post-Fall is another story. After the synod, Antonius Thysius (1565–1640) argued for the immortality of the soul on the basis of "the marvelous gifts, effects, and godlike functions of the soul" such as

> its clever genius...swift thinking...ease of perception...sharp discernment...discourse and reasoning about all things...recollection of past events...consideration of current events...ability to foresee future events, and especially its ability to turn towards itself and reflect upon itself.

Most of all, the immortality of the soul is evidenced by

> the soul's knowledge and worship of God that has been implanted in the soul, by the discernment and perception of true and false, fair and unfair, just and unjust, beautiful and base, honest and dishonest, and by the discovery and knowledge of countless arts.[49]

What Paul Means by "The Law"

When we turn to the New Testament we see that there is a varied used of the concept of "law." In Paul's letter to the Romans, Paul speaks broadly of "law" as something that binds. For example, the law of marriage binds a

---

[46] *Synopsis Purioris Theologiae/Synopsis of a Purer Theology: Volume 1*, ed. Deolf te Velde, trans. Riemer A. Faber (Leiden: Brill, 2015), 417.

[47] "Lumen naturae," in Muller, *Dictionary of Latin and Greek Theological Terms*, 206.

[48] Junius, *The Mosaic Polity*, 44.

[49] *Synopsis Purioris Theologiae: Volume 1*, 325.

husband and wife together (Rom. 7:2–3). More narrowly Paul speaks of "the law" in contrast to "the prophets" to mean the first five books of the Old Testament, the *Torah* (Rom. 3:21). But most specifically, he speaks of "the law" as the moral demands of God. We see this, for example, in Romans 2:12–29.[50]

Here Paul is challenging the hypocrisy and formalism of those who identified as law-keepers in contrast to Gentile sinners. His exhortation begins by speaking of the law as the moral demands of God in a twofold way. He says there is a law of nature on the Gentile conscience and that it is the same law that was written on Israel's tablets of stone (vv. 12–16). These are the same law just with different subjects. Then he hits the Jews or those Gentiles who have been swayed into a legalistic thinking. He says they relied on the law and sought to be teachers of the law, all the while they were breaking the law (vv. 17–24). His conclusion was that the symbol of law-keeping, circumcision, was powerless to save if it was merely an outward mark and not accompanied with heartfelt obedience.

The Limits of this Light

This **natural light** is on the heart of every human being. But it has its limits. Paul said, "For God has done what the law, weakened by the flesh, could not do" (Rom. 8:3). We'll come back to this verse, but it teaches that there's a limit to what the moral demands of God in the law can do. Article 4 goes on to say: **But so far is this light of nature** (*naturae lumine*) **from being sufficient to bring him to a saving knowledge of God and to true conversion** (*convertere*). Reason cannot change our lives in a saving way. Why not?

> **He is incapable of using it aright even in things natural and civil. Nay, further, this light, such as it is, man in various ways renders wholly polluted and holds it**

---

[50] On the Pauline use of "law" (*nomos*), see John Murray, "Paul's Use of 'Nomos'" in *Collected Writings of John Murray: Volume 4, Studies in Theology* (Edinburgh: Banner of Truth, 1982), 133–41; Herman Ridderbos, *Paul: An Outline of His Theology*, trans. John Richard De Witt (1966; Grand Rapids, MI: Eerdmans, 1975), 106–7; Jakob Van Bruggen, *Paul: Pioneer for Israel's Messiah*, trans. Ed M. van der Maas (2001; Phillipsburg, NJ: P&R, 2005), 214–53.

**in unrighteousness, by doing which he becomes inex-
cusable before God.**

Back in Romans 1 Paul said, "The wrath of God is [being] revealed
from heaven against all ungodliness and unrighteousness of men, who by
their unrighteousness suppress the truth" (v. 18). Both in natural things and
supernatural things, things of society and things of eternity, human beings
skew and suppress the truth of God on their hearts. Thysius said man under the state of sin in relation to spiritual and inward things evidences the
worst of his nature: "his intellect is largely ignorant of the substance of
God's law...[and] especially of the substance of the Gospel...the will, bound
by depravity, wills, choose, desires, and accomplishes things opposite to the
supernatural ones."[51]

What this Means for Us

Let me bring this home to you. When it comes to the regeneration of sinners, that is, being born again to new life in Christ, Paul's words in Romans
8:3 mean two things.

First, because our sin nature weakens any ability to free ourselves
spiritually, even the law of nature that God has implanted on our hearts is
unable to give us new life and to save us from our sins. This means there is
no "God-shaped hole" in our hearts, untouched by sin that we accessed to
believe in Jesus. This means we didn't grope around in the dark room of
our sins by following the one beam of light and that because we did that
God gave us more light until we found our way out of the room and into
salvation. This is what some people believe. This doctrine matters! The second is in relation to article 5, as we'll see below.

Article 5

In the same light are we to consider the law of the decalogue, delivered by God to His peculiar people the Jews by the hands of Moses. For
though it discovers the greatness of sin, and more and more convinces man
thereof, yet as it neither points out a remedy nor imparts strength to extricate him from misery, and thus being weak through the flesh leaves the
transgressor under the curse, man cannot by this law obtain saving grace.

---

[51] *Synopsis Purioris Theologiae: Volume 1*, 419.

THE LAW OF SINAI

The second thing Romans 8:3 means is because our sin nature weakens any ability to free ourselves spiritually, the law of nature that was republished in the form of the Ten Commandments is unable to give us new life and save us from our sins.[52] Article 5 says: **In the same light are we to consider the law of the decalogue, delivered by God to His peculiar people the Jews by the hands of Moses.**

In practical terms, this means that giving our friends some methods or rules and if they follow them they will come to Christ isn't true. "If you just start praying God will honor that and you'll be saved." I can remember being a believer who wanted so badly to speak in tongues—because I was told that's what true believers did—that I got ahold of a book on how to be filled with the Spirit. And I tried, and tried, and tried until I was in despair. I praise God for his grace!

What Paul Means by the Law (Again)

Turn back to Romans with me for a moment. In 3:19–20 Paul says the whole world is under the law and accountable to God. How does this call all humanity to account? By being unable to justify us from our sins before the holiness of God; instead, the law can only point out sin. To illustrate, we give our children lists of house chores and rules, but these cannot tell them *how* to clean their room, *how* to fold their laundry, or *how* to love and

---

[52] On the separate, but related, issue of the law as it relates to God's *covenant* with man, the Westminster Divine, Anthony Burgess (d. 1664) said, "I do not finde in any point of Divinity, learned men so confused and perplexed (being like *Abrahams* Ram, hung in a bush of briars and brambles by the head) as here." *Vindiciae Legis: or, A Vindication of the Morall Law and the Covenants, From the Errors of Papists, Arminians, Socinians, and more especially, Antinomians* (London, 1647), 229. For recent treatments on various sides of the issue see the following: for the view that the Mosaic *covenant* was a republication of the covenant of works, see *The Law Is Not of Faith: Essays on Works and Grace in the Mosaic Covenant*, ed. Bryan Estelle, J. V. Fesko, David VanDrunen (Phillipsburg, NJ: P&R, 2009); for the view that the Mosaic covenant was not, but was an administration of the covenant of grace, see Cornelis P. Venema, "The Mosaic Covenant: A 'Republication' of the Covenant of Works? A Review Article: *The Law Is Not of Faith: Essays on Works and Grace in the Mosaic Covenant*," *Mid-America Journal of Theology* 21 (2010): 35–101.

protect their siblings. If they break the rules and suffer the consequences, those lists are of no help to get them out of the punishment. The list just shows how bad they did; the list only accuses. In the same way the law of God says, "Love God" and "Love your neighbor," but only points out the sin and the consequence, but not the remedy. This is consistent with what Augustine said: "The Lord Himself...shows us what evil we should shun, and what good we should do, which is all that the letter of the law is able to effect."[53]

One of the great objections Paul addressed in Romans was, "Do we then overthrow the law by this faith?" (3:31). His extensive answer came in chapter 4. We uphold the law. How so? By giving it its proper place and power. This was illustrated in no better way than in the life of Abraham. Paul says he was justified not by works of law but by faith in Christ (4:13–16). This meant that Abraham was either an inheritor of God's promises because of his works or because of God's grace—there is no middle ground. The law brings wrath, but the promise of God rests on grace. In other words, the law does its work and the gospel does its work. "The word of the Law," Rivetus said, "only prepares the way for justifying faith."[54]

Article 5 of the canons expresses this common Christian conviction, saying, **For though it discovers the greatness of sin, and more and more convinces man thereof, yet as it neither points out a remedy nor imparts strength to extricate him from misery, and thus being weak through the flesh leaves the transgressor under the curse, man cannot by this law obtain saving grace.**

Article 6

What therefore neither the light of nature, nor the law could do, that God performs by the operation of the Holy Spirit through the Word or ministry of reconciliation, which is the glad tidings concerning the Messiah, by means whereof it hath pleased God to save such as believe, as well under the Old, as under the New Testament.

---

[53] Augustine, "On Rebuke and Grace," 2 (5:472).

[54] *Synopsis Purioris Theologiae: Volume 2*, 239.

REGENERATION DEFINED

With article 6 we come to the definitional article on regeneration. Taking what we've seen in articles 4–5 we read, **What therefore neither the light of nature** (*lumen naturae*)**, nor the law could do, that God performs.**[55] Again, this reflects Paul's climactic chapter 8 of his letter to the Romans: "God has done what the law, weakened by the flesh, could not do" (Rom. 8:3). What a God! What a comfort to us sinners! What a verse to memorize and repeat when down and out spiritually! This statement teaches that the law does not nor cannot rescue us from our bondage to sin; only God can. This verse brings to a glorious conclusion an argument Paul has been having since chapter 2 and that stretches all the way until chapter 7. This was also consistent with the language of the Second Council of Orange (529), which confessed with Paul in Galatians 5:4 that those who would be justified by the law have fallen from grace; then it confessed contrary to all forms of Pelagianism that the same is true of "those who think that nature is the grace which is commended and received by faith in Christ." Instead, Christ came to fulfill the law and to restore the nature that Adam destroyed (canon 21).[56] The role of the law and the power of the law was one of the struggles the Roman Christians were having—isn't it always a struggle? In simple terms, are we saved by law or are we saved by gospel?

The Means of Regeneration

Article 6 says we're saved by gospel. How does God **perform**[...] what his moral requirements in natural law and the Decalogue cannot do in us? **By the operation of the Holy Spirit through the Word or ministry of reconciliation, which is the glad tidings concerning the Messiah, by means whereof it hath pleased God to save such as believe, as well under the Old, as under the New Testament.** The Holy Spirit is the effective power of new birth. One of the ways Reformed people have sought to guard this truth was by saying the Spirit works "with the Word" (*cum verbo*). But our article also says he exercises that power "through the Word"

---

[55] *Synopsis Purioris Theologiae: Volume 2*, 211–21.

[56] Woods, *Canons of the Second Council of Orange*, 39.

(*per sermonem* or *verbum*) that is preached.[57] Rivertus said that "we must...not go head over heels to the extremes and pull apart what belongs together, or mix up what should be kept apart, by attributing to the instrument what belongs properly to the primary cause."[58] As John Calvin taught the Reformed church a generation prior to Dort, the Word and Spirit are inseparable:

> For by a kind of mutual bond the Lord has joined together the certainty of his Word and of his Spirit so that the perfect religion of the Word may abide in our minds when the Spirit, who causes us to contemplate God's face, shines; and that we in turn may embrace the Spirit with no fear of being deceived when we recognize him in his own image, namely, in the Word.[59]

In the language of the canons here and as we'll see below, regeneration is *mediate* not *immediate*.[60] Some Reformed theologians in the modern era have taught that regeneration is "immediate," meaning, the Spirit alone directly works regeneration. Others have taught that regeneration is "mediate," meaning, the Spirit alone works regeneration but by means of the preaching of the Word. Does it matter? Venema states:

> A genuine issue is at stake in this discussion. Advocates of immediate regeneration have been properly concerned to insist that the Spirit is the Author of regeneration, not the Word as such. The Word of God preached does not by itself possess an inherent power that can grant new life to otherwise dead sinners. Only God by his Spirit has the power to grant the new birth. However, once this point

---

[57] On this important distinction, see A. Baars, "The 'Appropriation of Salvation' in the Creeds: An Overview (Part 1)." *Clarion* 46, no. 24 (November 28, 1997): 528–31; "The 'Appropriation of Salvation' in the Creeds: An Overview (Part 2)," *Clarion*, December 1997, 566–68. The background to this distinction was within Lutheranism as Hermann Rahtmann went against the Lutheran Orthodox consensus in saying (as the Reformed did) the outward Word was without efficacy apart from the Holy Spirit. See Kenneth G. Appold, *Abraham Calov's Doctrine of Vocatio in its Systematic Context* (Tübingen: Mohr Siebeck, 1998), 112–24.

[58] *Synopsis Purioris Theologiae: Volume 2*, 241.

[59] Calvin, *Institutes*, 1.9.3.

[60] For the view that the Canons present a *mediate* view of regeneration, see Venema, *But for the Grace of God*, 68–69.

has been granted, it has to be acknowledged that the Reformed confessions typically insist that the Spirit ordinarily grants that new birth through the use of the means of grace. Consequently, though it is proper to be clear about *who* authors the new birth, it is just as proper to be clear about *how* (by what means) that new birth is authored. As always, the Reformed insist upon a *distinction, without separation*, between the Spirit and the Word of Christ.[61]

One twentieth-century advocate of *immediate* regeneration was Herman Hoeksema. One crucial text in this debate is 1 Peter 1:22–25:

> Having purified your souls by your obedience to the truth for a sincere brotherly love, love one another earnestly from a pure heart, since you have been born again, not of perishable seed but of imperishable, through the living and abiding word of God; for "All flesh is like grass and all its glory like the flower of grass. The grass withers, and the flower falls, but the word of the Lord remains forever." And this word is the good news that was preached to you.

Hoeksema granted to the advocates of mediate regeneration that "it is true that here the apostle presents regeneration as taking place through the Word of God…and also that he adds that this is the Word which by the gospel is preached unto the church."[62] Then Hoeksema presented his rebuttal: "But this does not imply at all that the apostle contends that regeneration occurs through the *preaching* of that living Word of God" (emphasis added).[63] This sounds at first like a contradiction, but he went on to base this on two distinctions: first, between "the living and abiding Word of God and the proclamation of that Word [being] two different things."[64] Second, between regeneration in a narrow sense of initial new life and regeneration in a broader sense of ongoing spiritual life.[65] Of the first distinction, Hoeksema said that in 1 Peter 1, "regeneration takes place through the liv-

---

[61] Cornelis P. Venema, *By His Spirit and Word: How Christ Builds His Church* (Grandville, MI: Reformed Fellowship, 2015), 59n10.

[62] Herman Hoeksema, *Reformed Dogmatics: Volume 2*, 2nd ed. (Jenison, MI: Reformed Free Publishing Association, 2005), 29.

[63] Hoeksema, *Reformed Dogmatics: Volume 2*, 30.

[64] Hoeksema, *Reformed Dogmatics: Volume 2*, 30.

[65] Hoeksema, *Reformed Dogmatics: Volume 2*, 30.

ing Word himself, that is, through Christ" and not "simply by the preaching of the gospel."[66] Of the second, he said, "It is true that the preaching of the Word stands in connection with regeneration in the broader sense…but this does not remove the fact that even in this broader sense regeneration does not take place through the preaching of the word, but through the living and abiding Word of God himself."[67] Where does he base his belief that regeneration in both its narrow and broad senses is restricted to the living Word and not the preached Word? He asserted that when the narrow sense of regeneration in verse 23 is described as occurring "not of perishable seed" and "through the living and abiding word of God," these are not synonymous as mediate regeneration advocates teach. In fact, he said, "The contrary is true" because Peter "makes a very careful distinction…us[ing]…different prepositions": "of" (ἐκ) and "by" (διὰ).[68] The point being that we are born again "of" or "from" the Spirit's implanting the seed of regeneration that is the principle of the new life, which then comes to life "by" means of the living and abiding Word—Christ himself.

In response, yes, there is a distinction between the Word and preaching; the Word ultimately is the Son himself who entered our world as a man to explain (ἐξηγήσατο) to us the Father (John 1:18). Yet Hoeksema is in danger of severing him from the preaching ministry he authorized. For example, the apostle Paul "thank[ed] God…that when [the Thessalonicans] received the word of God, which you heard from us, you accepted it not as the word of men but as what it really is, the word of God" (1 Thess. 2:13).[69] Note that well. Paul's preaching *was* the Word of God. We saw this above in canon 1.3 in connection with Romans 10. This is why our Reformed confessions stated the nature of preaching so strongly in the *Second Helvetic Confession*: "Wherefore when this Word of God is now preached in the church by preachers lawfully called, we believe that the very Word of God is preached, and received of the faithful."[70] As well, yes, there is a distinction between regeneration as the initial new life God gives and the ongoing

---

[66] Hoeksema, *Reformed Dogmatics: Volume 2*, 30.

[67] Hoeksema, *Reformed Dogmatics: Volume 2*, 30.

[68] Hoeksema, *Reformed Dogmatics: Volume 2*, 30.

[69] On this passage, see Daniel R. Hyde, *From the Pen of Pastor Paul: 1–2 Thessalonians* (Welwyn Garden City, UK: EP Books, 2015), 93–104.

[70] Dennison, *Reformed Confessions of the 16th and 17th Centuries*, 2:811.

life we are to pursue as new creatures. We see that here in 1 Peter where in 1:22–25 Peter speaks of initial new life and then in 2:1–3 he exhorts those who have been born again into spiritual "newborn infants" to leave their former sinful ways while longing for the "pure spiritual milk" of the Word.

Of this initial new life of regeneration in chapter 1, Hoeksema fails to incorporate the entire context. In verse 22 Peter begins by reminding his hearers that they "hav[e] *already* [perfect tense] purified [their] souls." He speaks of their already being cleansed and set apart for God. Notice how: "by your obedience to the truth." The connection is already made between a past action of purification and the truth. We typically speak of believing the truth, not obeying it, but both are apostolic modes of speech. Paul speaks of "obey[ing] the gospel" (Rom. 10:16; 2 Thess. 1:8) and "obeying the truth" (Gal. 5:7). The purpose of speaking this way "indicates that conversion is not simply a matter of intellectual change, but of a transformation of behavior."[71] The purpose of this past purification is "for [εἰς] a sincere brotherly love." Therefore he exhorts his hearers to "love one another earnestly *from* [ἐκ] *a pure heart*" (1 Pet. 1:22), which is the center of new life in these born again believers.

Verse 23 opens with another perfect tense verse: "Since you have been born again." Then he explains the means by which we were born again: "not of [ἐκ] perishable seed but of imperishable, through [διὰ] the living and abiding word of God" (λόγου ζῶντος θεοῦ καὶ μένοντος). He substantiates this with a quotation from Isaiah 40 in verses 24–25:

> All flesh is like grass
> and all its glory like the flower of grass.
> The grass withers,
> and the flower falls,
> But the word of the Lord remains forever. (τὸ ῥῆμα κυρίου
> μένει εἰς τὸν αἰῶνα)

The last phrase in verse 25 is Peter's explanation. He says, "This word" (τοῦτο...τὸ ῥῆμα) of the Lord that remains forever "is *the good news that was preached* [τὸ εὐαγγελισθὲν] to you."

---

[71] Peter H. Davids, *The First Epistle of Peter*, New International Commentary on the New Testament (Grand Rapids, MI: Eerdmans, 1990), 76.

To summarize: to implant the imperishable seed that initially regenerates into our hearts, God has used the means of his living Word that does not wither like the grass and the abiding Word that does not fall like the flower. This living and abiding Word that has given new life is the gospel that was preached to us! This interpretation is consistent with Johannes Polyander's (1568–1646) exposition immediately after the Synod of Dort when he said, "The primary efficient cause of the Gospel-call is God the Father, in the Son, and through (*per*) the Holy Spirit," and that the Son "calls these people to himself through (*per*) the Holy Spirit and the Word of truth."[72] As for "the ordinary instrumental cause," Polyander said it "is the ministry of the divine Word through (*per*) the preachers of the Gospel."[73] In further clarifying, he spoke of external and internal callings with "the former…achieved through (*per*) the administration of Word and sacraments, and the latter inwardly though (*per*) the working of the Holy Spirit."[74]

How we believe God saves fallen sinners like us is such an important question. You need to have an answer or else you will never have assurance of salvation. Are you saved wholly of God's grace, or are you saved because in some way or another you did something? Canons 3/4 have said our depravity in sin and our inability to escape that sin means God must do something. That something is regeneration or giving us new spiritual life. There's a beautiful antithesis and contrast between law and gospel when it comes to regeneration.

Article 7

This mystery of His will God discovered to but a small number under the Old Testament; under the New (the distinction between various peoples having been removed), He reveals Himself to many without any distinction of people. The cause of this dispensation is not to be ascribed to the superior worth of one nation above another, nor to their making a better use of the light of nature, but results wholly from the sovereign good pleasure and unmerited love of God. Hence they, to whom so great and so gracious a blessing is communicated above their desert, or rather notwithstanding their demerits, are bound to acknowledge it with humble and grateful hearts, and with the apostle to adore, not curiously to pry into the

---

[72] *Synopsis Purioris: Volume 2*, 211.

[73] *Synopsis Purioris: Volume 2*, 213.

[74] *Synopsis Purioris: Volume 2*, 221.

severity and justice of God's judgments displayed to others, to whom this grace is not given.

With articles 7–17 the canons expand in a series of articles the truth about regeneration. Article 7 relates back to a theme we saw in 1.8 and 1.RE 9: God's one electing plan of people in both the Old and New Testaments was based in his good pleasure and not based in one people being better or worthier than another. Article 7 relates this to the doctrine of the Holy Spirit's regenerating work.

By means of the prophets preaching of the Messiah to come (art. 6) **this mystery of His will God discovered** (*patefecit*; revealed) **to but a small number under the Old Testament.** This theme is seen as early as Genesis 4 where various descendants of Cain's line were known for their cultural exploits: city building, animal domestication, and music (Gen. 4:17–24). On the contrary, Seth's line was simply known as those who "began to call upon the name of the LORD" (Gen. 4:25). It continues with Noah and his family in contrast to the rest of the world, Abraham being called out of his father's house to make a new people, and Israel as they're surrounded by the nations.

The language of **mystery** denotes to us something unknown. In the New Testament the focus, though, is on something hidden for a time under the old covenant but now revealed under the new. Paul tells the Ephesians Christians that "the mystery [μυστήριον] was made known to me by revelation" (Eph. 3:3). Something was hidden to Paul that God revealed to him. Then he speaks of it as "the mystery of Christ [τῷ μυστηρίῳ τοῦ Χριστοῦ], which was not made known to the sons of men in other generations as it has now been revealed to his holy apostles and prophets by the Spirit" (Eph. 3:4–5). What was the mystery? "This mystery is that the Gentiles are fellow heirs, members of the same body, and partakers of the promise in Christ Jesus through the gospel" (Eph. 3:6).

Article 7 makes the contrast that **under the New (the distinction between various having been removed), He reveals** (*manifestat*) **Himself to many without any distinction of people.** Jesus commissioned his disciples/apostles to go into the world to preach the gospel (Matt. 28:18–20) just as the Lord told Abraham that he would be a blessing to all the nations (Gen. 12:3; 17:4–6). We see the fruit of that evidenced in Cornelius (Acts 10) and recognized at the Jerusalem Council, where the Holy Spirit's descent on the Gentiles testified that God accepted them alongside of the Jews into his kingdom (Acts 15).

Now that the boundaries of Israel have been removed in the new covenant, why is it that God **reveals** [his will] **to many?** Like earlier in 1.8 we read that **the cause of this dispensation is not be ascribed to the superior worth of one nation above another**—what a message we as Americans need to hear!—**nor to their making a better use of the light of nature** (*luminis naturae*), **but results wholly from the sovereign good pleasure and unmerited love of God.** This was consistent with the concluding definition of faith from the Council of Orange (529), which said the saints of old did not have faith implanted in them by nature as with Adam but it was bestowed on them by the grace of God, just as it is now after the coming of our Lord.[75]

This article concludes with the practicality of confessing this aspect of the truth about regeneration:

> **Hence they, to whom so great and so gracious a blessing is communicated above their desert, or rather notwithstanding their demerits, are bound to acknowledge it with humble and grateful hearts, and with the apostle to adore, not curiously to pry into the severity and justice of God's judgments displayed to others, to whom this grace is not given.**

Humility for grace, adoration for justice.

Article 8

As many as are called by the gospel are unfeignedly called. For God hath most earnestly and truly declared in His Word what will be acceptable to Him; namely, that all who are called, should comply with the invitation. He, moreover, seriously promises eternal life and rest to as many as shall come to Him and believe on Him.

GOD'S SINCERE AND SERIOUS CALL

My two brothers and I all have heard the good news of Jesus. Yet two of the three of us do not evidence a true faith. Only I do. I know many of you

---

[75] Woods, *Canons of the Second Council of Orange*, 45.

are in the same situation with your family. The question is why? Why is it that some hear and respond and others do not? It's also in that questioning that we empathize with Paul's deep anguish for his fellow brothers and sisters: "I have great sorrow and unceasing anguish in my heart. For I could wish that I myself were accursed and cut off from Christ for the sake of my brothers" (Rom. 9:2–3). Many do not receive the grace of God (art. 7); thus article 8 explains that **as many as are called by the gospel are unfeignedly** (*serio*; seriously) **called**.

Matthew 22 illustrates for us God's sincere and serious call to sinners like my brothers and I that we all come to Jesus Christ for salvation. Jesus speaks here in a "parable" (v. 1) of "the kingdom of heaven" (v. 2). There is "a king who gave a wedding feast for his son" (v. 2) and so he "sent his servants to call those who were invited to the wedding feast, but they would not come" (v. 3). So "he sent other servants" to do the same thing (v. 4), but this time while some "paid no attention" (v. 5), others "seized his servants, treated them shamefully, and killed them" (v. 6). This angered the king who "sent his troops and destroyed those murderers and burned their city" (v. 7). Jesus is speaking here of the religious leaders of Israel who refused him and the eventual destruction of their city, Jerusalem, in AD 70.

Jesus continues the parable, saying the king prepared even more "servants" (v. 8) to "go therefore to the main roads and invite to the wedding feast as many as you find" (v. 9), which led to "the wedding hall" being "filled with guests" (v. 10). He's speaking of his eventual Great Commission when he commanded his apostles to "go...and make disciples of all nations" (Matt. 28:19). "As many as you find" (v. 9) describes what we call the general call of the gospel, which is an indiscriminate offer to "both bad and good" (v. 10). This general call is sincere and serious: **as many as are called by the gospel are unfeignedly called** (*serio vocantur*, *seriously* called). As Hoekema pointed out, here the synod appropriated Remonstrant language.[76] In their *Sententiae Remonstrantium* they said, "Whomever God calls to salvation, He calls seriously [*serio vocat*]."[77] Yet note how the canon stops short of appropriating the rest of their language:

---

[76] Hoekema, "The Missionary Focus of the Canons of Dort," 217.

[77] "The Opinions of the Remonstrants," appendix H in De Jong, *Crisis in the Reformed Churches*, 226.

> That is, with a sincere and completely unhypocritical intention and will to save; nor do we assent to the opinion of those who hold that God calls certain ones externally whom He does not will to call internally, that is, as truly converted, even before the grace of calling has been rejected.[78]

Some such as Raymond Blacketer have taken this detail to mean the synod did "not accept [the Remonstrants'] requirement for such a call, namely, that God must sincerely intend and will to save anyone who receives that call." He went on to say that the synod's decision to appropriate a part and not the whole of the Remonstrants' language was to "explain how the call can really be serious when, in fact, God does not intend or will the salvation of the reprobate!"[79] No doubt some at the synod would've agreed; yet men like John Davenant could still affirm what the synod said while also affirming "in God a true will revealed in the Gospell of Saving all men that shall believe."[80]

Article 8 continues with an explanation of how God's call is serious: **For God hath most earnestly and truly declared in His Word what will be acceptable to Him; namely, that all who are called, should comply with the invitation.** Behind this popular language is the technical distinction, variously expressed as God's decretive will (*voluntas decreti*) and his preceptive will (*voluntas praecepti*), or the will of God's good pleasure (εὐδοκία) and the will of God's complacency (εὐαρεστία), and also the secret will (*voluntas arcana*) and the revealed will (*voluntas revelata*).[81] Article 8 first describes the latter in the list of terms above: God's preceptive, complacent, and revealed will. In the words of the article, **God hath…declared in His Word what will be acceptable to Him: that** his preceptive will is that **all who are called, should comply with the invitation.** Article 8 then describes

---

[78] "The Opinions of the Remonstrants," appendix H in De Jong, *Crisis in the Reformed Churches*, 226–27. For a meticulous response to Hoekema and others on this point, see Raymond A. Blacketer, "The Three Points in Most Parts Reformed: A Reexamination of the So-Called Well-Meant Offer of Salvation," *Calvin Theological Journal* 35 (2000): 39–51.

[79] Blacketer, "The Three Points in Most Parts Reformed," 42.

[80] John Davenant, *Animadversions written by the Right Reverend Father in God, John Lord Bishop of Sarisbury, upon a Treatise intitled Gods love to Mankinde* (London: 1641), 173.

[81] On these distinctions, see Muller, "voluntas Dei," in *Dictionary of Latin and Greek Theological Terms*, 399–402.

the former in the list of terms above: God's decretive, good pleasure, and secret will. In the words of the article, **He, moreover, seriously promises eternal life and rest to as many as shall come to Him and believe on Him** since those who do have been ordained in God's decretive, good pleasure, and secret will. Back to Jesus' parable, at the end he gives the punch line, distinguishing the general call from the effectual call, which we'll see below: "For many are called, but few are chosen" (v. 14).

MAN'S SINFUL REFUSAL TO COME

Matthew 22 illustrates in my situation why my two brothers don't believe: *man's sinful refusal to come.* The first time the king's servants go out to all those previously invited, we read, "But they would not come" (v. 3). Then the second time we read that some wouldn't even "pa[y]...attention and went off" on their daily routines, with some going "to his farm" and others "to his business" (v. 5). Even worse was that "the rest seized his servants, treated them shamefully, and killed them" (v. 6). This is the tragedy of unbelief. It pleases God **that all who are called, should comply with the invitation** because this call includes the **promise[...]** of **eternal life** to all those dead in trespasses and sins **and rest** for restless souls.

Article 9

It is not the fault of the gospel nor of Christ, offered therein, nor of God, who calls men by the gospel and confers upon them various gifts, that those who are called by the ministry of the Word refuse to come and be converted. The fault lies in themselves, some of whom when called, regardless of their danger, reject the word of life; others, though they receive it, suffer it not to make a lasting impression on their heart; therefore, their joy, arising only from a temporary faith, soon vanishes and they fall away; while others choke the seed of the Word by perplexing cares and the pleasures of this world, and produce no fruit. This our Savior teaches in the parable of the sower (Matt. 13).

Article 9 links back to article 8's mention of the "many as are called" by beginning in a way that our translation mutes: "The many who are called through the ministry of the gospel" (*Quod multi per ministerium Evangelii vocati*). It continues by connecting these to one of the canons' pervasive themes: personal responsibility for unbelief. The fault for my brothers' unbelief is not the gospel in which Christ is offered. The fault lies in them: **It is not the fault of the gospel nor of Christ, offered**[82] **therein, nor of God, who calls** *people*[83] **by the gospel and confers upon them various gifts, that those who are called by the ministry of the Word refuse to come and be converted** (*convertuntur*). **The fault lies in themselves.**

To illustrate this, article 9 picks up on another of Jesus' parables: the parable of the sower in Matthew 13. According to Jesus' parable, some seeds fall along the path but are eaten by birds, signifying those that reject the gospel (Matt. 13:4). Article 9 applies this: **some of whom when called, regardless of their danger, reject the word of life.** Then Jesus goes on to speak of various kinds of faith.[84] Some seeds fall on rocky ground and immediately spring up, but since the soil is not deep the sun scorches them to death, signifying those who receive the gospel with the joy that comes from a temporary faith but without a lasting impression (Matt. 13:5–6). Article 9 again makes the application: **others, though they receive it, suffer it not** (*do not*) **to make a lasting impression on their heart; therefore their joy, arising only from a temporary faith, soon vanishes and they fall away.** Jesus said some seeds fall among thorns that overgrow the seeds and choke them, signifying those who receive the gospel only to be choked spiritually by the perplexing cares and the pleasures of this world (Matt. 13:7). Article 9's application is that **others choke the seed of the Word by perplexing cares and the pleasures of this world, and produce no fruit.** But some seeds fall on good soil and produce grain a hundredfold, sixtyfold, and thirtyfold (Matt. 13:8). I genuinely received the gospel and was changed forever. My brothers still have not. The question is why? The answer is in article 10.

---

[82] Blacketer argues that *oblato* (from *offero*) is much more plausibly interpreted as Christ being exhibited or presented in the gospel. "The Three Points in Most Parts Reformed," 44–45.

[83] The translation we're using as our baseline inserts "men" here, which I've rendered neutrally as "people." However, this word is not in the text but is implied. The text actually speaks of "*many* who are called through the ministry of the gospel" (*Quod multi per ministerium Evangelii vocati*).

[84] On this, see *Synopsis Purioris Theologiae: Volume 2*, 231–37.

Article 10

But that others who are called by the gospel obey the call and are converted is not to be ascribed to the proper exercise of free will, whereby one distinguishes himself above others, equally furnished with grace sufficient for faith and conversion as the proud heresy of Pelagius maintains; but it must be wholly ascribed to God, who as He has chosen His own from eternity in Christ, so He confers upon them faith and repentance, rescues them from the power of darkness, and translates them into the kingdom of His own Son, that they may show forth the praises of Him who hath called them out of darkness into His marvelous light; and may glory not in themselves, but in the Lord according to the testimony of the apostles in various places.

GOD'S EFFECTUAL CALL

Article 10 takes up the opposite of article 9: **But that others who are called by the gospel** (*per ministerium Evangelii;* by the ministry of the gospel) **obey the call.** My brothers and I have all heard the general call of the gospel. But the reason that I came to Christ is God's effectual call: **and are converted** (*convertuntur*) **is not to be ascribed to the proper exercise of free will…but it must be wholly ascribed to God.**

Matthew 22 again illustrates this *effectual call.* Those who refused to come to the wedding feast did so because of their sin. But did those on "the main roads" (v. 9) whom the king's servants "gathered" whether "bad and good" (v. 10) have something different about them? Were they less sinful? Were they more spiritual? Obviously not because Jesus says some were "bad" and some were "good," which he illustrates further as one of those who are "bad" entered "without a wedding garment" (v. 12). Article 10 says the idea that I heard the gospel, came to Jesus Christ, and was converted by the power of the Holy Spirit because I **distinguishe[d]** myself **above others, equally furnished with grace sufficient for faith and conversion** is **the proud heresy of Pelagius.** Again, what distinguishes people who come from those who refuse? In Jesus' words, "Many are called [generally], but few are chosen" [effectually] (v. 14). God alone is the distinguishing "factor." In the words of article 10:

> **But it must be wholly ascribed to God, who as He has chosen His own from eternity in Christ** (first point of doctrine)**, so He confers upon them faith and repentance, rescues them from**

the power of darkness, and translates them into the kingdom of His own Son, that they may show forth the praises of Him who hath called them out of darkness into His marvelous light; and may glory not in themselves, but in the Lord according to the testimony of the apostles in various places.

While the general call of the gospel leads many to a profession of Christ, it is only the effectual call that enables some to a true possession of Christ.[85] These have been **chosen...in Christ** (first point of doctrine), then had **confer[red] upon them faith and repentance**, been **rescue[d]...from the power of darkness**, and finally **translate[d]...into the kingdom of His own Son**. As a preacher I can only knock at the door of the heart; only the Holy Spirit has the key to unlock, to enter, and to grace with salvation mentioned above.

Praise God! In response, article 10 says with Peter that the Holy Spirit has done this so that my new existence is "to proclaim the excellencies of him who called [me, effectually] out of darkness into his marvelous light" (1 Pet. 2:9). I still have two brothers who need this. Who do you have?

Article 11

But when God accomplishes His good pleasure in the elect or works in them true conversion, He not only causes the gospel to be externally preached to them and powerfully illuminates their mind by His Holy Spirit, that they may rightly understand and discern the things of the Spirit of God; but by the efficacy of the same regenerating Spirit, pervades the inmost recesses of the man; He opens the closed, and softens the hardened heart, and circumcises that which was uncircumcised, infuses new qualities into the will, which though heretofore dead, He quickens; from being evil, disobedient, and refractory, He renders it good, obedient, and pliable; actuates and strengthens it, that like a good tree, it may bring forth the fruits of good actions.

THE WORK OF REGENERATION

The born-again experience. Hardly anything describes American evangelicalism more than this phrase. Political candidates unashamedly grovel for

---

[85] Thomas Watson, *A Body of Divinity* (1692; repr., Edinburgh: Banner of Truth Trust, 2000), 221.

votes using these magic words. Football games end with all the born-again players praying at the fifty-yard line. Even our culture uses this phrase, for example, to describe an actor who came out of nowhere and get back into the biz. The biblical idea has been lost under a mountain of frivolous uses.

Sadly, Christians have caused this. Some suggest it means that you've accepted Jesus into your heart as your personal Lord and Savior. Others that it was the emotional experience they underwent when they believed in Jesus. But what did Jesus mean when he said we must be "born again" or regenerated? We cannot be confused on this vital doctrine! Article 11 gives us a clear and powerful elaboration on Jesus' words in John 3.

The Necessity of Regeneration

The story begins with "now there was a man" (John 3:1). You can't understand chapter 3 unless you link it to the end of chapter 2. Jesus has just cleansed the temple. "Many believed in his name when they saw the signs that he was doing" (John 2:23). This connects back to Jesus' turning water into wine when "his disciples *believed in him*" (2:11). Hallelujah! Not. So. Fast. Look at verse 24. The Greek is more striking than the ESV: "*He, though, Jesus,* did not entrust himself to them." Many trusted Jesus; but Jesus didn't entrust himself to them! The same word that is used of their faith in him is used of his not having faith in them. This should wake us up in the morning! It's possible to have what looks like faith because of a miracle God has done. But it's not true faith. How many people have we met who have gone forward at an altar call at a Billy Graham Crusade? How many people do we know who were lonely and were told Jesus would be the best friend ever; they believed, the void was filled, only to have something happen and they lost faith? How many people have been told, "God has a wonderful plan for your life," they trusted Jesus, something great happened, then something bad happened only to see them fall away? If that's you today, I say to you with all seriousness because I care for you: *You can deceive people; you cannot deceive Jesus!* True faith is giving yourself to Jesus for who he is, not for what he gives you.

Here's another surprising and unsettling aspect of Jesus you don't hear about in the Churchianity so popular today! Why wouldn't Jesus entrust himself to people? "Because he knew all people and needed no one to bear witness about man [ἀνθρώπου], for he himself knew what was in man" (ἀνθρώπῳ; vv. 24–25). The Jewish commentary tradition in Jesus' day said, "Seven things are hidden from man," like "the day of death" and "the time of restoration of the kingdom of David." Also on the list was "what is within another."[86] In contrast, the prophet Jeremiah said, "I the LORD search the heart and examine the mind" (Jer. 17:10). Jesus knows what only God knows: the heart.

What word did you just hear twice in verse 25? Look at how John 3 begins with a connection: "now"[87] or "*and* there was a man" (ἄνθρωπος; v. 1). One such "man" whose heart Jesus knew was "named Nicodemus."[88] He was "of the Pharisees," those strict observers especially of the traditions of the elders, and he was "a ruler," being part of the Sanhedrin or Jewish ruling council.[89] He's no ordinary person; he's a religious leader with the highest clearance level!

"This man came to Jesus by night" (v. 2) because he wanted to be incognito. More so, "night" is a double entendre—a word with two connotations. Yes it's dark at "night," but in this Gospel the connotation is spiritual darkness (John 3:2; 9:4; 11:10; 13:30). Nicodemus comes to Jesus in the dark not knowing he's still in the dark! He says seemingly so respectfully, "Rabbi, we know," and he speaks seemingly so impressively of their "faith": "we know that you are a teacher come from God" (v. 2). What's wrong? When the delegation of Pharisees went to John in chapter 1, they at least considered he was: the Messiah, Elijah, or the prophet like Moses! Nicodemus's respect on behalf of his group denigrates Jesus as merely a teacher! Get ready for the Nicodemus spirit on TV this Easter season as religious scholars all unite to deny the resurrection only to say quickly, "But he's one of the world's great teachers." Nicodemus knows this about Jesus, "for no one can do these signs that you do unless God is with him" (v. 2). Did you catch that? Nicodemus is a "man" like those Jesus knows and didn't entrust himself to; and he's just like them in believing because of his signs. "No one

---

[86] Cited in D. A. Carson, *The Gospel according to John* (Grand Rapids, MI: Eerdmans, 1991), 184.

[87] On the interpretation of δὲ see Carson, *The Gospel according to John*, 185–86.

[88] On the connection between John 2:23–25 and 3:1, see Herman Ridderbos, *The Gospel of John: A Theological Commentary*, trans. John Vriend (Grand Rapids, MI: Eerdmans , 1997), 121–23.

[89] Leon Morris, *The Gospel according to John*, New International Commentary on the New Testament (1971; repr., Grand Rapids, MI: Eerdmans, 1989), 210.

can do these *signs that you do*" (τὰ σημεῖα ποιεῖν ἃ σὺ ποιεῖς) alludes back to 2:23 and those who believed because of "the signs that he was doing" (τὰ σημεῖα ἃ ἐποίει). "Houston, we have a problem!" Nicodemus illustrates for you and me the problem of trying to enter God's kingdom on your own terms: He wants Jesus for what he can get from his miracles. He wants Jesus as a great teacher but still trusts observing what his tradition has taught him is his ticket to heaven. This selfish self-trust is *our* problem!

The Impossibility of Regeneration by Man

As if that isn't bad enough news, Jesus tells Nicodemus and us of *the impossibility of regeneration by man*. Why? How does Jesus answer Nicodemus's flowery words? "Truly, truly, I say to you" (v. 3), literally, "amen, amen." In the collective human wisdom of some Pharisees, Nicodemus said, "We know"; the Word-made-flesh says, "I say to you." He proclaims the solution to the problem: "Unless one is born again he cannot see the kingdom of God" (v. 3). That's an absolute!

The coming kingdom was the hope of the Old Testament. We hear the Law and the Prophets put to song in the refrains of the Psalms: "The LORD is king," "The LORD reigns over all," and "The LORD's kingdom extends from shore to shore." They longed for the coming kingdom to put an end to the world's wicked kingdoms. In Jesus' day the kingdom age was understood to be the age of resurrection life when every Israelite except serious apostates would be raised from the dead.[90] What does Jesus say? Even the Nicodemuses who belong the covenant people are a cut above as Pharisees, and the elite of the elite in the Sanhedrin, must be radically changed to enter!

Why is it absolutely necessary? Because as John 2:24–25 tells us, Jesus knows all people and what is in everyone. What is that? Unbelief! The Jews didn't believe. The false disciples didn't believe. You didn't believe. Why? I hardly even need to say why, because you know why. You were "dead in your trespasses and sins" (Eph. 2:1). "There is no one good, no one righteous, no one who understands, no one who seeks after God" (Rom. 3:10–12). It is absolutely necessary that you undergo rebirth because you are unfit for the presence of God!

---

[90] See Carson, *The Gospel according to John*, 189.

The Possibility of Regeneration by God

But what is impossible with man is possible with God. This is the beauty of the gospel: it is *God* who accomplishes what is impossible for us to do!

First, the meaning of "regeneration" is the act of giving life again. So can you give yourself a new life from the one you have? No. Even all the plastic surgery, dieting, exercise, makeup, and day spas are only taking the old you and making you a younger-*looking* old you! Nicodemus is incredulous: "How can a man be born when he is old? Can he enter a second time into his mother's womb and be born?" (v. 4). Physically speaking, naturally speaking, earthly speaking, humanly speaking there is no way you can be born again out of your mother's womb—it's impossible!

There's a second reason it is impossible to give yourself a new spiritual life. Jesus says you must be "born again," and Nicodemus understands it to mean physical life. But the word Jesus uses is a double entendre because every other time John uses that word "again" in his Gospel it means "above."[91] Does it mean "again," as Nicodemus understood it? Yes, but Jesus also understands it in a second way: you must be born anew "from above." Nicodemus, if you want to enter heaven you must be born from heaven. If you want to enter the kingdom of God you must be born "of God." Jesus' point is that if the lesser miracle of being born again physically is impossible for man to accomplish, how much more so is it to be born "from above"?

"Truly, truly [or *Amen, Amen*], I say to you [*all*], unless one is born of water and the Spirit, he cannot enter the kingdom of God" (v. 5). "See" in verse 3 is paralleled with "enter" here. "Born *again*" or "*from above*" in verse 3 is paralleled with "born of water and the Spirit."[92] What Nicodemus said was impossible physiologically is possible for God. In fact, it was promised by God in the prophets who said this would happen in the age of the Messiah. Write down Ezekiel 36 and read it this afternoon in comparison with John 3. To summarize, the prophet speaks to the exiled people of God in Babylon who once defiled the land by their idolatry like a woman was impure during her menstruation (Ezek. 36:17). Because of that the nations defiled his name in mockery (vv. 20–21). But the Lord would act for the

---

[91] E.g., John 3:31; 19:11, 23.

[92] On the interpretative options, see Carson, *The Gospel according to John*, 191–96; Morris, *The Gospel according to John*, 215–18.

sake of his holy name! (vv. 22–23). How? By returning them to the Promised Land (v. 24) with this promise: "I will sprinkle clean water on you, and you shall be clean.... I will give you a new heart, and a new spirit I will put within you.... I will put my Spirit within you, and cause you to walk in my statutes" (vv. 25–27). Impossible with you, yes; but with me, I've promised to do this! "That which is born of the flesh is flesh." In John 1:13, John said God's children are born "not of blood nor of the will of the flesh nor of the will of man, but of God." "That which is born of the Spirit is spirit" (v. 6). There's earthly life, and that's all Nicodemus and we are capable of hearing as sinners; but there's also heavenly life that we need and that only God can give. It's not about being born as a Jew that gives entrance into the kingdom, but being born anew. Jesus says, "Do not marvel at this because as the wind blows where it wishes...so it is with everyone who is born of the Spirit" (vv. 7–8). "Of the Spirit." That phrase is used twice here (vv. 6, 8). It means the Holy Spirit, not you and me, is the one who gives this new spiritual life. It also means he's the one who acts while we are acted upon. John uses passive voice here to say the action is performed *on* us, not *by* us. We don't sprinkle ourselves, we don't put the Spirit in ourselves, we don't give ourselves a heart transplant—this is *given to* us! This is the beauty of why the gospel is good news: it's something *God* does for us when we can't do it for ourselves! Amen? Oh, and I should mention what comes after Ezekiel 36? Ezekiel 37, of course! But what does that say? Israel was like a valley of dead, dry bones and when the Spirit blew over them like the wind they came alive![93] Biblically speaking, then, regeneration is being *given* a new heart (Ezek. 36:25–27), *becoming* a new creation (2 Cor. 5:17), and *being* resurrected (Eph. 2:5).

Article 11 of our canons applies Jesus' words to the issue of the sinful will of man and his being converted to God as the momentous change of life: **But when God accomplishes His good pleasure in the elect or works in them true conversion** (*conversionem*). Then it goes on to speak of the way sinners of changed, describing in particular the effects of the grace of regeneration: **He not only causes the gospel to be externally preached to them and powerfully illuminates their mind by His Holy Spirit, that they may rightly understand and discern the things of the Spirit of God.**

---

[93] See Carson, *The Gospel according to John*, 198.

In John's words, conversion comes about by being "born…of God" (John 1:13), and in Jesus' words it's being "born from above" (John 3:3). Note that the canon says conversion happens by more than mere outward preaching; it includes that, but it's more than that. It also includes the Holy Spirit's powerful work to give light to the blind minds of people **that they may rightly understand and discern the things of the Spirit of God**.

This comes right from Paul's first letter to the Corinthians, where he says he imparted not an earthly wisdom but a secret wisdom of God through preaching. While the rulers of this world cannot grasp this wisdom, "these things God has revealed to us through the Spirit" (1 Cor. 2:10). Why is this necessary? "The natural person does not accept the things of the Spirit of God, for they are folly to him, and he is not able to understand them because they are spiritually discerned" (1 Cor. 2:14).

Outward preaching and illumining the mind; but it's more than that! Look at how article 11 says **but by the efficacy of the same regenerating Spirit** does a heavenly, spiritual work we cannot do for ourselves.[94] Note the verbs used of the Spirit:

1. *Pervades* (*penetrat*; penetrates) **the inmost recesses of** *the person* (*hominis*): "For the word of God is living and active, sharper than any two-edged sword, piercing to the division of soul and of spirit, of joints and of marrow, and discerning the thoughts and intentions of the heart" (Heb. 4:12).

2. *Opens* **the closed…heart**: "The Lord opened [Lydia's] heart to pay attention to what was said by Paul" (Acts 17:14).

3. *Softens* **the hardened heart**: "I will give you a new heart…. I will remove the heart of stone from your flesh and give you a heart of flesh" (Ezek. 36:26).

4. *Circumcises* [the heart] **that was uncircumcised**: "The LORD your God will circumcise your heart and the heart of your off-spring, so that you will love the LORD your God with all your heart and with all your soul, that you may live" (Deut. 30:6); "In [Christ] also you were circumcised with a circumcision made without hands, by putting off the body of the flesh, by the circumcision of Christ" (Col. 2:11); "But a Jew is one inwardly, and circumcision is a matter of the heart, by the Spirit, not by the letter" (Rom. 2:29).

---

[94] On the efficient cause of regeneration, see *Synopsis Purioris Theologiae: Volume 2*, 237–39.

5. *Infuses* **new qualities into the will, which though heretofore dead, He** *quickens*; **from being evil, disobedient, and refractory, He renders it good, obedient, and pliable**: "Even when we were dead in our trespasses, [God] made us alive together with Christ.... For we are his workmanship, created in Christ Jesus for good works, which God prepared beforehand, that we should walk in them" (Eph. 2:5, 10).[95]

6. *Actuates* **and** *strengthens* [the will], **that like a good tree, it may be** *bring forth* **the fruits of good actions**: "For no good tree bears bad fruit, nor again does a bad tree bear good fruit, for each tree is known by its own fruit.... The good person out of the good treasure of his heart produces good, and the evil person out of his evil treasure produces evil" (Luke 6:43, 44, 45).

Augustine summarized this **efficacy** even at the beginning of the life of faith this way: "To desire the help of grace is the beginning of grace."[96]

All those who are born in sin from their mother's womb are sinners. Therefore, all of us who were born in such fashion cannot enter the kingdom of God. If the Jews couldn't enter heaven in their natural state, how much more so must we Gentiles undergo a radical new birth? If the Jews couldn't keep the law and thus were barred from heaven, how much more so are we barred from the kingdom of God? If those false disciples saw Christ's miracles and believed in His name, but were still in their sins, how much more so we who only pray the "Sinner's Prayer"?

Article 12

And this is the regeneration so highly celebrated in Scripture and denominated a new creation: a resurrection from the dead, a making alive, which God works in us without our aid. But this is in no wise effected merely by the external preaching of the gospel, by moral suasion, or such a mode of operation, that after God has performed His part, it still remains in the power of man to be regenerated or not, to be converted or to continue unconverted; but it is evidently a supernatural work, most powerful, and at the same time most delightful, astonishing, mysterious, and ineffable; not inferior in efficacy to creation or the resurrection from the dead, as the Scripture inspired by the author of this work declares; so that all in whose heart God works in this marvelous manner are certainly, infallibly, and ef-

---

[95] Michael S. Horton, *Covenant and Salvation: Union with Christ* (Louisville, KY: Westminster John Knox, 2007).

[96] "On Rebuke and Grace," 2 (5:472.)

fectually regenerated, and do actually believe. Whereupon the will thus renewed is not only actuated and influenced by God, but in consequence of this influence, becomes itself active. Wherefore also, man is himself rightly said to believe and repent, by virtue of that grace received.

BIBLICAL DESCRIPTIONS OF REGENERATION

"You must be born again." What a glorious gospel doctrine for us who have been made alive by the Holy Spirit. We should never be confused about such a core doctrine of our faith. As we saw in Jesus' words in John 3 and article 11 above, this is a work that is impossible for us to accomplish, but God the Holy Spirit performs it with the greatest ease.

Article 12 now elaborates further on the meaning of this work of the Holy Spirit describing it from various Scriptures: **And this is the regeneration** (*regeneratio*) **so highly celebrated in Scripture and denominated a new creation: a resurrection from the dead, a making alive, which God works in us without our aid**. It's called **regeneration** or being "born again" by Jesus (John 3:3), Paul (Titus 3:5), and Peter (1 Pet. 1:3, 23). It's called **a new creation** by Paul (2 Cor. 5:17). It's called **the resurrection from the dead** by Paul (Rom. 6:5; Eph. 2:6; Col. 2:12; 3:1). It's called **a making alive** by Paul (Eph. 2:6; Col. 2:13).

Article 12 goes on to contrast the power of this rebirth, saying it's not in us but in God himself. *The power is not in us* when the article says, **But this is in no wise** (way) **effected merely by the external preaching of the gospel** as we saw in article 11 above. Practically, I used to think along these lines: "If I could just get my friend to go to that evangelistic crusade God could really do a work in his heart." The focus was so much on the outward preacher and not the power of the Holy Spirit. *The power is not in us* when the article says **this is in no *way* effected...by moral suasion** (*moralem suasionem*). The Remonstrant position is echoed today when you hear people say things like, "The Holy Spirit is a gentleman and will never violate your free will." Through the preacher the Spirit merely seeks to persuade "morally," that is, outwardly through reason, but not effectively in the soul.[97] *The power is not in us* when the article says **this is in no *way* effected…by…such a mode of operation, that after God has performed His part, it still remains in *human* (*hominis*) power to be regenerated or not, to be converted or to continue unconverted** (*regenerari vel non regenerari, converti vel non converti*). I was converted in this kind of evangelical environment. We heard things like, "God loves you, now all you have to do is love him back"; "Jesus died for your sins, now all you have to do is believe"; "Jesus stands at the door and knocks, but you still have to open it."

The effective power of regeneration is in God: **but it is evidently a supernatural work.** Remember what Jesus said to Nicodemus. **most powerful** [being from God], **and at the same time most delightful** [to God], **astonishing, mysterious, and ineffable** (inexpressible). This is what Jesus said when he likened being born again by the Spirit to the wind: "The wind blows where it wishes, and you hear its sound, but you do not know where it comes from or where it goes. So it is with everyone who is born of the Spirit" (John 3:8). Then our article says this work of the Spirit is **not inferior in efficacy to creation or the resurrection from the dead, as the Scripture inspired by the author of this work declares.** In the beginning God spoke and everything came to be! Paul calls our new life in Christ a "new creation" where the old passes away and something new comes in its place (2 Cor. 5:17). This new thing in us is no less powerful than God speaking the Milky Way into existence! Because our regeneration is this powerful, the result is that **all in whose heart God works in this marvelous manner are certainly, infallibly, and effectually regenerated** (*regenerentur*), **and do actually believe.** When God wants to give us a new heart, he does! We have a new one forever! As well, **whereupon the will thus renewed is not only actuated and influenced by God, but in consequence of this influence, becomes itself active. Wherefore also, man is himself rightly said to believe and repent, by virtue of that grace received.** We saw in article 11 that God enlightens our minds. Now we read that he renews our hearts and our wills. All that we were made to be in Adam that his sin and our continual sinning has effaced and ruined, Christ

---

[97] On the internal debate within the synod concerning Matthias Martinius's assertion that "God was *causa physica conversionis*," see Sinnema, "Reformed Scholasticism and the Synod of Dort, 483–87.

renews in us by the power of his Holy Spirit. We're reborn into new men, women, and children of our heavenly Father.

Article 13

The manner of this operation cannot be fully comprehended by believers in this life. Notwithstanding which, they rest satisfied with knowing and experiencing that by this grace of God they are enabled to believe with the heart, and love their Savior.

Article 13 is a brief elaboration to say that while we can describe and define the Holy Spirit's work from Scripture, as above, it's still a mysterious work: **The manner of this operation cannot be fully comprehended by believers in this life**. To use Jesus' analogy, like the wind blows but you don't know its origin or destination, the Holy Spirit is powerful and uncontrollable by us. We cannot...fully comprehend[...] (plene comprehendere non possunt) him and his work. What's interesting is how this article 13 concludes: **Notwithstanding which, they rest satisfied with knowing and experiencing that by this grace of God they are enabled to believe with the heart, and love their Savior.** The Spirit's work is incomprehensible, meaning, we're not able to fully grasp and get our arms around it; yet his work is experienceable. This is one of the reasons why the canons are so unique among Protestant Reformation confessions. They not only express high truth to engage the mind, the canons reach down deep into the hearts of God's people. We cannot comprehend the Spirit's work, but we can be content that God's grace has been at work in us. He's touched our minds to know that we are sinners who have an even greater Savior. He's touched our hearts to lead us to believe and love him! All the theological and philosophical language we use to express the graciousness of the Holy Spirit's work is so that we can truly pray as "the frozen chosen," Reformed people:

> Eternal Spirit, God of truth,
> Our contrite hearts inspire;
> Kindle a flame of heavenly love,
> And feed the pure desire.[98]
> Come, Holy Spirit, heavenly Dove,

---

[98] From the hymn "Eternal Spirit, God of Truth," by Thomas Cotterill (1810).

With all Thy quickening powers;
Kindle a flame of sacred love
In these cold hearts of ours.[99]

Article 14

Faith is therefore to be considered as the gift of God, not on account of its being offered by God to man, to be accepted or rejected at his pleasure; but because it is in reality conferred, breathed, and infused into him; or even because God bestows the power or ability to believe, and then expects that man should by the exercise of his own free will, consent to the terms of salvation and actually believe in Christ; but because He who works in man both to will and to do, and indeed all things in all, produces both the will to believe and the act of believing also.

Article 14 elaborates on the line at the end of article 13 that **by this grace of God they are enabled to believe with the heart, and love their Savior.** Article 14, then, goes on to say, **Faith is therefore to be considered as the gift of God.** This is a theme we've seen previously in the first point of doctrine on predestination (1.5, 1.6, 1.7, 1.9) and in the second point of doctrine on redemption (2.7, 2.8, 2.RE 3). Article 14 goes on to explain how faith is a gift of grace: **not on account of its being offered by God to** *a person* (*homini*)**, to be accepted or rejected at his pleasure; but because it is in reality conferred, breathed, and infused into him.** How often have well-meaning evangelical preachers tried to illustrate that while God does his part in offering us the gift of salvation, it's still up to us to receive the gift and open it? Faith is not merely offered, it's bestowed, breathed, and infused into us. Article offers another explanation: **or even because God bestows the power or ability to believe, and then expects that** *a person* (*hominis*) **should by the exercise of his own free will, consent to the terms of salvation and actually believe in Christ; but because He who works in** *a person* (*homine*) **both to will and to do, and indeed all things in all, produces both the will to believe and the act of believing also.** While some Remonstrants granted that God gifted faith in the sense of the potential to believe, the Reformed used the language of Paul to say not only that "it has been granted to you that for the sake of

---

[99] From the hymn "Come, Holy Spirit, Heavenly Dove," by Isaac Watts (1707).

Christ you should not only believe in him" (Phil. 1:29) but also that "it is God who works in you, both to will and to work for his good pleasure" (Phil. 2:13).

Article 15

God is under no obligation to confer this grace upon any; for how can He be indebted to man, who had no previous gifts to bestow, as a foundation for such recompense? Nay, who has nothing of his own but sin and falsehood? He therefore who becomes the subject of this grace, owes eternal gratitude to God, and gives Him thanks forever. Whoever is not made partaker thereof, is either altogether regardless of these spiritual gifts and satisfied with his own condition, or is in no apprehension of danger and vainly boasts the possession of that which he has not. With respect to those who make an external profession of faith and live regular lives, we are bound, after the example of the apostle, to judge and speak of them in the most favorable manner. For the secret recesses of the heart are unknown to us. And as to others, who have not yet been called, it is our duty to pray for them to God, who calls the things that are not, as if they were. But we are in no wise to conduct ourselves towards them with haughtiness, as if we had made ourselves to differ.

Article 15 offers a practical response to the **delightful, astonishing, mysterious, and ineffable** (art. 12) as well as incomprehensible (art. 14) work of the Holy Spirit we've seen the foregoing articles.

GOD'S GRACE IS GRACIOUS

The article first opens with a statement of the sheer graciousness of God's grace: **God is under no obligation to confer this grace upon any.** This is one of the great theological principles of Scripture and the Western Augustinian tradition. To quote Paul, "But if it is by grace, it is no longer on the basis of works; otherwise grace would no longer be grace" (Rom. 11:6). Article 15 continues to apply Paul's great doxology in Romans 11:33–36, saying, **for how can He be indebted to *them* (*ei*), who had no previous gifts to bestow, as a foundation for such recompense? Nay, who has nothing of his own but sin and falsehood?**

OUR RESPONSE OF GRACIOUSNESS

God owes us nothing, yet he's bestowed on us everything! Unless you're a lump on a log this should evoke a response from you! Here's how article 15 expresses it: **He therefore who becomes the subject of this grace, owes eternal gratitude to God, and gives Him thanks forever.** In the words of the Psalm, believers exclaim: "What shall I render to the LORD, for all his benefits to me?" (Ps. 116:12). Yet some do not receive this grace. Why not? **Whoever is not made partaker thereof, is either altogether regardless of these spiritual gifts and satisfied with his own condition.** Those who do not receive are hardened in heart. Others seem to receive it: **or is in no apprehension of danger and vainly boasts the possession of that which he has not.**

As recipients of God's grace, article 15 continues, we are to treat these two other groups graciously. First, we are to treat those who boast in self-assurance this way: **With respect to those who make an external profession of faith and live regular lives, we are bound, after the example of the apostle, to judge and speak of them in the most favorable manner. For the secret recesses of the heart are unknown to us.** The **external** or outward profession of people is all that we can judge as human beings. Only God knows the human heart and can search them (Ps. 44:21; Rom. 8:27).

Second, we are to treat those who do not receive God's grace this way: **And as to others, who have not yet been called, it is our duty to pray for them to God, who calls the things that are not, as if they were. But we are in no wise to conduct ourselves towards them with haughtiness, as if we had made ourselves to differ.** Our calling is to pray for the lost. Our calling is to be humble before the lost. As Paul told Gentile believers who like wild olive branches were grafted onto the tree of God's covenant people, "Do not be arrogant toward the branches...do not become proud, but fear" (Rom. 11:18, 20). In the words of Ian Hamilton, "A proud Calvinist is an oxymoron."[100]

---

[100] Ian Hamilton, "Winsome Calvinism," *Banner of Truth* 526 (2007): 4.

Article 16

But as man by the fall did not cease to be a creature endowed with understanding and will, nor did sin which pervaded the whole race of mankind deprive him of the human nature, but brought upon him depravity and spiritual death; so also this grace of regeneration does not treat men as senseless stocks and blocks, nor takes away their will and its properties, neither does violence thereto; but spiritually quickens, heals, corrects, and at the same time sweetly and powerfully bends it; that where carnal rebellion and resistance formerly prevailed, a ready and sincere spiritual obedience begins to reign, in which the true and spiritual restoration and freedom of our will consist. Wherefore unless the admirable Author of every good work wrought in us, man could have no hope of recovering from his fall by his own free will, by the abuse of which, in a state of innocence, he plunged himself into ruin.

In article 16 the synod elaborates on the nature of regeneration. If, as we've seen, regeneration is a new creation, does this mean that God bypasses us completely in this work? Are we the same person after regeneration as we were before?

AN ANALOGY

The first thing we read is an analogy between creation and re-creation. First, article 16 speaks of the creation and fall of humanity: **as man** (*homo*), meaning Adam, **by the fall did not cease to be a *human being*** (*homo*)[101] **endowed with understanding and will**. God created Adam and Eve as human beings with intellect and will, and after their fall into sin they, and all humanity to come, still have intellect and will. The analogy continues: **nor did sin which pervaded the *whole human race*** (*universum genus humanum*) **deprive him of the human nature, but brought upon him depravity and spiritual death**. Speaking of the fall into sin, sin effaced human nature, it did not erase human nature.

Then the analogy comes full circle in speaking of regeneration: **so also this grace of regeneration** (*regenerationis*) **does not treat *people*** (*hominibus*) **as senseless stocks and blocks**. The imagery of **stocks and blocks** doesn't quite come through; it's *truncis et stipitibus*, tree trunks and

---

[101] Within this sentence is a particularly catchy axiom: *homo non desiit esse homo*, "man (Adam) did not cease to be man" (human).

stakes/posts. In other words, inanimate, lifeless things. This means when Reformed people speak of "irresistible grace" we're not saying human beings were like mindless zombies that God grabbed and made human. We're not saying God completely bypassed our human intellect and will in converting us. Going back to our introduction to this book and the popular language "the five points of Calvinism" or "TULIP," this language of "irresistible grace" is another phrase we need to consider carefully. This communicates to people that they had no authentic human response to the gospel. It also seems to contradict clear Scriptures that describe the people of God in Jesus' day and before as being "stiff-necked," "uncircumcised in heart and ears," and "always resist[ing] the Holy Spirit" (Acts 7:51). In fact, in the aforementioned response of Paraeus to the "horrid and barbarous" terms of resistible and irresistible grace he said we need to be clear on how we speak. Prior to conversion God issues a "calling grace" or what we call the outward call of the gospel. This outward call of the gospel as seen above from Acts 7 "is not irresistible, but too much resistible; yes, that the will before conversion can doe nothing but resist this calling grace."[102] There is also a "cooperating grace" after conversion in the life of the regenerated believer. In the context of the tension between the flesh and Spirit in Galatians 5 and Romans 7, Paraeus said, "This resistibilitie or resistance is not…between grace & the will, but between sensualitie, or that remainder of the flesh in the Saints, & between grace."[103] In these two senses grace *can* be resisted by the unregenerated and regenerated sinner. Yet there is also "operating grace" or "the motion of Gods mercie (as *Austin* [Augustine] calls it) by which hee worketh inwardly in the minds, wills, and hearts of the unregenerate these things which belong to mans conversion."[104] What this teaches us is that we ought to put our focus as preachers and teachers on the efficacy or effectiveness of grace, which first works *on* and *in* dead sinners who then genuinely respond *by* and *through* this grace.[105]

Further, the article state that **this grace of regeneration does not…take[…] away their will and its properties, neither does violence**

---

[102] Paraeus, "Epitome of Arminianisme," 834.

[103] Paraeus, "Epitome of Arminianisme," 834.

[104] Paraeus, "Epitome of Arminianisme," 834. For Paraeus's thirteen proofs that this work of grace is irresistible, see ibid., 835–36.

[105] I'm indebted to my colleague, Dr. Cornelis Venema, for this line of thought. *But for the Grace of God*, 67–68. See also Feenstra, *Unspeakable Comfort*, 96–97.

thereto. In other words, God didn't transplant a sinful will bent in on itself and give us a new one. He also didn't coerce us by force. Sometimes well-intentioned Reformed people say, "I was brought into the kingdom kicking and screaming; that's irresistible grace." Instead, **this divine grace of re-generation...spiritually quickens, heals, corrects, and at the same time sweetly and powerfully bends it**. God brings our spiritually dead wills back to life; he heals our mortally wounded will; he reforms that which was deformed in such a way that while it once was bent in upon itself, now it is bent outward toward its Maker.

One of the important truths this article affirms is that fallen man is still human in the image of God. On the contrary, Feenstra takes take the language of article 1 that by his sin Adam **forfeited these excellent gifts** to mean "man is no longer the image of God...no longer God's representative" and that "the remains of the image of God are no longer stamped upon him." Based on this, he goes on to say, "The Lord has to make an entirely new beginning with us."[106] This has been a view within Reformed circles from as far back as John Calvin's 1539 *Institutes*, although Calvin later modified his view to say, "In man's conversion what belongs to his primal nature remains entire...it is created anew; not meaning that the will now begins to exist, but that it is changed from an evil to a good will."[107] The *Dutch Annotations* explained in comments on the language of a "new heart" in Ezekiel 11:19: this is "a change of the spirit, not in substance and essence, but in qualities and powers." How? "By rooting out of the soul the evil qualities, powers and faculties wherewith through their own corrupt nature they oppose me, and by taking them away from them by the Spirit of regeneration."[108]

The best proof that God does not remake us entirely in regeneration is the overall context of article 1 as found in several other articles. Article 4 confesses:

> **There is...a certain light of nature remaining in *people* after the fall, by virtue of which he retains some notions about God, natural things, and the difference**

---

[106] Feenstra, *Unspeakable Comfort*, 100.

[107] Calvin, *Institutes*, 2.3.6. On Calvin's shift, see Lane, "Did Calvin Believe in Freewill?," *Vox Evangelica* 12 (1981): 81–83.

[108] *Dutch Annotations* on Ezekiel 11:19.

between what is moral and immoral, and demonstrates a certain eagerness for virtue and for good outward behavior.

Added to this is the language of article 16: **as man** (*homo*), meaning Adam, **by the fall did not cease to be a creature endowed with understanding and will, nor did sin…deprive him of the human nature.** In the words of Thysius, "God herein woks in his divine manner, and in fact with a grace, power, and efficacy…that he effectively takes the depravity out of the will and implants uprightness in it, so that man is changed from unwilling to willing, and from resisting God to obeying Him."[109] To use the distinction from above, the will still remains, it's just the depraved habit that's removed.

A RESULT

Because of this wonderful work of the Spirit we read **that where carnal rebellion and resistance formerly prevailed, a ready and sincere spiritual obedience begins to reign.** Those who once hated God now love God. Those who rebelled against God now rebel against their sins, the world, and the devil. Those who once resisted God now willingly acquiesce to his will. The irony is, against ancient Pelagianism and modern Arminianism, it is in this that **the true and spiritual restoration and freedom of our will consist.** The will was free before, but free to act consistent with our sinful and fallen human nature. Thysius said, "Inclines toward sin not by the force of necessity but out of pleasure…because this is the will of a man who has been sold under sin, who is its slave and dead in it, it should be called bound rather than free."[110] Now it's truly free to love and serve the Lord as the desire of a new heart.[111] Paul said to whomever you present yourself as an obedient slave you are a slave—either to sin or righteousness (Rom. 6:16). For the Romans he praised God: "But thanks be to God, that you who were once slaves of sin have become obedient from the heart to the standard of teaching to which you were committed" (Rom. 6:17). Notice that. We were once slaves to sin, but now we're obedient to God from

---

[109] *Synopsis Purioris Theologiae: Volume 1*, 421.

[110] *Synopsis Purioris Theologiae: Volume 1*, 419.

[111] Venema, *But for the Grace of God*, 68.

the heart, the very center of our being that only served sin, self, and Satan before! Paul then concluded in one of his most ironic but illuminating lines: "and having been set free from sin, have become slaves of righteousness" (Rom. 6:19). We're still slaves, it's just that we serve God now from the bottom of our hearts. One of my favorite lines from the Reformation Book of Common Prayer prays to God, saying, "whose service is perfect freedom."[112]

In concluding this article, the divines at Dort wrote: **wherefore unless the admirable Author of every good work wrought in us,** *people* (*homini*) **could have no hope of recovering from his fall by his own free will, by the abuse of which, in a state of innocence, he plunged himself into ruin.** This is such a profound image. Man was created *rectissimeque*, the image being *standing upright*, but by sin he fell down and was unable to get back up. Only God could do that work through the powerful yet pleasing work of regeneration.

Article 17

As the almighty operation of God, whereby He prolongs and supports this our natural life, does not exclude, but requires the use of means, by which God of His infinite mercy and goodness hath chosen to exert His influence, so also the beforementioned supernatural operation of God, by which we are regenerated, in no wise excludes or subverts the use of the gospel, which the most wise God has ordained to be the seed of regeneration and food of the soul. Wherefore, as the apostles, and teachers who succeeded them, piously instructed the people concerning this grace of God, to His glory, and the abasement of all pride, and in the meantime, however, neglected not to keep them by the sacred precepts of the gospel in the exercise of the Word, sacraments and discipline; so even to this day, be it far from either instructors or instructed to presume to tempt God in the church by separating what He of His good pleasure hath most intimately joined together. For grace is conferred by means of admonitions; and the more readily we perform our duty, the more eminent usually is this blessing of God working in us, and the more directly is His work advanced; to whom alone all the glory both of means, and of their saving fruit and efficacy is forever due. Amen.

---

112 "The Collect for Peace" in the service of Morning Prayer.

As we've seen, Jesus' powerful and memorable words in John 3 on being born again, or being regenerated, means that the Holy Spirit gives us who were dead in sins new spiritual life. This is so wonderful that we sing with Peter, "Blessed be the God and Father of our Lord Jesus Christ! According to his great mercy, he has caused us to be born again to a living hope" (1 Pet. 1:3). Perhaps surprisingly, he gave us this life by working within the confines of who we are as human beings with minds, wills, and affections. Now that we are born anew, how is this new life fed? Is it sustained supernaturally apart from means?

THE ANALOGY OF FOOD

Article 17 makes use of another analogy: that of food in relation to our ongoing new spiritual life: **As the almighty operation of God, whereby He prolongs** (*producit*; brings forth) **and supports** (*sustentat*; sustains) **this our natural life, does not exclude, but requires the use of means, by which God of His infinite mercy** (*sapientia*; wisdom) **and goodness hath chosen to exert His influence.** To give us earthly and temporal life God has used the means of our parents and to sustain that life he uses the means of food. The analogy continues: **so also the beforementioned supernatural operation of God, by which we are regenerated** (*regenerat*), **in no wise** (way) **excludes or subverts the use of the gospel, which the most wise God has ordained to be the seed of regeneration** (*semen regenerationis*) **and food of the soul.**

As newborn children of God, we have a twofold life. We have an outward life of the body and an inward life of the soul. We have a temporal life, and we have eternal life. And just like we need to eat food to nourish, strengthen, and sustain our outward and temporal life, so too with our spiritual life. This is why Peter can write about out inward and eternal life based on the analogy of our outward and temporal life. He speaks of our inwardly being "born *again*," just as we were born temporary; he speaks of the "perishable seed" that gave us temporal life and of the "imperishable" seed that gave us eternal life (1 Pet. 1:23); he speaks of our being made spiritual "newborn infants" who "long for the pure spiritual milk, that by it you may grow up into salvation" (1 Pet. 2:2). Our canons are on biblical footing in their statement.

One of the applications for us is to be concerned for our inward and eternal life as we are about our outward and temporal life. Paul told Timothy:

> If you put these things before the brothers, you will be a good servant of Christ Jesus, being trained in the words of the faith and of the good doctrine that you have followed. Have nothing to do with irreverent, silly myths. Rather train yourself for godliness; for while bodily training is of some value, godliness is of value in every way, as it holds promise for the present life and also for the life to come. (1 Tim. 4:6–8)

Notice that exercise has value; it's just that godliness has more because it's dealing with eternal realities. Eat well, sleep well, and exercise well; and take care of your soul!

THE FOOD OF THE SOUL

Let's focus in especially on the food of the soul here in 1 Peter chapters 1 and 2. Peter speaks of our new spiritual life in terms of our initial regeneration and our subsequent preservation here. We see that in our canon, which speaks of **the seed of regeneration and food of the soul**.

Peter speaks of our *regeneration* beginning in verse 23: "Since you have been born again" (1 Pet. 1:23). What's so powerful about this verb is that Peter puts it in the perfect tense. That means this is something that has already been accomplished. How were we born again? Jesus said in John 3 that the Holy Spirit is the one who does this work. But how? Peter explains with a quotation from Isaiah 40: "All flesh is like grass and all its glory like the flower of grass. The grass withers, and the flower falls, but the word of the Lord remains forever" (1:24–25). In Isaiah's day, the people of God were wasting away like grass and flowers in the desert in their exile in Babylon, but God comforted them with the truth that his reviving word remained and did not change. Then Peter applies this to us in that little explanation at the end: "And this word is the good news that was preached to you" (1:25). How were you and I regenerated? By the power of the Holy Spirit through the means of the preaching of the gospel.

Peter then speaks of our *preservation* as the children of God in 1 Peter 2:2–3: "Like newborn infants, long for the pure spiritual milk, that by it you may grow up into salvation—if indeed you have tasted that the Lord is good." I never knew what it was for a baby to long for milk until I became a dad. My firstborn son, Cyprian, was so big when he was born (12 lb. 5 oz.!) that for the first couple of days he was not able to be satisfied with just his mom's milk. So he was crying out in hunger. I had to supplement his milk with formula that I fed him with a little syringe and tube that I held inside his cheek. He guzzled that formula! Now, we all know that "milk" can be used negatively in Scripture of those who are so spiritually childish and immature that they old feed on milk (1 Cor. 3:1–2; Heb. 5:13). But Peter uses it positively because milk is appropriate for sustaining new life.

As God the Father's "newborn infants," we are called to "long for the pure spiritual milk." What is this "milk"? That's the big surprise here. In verse 1 Peter tells us that we have already and that we must continue to "put away all malice and all deceit and hypocrisy and envy and all slander." The surprise is that he does not now give a list of virtues in contrast, but simply mentions dependence on the Lord.[113] Notice that "the pure spiritual milk" is parallel to "if indeed you have tasted that the Lord is good" (v. 3). And how have we tasted of the Lord's goodness? Back to 1:25: the preaching of the gospel! Look at article 17 again with me:

> **Wherefore, as the apostles, and teachers who succeeded them, piously instructed the people concerning this grace of God, to His glory, and the abasement of all pride, and in the meantime, however, neglected not to keep them by the sacred precepts of the gospel in the exercise of the Word, sacraments and discipline; so even to this day, be it far from either instructors or instructed to presume to tempt in the church by separating what He of His good pleasure hath most intimately joined together.**

Why are we to long for it? Peter says "that by it you may grow up into salvation." Our children are born and they are members of our families; their status is not in doubt. In the same way when we are born again by the Father's will our status as his children does not change. "Grow[ing] up into salvation" (2:2) is our maturation in the salvation we already have. We are

---

[113] Davids, *The First Epistle of Peter*, 81.

to long for the Word so that we will grow! Look one last time at the canon, which says:

> For grace is conferred by means of admonitions; and the more readily we perform our duty, the more eminent usually is this blessing of God working in us, and the more directly is His work advanced; to whom alone all the glory both of means, and of their saving fruit and efficacy is forever due. Amen.

VI:

WHAT WE REJECT
REJECTION OF ERRORS 1-9

HAVING SET forth the orthodox teaching on humanity's sin and God's grace in the conversion of sinners, especially the Holy Spirit's work in regeneration, the synod again lists several rejections of errors on these same issues of the relationship between the Spirit's work in the lives of sinners. Let's look at these briefly.

Rejection of Errors 1

That it cannot properly be said that original sin in itself suffices to condemn the whole human race or to deserve temporal and eternal punishment.

For these contradict the apostle, who declares: "Wherefore, as by one man sin entered into the world, and death by sin; and so death passed upon all men, for that all have sinned" (Rom. 5:12). And: "The judgment was by one to condemnation" (Rom. 5:16). And: "The wages of sin is death" (Rom. 6:23).

The first rejection begins: *it cannot properly be said that original sin in itself suffices to condemn the whole human race.* This picks up a theme we've seen previously. In 1.1 we read the opposite: **as all men have sinned in Adam, lie under the curse, and are deserving of eternal death, God would have done no injustice by leaving them all to perish, and delivering them over to condemnation on account of sin.** This orthodox Reformed doctrine is in direct continuity with the Council of Carthage (418) while the Remonstrant doctrine is in direct contradiction. In its second canon, Carthage confessed the reason infants of believers were to be baptized was precisely because they derived sin from Adam that needed the grace of remission. The translators of the Dutch Bible continued this catholic theme when they said: "For all men that die have not committed any actual sin in themselves, as appears in infants, many of which die in their infancy; and therefore must have sinned in this one man in whose loins they were."[1]

The first rejected error continues: *it cannot properly be said that original sin in itself suffices...to deserve temporal and eternal punishment*. Again, this picks up on a theme we saw in 2.1: **God is...supremely just. And His justice requires...that our sins committed against His infinite majesty should be punished, not only with temporal, but with eternal punishment, both in body and soul**. The Second Council of Orange (529) rejected the ancient Pelagian view that Adam's sin only brought about bodily death as a punishment on the human race, but that his sin was not passed down. In fact, canon 2 went on to define sin as "the death of the soul" (*mors...animae*).[2] In response the synod looked to several Scriptures we've seen and commented on already.

First, the article cited Romans 5:12, which we saw in connection with 1.1 and 3/4.2. Paul tells us that Adam brought sin and death into the world, which are then passed on to all humanity on the basis of Adam's representative action.

Second, although the canons haven't cited Romans 5:16 in particular to this point, its overall context of 5:12 makes it poignant: **The judgment was by one to condemnation**. Adam's sin brought judgment upon our race and therefore eternal condemnation in direct contrast to Pelagianism and the Remonstrants.

Third, the article cited Romans 6:23 again, as it had done at the very beginning in 1.1: **"The wages of sin is death"** (death being understood as *eternal* death).

---

[1] *Dutch Annotations* on Romans 5:12.

[2] Woods, *Canons of the Second Council of Orange*, 19.

Rejection of Errors 2

That the spiritual gifts or the good qualities and virtues, such as goodness, holiness, righteousness, could not belong to the will of man when he was first created, and that these, therefore, could not have been separated therefrom in the fall.

For such is contrary to the description of the image of God which the apostle gives in Ephesians 4:24, where he declares that it consists in righteousness and holiness, which undoubtedly belong to the will.

The second rejection also deals with issues related to Adam as originally created in terms of his constitution and by extension our creation after the Fall. The Remonstrants taught *that the spiritual gifts or the good qualities and virtues, such as goodness, holiness, righteousness, could not belong to human (hominis) will when he was first created, and that these, therefore, could not have been separated therefrom in the fall.* After their original *Remonstrance* of 1610, when the state and church sought reconciliation at the 1611 *Collatio Hagiensis*, the Remonstrants asserted this same truth this way: "Infusion [of spiritual gifts] could not occur" at creation and the reason was "because it [the will] is of itself free to will either good or evil."[3]

Although this seems like an obscure theological discussion akin to how many angels can dance upon the head of a pin or that we're on thin biblical ground trying to prove the contrary, the synod takes us back to a text we began with in this point of doctrine: **For such is contrary to the description of the image of God which the apostle gives in Ephesians 4:24, where he declares that it consists in righteousness and holiness, which undoubtedly belong to the will.** In other words, as mentioned before, what is *renewed* in us in Christ *resided* in Adam prior to his fall. Since our wills are renewed so that we pursue righteousness and holiness as new creations in Christ, Adam's will possessed these gifts.

Rejection of Errors 3

That in spiritual death the spiritual gifts are not separate from the will of man, since the will in itself has never been corrupted, but only hindered through the darkness of the understanding and the irregularity of the affections; and that, these hindrances having been removed, the will can then bring into operation its native powers, that is, that the

---

[3] Cited in Goudriaan, "The Synod of Dordt on Arminian Anthropology," 97.

will of itself is able to will and to choose, or not to will and not to choose, all manner of good which may be presented to it.

This is an innovation and an error, and tends to elevate the powers of the free will, contrary to the declaration of the prophet: "The heart is deceitful above all things, and desperately wicked" (Jer. 17:9); and of the apostle: "Among whom (sons of disobedience) also we all had our conversation in times past in the lusts of our flesh, fulfilling the desires of the flesh and of the mind" (Eph. 2:3).

Rejection 3 continues the themes introduced in the first two: *That in spiritual death the spiritual gifts are not separate from human* (*hominis*) *will.* At the 1611 *Collatio Hagiensis*, the Remonstrants said it like this: "Spiritual gifts are not in the literal sense separated from the human will since they never were engraven into it, but only the freedom by which it would be capable of doing either good or bad."[4] The Remonstrants actually had a doctrine of humanity's creation in a state of "pure nature" that came from a strand in medieval theological debates. This meant, therefore, Adam did not have any supernatural gifts above what he had by virtue of his creation. The reason for this, according to the Remonstrant Caspar Barlaeus, was that God wanted Adam's obedience to be entirely free.[5]

The first reason the Remonstrants offered for this position was *since the will in itself has never been corrupted, but only hindered through the darkness of the understanding and the irregularity of the affections.* Yet the Reformed were consistently rejecting a view the Council of Carthage (418) had long ago rejected. The Pelagians taught that grace helps us in not sinning "by opening to our understanding the commandments, so that we may know what to seek, to avoid, and also love to do" (canon 4). In other words, one issue between the Remonstrant Reformed and the orthodox Reformed was that the *mind* (Remonstrant), not the *will* (Reformed), was seen as in need of grace. Again, the Reformed were on catholic ground with the Second Council of Orange (529) that said Adam's sin affected the whole person in body *and* soul, meaning, it weakened the human will (canon 1).[6]

---

[4] Cited in Goudriaan, "The Synod of Dordt on Arminian Anthropology," 97.

[5] See Goudriaan, "The Synod of Dordt on Arminian Anthropology," 99.

[6] Woods, *Canons of the Second Council of Orange*, 17–19.

The second reason for the Remonstrant view that spiritual gifts were not given to Adam and in him all humanity before the Fall was *that, these hindrances having been removed, the will can then bring into operation its native powers, that is, that the will of itself is able to will and to choose, or not to will and not to choose, all manner of good which may be presented to it.* For the Remonstrant, the will in itself was neutral and able to sin or not to sin even after the Fall.[7] To put it in terms of the Pelagianism the Council of Carthage (418) rejected: "Grace…was given to us only that we might be able more readily by grace to perform what we were ordered to do through our free will" (canon 5). The Second Council of Orange (529), in fact, rejected the view that "the free choice of all men was not weakened by the sin of the first man; or at least, thinks that it was only so far injured as to admit of the possibility of some being able to seek for themselves the mystery of eternal salvation with the revelation of God" (canon 8).[8]

In response to this error and its reasons, the synod said: **This is an innovation and an error, and tends to elevate the powers of the free will** (*vires liberi arbitrii*). What this means is that the debate at the time of Dort was not about "free will" so much as the power of free will to make choices from a neutral stance. The freedom of the will remains intact even after the Fall. Yet its power to choose or not to choose is damaged and affected by our sinful nature. In the words of the Gelderland delegates to the synod, "The will has not been lost by sin; nor the freedom of the will. For freely the human being wills everything he wills, but as long as a man is a prisoner of the devil and a servant of sin, he wills nothing but evil (albeit under the appearance of the good),"[9] As such, it was **contrary to the declaration of** both **the prophet** Jeremiah…**and of the apostle** Paul. Jeremiah said centuries before the coming of Jesus, **"The heart is deceitful above all things, and desperately wicked (Jer. 17:9)."** Taking the heart as the center of human willing, the prophet is saying it is not neutral but bent to sin. In the New Testament Paul said of converts to Christ: **Among whom (sons of disobedience) also we all had our conversation** (i.e., lived among them) **in times past in the lusts of our flesh, fulfilling the**

---

[7] See the discussion in Goudriaan, "The Synod of Dordt on Arminian Anthropology," 96–98.

[8] Woods, *Canons of the Second Council of Orange*, 27.

[9] Cited in Goudriaan, "The Synod of Dordt on Arminian Anthropology," 95.

desires of the flesh and of the mind (Eph. 2:3). In other words, unbelievers will or do what the sinful affections desire.

Rejection of Errors 4

That the unregenerate man is not really nor utterly dead in sin, nor destitute of all powers unto spiritual good, but that he can yet hunger and thirst after righteousness and life, and offer the sacrifice of a contrite and broken spirit, which is pleasing to God.

For these are contrary to the express testimony of Scripture. "Who were dead in trespasses and sins"; "Even when we were dead in sins" (Eph. 2:1, 5); and: "every imagination of the thoughts of his heart was only evil continually" (Gen. 6:5); "for the imagination of man's heart is evil from his youth" (Gen. 8:21). Moreover, to hunger and thirst after deliverance from misery, and after life, and to offer unto God the sacrifice of a broken spirit, is peculiar to the regenerate and those that are called blessed. "Create in me a clean heart, O God; and renew a right spirit within me"; "Then shalt Thou be pleased with the sacrifices of righteousness, with burnt offering and whole burnt offering: then shall they offer bullocks upon Thine altar" (Ps. 51:10, 19); "Blessed are they which do hunger and thirst after righteousness: for they shall be filled" (Matt. 5:6).

Because of the errors above related to Adam, his creation, his sin, and our subsequent creation after his sin, the Remonstrants taught *that the unregenerate person (hominem) is not really nor utterly dead in sin, nor destitute of all powers unto spiritual good, but that he can yet hunger and thirst after righteousness and life, and offer the sacrifice of a contrite and broken spirit, which is pleasing to God.* One of the things this language shows is that by 1618–1619 the Remonstrant doctrine had developed and devolved, in fact, in terms of how it viewed the necessity of grace. Article 3 of the original 1610 *Remonstrance* said, "Man does not have saving faith of himself nor by the power of his own free will...and sin can not of and through himself think, will or do any good which is truly good"; therefore, "it is necessary that he be regenerated by God, in Christ, through his Holy Spirit, and renewed in understanding, affections or will, and all powers."[10] The will needed complete renewal. One of the reasons for developing a system in which *the unregenerate person is not really nor utterly*

---

[10] As cited in "The *Remonstrance* of 1610," appendix C in De Jong, *Crisis in the Reformed Churches*, 208.

dead in sin, nor destitute of all powers unto spiritual good was the priority of the intellect in Remonstrant theology over the will as in orthodox Reformed theology. What this means is that the intellect was in need of repair so that the will could exercise its powers in the right way.[11]

The synod responded line by line to this large error that was **contrary to the express testimony of Scripture** with several passages.

In Ephesians 2:1 and 2:5 the apostle Paul said before conversion and regeneration the Ephesians **"were dead in trespasses and sins."** The meaning of this is that unregenerate people are "not only subject to temporal and eternal death, but also without any life and motion in spiritual things."[12]

In Genesis 6:5 and 8:21 we read that **"every imagination of the thoughts of his heart was only evil continually"** and **"for the imagination of the human (*hominis*) heart is evil from his youth."** In the *Dutch Annotations* we read on Genesis 6:5 that this is "a very naked and fundamental description of original sin and the fruits thereof."[13]

Finally, the rejection links together texts like David's prayer of confession in Psalm 51 and Jesus' teaching on the Sermon on the Mount in Matthew 5 to say: **to hunger and thirst after deliverance from misery, and after life, and to offer unto God the sacrifice of a broken spirit, is peculiar to the regenerate and those that are called blessed.**

Rejection of Errors 5

That the corrupt and natural man can so well use the common grace (by which they understand the light of nature), or the gifts still left him after the fall, that he can gradually gain by their good use a greater, namely, the evangelical or saving grace and salvation itself. And that in this way God on His part shows Himself ready to reveal Christ unto all men, since He applies to all sufficiently and efficiently the means necessary to conversion.

For the experience of all ages and the Scriptures do both testify that this is untrue. "He sheweth His word unto Jacob, His statutes and His judgments unto Israel. He hath not dealt so with any nation: and as for His judgments, they have not known them" (Ps. 147:19, 20). "Who in times

---

[11] See Richard A. Muller, "The Priority of the Intellect in the Soteriology of Jacob Arminius," *Westminster Theological Journal* 55, no. 1 (1993): 55–72.

[12] *Dutch Annotations* on Ephesians 2:1.

[13] *Dutch Annotations* on Genesis 6:5.

past suffered all nations to walk in their own ways" (Acts 14:16). And: "Now when they (Paul and his companions) had gone throughout Phrygia and the region of Galatia, and were forbidden of the Holy Ghost to preach the word in Asia, after they were come to Mysia, they assayed to go into Bithynia: but the Spirit suffered them not" (Acts 16:6, 7).

Rejection 5 is related back to articles 4 and 5 and the Reformed teaching "natural light" cannot convert or regenerate sinners. The Remonstrant teaching being rejected was *that the corrupt and natural person (hominem) can so well use the common grace (gratia communi) (by which they understand the light of nature [lumen naturae]), or of the gifts still left him after the fall.* One of the great differences between the Remonstrant Reformed and the orthodox Reformed was the Remonstrants' much more positive role of natural light (*lumen naturae*) or reason. One of the things Arminius taught that was carried on by his followers was that those who use their natural abilities aright are given a more supernatural grace by God.[14] Arminius spoke of "that promise by which God binds Himself to illuminate with supernatural grace (*gratia supernaturali*) the man who shall make right use of natural light (*lumine naturali*), or at least, so far as he is able, shall not make a bad use thereof."[15] Johannes Arnoldus was one such disciple: "Arminius prefers saying God gives further grace to him who makes the right use of the first [grace], but denies further [grace] to him who does not make the right use of it."[16] This was an adaptation of medieval covenant theology that those who did what was in them would receive grace.[17] Some even called natural light *"common grace"* in distinction from the further supernatural grace.[18] Because of this natural light within, some like Simon Episcopius said everyone has the ability to read and understand the Word of God and the spiritual truths it contains.[19] This was in contrast to the Second Council of Orange (529), which rejected the view that we can form any right opinion or make any right choice that relates to salvation, or

---

[14] Cited in Goudriaan, "The Synod of Dordt on Arminian Anthropology," 91.

[15] "Modest Examination," in *The Works of James Arminius: Volume 3*, 449; cf. 483–84. For the Latin text, see *Examen modestum libelli* (Leiden, 1612), 218; cf. 259–60.

[16] Cited in Goudriaan, "The Synod of Dordt on Arminian Anthropology," 92.

[17] On this, see Oberman, *The Harvest of Medieval Theology.*

[18] See Goudriaan, "The Synod of Dordt on Arminian Anthropology," 92.

[19] Goudriaan, "The Synod of Dordt on Arminian Anthropology," 93–94.

that we can assent to the preaching of the gospel through our natural powers; instead, these proceed from the illumination and inspiration of the Holy Spirit (canon 7).[20]

The result of this high view of natural light was twofold. First, one could scale the ladder of grace: *that he can gradually gain by their good use a greater, namely, the evangelical or saving grace and salvation itself.* Second, this ladder was sent into all the world: *that in this way God on His part shows Himself ready to reveal Christ unto all men, since He applies to all sufficiently and efficiently the means necessary to conversion.*

Dort offered a response as we would expect from Scripture that it testif[ies] **that this is untrue.** But it's interesting it also rooted its rejection in **the experience of all ages.** The Reformed teaching was a biblical teaching but also one that had been confirmed in the crucible of experience in the lives of God's people for millennia. Three texts illustrated this rejection.

First, the Psalter praises the Lord who **"sheweth His word unto Jacob, His statutes and His judgments unto Israel. He hath not dealt so with any nation: and as for His judgments, they have not known them" (Ps. 147:19–20).** In other words, by God revealing himself through his Word to his people, those outside could not then use natural light to ascend into the supernatural light of God. Salvation was a matter of revelation, and God revealed himself to some in the time of the old covenant; he did not also reveal himself partway to the world.

Second, in Acts 14:16 Paul states that God **"in times past suffered** ["permitted"] **all nations to walk in their own ways."** The human race is sinful and God has permitted our race to live in the sins they desired. As we saw earlier from Romans 3, "no one seeks God" in their natural state.

Third, as we've already seen in Acts 16:6–7, Luke records for us that **"when they (Paul and his companions) had gone throughout Phrygia and the region of Galatia, and were forbidden of the Holy Ghost to preach the word in Asia, after they were come to Mysia, they assayed to go into Bithynia: but the Spirit suffered them not."** Those in Asia and Bithynia could not reason their way into the kingdom apart from God's gracious revelation of himself.

---

[20] Woods, *Canons of the Second Council of Orange*, 25.

Rejection of Errors 6

That in the true conversion of man no new qualities, powers or gifts can be infused by God into the will, and that therefore faith through which we are first converted, and because of which we are called believers, is not a quality or gift infused by God, but only an act of man, and that it cannot be said to be a gift, except in respect of the power to attain to this faith.

For thereby they contradict the Holy Scriptures which declare that God infuses new qualities of faith, of obedience, and of the consciousness of His love into our hearts: "I will put My law in their inward parts, and write it in their hearts" (Jer. 31:33). And: "I will pour water upon him that is thirsty, and floods upon the dry ground: I will pour My Spirit upon thy seed" (Is. 44:3). And: "the love of God is shed abroad in our hearts by the Holy Ghost which is given unto us" (Rom. 5:5). This is also repugnant to the continuous practice of the Church, which prays by the mouth of the prophet thus: "turn Thou me, and I shall be turned" (Jer. 31:18).

So far we've seen that the Remonstrants taught that man in the state of innocence in the Garden was created with free will and that no other gifts were granted to him above and beyond his creaturely capacity. Under the state of misery he still has this capacity as nothing was lost. With article 6 we learn they also taught that in the state of grace nothing was added to him: *that in the true conversion* (vera conversione) *of people* (hominis) *no new qualities, powers or gifts can be infused by God into the will.* They cannot be added because as we saw above (3/4.RE 2, 3) they were not there in the first place.

The Remonstrant teaching goes on: *and that therefore faith through which we are first converted* (convertimur), *and because of which we are called believers, is not a quality or gift infused by God, but only a human* (hominis) *act, and that it cannot be said to be a gift, except in respect of the power to attain to this faith.* All the biblical language we've seen so far in every point of doctrine that faith is a supernatural gift of God's grace was reduced to *a human act* and the language of *gift* was redefined as only a way of speaking of *the power to attain.* According to the Remonstrants, what was *native* or natural to created and even fallen human beings was an active power to exercise supernatural faith (cf. 3/4.RE 3).

Following the Second Council of Orange (529), though, we see that this was an ancient error that said grace was conferred as a result of human prayer (canon 3), that God awaits our desire to be cleansed from sin (canon 4), that the desire for faith's beginning and increase belongs to us by nature (canon 5); instead, all these proceed from grace.[21] More importantly, these views **contradict the Holy Scriptures which declare that God infuses new qualities of faith, of obedience, and of the consciousness of His love into our hearts.** As proof, the synod offered the following set of biblical passages:

> **"I will put My law in their inward parts, and write it in their hearts." (Jer. 31:33)**

> **"I will pour water upon him that is thirsty, and floods upon the dry ground: I will pour My Spirit upon thy seed." (Isa. 44:3)**

> **"the love of God is shed abroad in our hearts by the Holy Ghost which is given unto us." (Rom. 5:5)**

> **This is also repugnant to the continuous practice of the Church, which prays by the mouth of the prophet thus: "turn Thou me, and I shall be turned." (Jer. 31:18)**

What are these texts teaching in this context? First, God has to radically perform something we cannot perform on our own in order for us to be saved, which this rejection calls **infus[ing] or pour[ing].** Second, this **infus[ing] or pour[ing]** involves granting to us what the rejection calls **new qualities.** This means these are gifts **of faith, of obedience, and of the consciousness of His love into our hearts** we did not have before in the state of misery; yet again, this implies we did have them, in Adam, in the state of innocence.

Rejection of Errors 7

That the grace whereby we are converted to God is only a gentle advising, or (as others explain it), that this is the noblest manner of working in the conversion of man, and that this manner of working, which consists in advising, is most in harmony with man's nature; and that there is no reason why this advising grace alone should not be sufficient to make the natural man spiritual, indeed, that God does not produce the consent of the will except through this manner of advising; and that the power of the divine

---

[21] Woods, *Canons of the Second Council of Orange*, 19–23.

working, whereby it surpasses the working of Satan, consists in this, that God promises eternal, while Satan promises only temporal goods.

But this is altogether Pelagian and contrary to the whole Scripture which, besides this, teaches yet another and far more powerful and divine manner of the Holy Spirit's working in the conversion of man, as in Ezekiel: "A new heart also will I give you, and a new spirit will I put within you: and I will take away the stony heart out of your flesh, and I will give you an heart of flesh" (Ezek. 36:26).

Rejection 7 takes up another Remonstrant redefinition of the grace of conversion. What did it mean to be converted according to the Remonstrants? *The grace whereby we are converted* (*convertimur*) *to God is only a gentle advising* (*lenem suasionem*; gentle persuasion). We've already seen in article 12 the distinction between grace as inwardly effectual and grace as merely outwardly reasonable and persuasive. The rejection goes on to explain this Remonstrant view:

> *Or (as others explain it), that this is the noblest manner of working in the conversion of a person* (*conversion hominis*), *and that this manner of working, which consists in advising* (*suasionibus*; persuasion), *is most in harmony with human nature* (*naturae humanae*); *and that there is no reason why this advising grace* (*moralis gratia*; persuading grace) *alone should not be sufficient to make the natural man spiritual.*

The Remonstrants understood the Reformed system of conversion to be one of coercion while theirs was a system of persuasion: *indeed, that God does not produce the consent of the will except through this manner of advising* (*morali*; persuading); *and that the power of the divine working, whereby it surpasses the working of Satan, consists in this, that God promises eternal, while Satan promises only temporal goods.* In other words, the manner of God's grace is that he promises more goods than Satan; that's it! It's up to our will to consent.

When the synod responded, it did not mince words: **But this is altogether Pelagian and contrary to the whole Scripture which, besides this, teaches yet another and far more powerful and divine manner of the Holy Spirit's working in the conversion of man.** We then get a glimpse into this **far more powerful and divine manner** of converting sinners in Ezekiel 36:26: **"A new heart also will I give you, and a new spirit will I put within you: and I will take away the stony heart out of your flesh, and I will give you an heart of flesh."** In other words, as we saw in article 12 above, conversion is a completely efficacious act of God alone. Augustine said it like this in the context of his will being done in the Old Testament: "If, then, when God wills to set up kings in the earth, He has the wills of men more in His power than they themselves have."[22]

Rejection of Errors 8

That God in the regeneration of man does not use such powers of His omnipotence as potently and infallibly bend man's will to faith and conversion; but that all the works of grace having been accomplished, which God employs to convert man, man may yet so resist God and the Holy Spirit when God intends man's regeneration and wills to regenerate him, and indeed that man often does so resist that he prevents entirely his regeneration, and that it therefore remains in man's power to be regenerated or not.

For this is nothing less than the denial of all the efficiency of God's grace in our conversion, and the subjecting of the working of the Almighty God to the will of man, which is contrary to the apostles, who teach: "who believe, according to the working of His mighty power" (Eph. 1:19). And: "That our God would...fulfil all the good pleasure of His goodness, and the work of faith with power" (2 Thess. 1:11). And: "According as His divine power hath given unto us all things that pertain unto life and godliness" (2 Pet. 1:3).

Continuing the theme of the previous rejection, rejection 8 records the Remonstrant teaching *that God in people's (hominis) regeneration does not use such powers of His omnipotence as potently and infallibly bend his (ejus) will to faith and conversion (conversionem)*. Because of the Fall, humanity's will is bent in upon itself (*incurvatus in se*), but by the power of God's grace our will is bent back outward that we might return to God from ourselves. The Remonstrants rejected this.

The rejection continues to chronicle Arminian teaching *that all the works of grace having been accomplished, which God employs to convert people (hominem convertendum), people (hominem) may yet so resist God and the Holy Spirit when God intends man's regeneration (regenerationem) and wills to regenerate (regenerare) him, and indeed that man often does so*

---

[22] Augustine, "On Rebuke and Grace," 45 (5:490).

resist that he prevents entirely his regeneration (*regenerationem*), *and that it therefore remains in their* (*ipsius*) *power to be regenerated or not to be regenerated* (*regeneretur vel non regeneretur*). The resistibility of God's efficacious grace was a distinguishing characteristic of Remonstrant theology.[23] The reason for it was the power of the will: *it…remains in their power to be regenerated or not to be regenerated.*

In response, the synod summarized this particular error as teaching that **this is nothing less than the denial of all the efficiency of God's grace in our conversion, and the subjecting of the working of the Almighty God to** *human* **will** (*voluntati hominis*). Further it **is contrary to the apostles, who teach** three key truths.

First, in the words of the apostle Paul in Ephesians 1:19 we **"believe, according to the working of His mighty power,"** not the other way around. Here in Paul's first great prayer for the Ephesians, he prayed God would give them the Spirit of wisdom and revelation so their eyes would be opened to the truth of "the immeasurable greatness of his power toward us who believe, according to the working of his great might that he worked in Christ when he raised him from the dead" (Eph. 1:19–20). Paul wanted believers to know that the same power God used to raise Jesus is the same power he used to enable us to believe!

The second key truth the synod brought up in response was from another of Paul's prayers **"that our God would…fulfil all the good pleasure of His goodness, and the work of faith with power"** from 2 Thessalonians 1:11. Again, Paul said this in the context of prayer, that the Thessalonicans would be made worthy of being called by God and that he would "fulfill every resolve for good and every work of faith by his power" to the glory of Jesus.

The third truth was **"according as His divine power hath given unto us all things that pertain unto life and godliness"** from 2 Peter 1:3. The use of these texts was clear: while the Remonstrants viewed God as a gentleman who would never violate man's free will, the Reformed viewed God as an almighty Savior who rescues sinners whose free will only led them deeper down the path of perishing forever.

---

23 See Goudriaan, "The Synod of Dordt on Arminian Anthropology," 102–3.

Rejection of Errors 9

That grace and free will are partial causes, which together work the beginning of conversion, and that grace, in order of working, does not precede the working of the will; that is, that God does not efficiently help the will of man unto conversion until the will of man moves and determines to do this.

For the ancient Church has long ago condemned this doctrine of the Pelagians according to the words of the apostle: "So then it is not of him that willeth, nor of him that runneth, but of God that sheweth mercy" (Rom. 9:16). Likewise: "For who maketh thee to differ from another? and what hast thou that thou didst not receive?" (1 Cor. 4:7). And: "For it is God which worketh in you both to will and to do of His good pleasure" (Phil. 2:13).

Finally, rejection 9 records the error *that grace and free will (liberum arbitrium) are partial causes, which together work the beginning of conversion (conversionis).* Conversion was a cooperative effort between God and man who each did their part. The result of saying this was *that grace, in order of working, does not precede the working of the will.* For all the Remonstrants' talk of "prevenient grace," they actually didn't believe it was effectual. The Council of Orange's (529) concluding definition of faith said because Adam's sin so impaired and weakened free will, no one can either love God as he ought, believe in God, or do good for God's sake unless the grace of divine mercy has preceded him.[24] The sum of the Remonstrant error was *that God does not efficiently help the human will (hominis voluntatem) unto conversion until the human will (voluntas...hominis) moves and determines to do this.* In contrast, Orange (529) spoke of God's grace in baptism as changing man for the better in contrast to how the sin of Adam changed him for the worse (canon 15).[25]

In response the synod mentioned that **the ancient Church has long ago condemned this doctrine of the Pelagians according to the words of the apostle.** Where did the **ancient Church** do this? As we saw in the introduction to this point of doctrine, at the Council of Carthage in 418 and then later at the Council of Orange in 529. On what basis did the **ancient Church** make this judgment? Paul's teaching as summarized by three passages.

---

[24] Woods, *Canons of the Second Council of Orange*, 45.

[25] Woods, *Canons of the Second Council of Orange*, 33.

First, Romans 9:16: **"So then it is not of him that willeth, nor of him that runneth, but of God that sheweth mercy."**

Second, 1 Corinthians 4:7: **"For who maketh thee to differ from another? and what hast thou that thou didst not receive?"**

Third, Philippians 2:13: **"For it is God which worketh in you both to will and to do of His good pleasure."** Paul added this clause to his previous exhortation that the Philippians "work out [their] own salvation with fear and trembling," according to the *Dutch Annotations* "so that we would know that it was not according to any foregoing good disposition or preparation, which [God] should find in man, but according to his pleasure of good grace that a man of himself and by his own abilities, could work out salvation."[26]

---

[26] *Dutch Annotations* on Philippians 2:13.

THE GRACE OF PRESERVATION

VII:

WHAT WE CONFESS

ARTICLES 1-15

THE REMONSTRANT DOCTRINE

WE'VE COME to the fifth and final doctrine of the Remonstrants and the response of the orthodox Reformed. The title of this point of doctrine and subsequent articles speak of "perseverance"[1] while other articles speak of "preservation."[2] The original *Remonstrance* of 1610 said the following in its article 5 on this doctrine:

> That those who are incorporated into Jesus Christ and thereby become partakers of his life-giving Spirit have abundant strength to strive against satan, sin, the world, and their own flesh and to obtain the victory; it being well understood (that this is) through the assistance of the grace of the Holy Spirit, and that Jesus Christ assists them through his Spirit in all temptations, extends the hand, and—if only they are prepared for warfare and desire his help and are not negligent—keeps them standing, so that by no cunning or power of satan can they be led astray or plucked out of Christ's hands, according to the word of Christ, John 10, "No one shall pluck them out of my hands."

---

[1] *perseverantia* (arts. 9, 15); *perseverantiae* (arts. 11, 12, 13).

[2] *conservat* (arts. 3, 7, 14); *conservantis* (art. 4); *custodia* (arts. 8, 9).

As with all the original Remonstrant articles we've seen before, the Reformed agree in many things in this fifth point. What this first part of article 5 says is *mostly* consistent with what we've seen in the Council of Carthage (418), which rejected the view "that whoever says the grace of God that justifies through Christ avails only for the remission of past sins, and not for assistance against sins in the future" (art. 3). God's grace justifies and also sanctifies. Later at the Second Council of Orange (529) it was declared that God's assistance is necessary for doing good (canon 9), that this assistance is always to be sought in order to persevere in good works (canon 10), and that a person can do no good without God (canon 20).[3] In its concluding definition of faith it was confessed that after grace has been received through baptism all baptized persons have the ability and responsibility, if they desire to labor faithfully, to perform with the aid and cooperation of Christ what is of essential importance in regard to the salvation of their soul. It also said that in every good work it is not we who take the initiative and are then assisted through the mercy of God, but God who first inspires in us faith in him and love for him without any previous good works that deserve reward. This leads us to seek the sacrament of baptism and after baptism be enabled by his help to do what is pleasing to him. Article 5 of the *Remonstrance*, though, went on to state:

> But whether they can through negligence fall away from the first principle of their life in Christ, again embrace the present world, depart from the pure doctrine once given to them, lose the good conscience, and neglect grace, must first be more carefully determined from the Holy Scriptures before we shall be able to teach this with the full persuasion of our heart.

Initially, the Remonstrants considered final perseverance an issue that was unclear in Scripture.[4]

---

[3] Woods, *Canons of the Second Council of Orange*, 27–29, 39.

[4] On the debate with the Remonstrants at Dort, see Berkouwer, *Faith and Perseverance*, 39–45.

THE ISSUE

By the time of the synod, though, the Remonstrants were of the opinion that "true believers are able to fall through their own fault into shameful and atrocious deeds, to persevere and to die in them; and therefore finally to fall and to perish."[5] The main issue, though, of the "if only" language of the *Remonstrance* was viewing faith's interaction with grace as a hypothetical condition of final perseverance. "If" the believer is prepared for spiritual warfare, "if" the believer desires God's help, "if" the believer isn't negligent—as antecedent conditions—then God will preserve. In the words of Paraeus, "Their assertion is not categoricall, but conditionall, that Christ, by his Spirit, is present with them, that hee stretcheth out his hand to them, and confirmes them that are inserted into him by true faith, if..." To this he asked: "But, I pray, what kind of God doe they feigne here...What kind of Christ? What kind of Spirit?"[6] For example, in Romans 8 Paul speaks a series of "ifs": "*if* in fact the Spirit of God dwells in you...*if* Christ is in you...*if* the Spirit of him who raised Jesus from the dead dwells in you" (Rom. 8:9, 10, 11). As Colin Kruse said, the possession of the Holy Spirit "is the *sine qua non* of Christian existence."[7] To use Paraeus' distinction, Paul's purpose in using εἴπερ and εἰ ("if") is not to cast into doubt the Roman believers' status because this is conditional but to state something as categorically true. Hence the sense of these words is "since."[8] The conditions in Paul's argument are fulfilled conditions.[9] Returning to the canons, Berkouwer ironically said of the Remonstrant position, "*If* we grasp the real meaning of this objection...we have understood in principles the whole controversy."[10]

---

[5] "The Opinions of the Remonstrants," appendix H in De Jong, *Crisis in the Reformed Churches*, 228. See also *The Arminian Confession of 1621*, trans. and ed. Mark A. Ellis, Princeton Theological Monograph Series 51 (Eugene, OR: Pickwick, 2005), 112–13.

[6] Paraeus, "Epitome of Arminianisme," 839.

[7] Kruse, *Paul's Letter to the Romans*, 332.

[8] Schreiner, *Romans*, 413, 414.

[9] Kruse, *Paul's Letter to the Romans*, 333. See the discussion also in Schreiner, *Romans*, 395, 409, 410.

[10] Berkouwer, *Faith and Perseverance*, 40. Emphasis added.

One of the ways that modern evangelicals have tried to find the ever-elusive "middle way" between Arminianism and Calvinism is to affirm the exhortations and warnings about perseverance while affirming the promises about ultimate salvation. This doctrine is called "eternal security." We'll return to George Bryson's popular polemical book for an example. He asks, "If all true believers persevere, why does Scripture so often encourage the saints to persevere and just as often warn them of the consequences of not persevering?"[11] We'll come back to how he misunderstands the Reformed position that perseverance comes *through means of* encouragements and exhortations.[12] For now, note how he sets up the scenario between the encouragement to perseverance and the exhortation that there are consequences if you don't. He then points to Jesus' image of branches abiding in the vine to bear fruit and the consequences of not abiding, saying, "This warning is totally meaningless and unnecessary if the Calvinistic position on Perseverance is correct."[13] How does Bryson reconcile these two "sides"? He does so with a doctrine of eternal security but loss of rewards in eternity:

> The saved *should* persevere in faith and holiness to the end of their life on earth, thereby proving their love for the Lord. The truly saved, to the degree they fail to persevere in faith and holiness, have to that same degree demonstrated a lack of love for the Lord. Although saved, they experience a loss of fellowship with the Lord in this life, and a loss of rewards in the next.[14]

What's ironic about Bryson's rejection of the perseverance of the saints but advocating for eternal security is that his own Dispensationalist tradition originally reflected the Calvinistic point of view.[15]

---

[11] Bryson, *The Five Points of Calvinism*, 109.

[12] For an excellent exposition of the relationship between perseverance and the admonitions of Scripture, see Berkouwer, *Faith and Perseverance*, 83–124.

[13] Bryson, *The Five Points of Calvinism*, 112.

[14] Bryson, *The Five Points of Calvinism*, 120.

[15] See for example, Lewis Sperry Chafer, *Salvation* (New York: Charles C. Cook, 1917). See also the notes to Hebrews 6:4–6 in *The New Scofield Reference Bible*, ed. C. I. Scofield (New York: Oxford University, 1967), 1315.

HISTORICAL BACKGROUND

Augustine

Our survey of the doctrine of the perseverance of the saints takes us back again to one of the four Latin doctors of the church (*Doctores Ecclesiae*), Augustine. In the context of his debates with Pelagius on sin and grace, discussed in chapter 5 above, Augustine wrote the church's first extensive reflection on perseverance in his 428/429 *On the Gift of Perseverance (De Dono Perseverantiae)*. Yet Augustine consciously explained this treatise and two others like it were following the teaching of Cyprian, Ambrose, and Gregory of Nazianzus.[16] Even Augustine engaged in recapturing and retrieving earlier sources to demonstrate his own catholicity on the doctrine of the perseverance of the saints.

Consistent with his doctrine of double predestination, discussed in chapter 1, the gift of final perseverance is based in God's gift of predestination. This means his grace is the ultimate reason a believer finally perseveres: "I assert...that the perseverance by which we persevere in Christ even to the end is the gift of God."[17] This gift given to some (the elect/predestined) and not others is the only reason for the difference between one person and another.[18] Why perseverance is given to some in the church and not to others is a mystery left to the judgment of God. Augustine simply said, "I do not know" and "be ignorant, without a murmur against God."[19] Ultimately, the one who perseveres shows he's been predestined while the other hasn't.[20]

---

[16] For references to Cyprian, see "On Rebuke and Grace," 10, 12; "On the Predestination of the Saints," 7, 8, 15, 26, 28; "On the Gift of Perseverance," 4, 7, 8, 12, 36, 43, 48, 49, 55. For references to Ambrose, see "On the Gift of Perseverance," 19, 20, 33, 48, 49, 64. For reference to Gregory of Nazianzus, see "On the Gift of Perseverance," 49.

[17] Augustine, "On the Gift of Perseverance," ch. 1, *NPNF: First Series*, 5:526. See also "On Rebuke and Grace," 10 (5:475–76).

[18] Augustine, "On Rebuke and Grace," 12 (5:466–67).

[19] Augustine, "On Rebuke and Grace," 17 (5:478); 19 (5:479).

[20] Augustine, "On the Gift of Perseverance," ch. 21, *NPNF: First Series*, 5:532–33; "On Rebuke and Grace," 12 (5:476).

The grace of God, which both begins a man's faith and which enables it to persevere unto the end, is not given according to our merits, but is given according to His own most secret and at the same time most righteous, wise, and beneficent will; since those whom He predestinated, them He also called, with that calling of which it is said, "The gifts and calling of God are without repentance."[21]

We shouldn't jump to the anachronistic conclusion that Augustine was "Reformed" in his doctrine of perseverance. While the predestined will persevere by grace, the Christian cannot know in this life with infallible certainty that he is among the elect and that he will finally persevere since he lives his life in a state of trial.[22] Further, it's possible for one to experience the spiritual graces of regeneration in baptism and the justifying grace of God, and yet not persevere to the end.[23] To summarize, Augustine's position on perseverance includes the following:

- Perseverance is a gift of grace.

- The predestined cannot lose this gift.[24]

- While the elect cannot lose this gift, "believers," who have been regenerated in baptism, have been given faith, hope, and love, and have been called (but not according to God's purpose of election), can fall away to condemnation.[25]

---

[21] Augustine, "On the Gift of Perseverance," ch. 33, *NPNF: First Series*, 5:538.

[22] Augustine, "On the Gift of Perseverance," chs. 1, 33, *NPNF: First Series*, 5:526, 538; "On Rebuke and Grace," 40 (5:488).

[23] Augustine, "On the Gift of Perseverance," ch. 21, *NPNF: First Series*, 5:532–33; "On Rebuke and Grace," 9 (5:474–75), 11 (5:476), 16 (5:478), 18 (5:478–79), 20 (5:479–80), 22 (5:480).

[24] On these first two points especially, John Owen said, "Thus far Austin is clearly engaged with us." "The Doctrine of the Saints' Perseverance Explained and Confirmed," in *Works*, 11:2.

[25] For the similarity of this point in John Owen's theology, see Henry Knapp, "Augustine and Owen on Perseverance," *Westminster Theological Journal* 62, no. 1 (Spring 2000): 78–83. Similarly, Owen spoke of "an inferior, common work of the Holy Spirit" that caused "great alteration and change" in a person's life; these assent to the realities of the gospel; these are not technically hypocrites as they did not believe for show; these have gifts and abilities that are even used for the cause of the church; yet they ultimately are not regenerated.

- The purpose of these apostates in the church was to cause the elect to fear apostasy and strive against it and keep them from pride.[26]

- The subjective effect of this doctrine is that the elect cannot know for certain that they have the gift of perseverance in this life until they die. This is the main pastoral difference between Dort and Augustine.[27]

Aquinas

In the shadow of Augustine, "Western Christian thinkers have more or less attempted to base their understanding of the doctrine of perseverance on ideas of Augustine or of those he reacted to."[28] In his *Summa Theologica*, Thomas Aquinas builds upon the teaching of Augustine. Aquinas distinguished three senses of the term "perseverance."[29] First, it's a disposition (*habitus*) of mind whereby "a man stands steadfastly, lest he be moved by the assault of the sadness from what is virtuous." Second, it's the inclination whereby "a man has the purpose of persevering in good unto the end." Third, it's "the abiding in good to the end of life" or "final perseverance." Like Augustine, Aquinas believed the justified person was in continual need of God's grace in view of the fact that the same person could fall away and be finally lost: "For to many grace is given to whom perseverance in grace is not given."[30] Like Augustine, perseverance has both historical and eschatological dimensions.[31] This potential to fall away stemmed from the fact that human free will by nature is changeable, even after the effects of God's grace upon it. While the grace-repaired will has the power to choose the good even to the end, it is also in our power to choose the opposite.[32]

---

[26] Augustine, "On the Gift of Perseverance," ch. 33.

[27] For this helpful summary, see Knapp, "Augustine and Owen on Perseverance," 65–87.

[28] Ján Henžel, "When Conversion Is Joy and Death Victory: Historical Foundations of the Doctrine of Perseverance," *Tyndale Bulletin* 54, no. 2 (2003): 127–28.

[29] Aquinas, *Summa Theologica*, I–II, Q. 109, art. 10 (p. 1131).

[30] Aquinas, *Summa Theologica*, I–II, Q. 109, art. 10.

[31] Henžel, "When Conversion Is Joy and Death Victory," 129.

[32] Aquinas, *Summa Theologica*, II–II, Q. 137, art. 4.

A REFORMED "DISTINCTIVE"?

Because of the above, Louis Berkhof said, "The Reformed or Calvinistic Churches stand practically alone in giving a negative answer to the question, whether a Christian can completely fall from the state of grace and be finally lost."[33] More recently Jay Collier has followed Seán Hughes in arguing that of the points of Dort, only that of perseverance seems to be a distinctly Reformed doctrine.[34] One of the arguments Collier offers is that the 1592 Lutheran *Saxon Visitation Articles* lists perseverance as a Reformed false and erroneous doctrine.[35]

In response, while stating "the pure and true Doctrine of our [Lutheran] Churches" concerning Holy Baptism, article 3 of the *Visitation Articles* does state its own doctrine of perseverance of the saints in which regenerated (baptized) people who persevere enter eternal life:

> By Baptism, as a bath of the regeneration and renovation of the Holy Ghost, God saves us, and works in us such justice and purgation from our sins, that he who perseveres to the end in that covenant and hope does not perish, but has eternal life. (3.2)[36]

In relation to perseverance, the *Visitation Articles* express a doctrine of apostasy: God not only "commands all to hear Christ, his Son, in the gospel" but also "promises, by his hearing, the virtue and operation of the Holy Ghost for conversion and salvation" (4.2). Despite this promise "many men, by their own fault, perish: some, who will not hear the gospel concerning Christ; some, who again fall from grace, either by fundamental error, or by sins against conscience" (4.3).[37] Then the *Visitation Articles* reject "the false and erroneous doctrine of the Calvinists." One of the errors of the Calvinists from the vantage point of the Lutherans was "that Baptism does not work nor confer regeneration, faith, the grace of God, and salva-

---

[33] Berkhof, *Systematic Theology*, 545.

[34] Collier, *Debating Perseverance*, 9–12. Hughes, "The Problem of 'Calvinism,'" 245–47.

[35] Collier, *Debating Perseverance*, 10–11.

[36] Schaff, *Creeds*, 3:184–85.

[37] Schaff, *Creeds*, 3:185.

tion, but only signifies and seals them" (On Holy Baptism, 2).[38] Then is also rejected "that the elected and regenerated can not lose faith and the Holy Spirit, or be damned, though they commit great sins and crimes of every kind" (On Predestination and the Providence of God, 3).[39] The Lutheran distinction is similar to that of Augustine between the perseverance of the saints or believers (asserted by the Reformed but rejected by Augustine and Lutheranism) and of the perseverance of the elect (asserted by all). Of this the Reformed theologian Rivetus would say after Dort in the *Synopsis*:

> Therefore they [Lutherans] are led astray and they lead others astray who posit that there are two species of truly justified people: the one, of the elect who do persevere, and the other, of those who are not elect, who although they were granted true faith at some point in time and were justified, till die in apostasy without repenting.[40]

In agreement, therefore, with Augustine, Luther and the tradition that followed him said the regenerating grace that came through the waters of baptism could be lost. On 2 Peter 2:22 Luther said, "Through baptism these people threw out unbelief, had their unclean way of life washed away, and entered into a pure life of faith and love. Now they fall away into unbelief and their own works, and they soil themselves again in filth."[41] Therefore the believer must always take heed lest he fall.[42]

In contrast, though, to Augustine and late medieval Roman theology, Luther and the tradition that followed him taught assurance."[43] Assurance of being in a state of grace was foundational to the Christian life according

---

[38] Schaff, *Creeds*, 3:188.

[39] Schaff, *Creeds*, 3:189.

[40] *Synopsis Purioris Theologiae: Volume 2*, 269.

[41] Martin Luther, "Sermons on the Second Epistle of St. Peter," in *Luther's Works: The Catholic Epistles*, ed. Jaroslav Pelikan, trans. Martin H. Bertram (St. Louis, MO: Concordia, 1967), 30:190. "To be sure, we are all called Christians. We are baptized and regenerated through Baptism. But all of us do not remain with our Baptism. Many fall away from Christ and become false Christians. But the honest Christians are thinly sown." Cited in Martin Luther, *What Luther Says*, ed. Ewald M. Plass (St. Louis, MO: Concordia, 1959), 1:280.

[42] See Julius Köstlin, *The Theology of Luther in Its Historical Development and Inner Harmony*, trans. Charles E. Hay, 2 vols. (Philadelphia: Lutheran Publication Society, 1897), 2:454–65.

[43] Cited in Köstlin, *The Theology of Luther*, 2:462.

to Luther: "I must be able to say, 'I know that I have a gracious God and that my works, performed in this faith and according to this Word, are good fruits and are pleasing to Him.'"[44] While God's eternal decree of election is known infallibly only to him, by focusing on Jesus Christ as preached in the gospel and presented by the promises of Scripture, the believer can find "very useful, salutary, and comforting teaching. For it confirms most powerfully the article that we become righteous and are saved apart from all our works and merit, purely on the basis on grace, solely for Christ's sake." Concerning Christ, "people [are] to seek eternal election in Christ and in his holy gospel as in the Book of Life."[45] At the same time, final apostasy is a genuine possibility for the baptized and justified believer. This paradox of the Lutheran position has been called "secure in Christ, insecure in one's self."[46]

Seeing that confessional Lutherans affirm an eternal, unconditional, and unchangeable election as the cause of the definite number of the children of God's salvation,[47] that Christ promises the powerful work of the Holy Spirit to assist believers for perseverance unto an eternal salvation,[48] and that assurance of election can be obtained *a posteriori* through repentance from sin and faith in Christ the Book of Life,[49] the differences be-

---

[44] Martin Luther, *Luther's Works*, ed. J. Pelikan (St. Louis, MO: Concordia, 1961), 24:218.

[45] *The Solid Declaration*, XI, 43, 89, in *The Book of Concord*, 648, 655.

[46] John Jefferson Davis, "The Perseverance of the Saints: A History of the Doctrine," *Journal of the Evangelical Theological Society* 34, no. 2 (June 1991): 216.

[47] The Epitome of the Formula of Concord, 11.5, 7, 13, 15 in *The Book of Concord*, 517–510.

[48] The Epitome of the Formula of Concord, 11.8. 11.13 even cited John 10 that no one can pluck us from Jesus' hand.

[49] The Epitome of the Formula of Concord, 11.11, 13. Citing Thomas Manteufel, *Churches in America* (St. Louis, MO: Concordia, 1994), 41, the Lutheran Church—Missouri Synod says of the "P" in TULIP:

> P (Perseverance in grace) We affirm with Scripture that those who are predestined to salvation cannot be lost but will continue by God's power to a blessed end (Rom. 8:30; 1 Pet. 1:5). Scripture does not teach, however, that those who come to faith cannot lose that faith (Heb. 6:4–6; 10:26–29; Ps. 51:11). God urges His people not to continue in sin but to live in repentance and faith (Rom. 6:1–4).

tween Lutheran and Reformed, I believe, are more verbal than substantive. Where the Lutheran speaks of the *regenerated* losing faith and the Holy Spirit, the Reformed would use more covenantal categories to describe apostasy: those merely within the sphere of the adminsteration of the covenant and those who possess the substance of the covenant. While Dort grounds final perseverance in God's "unchangeable purpose of election" (5.6), in agreement with Augustine and Aquinas, it goes on to ground it also in the nature of "the incorruptible seed of regeneration," which God "preserves in them [that fall] from perishing or being totally lost" (5.7). This understanding of regeneration as permanent differs from Augustine, Aquinas, and even fellow Protestant Lutherans. In other words, what is distinctly Reformed is the doctrine of the perseverance of the *saints*. Yet even with the doctrinal canons below, there is enough breadth of expression that does not explicitly condemn the views even the fellow Reformed delegates at the synod in the British suffrage.[50]

What follows is the most practical of the Canons of Dort on the perseverance of the saints. After two short common Christian convictions and a definition, most of the fifth point is taken up with pastoral issues such as the believer's struggle with sin, assurance, and using the means of grace. The Utrecht theologian of the nineteenth century Jan Jacob van Oosterzee (1817–1892) said this doctrine was "defended at the Synod of Dort with such warmth."[51]

COMMENTARY

Article 1

Whom God calls, according to His purpose, to the communion of His Son, our Lord Jesus Christ, and regenerates by the Holy Spirit, He delivers also from the dominion and slavery of sin in this life; though not altogether from the body of sin and from the infirmities of the flesh, so long as they continue in this world.

As found at https://www.lcms.org/about/beliefs/faqs/denominations (accessed August 21, 2018).

[50] For the text, see Milton, *The British Delegation and the Synod of Dort*, 265–93.

[51] Van Oosterzee, *Christian Dogmatics*, 664.

SALVATION'S TRIUMPH

The first common Christian conviction deals with the results of regeneration: freedom from the slavery of sin but not the struggle with sin.

There's no question we live in a quick-fix world. If your lawn mower breaks, buy a new one. If you have problems in your marriage, read *The Idiot's Guide to a Perfect Marriage*. When it comes to spirituality, religion, or faith, this is even more the case it seems. We can almost hear the echo as evangelical Christians chant: "What do we want? Our relationship with God! When do we want it? Now!" Once there was the *Experiencing God Bible*, but that took too long, so then there was the *One Minute Bible*. Once there was *Forty Days of Purpose*, but that was too long, so *Your Best Life Now* took its place. The list goes on.

Hebrews 11 memorably describes the Christian life as a *race*, but not a short race like a sprint or even a lap around the track; instead, it's a lifelong *race* like a marathon. The apostolic writer says, "Therefore, since we are surrounded by so great a cloud of witnesses, let us also lay aside every weight, and sin which clings so closely, and let us run with endurance the race that is set before us." Paul speaks about the Christian life as a race elsewhere in 1 Corinthians 9:24–26, saying:

> Do you not know that in a race all the runners run, but only one receives the prize? So run that you may obtain it. Every athlete exercises self-control in all things. They do it to receive a perishable wreath, but we an imperishable. So I do not run aimlessly; I do not box as one beating the air. But I discipline my body and keep it under control, lest after preaching to others I myself should be disqualified.

Kenneth Wuest once said, "The frequency with which Paul refers to the Greek athletic games far surpasses his illustrations from any other single department of first century life."[52] Just as a runner in the Greek games would undergo a ten-month preparation including "self-control" so that when he ran he would win a perishable crown of oak leaves, the Christian life is a lifelong exercise of self-control and running toward the imperishable crown of heaven.

---

[52] Kenneth S. Wuest, "Bypaths in the Greek New Testament," in *Wuest's Word Studies from the Greek New Testament: Volume 3* (1940; repr., Grand Rapids, MI: Eerdmans, 2004), 51.

A while back my wife and I zip-lined across and over a cloud forest high in the mountains of Costa Rica. As one who has acrophobia (a fear of heights)—says the guy who is 6'4"; go figure!—this was a conquest for me. When you're up there on the platform and you see the wires, the anchors, and the supports, you realize the line in between is held together from one strong end to the other. It's really a great illustration of the doctrine of God's grace. At one end God's "grace" was planned for me "in Christ Jesus before the ages began" (2 Tim. 1:9). We saw this in the first point of doctrine. In between, God's grace was purchased for me as Christ "loved me and gave himself for me" on the cross (Gal. 2:20). This is the second point of doctrine. God's grace was "poured into [my] heart[…]through the Holy Spirit who has been given to us" (Rom. 5:5). That is the third and fourth points of doctrine. Finally, the other end of God's grace is that I will be preserved "by [his] power" as I am "being guarded through faith for a salvation ready to be revealed in the last time" (1 Pet. 1:5). This is the fifth and final point of doctrine.

I don't think there is any doctrine more practical than the perseverance of the saints! Why? Because this is no mere doctrine; this is our life. What is *the "normal" Christian life*? Some say it's health and wealth. Some say it's getting saved and then moving on. Some say it's about finding yourself and becoming your potential. But I want us to turn to Scripture as it's summarized in our canons.

The first thing we see in the fifth point of doctrine is *salvation's triumph*. Article 1 takes us back to the first point of doctrine where we confessed God's eternal grace of election: **Whom God calls, according to His purpose**. We're then taken back to the second point of doctrine: **calls…to the communion His Son, our Lord Jesus Christ**. Finally, we're taken back to the third and fourth points of doctrine: **and regenerates by the Holy Spirit, He delivers also from the dominion** (*dominio*) **and slavery** (*servitute*) **of sin in this life**.

What's interesting is the close connection grammatically in this article. **Whom** (*quos*) God elected in his purpose, called, and regenerated are **also** delivered. But it's stronger and closer than this: **Whom** (*quos*) God elected, called, and regenerated are the same—**who indeed** (*eos quidem*)—that are delivered.[53] God saves sinners from beginning to end, conception to consummation. What this article highlights is the past tense, or, "already"

---

[53] See Hoeksema, *The Voice of Our Fathers*, 634.

aspect of our salvation. This comes right from Romans 6, which describes our deliverance in several ways.

First, "our old self was crucified" (Rom. 6:6). "Old self" interprets the phrase "old man" (παλαιὸς ἄνθρωπος). Notice the parallel in Paul's language: just as surely as Christ died, so surely we have died to the sin we inherited from the first man Adam. How sure was Christ's death? "For the death he died he died to sin, once for all" (Rom. 6:10). It's the same for me.

Second, the purpose was in order that "the body of sin might be brought to nothing" (Rom. 6:6). The "body of sin" is our sinful and selfish nature. The word behind the phrase "brought to nothing" (καταργηθῇ) is a violent verb that speaks of destruction and even annihilation.[54] It's the same word Paul uses when he says in Ephesians 2:15 that the enmity between Jew and Gentile was "abolished." In the same way it is with our sin nature.

Third, the end result is that "we would no longer be enslaved to sin" (Rom. 6:6). Just as Paul spoke of himself as a "servant of Jesus Christ" (Rom. 1:1) and us as "slaves of righteousness" (Rom. 6:17) and "slaves of God" (Rom. 6:22). In contrast to being "slaves of sin" (Rom. 6:17, 20), in which we were once willing lovers of sin, now we are willing lovers of God. Paul goes on to summarize, saying, "For one who has died has been set free from sin" (Rom. 6:7). Practically speaking, this means that you "must consider yourselves dead to sin" (Rom. 6:11).

To be delivered, then, is to be totally set free from captivity and oppression. We have been delivered from sin's dominion and its slavery of our lives. We were once slaves of darkness, that is, the world, sin, and the devil. But we have been delivered, redeemed, by the blood of the Son. We are under new ownership now. The language of the Holy Spirit is to use such momentous language when it describes our salvation! Some might think merely of the human authors of Scripture and be tempted to think Paul is overstating the case for effect. Is he using hyperbole? What he says the Holy Spirit says; and it's true. It speaks of the already aspect of our salvation.

Look at another powerful verse in Colossians 1:13–14: "He has delivered us from the domain of darkness and transferred us to the kingdom of his beloved Son, in whom we redemption, the forgiveness of sins." Here Paul says we have already been delivered from the dominion of darkness,

---

[54] καταργέω in *A Greek-English Lexicon of the New Testament*, 417. See the comments of Schreiner, *Romans*, 316.

meaning, the Satan's realm of sin. Later in 3:1 Paul says we have already been raised with Christ to the right hand of God. He says this because in 3:3 he goes on to say that we've already died with Christ. This in 3:10 he says we've already put on the "new man" (νέος ἄνθρωπος). Our Lord said it like this in John 8:34–36: "Jesus answered them, 'Truly, truly, I say to you, everyone who commits sin is a slave to sin. The slave does not remain in the house forever; the son remains forever. So if the Son sets you free, you will be free indeed.'"

Article 2

Hence spring daily sins of infirmity, and hence spots adhere to the best works of the saints, which furnish them with constant matter for humiliation before God, and flying for refuge to Christ crucified; for mortifying the flesh more and more by the spirit of prayer, and by holy exercises of piety; and for pressing forward to the goal of perfection, till being at length delivered from this body of death, they are brought to reign with the Lamb of God in heaven.

SALVATION'S TOIL

The second Christian conviction follows from the first: because of our new life but continual struggle with sin, those regenerated must strive for holiness.

Some Christian traditions stop where we left off above, ending up in error. I cannot tell you how many emails I get each week with the latest fads to teach God's people that they can cease from consciously sinning in this life, that they can progress from a carnal Christian life to a Spirit-filled life, and that they can reach the proverbial top of the mountain in sanctification. That's because they read Romans 6 and stop. But the same apostle also wrote Romans 7 and Philippians 3 that teach us another common truth: *salvation's toil*.

You should've noticed that I left off article 1 above without commenting on its last phrase: **though not altogether from the body of sin** (*corpore peccati*) **and from the infirmities of the flesh** (*carne*), **so long as they continue in this world.** Sin's dominion has been abolished; it's no longer my master. Yet, sin's corruption still affects us. Because of this, article 2 goes on to say: **Hence spring daily sins of infirmity, and hence**

spots adhere to the best works of the saints. Christians are still sinful and still think, say, and do sinful things. In the words of the apostle John, "If we say we have no sin, we deceive ourselves, and the truth is not in us" (1 John 1:8). We still have a present struggle with sin. Of course, the good news is that "if we confess our sins, [God] is faithful and just to forgive us our sins and to cleanse us from all unrighteousness" (1 John 1:9). Because of our constant struggle with the vestiges of our sinful nature inherited from Adam, in this life we never perform a perfectly good work that is untainted by sin. Praise God he accepts our works done in reliance on the Holy Spirit in Christ! Since we have this ongoing struggle, article 2 goes on to say it **furnish[es] them with constant matter** to perform the actions expressed by four verbs.

First, *God wants me to be humble*: **for humiliation before God**. Paul says it like this in Philippians 3:12, "Not that I have already obtained this [the glory of the resurrection] or am already perfect." This is why our Lord commands you and me still to ask our heavenly Father for forgiveness daily: "Forgive us our debts." Humility is such a key to the Christian life because it is a means by which we experience that "the LORD is near to the brokenhearted and saves the crushed in spirit" (Ps. 34:18).

Second, *God wants me to be centered on Jesus Christ*: **flying for refuge to Christ crucified**. Look again at Philippians 3. Paul says, "But whatever gain I had" in my former life according to the law and the flesh "I counted as loss for the sake of Christ. Indeed, I count everything" in this life "as loss because of the surpassing worth of knowing Christ Jesus my Lord. For his sake I have suffered the loss of all things and count them as rubbish, in order that I may gain Christ and be found in him, not having a righteousness of my own" (Phil. 3:7–9). In the image of the marathon runner above, we are to get our eyes off ourselves, our accomplishments, and our circumstances and onto Jesus Christ in the toil of life until we reach glory.

Third, *God wants me to mortify my sin*: **for mortifying the flesh more and more by the spirit of prayer, and by holy exercises of piety**. I must put to death, kill, and slay the sin that constantly clings to me. As Paul says in Philippians 3: "forgetting what lies behind" (Phil. 3:13). How do I do this? The article alludes to Paul's language in Romans 8: "For if you live according to the flesh [my sin nature that had dominion in my former phase of life] you will die, but if by the Spirit you put to death the deeds of the body, you will live" (Rom. 8:13). He's just said "We are debtors, *not to the* *flesh*," meaning, "we are debtors to the Spirit!" (Rom. 8:12). We expect to hear that we are indebted to God the Father; after all' he sent his Son for us (Rom. 8:3). Or, we expect to hear that we are indebted to the Son; after all' he was condemned for us on the cross (Rom. 8:4). Yet Paul says we are especially debtors to the Holy Spirit. We are to do so not only by turning from ourselves as we saw above, but by turning away from ourselves in mortification of our sins. The principle of our existence is that we're in the Spirit and not in the flesh. In practice, though, we actually need to turn from our sinful nature that we inherited from Adam that still clings to us like a "body of death" (Rom. 7:24). Life outside of Christ and under the power of your sinful nature leads down a path of life that only ends in one place: death (Rom. 8:6). He does not shy away from warning us: "if you" as a member of the church in Rome or a member of your church "live according-ing to the flesh you will die" (Rom. 8:13). In the memorable words of John Owen, "Be killing sin or it will be killing you."[55] Thomas Manton said it like this: "If you enter not into a war with sin, you enter into a war with God."[56]

We need to stand our ground and do battle with ourselves. Paul goes on to say, "but if by the Spirit you put to death [mortify; KJV] the deeds of the body, you will live" (Rom. 8:13).

What are we to mortify? "The deeds of the body." Paul is not saying anything about our bodies being bad while our souls are good. What he is doing is using a synecdoche, which is a rhetorical way of speaking of a part for the whole. It's not just our bodies but also everything that leads up to our bodies sinning. In our *bodies* we see our sins revealed and manifested, but our sins do not originate there. Remember Jesus' words "that everyone who looks at a woman with lustful intent has *already* committed adultery with her in his heart" (Matt. 5:28). The eyes manifest the heart. Thus we need to mortify what our eyes look at. Like Job, we must say, "I have made a covenant with my eyes; how then could I gaze at a virgin?" (Job 31:1). Again, Jesus said to the Pharisees, "You brood of vipers! How can you speak good, when you are evil? For out of the abundance of the heart the mouth speaks" (Matt. 12:34). The *words* manifest the heart. And so we need to mortify what we speak. Finally, in Matthew 15 Jesus speak of the *thoughts*,

---

[55] Owen, "Of the Mortification of Sin in Believers," *Works*, 6:9.

[56] Thomas Manton, "Sermons upon the Eighth Chapter to the Romans," in *The Works of Thomas Manton* (repr., Birmingham, AL: Solid Ground Christian Books, 2008), 12:72. Emphasis mine.

words, and *deeds*, saying, "But what comes out of the mouth proceeds from the heart, and this defiles a person. For out of the heart come evil thoughts, murder, adultery, sexual immorality, theft, false witness, slander. These are what defile a person" (Matt. 15:18–20). The deeds manifest the heart. Therefore mortify them! This is not merely changing what we look at, how we speak, and what we do. It includes that because of an inner change. Manton once said, "We must so oppose sin, that in some sort we may kill it or extinguish it, *not only scratch the face of it, but seek to root it out*; at least that must be our aim."[57] We do not view this like the priests of Baal in the Old Testament, who threw dust on themselves and beat their bodies to show how holy they were. We do not view this like the Roman religion with its Lenten ritual of giving up something for forty days, only to return to it afterward. We do not view this like hypocrites among us, who merely conform outwardly but inwardly despise their conformity. Mortification is holy war that begins deep in the heart and begins to manifest itself in looks, words, and acts. In ancient siege warfare, armies would not only use archers against their enemies on the wall or catapults and other weapons, but they would also use tunneling experts to dig deep under walls to bring them down.[58] Then they would fight hand to hand. In the same way we need to fight the sin in our hearts in order to collapse the sins of the body.

Why must we mortify? In contrast to living "according to the flesh" (Rom. 8:12), which leads to death (Rom. 8:13), if we mortify our sins we will "live" (Rom. 8:13). Sanctification produces in us a vibrant and living spirituality now in this life and leads us to the fullness of that in eternity. When we pursue holiness in this life, we enjoy a foretaste of what we are preparing ourselves for: the presence of God. And what is that place like? Peter describes it as the place "in which righteousness dwells" (2 Pet. 3:13). Manton is so quotable here: "Heaven would be a burden to a carnal heart, that hath no delight in communion with God, or the company of the saints, or an holy life."[59] Look at Paul's logic at the end of Romans 8:13: mortification *leads to* vivification. I didn't say that mortification *causes* vivification.

---

[57] Manton, "Sermons upon the Eighth Chapter to the Romans," 12:55. Emphasis added.

[58] For a description of "undermining," see Leif Inge Ree Petersen, *Siege Warfare and Military Organization in the Successor States (400–800 AD): Byzantium, the West and Islam* (Leiden: Brill, 2013), 286–88.

[59] Manton, "Sermons upon the Eighth Chapter to the Romans," 12:83.

Sanctification is not the *cause* of our glorification, but it is the *means* through which we come enjoy and experience glorification.[60] As we saw in 1.8, God has elected us **to grace and glory** (*ad gratiam et ad gloriam*). This was then paralleled by the phrase "to salvation and the way of salvation" (*ad salutem et ad viam salutis*). The **way of salvation** was then defined with an allusion to Ephesians 2:10: **He hath ordained that we should walk therein**.

How do we mortify? **By the Spirit**. We do not mortify sin by the force of our wills. We do not mortify sin by the strength of our resolve. We mortify sin **by the Spirit**. This means that we do so in total reliance upon and only through the means that he has appointed. The Holy Spirit is the one who sanctifies us freely and merely of his grace. But the means by which he does this work is through you and me.[61] When we are tempted, we need to be conscious of our need of the Spirit's help. When we feel anger or jealousy rising up within us, we need to pray for him to strengthen us. The canons tells us we mortify **by the spirit of prayer, and by holy exercises of piety**. When we are feeling helpless we need to use his means of the Word read privately and publicly, we need to hear the Word preached publicly, we need to partake of the sacraments publicly in the midst of the congregation, we need to pray privately and on the Lord's Day in public worship and at prayer meetings, we need to join our prayers with fasting, we need to meditate on the glories of Christ, we need to engage in self-examining, and we need godly conversation and accountability.

Fourth, *God wants me to long for heaven*: **for pressing forward to the goal of perfection, till being at length delivered from this body of death, they are brought to reign with the Lamb of God in heaven.** Back to Philippians, we hear Paul say we are to "press on toward the goal for the prize of the upward call of God in Christ Jesus," which is perfection (Phil. 3:14). All this sounds so active? I thought we were Reformed? Vene-

---

[60] Owen, "Of the Mortification of Sin in Believers," *Works*, 6:6, 9.

[61] Thomas Manton once said, "For to dream of a mortification which shall be wrought in us without our consent or endeavours, as well as whilst we are sleeping, as whilst we are waking, is to delude ourselves with a vain fancy." Manton, "Sermons upon the Eighth Chapter to the Romans," 12:73. The active nature of sanctification and holiness was expressed by Hendriksen, who said, "The recipients of these favors [mentioned in vv. 1–11] must go into action." William Hendriksen, *Romans*, New Testament Commentary (1980, 1981; repr., Grand Rapids, MI: Baker Book House, sixth printing 1989), 254.

ma states it like this: "God's gracious *gift* of preservation issues in and provokes the believer's responsible *task* of perseverance."[62]

One pastoral question that I've faced for years is if we cling to the promise of salvation's triumph, why does God allow sin to still dwell in his children in this life so that we have to engage in salvation's toil? One of the best answers to this I've read over the years comes from Thomas Boston (d. 1732).[63] In typical Puritan fashion, it includes many points! I'll summarize them below.

First, God has ordered our sanctification this way *for our further humiliation.* For example, God gave Paul a thorn in the flesh to keep him low and permitted David to fall so that he'd grow in the grace of humility.

Second, by this the Lord *stirs us up to frequent prayer* like a small child who gets burned and cries out to its father.

Third, this *makes us more watchful of our hearts that are prone to wander.*

Fourth, just as God allowed some Canaanites to remain in the land to try his people, so he has left remains of sin *for our exercise and trial.* God gave us armor; it shouldn't lie beside us rusting!

Five, this makes us more and more to *feel our need for Christ.*

Sixth, *this is God's ordinary way to bring about degrees of progress in us.* God could have created all things in one moment; instead, he was pleased to take six days, including one day to create us. He could have sent Christ immediately after Adam fell; instead, he was pleased to let thousands of years pass. He could have brought Israel to the Promised Land immediately; instead, because of their disobedience they wandered for forty years and he used that time. So it is with our sanctification.

Seventh, this way *Christ is glorified.* How? While the enemy (sin) does dwell within us, Christ's grace and Holy Spirit are at work in us so that the enemy cannot overcome, domineer, or destroy us. Because of indwelling sin, we know that we cannot justify ourselves, but can only be justified by the perfect obedience of Christ.

After these points, Boston wrote, "To see how God makes such an excellent medicine of such poisonous ingredients cannot be but very de-

---

[62] Venema, *But for the Grace of God,* 75.

[63] Thomas Boston, "Why the Lord Suffereth Sin to Remain in the Regenerate?," in *The Whole Works of the Late Reverend Thomas Boston of Ettrick: Sermons and Discourses on Several Important Subjects in Divinity,* ed. Samuel M'Millan (Aberdeen, Scotland: George and Robert King, 1849), 6:110–24.

lightful."[64] Your and my toil against our indwelling sin is difficult. Remembering that God uses it for his glory and our good motivates us
to pursue by faith Jesus. In the end of his answers, Boston wrote:

> It is plain, that the more difficulties the work of man's sal-
> vation is carried through, the free grace of God is the more
> exalted; our Lord Jesus, the author of eternal salvation,
> hath the greater glory: but in this way it is carried on over
> the belly of more difficulties, than it would have been, if by
> the first grace the Christian had been made perfect.[65]

My normal life is to celebrate my triumph already in Christ all the
while I struggle and toil with my sins longing for salvation not yet. It's only
when we hold these two truths together that we experience the normal
Christian life.

Article 3

*By reason of these remains of indwelling sin, and the temptations of sin and of the
world, those who are converted could not persevere in a state of grace if left to their own
strength. But God is faithful, who having conferred grace, mercifully confirms and powerfully preserves them therein, even to the end.*

PERSEVERANCE DEFINED

With article 3 the canons give us its definition of the orthodox Reformed
view of the perseverance of the saints.

You've been born again (1 Pet. 1:3). You now have a living hope in
this life and an eternal inheritance in the life to come (1 Pet. 1:3–4). Yet you
can wake up tomorrow morning without your new life, without your hope,
and without your inheritance. In the words of the Assemblies of God (AG):

> The Bible also teaches that believers who have accepted
> Christ as Savior can be lost if they repeatedly disregard the
> teachings of Scripture, continue to resist the conviction of

---

[64] Boston, "Why the Lord Suffereth Sin to Remain," in *Works*, 6:117.

[65] Boston, "Why the Lord Suffereth Sin to Remain," in *Works*, 6:124.

the Holy Spirit, and finally reach the point where they have turned away from their Savior.[66]

In the words of another of its Position Papers, the AG said:

> Most current Wesleyan or Arminian thinkers agree that just as God does not force persons into relationship with himself, so also He does not force those who change their mind to stay in that relationship....The believer's salvation is secure in Christ but can be abandoned by willful choice.[67]

This is exactly what so many believers today adhere to. I call this a gospel of sand.[68] It's as if God grabbed hold of the world like a child grabs a handful of sand on the beach, only to have grains start falling through the cracks in his fingers. Those remaining are the saved. This is the kind of gospel our forefathers labored against before, during, and after the Synod of Dort. While it would undoubtedly be true **by reason of these remains of indwelling sin, and the temptations of sin and of the world** [that] **those who are converted could not persevere in a state of grace if left to their own strength,** we see something else in the article as well as in Scripture.

While many professing believers deny the ultimate perseverance of the saints, the apostle Peter didn't. He says, "By God's power [we] are being guarded through faith for salvation ready to be revealed in the last time" (1 Pet. 1:5). In the words of the article: **But God is faithful, who having conferred grace, mercifully confirms and powerfully preserves them therein, even to the end.** Our heavenly Father will guard his entire church, whether dead or living, in heaven or on earth, from creation to consummation, in his almighty and ever-present power. He will do so "through [our]

---

[66] "Assurance of Salvation" (adopted by the General Presbytery in Session August 5 & 7, 2017), as found at https://ag.org/Beliefs/Topics-Index/Assurance-Of-Salvation (accessed August 2, 2018).

[67] "An Assemblies of God Response to Reformed Theology" (adopted by the General Presbytery in Session August 1 & 3, 2015), as found at https://ag.org/Beliefs/Topics-Index/Reformed-Theology-Response-of-the-AG-Position-Paper (accessed August 2, 2018).

[68] Based on the imagery of C. H. Spurgeon's sermon "The Perseverance of the Saints," as found at https://www.spurgeongems.org/vols13-15/chs872.pdf (accessed August 6, 2018).

faith (which is his gift to us) for salvation, ready to be revealed on the last day." In the words of Paraeus, "Perseverance is nothing else, but faith it selfe persevering to the end."[69] To the question of whether saving faith includes perseverance, the Reformed answer yes because "if not, faith would not be saving faith or justifying faith, for no-one except 'he who believes' (Mark 16:16) and no-one except 'he who endures to the end will be saved' (Matthew 24:13)."[70] This is what G. C. Berkouwer described as "the eschatological perspective of this doctrine." Beginning with article 4 below, we'll explore its "existential tension."[71]

The Certainty of the Salvation

In 1 Peter 1 we hear the promise of the certainty of the salvation of God. Peter speaks of our "inheritance" being "kept" by the power of God (1 Pet. 1:4, 5). Peter uses this verb "kept" (τετηρημένην; *tetērēmenēn*) in the perfect passive tense. It's noteworthy that the perfect tense is used less frequently than the other tenses in the New Testament, leading Daniel Wallace to say, "When it is used, there is usually a deliberate choice on the part of the writer."[72] What Peter is signifying is that our inheritance was accomplished in the past and the results of that past action continue into the present.[73] The New Testament authors use the verb τηρέω (*tēreō*) to speak of something that is "kept" until a definite time in the future. As such, it has eschatological overtones. For example, the guests at the wedding in Cana say of Jesus (unwittingly) that he has "kept (τετήρηκας; *tetērēkas*) the good wine until now" (John 2:10). In the Gospel Jesus would later tell Judas to leave Mary alone "that she may keep (τηρήσῃ; *tērēsē*) [the expensive ointment] for the day of my burial" (John 12:7). In the Epistles it's also used with this sense. Jude describes the fallen angels "who did not stay (τηρήσαντας; *tērēsantas*) within their own position of authority" whom God "has kept (τετήρηκεν;

---

[69] Paraeus, "Epitome of Arminianisme," 838. See *Synopsis Purioris Theologiae: Volume 2*, 263, which defines perseverance as "the continuous safe-keeping of faith, hope, and love, the deeds of which ought to last throughout one's entire life."

[70] *Synopsis Purioris Theologiae: Volume 2*, 263.

[71] G. C. Berkouwer, *Faith and Perseverance*, trans. Robert D. Knudsen, Studies in Dogmatics (1958; Grand Rapids, MI: Eerdmans, second printing 1973), 11, 12.

[72] Wallace, *Greek Grammar beyond the Basics*, 573.

[73] On the perfect tense, see Wallace, *Greek Grammar beyond the Basics*, 573–82.

tetērēken) in eternal chains under gloomy darkness until the day of judgment" (Jude 6). Peter himself uses this verb with eschatological overtones in his second Epistle (2 Pet. 2:4; 2:9; 3:7).

The certainty of the saints' salvation is also confirmed by the adjectives Peter uses to describe it: "imperishable" meaning it is incorruptible and immortal, "undefiled" meaning it is pure, and "unfading" meaning it does not lessen over time. The salvation God bestows is certain.

The Certainty of the Saved

Not only is the salvation certain but those who participate in it—the saved—are described with certainty. First Peter 1:5 continues with "who by God's power are being guarded." Peter uses a present participial verb here: φρουρουμένους (*phrouroumenous*), "guarding." But it's in the passive voice, meaning, God is the one active in guarding while believers are the recipients of this action. I like to illustrate this to the children in my congregation like this: think of a jar of peanut butter. The peanut butter is in the jar. The lid is opened and closed by your action. The peanut butter is passive. Why is there a lid? To preserve the peanut butter inside from the air outside that causes it to go bad. This same verb is both powerful and personal. It's used for a guard inside a city's walls whose job is not to let people out (2 Cor. 11:32). Elsewhere Paul says before we came to faith in Jesus Christ "we were held captive under the law" (Gal. 3:23). The law kept us in its custody. It owned us. It condemned us. In the context of 1 Peter 1, though, having been born again, we are now being powerfully guarded by God under his custody. We're under new ownership. We're no longer condemned; we're acquitted. When the last day comes, our rightful owner Jesus will take full possession of us.

Who are the "who" of verse 5? It's important to ask this question so that we don't end up saying every baptized person *is* elect, *is* regenerated, *is* justified, and *is* going to be preserved. One helpful way of answering this question was written later in the seventeenth century by Herman Witsius. In his work *The Economy of the Covenants*, he said that those whom God preserves can be described with five words:

> *Elect*—not to an external communion within a national
> covenant as all Israel was (Deut. 8:6), but these are elected

to an internal glory as Paul describes election in Ephesians 1:4–5;

Redeemed—not only for common blessings of a family, but these are redeemed from the bondage of sin as members of God's adopted family;

Regenerated—not only do they resemble having a spiritual life as the church in Sardis, "You have the reputation of being alive, but you are dead" (Rev. 3:1), but these actually have spiritual life according to Paul's words: "For the law of the Spirit of life has set you free in Christ Jesus from the law of sin and death" (Rom. 8:2);

Faithful—not only assent to the truth, even as the demons assent to the one God's existence (James 2:19), but these have a true, "sincere faith" (1 Tim. 1:5);

Sanctified—not only a federal holiness as our children have (1 Cor. 7:14) or an external holiness (2 Pet. 2:20; John 15; Heb. 10), but these have a true and thorough holiness (Eph. 4:24).[74]

One aspect of the illustration above that breaks down is the peanut butter itself. While God is preserving us, we're not passive. Yes, God is actively working out his preserving work for us, but he's also activating us to persevere. Peter tells us God's power is guarding us "through faith for a salvation ready to be revealed in the last time" (1 Pet. 1:5). God's preserving power is realized "through [our] faith," which, as we've seen many times above, was his gift to us. To cite the words of our article again: **But God is faithful, who having conferred grace, mercifully confirms and powerfully preserves them therein, even to the end**.

We'll explore this more in the articles below, but it's important to recognize that while faith and perseverance are gifts of God that have been bestowed upon us and that remain as dispositions in our soul, at the same time we recognize that the actions and senses of faith and perseverance may

---

[74] Herman Witsius, *The Economy of the Covenants between God and Man: Comprehending a Complete Body of Divinity*, trans. William Crookshank, 2 vols. (1822; repr., Escondido, CA: den Dulk Foundation, 1990), 2:55–56.

be interrupted for a time. As Rivetus said, "The person always remains tied to God, as if by a chain."[75]

The Certainty of the Savior

The inheritance of salvation is certain. Those saved and thus sharing in the inheritance are certain. All this is true because of the certainty of the Savior.

In contrast to his certainty, article 3 speaks of the uncertainty of our perseverance to **persevere in a state of grace if left to their own strength.** Why? Because we have three "deadly enemies" (Heidelberg Catechism, Q&A 127). There is a triple allegiance against us: first, the flesh, or the **remains of indwelling sin.** This remnant causes us to be beset all our life by "the sin" of unbelief (Heb. 12:1) and is at war within us (Rom. 7:15, 18–20). The second enemy is **the temptations...of the world** (Rom. 12:2; James 4:4; 1 John 2:15–17). The third is **the temptations of Satan** also called the devil (2 Cor. 11:14; Eph. 6:12, 16; James 4:7; 1 Pet. 5:8–9).[76]

In contrast to the uncertainty within us, God's ability to preserve is emphasized in article 3. He is **faithful** to himself and what he has promised. He is faithful **having conferred grace,** [he] **mercifully confirms and powerfully preserves them therein** (1 Cor. 1:8–9; Phil. 1:6; 2 Thess. 3:3; 1 Pet. 5:10). He is faithful in his power as he **preserves them...even to the end** (John 10:28–30; 1 Pet. 1:5; Jude 24).

Where did Peter get his teaching that the Savior is certain to save his people? The Gospel of John records Jesus rebuking the Pharisees as false shepherds while proclaiming himself the "good shepherd" (John 10:11). Jesus goes on to give three reasons he is *the certain shepherd who preserves his sheep.*

First, *Jesus is the door of the sheep* (John 10:7–10). In verse 7 he speaks one of his "I am" statements: "Truly, truly, I say to you, I am the door of the sheep." Whenever you read Jesus saying, "truly, truly," that's translating the words "amen, amen." It's Old Testament oath language and thus one of the most serious ways Jesus speaks as if to say, "Now listen up; this is absolutely serious." He then compares himself to the false shepherds of the Pharisees: "All who came before me are thieves and robbers, but the sheep

---

[75] *Synopsis Purioris Theologiae: Volume 2,* 265.

[76] The translation I'm utilizing somehow rendered *satanae tentationes* as **the temptations of sin** and not **of Satan.**

did not listen to them" (John 10:8). Now, listen to the importance of his saying again, "I am the door" (John 10:9): "If anyone enters by me, he *will be* saved and *will* go in and out and find pasture. The thief comes only to steal and kill and destroy. I came that they *may* have life and *have* it abundantly" (John 10:9–10).

Second, *Jesus is the shepherd of the sheep* (John 10:11–18). He speaks another "I am" statement: "I am the good shepherd" and as the good shepherd Jesus says he "lays down his life for the sheep" (John 10:11). Would he die for us only to have us not live for him? Then again, in contrast to a false shepherd who flees the sheep when the wolf comes near because he does not care about them (John 10:12–13), Jesus says, "I am the good shepherd" (v. 14). As this kind of shepherd he says, "I know my own and my own know me" (v. 14). Can Jesus disown what is his? Can we run away so far that he who knows us so well cannot find us? And look at how powerful this image is in verse 15: "just as the Father knows me and I know the Father." Did you get that? How does Jesus know us and we know him? In the same way that the Father knows the Son and the Son knows the Father. Can the Father disown his Son? Can the Son not love the Father? You see why it's ridiculous to say a true believer can lose salvation.

Third, *Jesus is the Son of God* (John 10:28–30). Look at verse 28: "I give them eternal life, and they will never perish, and no one will snatch them out of my hand." This verse in itself should eliminate the objection completely, forever! Look at it again: "I," the eternal, almighty Son of God through whom the universe came to be, "give them eternal life, and" therefore because I have given this "they will never perish." Literally Jesus says, "they will not perish forever" (οὐ μὴ ἀπόλωνται εἰς τὸν αἰῶνα). This is the strongest way of saying something in Greek. Jesus uses a double negative, aorist subjunctive. And how long is "never"? Forever, and ever, and ever! And because this is such an absolute statement, Jesus says, "No one will snatch them out of my hand." No one! Not Satan. Not the false shepherds. Not even yourself. "No one" means "no one."

Then notice how much stronger Jesus says this in John 10:29: "My Father, who has given them to me, is greater than all, and no one is able to snatch them out of the Father's hand." The Father gave the sheep to the Son, Jesus Christ, and Jesus gives the sheep eternal life. We cannot be snatched from Jesus' hand; we cannot be snatched from the Father's hand.

No one has the right, the might, the ability, or the authority to take us! Then in verse 30 he tells us why this is true: "I and the Father are one."

This is your powerful Savior! This is a gospel that powerfully saves! This is no gospel of sand but a gospel that withstands all assaults! What a reason to praise him when I feel low and lost! What a reason to be assured! What a reason to tell a lost sinner there is hope in Jesus' name.

Article 4

Although the weakness of the flesh cannot prevail against the power of God, who confirms and preserves true believers in a state of grace, yet converts are not always so influenced and actuated by the Spirit of God, as not in some particular instances sinfully to deviate from the guidance of divine grace, so as to be seduced by, and comply with the lusts of the flesh; they must, therefore, be constant in watching and prayer that they be not led into temptation. When these are neglected, they are not only liable to be drawn into great and heinous sins by Satan, the world and the flesh, but sometimes by the righteous permission of God actually fall into these evils. This the lamentable fall of David, Peter, and other saints described in Holy Scripture demonstrates.

In articles 4–8 the canons delve into the relationship between perseverance and the continuing problem the saints have with indwelling sin. This is the existential perspective of this doctrine mentioned above. As Berkouwer said, perseverance is not about my experiences or feelings: "an experience of consolation that flickers and dies and flickers again in the shadows of life's uncertainties" or "an experience of joyful communion with the Lord that perhaps tomorrow could be partial, and later even totally, threatened and destroyed." Instead, perseverance "is a continuity amidst all the transitoriness of our lives, as we proceed by devious paths through numberless circumstances and dangers toward the consummation, toward the day of Jesus Christ."[77]

ONCE SAVED, ALWAYS SAVED?

"Once saved, always saved." Do we believe that those God in his love chose in eternity will spend an eternity loving him? Yes. Yet, how is this

---

[77] Berkouwer, *Faith and Perseverance*, 10.

slogan so often used? It's used to say that a person who claims to be a Christian can live like an unbeliever his or her whole life and still be saved. This is the so-called doctrine of "eternal security" we saw above. It's used to justify sin and apathy about godliness. So do we believe "once saved, always saved"? Not in this familiar sense. But yes, if understood rightly.

What Scripture teaches us and what article 4 confesses is that while a true believer cannot completely fall *from* grace, a true believer can fall *into* heinous sins. To say that we can fall from grace is to say that we become unsaved and outside the grip of God's hand. But to say that we can fall into sin, even heinous sin, is to say that even then we are in the grip of grace, albeit not a very tight grip. The question before us is "Can I fall into heinous sins?"

The Real Potential in Ourselves

Can I fall into heinous sins? Article 4 begins: **Although the weakness of the flesh cannot prevail against the power of God.** We saw this power above in 1 Peter 1. Yet we have the potential in ourselves to fall because of our sin nature: **yet converts are not always so influenced and actuated by the Spirit of God, as not in some particular instances sinfully to deviate from the guidance of divine grace, so as to be seduced by, and comply with the lusts of the flesh.** Note we're not talking here about a *complete* lifestyle that lasts a lifetime; we're talking about **some particular instances.** In the words of Van Oosterzee, "Even in the regenerate heart lie perhaps hidden depths of Satan, from which the indwelling corruption breaks out sometimes with a force and violence, which seems almost inconceivable to ourselves and others."[78]

We see the potential of that force and violence break out in the *example of the saints*: **This the lamentable fall of David, Peter, and other saints described in Holy Scripture demonstrates.** *Lamentable.* This certainly describes David's fall in 2 Samuel 11 as he committed adultery with Bathsheba and then covered it up by having Uriah placed at the front of the battle line so he would assuredly be killed.[79] Instead of watching out for sin, he was watching to sin. *Lamentable.* This certainly describes Samson, who told

---

[78] Van Oosterzee, *Christian Dogmatics*, 665.

[79] Henry Peterson, *The Canons of Dort: A Study Guide* (Grand Rapids, MI: Baker Book House, 1968), 80.

the secret of his strength to Delilah because he underestimated her power over him (Judges 16). *Lamentable.* This certainly describes Peter. He was called by the Lord, trained by the Lord, accompanied the Lord as he did his miracles and preached the gospel of the kingdom, but there he was, falling and denying our Lord; there he was not able to stay awake while our Lord agonized in prayer over the cross to come (Matt. 26:36–44). After our Lord spoke to him about denying him three times, Peter goes and places himself "outside" the very place our Lord was interrogated (Matt. 26:69). There he said, "I do not know what you mean" (v. 70); there he "denied...with an oath: 'I do not know the man'" (Matt. 26:72); there he "invoke[d] a curse on himself and sw[ore], 'I do not know the man'" (Matt. 26:74). He should not have been in the place as this shows he underestimated his propensity to sin and overestimated his ability to withstand. This sad potential in use should cause us to lament like Peter: "And he went out and wept bitterly" (Matt. 26:75).

The same sin nature that ran through Peter's veins runs through us. With Peter, we can be prideful: "Though they all fall away because of you, I will never fall away.... Even if I must die with you, I will not deny you!" (Matt. 26:33, 35). Like Peter, while "the spirit indeed is willing...the flesh is weak" (Matt. 26:41). The potential lies within us too. Our hearts are full of flammable material with a big bright sign in all capital letters: EXPLOSIVE. All it takes is the smallest of sparks. To use another illustration, our sins are like the cold of winter that cause a fruitful tree to nearly go dormant.[80]

Article 4 corrects the misunderstanding of the doctrine of perseverance that it's "a fatal attempt to bring a bruising life that is tossed to and fro, with heights and depths, into a system; drawing lines, *straight lines*, while in real life only zig-zag lines are to be seen."[81]

The Righteous Permission in God

Can I fall into heinous sins? Yes, because of *the righteous permission in God.* Article 4 says: **when** believers **neglect[...]** to be watchful and prayerful, **they are not only liable to be drawn into great and heinous sins by Satan, the world and the flesh, but sometimes by the righteous permission of God actually fall into these evils.**

---

[80] Witsius, *The Economy of the Covenants*, 2:57.

[81] Berkouwer, *Faith and Perseverance*, 26. Emphasis added.

Don't forget that God is in control of all aspects of our lives. If he weren't, there would be no hope of change! Jesus tells them, "You will all fall away because of me this night" (Matt. 26:31). Jesus quotes Zechariah 13:7: "For it is written, 'I will strike the shepherd, and the sheep of the flock will be scattered'" (Matt. 26:31). Note again our article:

> When [watchfulness and prayer] **are neglected,** [believers] **are not only liable to be drawn into great and heinous sins by Satan, the world and the flesh, but sometimes by the righteous permission of God actually fall into these evils. This the lamentable fall of David, Peter, and other saints described in Holy Scripture demonstrates.**

Let's look at how this is illustrated in Luke 22:31–34, the parallel to our text: "'Simon, Simon, behold, Satan demanded to have you, that he might sift you like wheat, but I have prayed for you that your faith may not fail. And when you have turned again, strengthen your brothers" (Luke 22:31–32). What did you notice about our Lord's words? Did he say he turned Satan down? Did he say Satan had no business asking such a thing? No. Our Lord's answer shows that he did give Satan permission to "sift" Peter. Why? It was so that Peter's faith would be refined and purified, as he was to strengthen his brothers in faith after he repented and returned to the Lord. What this means is that the Lord can allow us to fall into sin on our own accord and that we need to be aware of this. He wants our faith to be strengthened even more through the experience so that we'll come out more assured than before.

The Remedy Prescribed in Scripture

Because we can fall into heinous sins, let's look at *the remedy prescribed in Scripture*: **they must, therefore, be constant in watching and prayer that they be not led into temptation.** Should we rest secure in a carnal security because we know we are impervious? Should we just give us because we might fall anyway? We cannot respond like this!

"Watch and pray," as Jesus said to his disciples (Matt. 26:41). We are to keep watch for our brothers and sisters (Gal. 6:1). Are you concerned when a brother or sister is not in worship week in and week out? Are you aware that a brother or sister may be falling? We are to keep watch for ourselves (1 Thess. 5:6; 1 Pet. 5:8). Are you aware of your weaknesses? We are to watch for ourselves as Jesus said to his disciples (Matt. 26:41). We are to pray (Eph. 6:18; 1 Thess. 5:6, 17). Engaging in warfare! Perseverance exists in the existential tension of the Christian life. It doesn't exist "in a static, lifeless relationship" between God and us "but in the mobile, living relationship of the entire human life to the Father."[82]

Article 5

By such enormous sins, however, they very highly offend God, incur a deadly guilt, grieve the Holy Spirit, interrupt the exercise of faith, very grievously wound their consciences, and sometimes lose the sense of God's favor for a time, until on their returning into the right way of serious repentance, the light of God's fatherly countenance again shines upon them.

WHY DO I FEEL SPIRITUALLY DESERTED?

Article 5 picks up on the **great and heinous sins** mentioned in article 4, into which believers may fall, by dealing with the consequences of such sins.

Spiritual desertion is real.[83] It's the feeling and sense that God's good presence has deserted you. The sensitive believer who knows God, knows his or her own sins, expresses in heartfelt ways from time to time this spiritual experience of feeling far from God or that he is far from us.

Look at Psalm 6. Here this feeling is expressed in an agonizing question: "Be gracious to me, O LORD, for I am languishing; heal me, O LORD, for my bones are troubled. My soul also is greatly troubled. But you, O LORD—how long?" (Ps. 6:2–3). Look at Psalm 32. Here it is expressed as past pain: "For when I kept silent, my bones wasted away through my groaning all day long" (Ps. 32:3). Look at Psalm 38. Here it is expressed as deep pain: "For your arrows have sunk into me, and your hand has come down on me" (Ps. 38:2). Notice how this affects David: "My heart throbs; my strength fails me, and the light of my eyes—it also has gone from me" (Ps. 38:10). Then notice the language of feeling distant: "My friends and

---

[82] Berkouwer, *Faith and Perseverance*, 29.

[83] Gisbertus Voetius and Johannes Hoornbeeck, *Spiritual Desertion*, trans. John Vriend & Harry Boonstra, ed. M. Eugene Oosterhaven, Classics of Reformed Spirituality (Grand Rapids, MI: Baker Academic, 2003).

companions stand aloof from my plague, and my nearest kin stand far off.... Do not forsake me, O LORD! O my God, be not far from me!" (Ps. 38:11, 21).

These Psalms and many other Scriptures are summarized in article 5 in terms of why true believers can feel spiritually deserted.

Because You've Sinned

Why do I feel spiritually deserted is a huge question. But it has a basic "Christianity 101" kind of answer. Recently I went to my dentist. I told him I was having pain near the one filling I have. He x-rayed, drilled out the old silver filling, and did everything to get to the proverbial root of the problem. His answer: "Get back to basics, Danny. You need to floss more!" When we feel spiritually deserted we need to get back to basics: God feels far from you *because you've sinned*: **By such enormous sins.**

What's the one thing that links Psalms 6, 32, 38, and 51? They all lament sin. Notice how.

> Psalm 6:1: "Rebuke me not in your anger, nor discipline me in your wrath."
>
> Psalm 32:5: "I acknowledged my sin to you, and I did not cover my iniquity. I said, 'I will confess my transgressions to the LORD.'"
>
> Psalm 38:3–4: "There is no health in my bones because of my *sin*, for my *iniquities* have gone over my head; like a heavy burden, they are too heavy for me." And then again in verse 18: "I confess my *iniquity*; I am sorry for my *sin*."
>
> Psalm 51:1, 3–4: "Have mercy on me, O God, according to your steadfast love; according to your abundant mercy blot out my transgressions. For I know my transgressions, and my sin is ever before me. Against you, you only, have I sinned and done what is evil in your sight."

One of the wonderful truths before us in these Psalms is the pronoun used in article 5: **By such enormous sins, however,** *they*. The Psalms above are David's confessions of sin. These are *our* confessions of sin as believers.

Because of Sin's Effects

Get back to basics. One of those basics is knowing that your sin has consequences in this life even for believers. Especially of note is that major sin causes a major consequence like feeling far and separate from God. When you feel this way, recognize it's *because of sin's effects.*

By such sins we **very highly offend God**. We talk so much as a society of being "offended." But do you realize that your sins offend God himself? Psalm 51:4: "Against *you, you only* have I sinned, and done what is evil in *your sight.*" Get over yourself and think of him! Because sin offends God, we pray in Psalms 6:1 and 38:1, "Rebuke me not in your anger nor discipline me in your wrath."

By such sins we **incur a deadly guilt**. It's not only that you know you have sinned against God, but that you know that *he* knows that you've sinned! This leads to feeling mortified and petrified. Psalm 32:3 says, "For when I kept silent, my bones wasted away." Look at Psalm 38:6: "I am utterly bowed down and prostrate." Look at Psalm 38:8: "I am feeble and crushed; I groan because of the tumult of my heart." Then David says this in verses 13–14:

> But I am like a deaf man; I do not hear,
> like a mute man who does not open his mouth.
> I have become like a man who does not hear,
> and in whose mouth are no rebukes.

By such sins we **grieve the Holy Spirit**. The Spirit who lives within us and is the down payment of our living with the triune God in eternity is grieved by our sins according to Paul in Ephesians 4:30 (cf. Isa. 63:10).

By such sins we **interrupt the exercise of faith**. Notice that. A man who is paralyzed from the waist down still has life within him, but he cannot exercise his legs. In the same way, we still have spiritual life within us, but there are times we can be spiritually paralyzed like Peter, whom we saw above outside Jesus' trial and when asked if he was a Christian, he did not exercise faith but was paralyzed in fear and denial (Matt. 26:69–75). Rivetus said, "We do not deny the facts that saints are able to fall from time to time, and through the weakness of their flesh they can fall seriously into trivial and even very grievous sins…it is impossible for saints to lose their faith; but it is possible in a limited way."[84]

By such sins believers **very grievously wound their consciences**. The prophet Nathan told David, "You are the man," and then his conscience was wounded. The apostle John assures us in 1 John 3:20 that "whenever our heart condemns us, God is greater than our heart." That's a promise! But contained in it is the realization that our hearts *do* condemn us because of our sins.

By such sins we **sometimes lose the sense of God's favor for a time**. This is the worst of all experiences! "But you, O LORD, how long?" (Ps. 6:3). "But for you, O LORD, do I wait" (Ps. 38:15). "Do not forsake me, O LORD! O my God, be not far from me!" (Ps. 38:21). "Cast me not away from your presence, and take not your Holy Spirit from me. Restore to me the joy of your salvation" (Ps. 51:11–12). That phrase **for a time** is so important. This article reflects the teaching of Augustine who said that while it was true that elect believers could fall away, it was a partial or temporary fall only.[85]

Because You Need to Repent

Get back to basics. Our sinning causes us to feel the effects of sin. The basic response we need to have to *why do I feel spiritually deserted* is *repent!* All those very real and painful effects of sin can cease, and be reversed. They last **until on their returning into the right way of serious repentance, the light of God's fatherly countenance again shines upon them**.

Are there any better examples of serious repentance than Psalms 6, 32, 38, and 51? As we see their words in our open Bibles, I pray your hearts have been opened to the Holy Spirit's gracious invitation to return to God as a Father through Jesus his Son.

One of the truths we learn in this discussion is that for the Reformed, the issue is not that we can't resist God's grace, but that this resistance isn't final and ultimate.[86] It's to that truth the next article explains.

---

[84] *Synopsis Purioris Theologiae: Volume 2*, 271.

[85] Augustine, "On Rebuke and Grace," 13, 23 (4:476–77, 480–81).

[86] Berkouwer, *Faith and Perseverance*, 41–43.

Article 6

But God, who is rich in mercy, according to His unchangeable purpose of election, does not wholly withdraw the Holy Spirit from His own people, even in their melancholy falls; nor suffers them to proceed so far as to lose the grace of adoption, and forfeit the state of justification, or to commit the sin unto death; nor does He permit them to be totally deserted, and to plunge themselves into everlasting destruction.

CAN GOD RENEW MY BACKSLIDING?

The **light of God's fatherly countenance** that **again shines upon** the repentant believer is grounded not in the believer's repentance, but in the grace of God himself. This is what article 6 takes up in dealing with renewal from backsliding.

A Renewing God

Spiritual struggles can lead to a lack of faith, which leads into sin, which may lead to even worse sins, which leads to an interruption of the exercise of faith. As you can see, it's a vicious cycle. Yet in it all, we still have faith. To give a couple of illustrations, in these times our faith is like a smoldering piece of charcoal that is buried under the ashes. In these times our faith is like the sun when it is concealed by dark storm clouds. In these times our faith runs to the corner of our hearts and is ashamed to come out. The question is, in these times of backsliding to Egypt instead of moving forward to the Promised Land of the pilgrimage of faith, *can God renew my backsliding?*

The answer is yes because we have *a renewing God*. Echoing Ephesians 2:4 the article opens: **But God, who is rich in mercy** (*dives misericordia*). For example, ten times in Psalm 30 David invokes the name of the LORD (vv. 1, 2, 3, 4, 7, 8 [2x], 10 [2x], 12). You know that whenever you see the word "LORD" in all caps in your Bible, this is his Name he revealed to Moses at the burning bush: "I AM WHO I AM" (Ex. 3:14). His name expresses his faithfulness to his covenant. Listen to how Matthew Henry (1662–1714) expressed the ability of God to renew us:

> If *weeping endureth for a night,* and it be a wearisome night, yet
> as sure as the light of the morning returns after the dark-

ness of the night, so sure will joy and comfort return in a short time, in due time, to the people of God; for the covenant of grace is as firm as the covenant of the day.[87]

Look also with me at Jeremiah 31. Here the Lord promises renewal to his people out of their exile. Notice that this promise comes to "the people who survived the sword" and who were "in the wilderness" (Jer. 31:2). Then we read, "I have loved you with an everlasting love; therefore I have continued my faithfulness to you" (Jer. 31:3).

Can God renew my backsliding? The answer is that he's faithful to his promises. He's **rich in mercy** to use the language of article 6. Being so merciful **according to His unchangeable purpose of election, does not wholly withdraw the Holy Spirit from His own people, even in their melancholy** (*tristibus*; sorrowful) **falls.** What we saw in the first point of doctrine is connected to our regeneration in the third and fourth points and applied here in the fifth point. Even when I sorrowfully fall into sin like David, I can pray, not hypothetically but repentantly in confidence: "Take not your Holy Spirit from me" (Ps. 51:11).

Can God renew my backsliding? Being **rich in mercy** God does not allow me **to proceed so far as to lose the grace of adoption.** He's brought me into his family, changing my status from orphan to son; he will not reverse this work!

Can God renew my backsliding? Being **rich in mercy** God does not allow me **to proceed so far as to lose...the state of justification.** I once was in a state or status of misery, but that was changed to a state or status of justification (*iustificationis statu*). Being clear on this is necessary for our comfort. We're not merely innocent and back to Adam's Garden status; we're not merely freed from guilt and punishment; no, we're positively righteous in our status and standing before almighty God. He's declared us righteous in his Son, and we do not lose this![88]

---

[87] Matthew Henry, *Commentary on the Whole Bible* (1991; repr., Peabody, MA: Hendrickson, eighth printing 1997), 782 col. 3 [loc. Ps. 30:1–5].

[88] While the canons don't get into the issues of whether justification is forgiveness only or includes the imputation of the active obedience of Christ, I believe the latter. This is where Feenstra, errs, speaking of justification merely as God declaring the believer innocent, freeing from guilt and punishment, and granting eternal life. Missing in his exposition is any mention of the imputation of Christ's righteousness. Feenstra, *Unspeakable Comfort*, 162.

Can God renew my backsliding? Being **rich in mercy** God does not allow me **to proceed so far as to…commit the sin unto death; nor does He permit** [me] **to be totally deserted, and to plunge** [myself] **into everlasting destruction.** As a pastor I've been asked from time to time, "Pastor, have I committed the sin against the Holy Spirit?" My response has always been the same. First, if you're concerned about it, perhaps you haven't committed that sin; second, this particular sin is one in this redemptive historical age in which a person completely and finally cuts him- or herself off from grace and there is no longer is any excuse for that person. In the time of Jesus, the Pharisees spoke against him in his state of humiliation; now, a person rejects him finally in his state of exaltation. It is sin "which certainly brings death with it, which is the blasphemy against the Holy Ghost, when any one denies the truth of the Christian doctrine, whereby he was enlightened and convinced by the Holy Spirit, and maliciously blasphemes and persecutes the same."[89] Third, this is not a sin of weakness like with Peter, or fear, like with Saul of Tarsus, "but out of mere hatred and obstinacy, against the conviction of the Holy Spirit, resists, blasphemes, and persecutes the same."[90] Of this **sin unto death** Augustine said those delivered from the servitude of sin "do not any more obey the sin which is unto death…concerning which sin…many and different notions may be entertained. I, however, say that that sin is to forsake even unto death the faith which worketh by love. This sin they no longer serve."[91]

Article 7

For in the first place, in these falls He preserves in them the incorruptible seed of regeneration from perishing or being totally lost; and again, by His Word and Spirit, certainly and effectually renews them to repentance, to a sincere and godly sorrow for their sins, that they may seek and obtain remission in the blood of the Mediator, may again experience the favor of a reconciled God, through faith adore His mercies, and henceforward more diligently work out their own salvation with fear and trembling.

Article 7 continues the theme that God renews the believer who has fallen very low in serious sin.

---

[89] *Dutch Annotations* on 1 John 5:16.

[90] *Dutch Annotations* on Matthew 12:31.

[91] Augustine, "On Rebuke and Grace," 35 (5:486).

A Renewed People

As we've seen above, we have a renewing God. Article 6 described his rich mercy in renewal from the vantage point of his electing grace. Here in article 7 his rich mercy is described in historical terms: regeneration and repentance.

Can God renew my backsliding? Yes, because *he preserves regeneration*: **For in the first place, in these falls He preserves in them the incorruptible seed of regeneration from perishing or being totally lost.** We've seen this above in 1 Peter 1.

Can God renew my backsliding? Yes, because *he provides repentance*: **again, by His Word and Spirit, certainly and effectually renews them to repentance, to a sincere and godly sorrow for their sins.** When the Lord brought back his people, he said this through Jeremiah:

> Behold, I will bring them from the north country and gather them from the farthest parts of the earth, among them the blind and the lame, the pregnant woman and she who is in labor, together; a great company, they shall return here. With weeping they shall come, and with pleas for mercy I will lead them back, I will make them walk by brooks of water, in a straight path in which they shall not stumble, for I am a father to Israel, and Ephraim is my firstborn. (Jer. 31:8–9)

Augustine discussed the pastoral case of those whose faith had been upset by Hymnanaeus and Alexander's doctrine that the resurrection had already happened (2 Tim. 2:16–18). He cited Paul's next words: "The Lord know those who are his" (2 Tim. 2:19). In other words, the elect not only will persevere, but those elect persons whose faith partially ceased or even for a time ceased would be renewed: "The faith of these…either actually does not fail at all, or, if there are any whose faith fails, it is restored before their life is ended, and the iniquity which had intervened is done away, and perseverance even to the end is allotted to them."[92]

---

[92] Augustine, "On Rebuke and Grace," 16 (5:478). "For these in their love for God continue even to the end; and they who for a season wander from the way return, that they may continue unto the end what they had begun to be in good." *Ibid.*, 23 (5:480–481).

By such renewing work God makes us *a renewed people*. There are several characteristics of a renewed people according to article 7.

A renewed people *seek remission*: **that they may seek and obtain remission in the blood of the Mediator**. David's says in Psalm 30: "O LORD my God, I cried to *you* for help, and *you* have healed me" (v. 2); "To *you*, O LORD, I cry, and to the *Lord* I plead for mercy" (v. 8); "Hear, O LORD, and be merciful to me! O LORD, be my helper!" (v. 10).

A renewed people *experience God's favor*: **that they...may again experience the favor of a reconciled God**. Listen again to the amazing words of Psalm 30: "For his *anger* is but for a *moment*, and his *favor* is for a *lifetime*. *Weeping* may tarry for the *night*, but *joy* comes in the *morning*" (v. 5). This anger and weeping only lasted a moment in the night, but even this is so horrific that David likened it to death itself: "You have brought up my soul from Sheol; you restored me to life from among those who go down to the pit" (v. 3). Listen to what John Calvin said about this phrase:

> He reckoned that he could not sufficiently express in words the magnitude of the favor which God had conferred upon him, unless he compared the darkness of that period to a grave and pit, into which he had been forced to throw himself hastily, to protect his life by hiding, until the flame of insurrection was quenched.[93]

A renewed people *adore God's mercies*: **that they...through faith adore His mercies**. "I will extol you, O LORD" (Ps. 30:1); "Sing praises to the LORD, O you his saints, and give thanks to his holy name" (Ps. 30:4); "You have turned for me my mourning into dancing; you have loosed my sackcloth and clothed me with gladness, that my glory may sing your praise and not be silent. O LORD my God, I will give thanks to you forever!" (Ps. 30:11–12).

What these aspects of our renewal are describing is the life of prayer. Augustine explained the relation between perseverance and prayer saying that the fact that the church prays daily "hallowed be Thy name" is proof that perseverance is a gift of grace.[94] In terms of our renewal, then, God

---

[93] John Calvin, *Commentary on the Book of Psalms: Volume First*, trans. James Anderson, Calvin's Commentaries 4 (repr., Grand Rapids, MI: Baker Book House, 1996), 4:486.

[94] Augustine, "On Rebuke and Grace," 10 (5:476).

renews in us this life of persevering prayer asking him, "Lead us not into temptation."[95]

A renewed people *work out their salvation*: **that they...henceforward more diligently work out their own salvation with fear and trembling.** Here the article quotes Philippians 2:12. That's what David did as he "cried to" the Lord "for help, and" the Lord "healed" him; therefore, he praised the Lord (Ps. 30:2). And he asks in Psalm 30:9, "What profit is there in my death, if I go down to the pit? Will the dust praise you? Will it tell of your faithfulness?" "No, but I will," is what he is saying!

You can fall into sin; you cannot fall out of grace. God is a renewing God; God promises to make you a renewed people.

Article 8

Thus, it is not in consequence of their own merits or strength, but of God's free mercy, that they do not totally fall from faith and grace, nor continue and perish finally in their backslidings; which, with respect to themselves, is not only possible, but would undoubtedly happen; but with respect to God, it is utterly impossible, since His counsel cannot be changed nor His promise fail, neither can the call according to His purpose be revoked, nor the merit, intercession and preservation of Christ be rendered ineffectual, nor the sealing of the Holy Spirit be frustrated or obliterated.

PRESERVED BY A TRIUNE GOD

Article 8 goes on to summarize the canons' discussion of the relationship between perseverance and the saints' ongoing struggles with sin.

We are weak, but God is strong. We are able in ourselves to fall totally from grace, but God is not able to let us fall totally. When we think of ourselves, all that happens is despair, but when we think of God, all that happens is hope. We've seen the ups and downs, the joys and pains of the Christian life in the past several articles. Article 8 begins with a summary:

> **Thus, it is not in consequence of their own merits or strength, but of God's free mercy, that they do not totally fall from faith and grace, nor continue and perish**

---

[95] Augustine, "On the Gift of Perseverance," 63 (5:551). For Augustine's application of the Lord's Prayer to perseverance, see ibid., 3–11 (5:527–29).

finally in their backslidings; which, with respect to themselves, is not only possible, but would undoubtedly happen; but with respect to God, it is utterly impossible.

What relevance does the doctrine of the Trinity have for your practical Christian life?[96] Maybe you've never thought of that before. I mean, we believe the doctrine of there being one God in three persons, we confess it in the creeds, and we sing about it in our songs, right? But how does this inexpressible, mysterious doctrine come down to our level of experience and comfort, help, and aid us? Let me say unequivocally that the doctrine of the Trinity is the guarantee of your preservation.

How so? It's not by prying into the mysteries of how three can be one, but for our weakness, God has revealed himself in Scripture by teaching us that each person of the Trinity has a distinct role in our salvation. Let's pause and reflect upon the work of each person of the triune God and how that work strengthens us with the knowledge that we are preserved children of God.

By the Work of the Father

We know that if left to ourselves we would fall flat on our faces and fall from grace totally. **With respect to God, it is utterly impossible, since His counsel cannot be changed nor His promise fail, neither can the call according to His purpose be revoked.**

God's **counsel** concerning you **cannot be changed**. Listen to Psalm 33:11, which says, "The counsel of the LORD stands forever, the plans of his heart to all generations." When the prophet Isaiah described the Lord against the idols of the nations, God said, "I am God, and there is none like me, declaring the end from the beginning and from ancient times things not yet done" (Isa. 46:10). Is this clear yet? Well, those verses talk about his counsel for everything in general; there's nothing there *for me.* "For the mountains may depart and the hills be removed, but my steadfast love shall not depart from you, and my covenant of peace shall not be removed" (Isa. 54:10).

---

[96] On this, see Ryan M. McGraw, *Knowing the Trinity: Practical Thoughts for Daily Life* (Lancaster, PA: Alliance of Confessing Evangelicals, 2017).

When you think of God the Father, meditate upon the fact that "before the foundation of the world" he chose and predestined *you*! Of all people, he chose *you*! Don't tell me that does not comfort you. Don't tell me that does not enliven you. Don't tell me that does not move you to cry out with Paul, "Blessed be the God and Father of our Lord Jesus Christ!" Don't tell me Calvinism is boring, that we are the so-called frozen chosen, or that the doctrine of election is all hear and no heart! For in the aeons of eternity, when the Father, Son, and Holy Spirit dwelt in perfect love with one another, "in love"—that same love—he predestined *you*!

God's **promise** concerning you **[cannot] fail**. If the Father chose us and that is immutable, then his promise to us is an extension of that immutable love. What promise is that? Listen to 1 John 2:25: "And this is the promise that he made to us—eternal life." Whose promise? The Father's promise! And unlike our promises as fathers or the promises our fathers made to us, God the Father's promises are never forgotten, are never pushed aside because he is too busy, are never said in haste, but are always realized in our lives!

God's **calling** of you **according to His purpose [cannot] be revoked**.

By the Work of the Son

Once again, if we were left on our own, we would fall completely away from God. But God! Article 8 goes on to say this about God the Son, our Lord Jesus Christ: **with respect to God, it is utterly impossible, since…the merit, intercession and preservation of Christ [cannot] be rendered ineffectual**. Paul continues on in Ephesians 1 to praise Jesus Christ for his work of redemption, saying, "In him we have redemption through his blood, the forgiveness of our trespasses, according to the riches of his grace" (Eph. 1:7). The death of Christ on the cross, by which his blood was shed for the remission of our innumerable sins, was the final, culminating act of his obedience on our behalf. When we think of the obedience of Jesus, we make a helpful distinction between his active and his passive obedience, that is, his obedience in fulfilling the law and his obedience in suffering death for us. But do not think that his active obedience ended right before the cross began. Instead, the cross is described as the final act of his obedience. Look with me at Romans 5:18–19:

Therefore, as one trespass led to condemnation for all men, so one act of righteousness leads to justification and life for all men. For as by one man's disobedience the many were made sinners, so by the one man's obedience the many will be made righteous.

How can we say that the Son of God came from heaven to earth with those the Father in his counsel chose in his mind and on his heart, lived in their place all his thirty-three years, and died on the cross for their particular sins, can have that work wiped out by us? *He* merited eternal life for you, you didn't!

And after our Lord merited our eternal life, he went to heaven and "is interceding for us" (Rom. 8:34), where he "always lives to make intercession for them" (Heb. 7:25) as our "advocate" when we sin (1 John 2:1). That last section of verses from John 17, our Lord's "high priestly prayer," reminds us that our Lord preserves us. Right now he is holding you in his hand and Satan himself cannot snatch you from it (John 10:28). Satan may test like he did with Job, Satan may sift like he did with Peter, and Satan may buffet like he did with Paul, but Satan may not snatch!

By the Work of the Holy Spirit

Finally, when we understand that on our own we most certainly would fall from grace totally and completely, we are sent back by the canons to the work of the Holy Spirit: **with respect to God, it is utterly impossible, since...the sealing of the Holy Spirit [cannot] be frustrated or obliterated**. He is the seal (Eph. 1:13). This means his grace in your life is authentic and guaranteed. It also means we are rendered inviolable. As Paul goes on to say of the Holy Spirit, it is "by whom you were sealed for the day of redemption" (Eph. 4:30). As well, the Spirit is the earnest payment (Eph. 1:14), a part of the whole payment in the future. Paul puts these two images of seal and earnest payment about us together in 2 Corinthians 1:22, where he says God "has also put his seal on us and given us his Spirit in our hearts as a guarantee."

Article 9

Of this preservation of the elect to salvation and of their perseverance in the faith, true believers for themselves may and do obtain assurance according to the measure of their faith, whereby they arrive at the certain persuasion that they ever will continue true and living members of the church; and that they experience forgiveness of sins, and will at last inherit eternal life.

ARE YOU ASSURED?

Articles 9–13 transition from the struggles faith has with sin to deal with the relationship between perseverance of the saints and their assurance of faith.

Its Possibility

Doubt is the new assurance. There was a faddish movement of churches a while back known as the Emergent Church and also the Emerging Church, and its leaders were so hip and avant-garde. One of its fresh faces at one point was Rob Bell, who has subsequently left his church to do spirituality shows for Oprah. In his book *Velvet Elvis*, he asked whether our faith would fall if archeologists found the DNA of a guy named Larry, who happened to be Jesus' father. Now, Bell went on to affirm the virgin birth, but his point was that we shouldn't be so dogmatic about something that really doesn't change the way we live.[97] Another leader was Brian McLaren, who, when asked, "What is the good news?" answered that it was better to be a Muslim peace activist than a Christian who debates theology.[98] The only assurance they preached was to doubt everything. Article 9 goes on to speak of the possibility of assurance.

Note how the article begins by recognizing the two aspects of the doctrine being confessed in the fifth point: **Of this** *preservation (custodia)* **of the elect to salvation and of their** *perseverance (perseverantia)* **in the faith**. These are the two sides of the same doctrine. Then the divines confessed **true believers** *(verequa fidelium)* not only *may* but *do* **obtain assurance** of their preservation and perseverance. Note well that its actual, *true* believers who can have this assurance. The church as with the ancient people of God is a mixed assembly of people. As Paul states it in Romans 9:6, "not all Isra-

---

[97] Rob Bell, *Velvet Elvis: Repainting the Christian Faith* (Grand Rapids, MI: Zondervan, 2005), 26–27.

[98] http://beholdingandbecoming.blogspot.com/2008/09/brian-mclaren-on-gospel.html (accessed August 8, 2018).

el"—meaning, ethnic Israel—"are Israel"—meaning, truly Israelites. In the language of the Belgic Confession (BC), not all in the church are of the church (see BC, art. 29).

It's this **certain persuasion** (*certo dredunt*) **that they ever will continue true and living members of the church; and that they experience forgiveness of sins, and will at last inherit eternal life** of which Paul speaks of in Romans 8. "There is therefore now no condemnation for those who are in Christ Jesus" (Rom 8:1). That's assurance! "For I am sure that" [nothing] "will be able to separate us from the love of God in Christ Jesus our Lord" (Rom. 8:38–39). That's confidence! Hebrews 5:13–14 contrasts babes from men. Faith contains the element of trust, but believers do not always exercise faith so that they are assured. In other words, faith is rooted in the objectivity of Christ and his salvation, although subjectively I may or may not feel that at any given time.[99]

"But I don't have *that* kind of confidence! After all, Paul is an apostle." Yes, he was, and he was assured. But he was assured by the same faith you have in the same Savior. That's why our article speaks with the biblical phrase of assurance being **according to the measure of their faith** (cf. Rom. 12:3). For example, in Hebrews 5:13–14 the author contrasts spiritual babies in Christ with mature adults in Christ. Both have faith, and faith contains the element of trust, but an immature, childish believer doesn't always exercise faith as a mature believer does.[100] Assurance is a possibility for all of us although it may not be a possession yet.

Article 10

This assurance, however, is not produced by any peculiar revelation contrary to, or independent of the Word of God; but springs from faith in God's promises, which He has most abundantly revealed in His Word for our comfort; from the testimony of the Holy Spirit witnessing with our spirit that we are children and heirs of God (Rom. 8:16); and lastly, from a serious and holy desire to preserve a good conscience and to perform good works. And if the elect of God were deprived of this solid comfort that they shall finally obtain the victory and of this infallible pledge or earnest of eternal glory, they would be of all men the most miserable.

---

[99] Louis Berkhof, *The Assurance of Faith: The Firm Foundation of Christian Hope* (1939; repr., Birmingham, AL: Solid Ground Christian Books, 2004), 24.

[100] Berkhof, *The Assurance of Faith*, 24.

Its Source

Assurance is possible for the true believer in Christ. The question remains, where do we get it? Article 10 focuses on the source of its production. Article 10 gives us the source, first, in terms of what it *is not*: **This assurance, however, is not produced by any peculiar revelation contrary to, or independent** (*extra*; outside) **of the Word of God.** The canons say this in contrast to the Roman Catholic Church. At the Council of Trent in 1546 Rome said: "If any one saith, that he will for certain, of an absolute and infallible certainty, have that great gift of perseverance unto the end,— unless he have learned this by special revelation: let him be anathema."[101] To return to Romans 8 quoted above, this means Rome says Paul could speak as he did because God gave him a special revelation that he was elect.

Yet note that Paul who began saying, "There is therefore now no condemnation for *those* who are in Christ Jesus," goes on to say:

> What then shall *we* say to these things? If God is for *us*, who can be against *us*? He who did not spare his own Son but gave him up for *us* all, how will he not also with him graciously give *us* all things? Who is to condemn? Christ Jesus is the one who died…who is at the right hand of God, who indeed is interceding for *us*. Who shall separate *us* from the love of Christ? No, in all these things *we* are more than conquerors through him who loved *us*. For *I* am sure that neither death nor life, nor angels nor rulers, nor things present nor things to come, nor powers, nor height nor depth, nor anything else in all creation, will be able to separate *us* from the love of God in Christ Jesus *our* Lord. (Rom. 8:31–32, 34, 35, 37, 39)

Instead of the source of assurance being private revelation, article 10 points us to three legitimate sources. It's important to note these are not magic remedies taken once. They must be cultivated over the course of your life.

First and foremost is *God's promise*: **but springs from faith in God's promises, which He has most abundantly revealed in His Word for**

---

[101] Session 6, canon 16.

our comfort. Romans 8 is God promise to your soul, believer, apostle or not![102]

Second, the *witness of the Spirit*: **from the testimony of the Holy Spirit witnessing with our spirit that we are children and heirs of God (Rom. 8:16).** Romans 8:16–17 says the Holy Spirit witnesses *to* our spirit through the promises of the Word and *with* our spirit as we believe those promises and see the fruit in our lives.[103] We also recognize that this "testimony although it be not always alike powerful in believers, yet notwithstanding it manifests itself many times in their greatest humiliation and distress 'that we are children of God.'"[104]

Third, the *good works* we do: **lastly, from a serious and holy desire to preserve a good conscience and to perform good works.** As 1 John 3 says, "By this we know love, that he laid down his life for us, and we ought to lay down our lives for the brothers.... By this we shall know that we are of the truth and reassure our heart before him" (vv. 16, 19).[105]

In fact, without this possibility of assurance and its cultivation by means of God's promises, the work of the Holy Spirit, and our growth in godliness, article 10 describes us as miserable: **And if the elect of God were deprived of this solid comfort that they shall finally obtain the victory and of this infallible pledge or earnest of eternal glory, they would be of all men the most miserable.**

Article 11

The Scripture moreover testifies that believers in this life have to struggle with various carnal doubts and that under grievous temptations they are not always sensible of this full assurance of faith and certainty of persevering. But God, who is the Father of all consolation, does not suffer them to be tempted above that they are able, but will with the temptation also make a way to escape that they may be able to bear it (1 Cor. 10:13),

---

[102] See also 1 John 3:16; John 3:16, 18; 5:24–25; 6:40, 47, 51, 54, 56, 58; 2 Cor. 1:20; Heb. 6:18.

[103] See also 1 John 3:24; 1 John 2:20, 27; Rom. 8:9, 14–17; Gal. 4:6–7; Rom. 8:16–17; 1 John 3:1–2. The *Dutch Annotations* on Romans 8:16–17 spoke of the twofold witness of the Spirit *to* our spirits and *with* our spirits as we see the work of his grace in our lives.

[104] *Dutch Annotations* on Romans 8:16–17.

[105] See also 1 John 3:16–19, 24; 2:3, 5; 3:10; 4:7.

and by the Holy Spirit again inspires them with the comfortable assurance of persevering.

LIVING OUT OUR ASSURANCE

The Struggle and the Strength

As we've seen, while we can fall *into* sin, God preserves us so that we cannot fall *from* grace. And we can be assured of his preserving work and our own perseverance unto glory. Does assurance mean no more spiritual doubts? Absolutely not. As article 11 goes on confess, assurance of God's perseverance and our preservation is lived out in the context of *assurance and temptation*: **The Scripture moreover testifies that believers in this life have to struggle with various carnal doubts and that under grievous temptations they are not always sensible of this full assurance of faith and certainty of persevering.**

Just because we are believers does not mean that our faith never doubts. Just because we are forgiven does not mean that we are not tempted to fall. Remember, while the guilt and penalty of sin has been nullified in our lives we still have a sin nature that pollutes us. This sinful pollution leads to **various carnal doubts**, and when it undergoes **grievous temptation** we're **not always sensible of this full assurance of faith and certainty of persevering**. To struggle with carnal doubts is to struggle with sinful doubts that arise from our sin nature. To struggle with grievous temptations is to struggle with things that seem so strong that we have no way of resisting.

We see that in 1 Corinthians 10. Everything that happened to our forefathers happened as "examples for us" (v. 6) and "for our instruction" (v. 11). When Paul says, "No temptation has overtaken you that is not common to man" (v. 13), he's speaking of their being tempted to idolatry (v. 7), to sexual immorality (v. 8), to test Christ (v. 9), and to grumble (v. 10). What hope is there, then, for sinners like us? Article 11 goes on to apply Paul's words from 2 Corinthians 1 to the struggles of 1 Corinthians 10:

> **But God, who is the Father of all consolation, does not suffer them to be tempted above that they are able, but will with the temptation also make a way to escape that they may be able to bear it (1 Cor. 10:13),**

and by the Holy Spirit again inspires them with the comfortable assurance of persevering.

Article 12

This certainty of perseverance, however, is so far from exciting in believers a spirit of pride or of rendering them carnally secure, that on the contrary, it is the real source of humility, filial reverence, true piety, patience in every tribulation, fervent prayers, constancy in suffering, and in confessing the truth, and of solid rejoicing in God; so that the consideration of this benefit should serve as an incentive to the serious and constant practice of gratitude and good works, as appears from the testimonies of Scripture and the examples of the saints.

Assurance and Motivation

Article 12 speaks of a second practicality of living out our assurance: the relationship between *assurance and motivation*. If our God and Father of all consolation does not allow us to be tempted more than we can handle, provides us with the way of escaping temptation, and renews us by the Holy Spirit, why should we even try in the Christian life? In the terms of American bumper sticker theology: "Let Go and let God." Is this the motivation of the true believer?

On the contrary, article 12 begins, **this certainty of perseverance, however, is so far from exciting in believers a spirit of pride or of rendering them carnally secure**. The certainty of perseverance excites or stimulates us not to carelessness in godliness but carefulness to godliness; not self-gratification but glorification of God; not laziness but love.

Why does this article begin this way? One of the charges of the Remonstrants was that assurance would lead to pride and carnal self-assurance. We'll return to this later, but for now just note the rejection of errors that says "the doctrine of perseverance and the assurance of salvation from its own character and nature is a cause of indolence and is injurious to godliness, good morals, prayers, and other holy exercises, but that on the contrary it is praiseworthy to doubt" (CD 5.RE 6).

You've heard this before, right? "If you believe in election, irresistible grace, and eternal security you can live any way you want." The apostle Paul did. He had to answer this slippery slope argument in Romans 6. After he proclaimed the doctrine of justification by faith alone he asked, "What shall we say then? Are we to continue in sin that grace may abound? By no means!" (Rom. 6:1–2).

We have to be aware that this charge will always be thrown at us. But we also have to be aware of our own "spirit of pride" within us that turns our liberty in our Savior into a license for our sins, the grace of God for self-gratification (Gal. 5:13; 1 Pet. 2:16). But, in every error there is a grain of truth. I asked you why this article of the canons begins the way it does and there is a second reason: we must beware of using liberty for license, the grace of God for self-gratification. Here is where we have to get personal. Have you ever said to yourself, "I can indulge in the flesh because God will forgive me"? Not only do we have to set an example to those who reject this doctrine, but we have to be aware that we by nature will use the certainty of perseverance as a reason for sinning.

In contrast to the Arminian charge and our natural inclination to turn certainty into an excitement for sin, the canons proclaim in no uncertain terms that certainty is

> **on the contrary, it is the real source of humility, filial reverence, true piety, patience in every tribulation, fervent prayers, constancy in suffering, and in confessing the truth, and of solid rejoicing in God; so that the consideration of this benefit should serve as an incentive to the serious and constant practice of gratitude and good works, as appears from the testimonies of Scripture and the examples of the saints.**

Our doctrine is the **real source** (*vera radix*; true root) and the **incentive** (*stimulus*) for good works. Listen to Witsius, who said, "Nothing is more powerful for inflaming our hearts with love to God, than to know, sense, and taste of the divine love shed abroad in them."[106] What "excites" you? I ask that as our English word "excited" can mean to stir up the emotions, or, it can also mean to stir up or stimulate to action. Behind our English translation **incentive** is the word *stimulus*, that is, a spur, an incentive to good works. Article 12 is speaking of what stimulates or motivates us to perseverance. It's not speaking of merely being stirred up emotionally but

---

[106] Witsius, *The Economy of the Covenants*, 2:78.

by the work of God the Holy Spirit we are stimulated to good works in response to his amazing grace.

We can certainly assert the above words against our Arminian friends and then they can assert their charge, and nothing changes. But why is being certain that you will persevere the source and incentive to living a holy life? The power of God's grace. Listen to 1 John 3:1: "How great is the love of the Father!" It is God who excites us; it is not our own doing. The God who excites us—who stimulates us to action—causes us to be excited with all our being, body and soul, mind and emotions. We see the working of the indwelling Holy Spirit in us, exciting us to live righteously. Consider this, beloved. You are the temple of the Holy Spirit. Because the promises of God "breathe his love and grace," we are moved to gratitude. As Witsius said, "All our religion is nothing but gratitude."[107]

Article 13

Neither does renewed confidence of persevering produce licentiousness or a disregard to piety in those who are recovering from backsliding; but it renders them much more careful and solicitous to continue in the ways of the Lord, which He hath ordained, that they who walk therein may maintain an assurance of persevering, lest by abusing His fatherly kindness, God should turn away His gracious countenance from them, to behold which is to the godly dearer than life, the withdrawing whereof is more bitter than death, and they in consequence hereof should fall into more grievous torments of conscience.

Assurance and Restoration

Article 13 brings up a third practicality of living out our assurance: the relationship between *assurance and restoration*. If we fall into sin and the Lord's promise to preserve us means he will restore us again, what does that look like in real life? As we saw above, the reality of God's renewal of our lives does not lead us to carelessness in persevering: **Neither does renewed confidence of persevering produce licentiousness or a disregard to piety in those who are recovering from backsliding**.

We cannot be careless because the power of God's grace is at work within us. As Paul says later in 2 Corinthians 5, we are new creations in

---

[107] Witsius, *The Economy of the Covenants*, 2:80.

Christ. Then he says in 2 Corinthians 6 that we cannot be careless because the Holy Spirit is at work within us as his temples. Instead, God's renewing work leads us to carefulness:

> **But it renders them much more careful and solicitous to continue in the ways of the Lord, which He hath ordained, that they who walk therein may maintain an assurance of persevering, lest by abusing His fatherly kindness, God should turn away His gracious countenance from them, to behold which is to the godly dearer than life, the withdrawing whereof is more bitter than death, and they in consequence hereof should fall into more grievous torments of conscience.**

We are going to be tempted to sin, but we have the assurance of the Lord's care for us even in those temptations. We are going to struggle with motivation, but we have the Lord's promise that he is at work within us to will and to do his good pleasure. We are to going to fall into sin, but we have the assurance not only that we won't fall out of grace but that our faithful God will restore and renew us again. Grace should not lead to not to carelessness but to carefulness.

Article 14

And as it hath pleased God, by the preaching of the gospel, to begin this work of grace in us, so He preserves, continues, and perfects it by the hearing and reading of His Word, by meditation thereon, and by the exhortations, threatenings, and promises thereof, as well as by the use of the sacraments.

HOW DOES GOD PRESERVE ME?

Here in article 14 the canons offer a brief article on the relationship between the saints' perseverance and the saints' use of the means of grace.

The canons have followed the outline of Scripture in celebrating God's "grace" that was *planned* for you and me "in Christ Jesus before the ages began" (2 Tim. 1:9). God's grace led Christ to *purchase* you and me as he "loved me and gave himself for me" on the cross (Gal 2:20). God's grace was "*poured* into [our] heart[s]...through the Holy Spirit who has been given to us" (Rom. 5:5). And God's grace will be *preserved* "by [his] power" as we are "being guarded through faith for a salvation ready to be revealed in the last time" (1 Pet. 1:5). It's no wonder we sing, "Amazing grace, how sweet the sound, that saved a wretch like me!"

As we come to the end we sing to God because he preserves our souls by this infinite and supernatural power.[108] We experience this preserving power through faith (1 Pet. 1:5). What does faith embrace? God preserves us through the power of the Holy Spirit, the seal and down payment of our redemption on the last day (Eph. 1:13–14). How do we come to know this? Article 14 is all about the external means God uses that my faith grabs hold of in initial regeneration and the life of perseverance.

He Uses Means

As we sing of God's power to preserve, we need to know that *he uses means* to accomplish his preserving work. In the beginning when he created, how did he execute this eternal plan? Genesis 1 says over and over, "And God said." God used the means of his Word to create. "But isn't he almighty?" He is. His use of means was not for his sake, but for ours. All throughout the narrative of Scripture God used the things he made to accomplish his purpose. He used rain to flood the earth in his judgment. He used a rainbow to signify his grace. He used a lamb and its blood to signify his salvation to Israel. John 6 tells us that Jesus used bread to feed people. Then Peter confessed that Jesus' words were the means of eternal life. A 2014 Pew Research Center study showed that *only 42 percent* of Christians said it was essential to being a Christian to read the Word of God![109] In contrast, John recorded an important statement by Peter so that we would cling to Jesus by clinging to the means of his Word as if Jesus were right in front of you speaking face-to-face: "Lord, to whom shall we go? You have the words of eternal life" (John 6:68).

This concept that God uses means separated the Protestants from the Anabaptists, which is manifested today in our hyperspiritual world. This is also one of the great confusions non-Reformed writers such as George Bryson have. Not only does he *not* cite the Canons of Dort, which explicitly express that God uses in means in perseverance, but he does not get that

---

[108] Witsius, *The Economy of the Covenants*, 2:76.

[109] http://www.pewresearch.org/fact-tank/2017/04/14/5-facts-on-how-americans-view-the-bible-and-other-religious-texts/ (accessed August 8, 2018).

the Reformed view is that God preserves us *through* means: **as it hath pleased God, by** (*per*) **the preaching of the gospel, to begin this work of grace in us, so He preserves, continues, and perfects it** [his work] **by** (*per*) **the hearing and reading of His Word**.

Bryson's caricature is that "if the saints persevere because they are Saints and cannot do otherwise, then no lack of exhortation or warning is going to prevent them from persevering."[110] He goes on to cite specific passages such as Colossians 2:6, John 15, and 2 Peter 1:1–7 and then comment: "If it is a foregone conclusion that a true believer will always continue to walk in Christ in the sense that Paul is speaking, why encourage him to do so?"[111] This version of "once saved, always saved," "eternal security," or "easy believism" is *not* the view of the Canons of Dort. Venema says:

> The *Canons* speak of the *perseverance* of the *saints*. They affirm that those whom God preserves in the way of salvation, He preserves through the use of means by which believers persevere in faith, hope, and love.... Not just anyone who professes to believe, however much he may deny this profession by an ungodly life, is said to be preserved in the way of salvation. Not at all. The *Canons* expressly reject this misunderstanding, and underscore the believer's responsible use of the means of grace as indispensable to his perseverance.[112]

Before Dort, though, this was an issue Augustine addressed. Augustine's doctrine of predestination, grace, and free will caused some monks in Southern Gaul to say that since perseverance is a gift, rebuke and exhortation to persevere is unnecessary.[113] Instead, they said all that was needed was prayer for them to eventually do what was required.[114] In response, Augustine said, "The teachers of the churches, the apostles, were in the habit of...prescribing what things should be done, as rebuking if they were

---

[110] Bryson, *The Five Points of Calvinism*, 109. This was also a caricature of the Remonstrants. See Paraeus, "Epitome of Arminianisme," 840.

[111] Bryson, *The Five Points of Calvinism*, 112.

[112] Venema, *But for the Grace of God*, 79, 80. Emphasis in original.

[113] Augustine, "On Rebuke and Grace," 4 (5:473).

[114] Augustine, "On Rebuke and Grace," 5 (5:473).

not done, and praying that they might be done."[115] We saw this above in connection with 3/4.17:

> **Wherefore, as the apostles, and teachers who succeeded them, piously instructed the people concerning this grace of God...and in the meantime, however, neglected not to keep them by the sacred precepts of the gospel...so even to this day, be it far from either instructors or instructed to presume to tempt God in the church by separating what He of His good pleasure hath most intimately joined together. For grace is conferred by means of admonitions; and the more readily we perform our duty, the more eminent usually is this blessing of God working in us, and the more directly is His work advanced.**

Augustine went on to say there is a connection between rebuke and grace: "Let men then suffer themselves to be rebuked when they sin, and not conclude against grace from the rebuke itself, nor from grace against rebuke." Why? He gave the image of rebuke as medicine to the elect: "if he who is rebuked belongs to the number of the predestinated, rebuke may be to him a wholesome medicine." To those not predestined "rebuke may be to him a penal infliction." Therefore out of love the pastor must apply the rebuke of the Word and pray for those in sin "that he may be healed." This healing comes *by means of* the rebuke: "when men either come or return into the way of righteousness by means of rebuke, who is it that works salvation in their hearts but that God who gives the increase, whoever plants and waters, and whoever labours on the fields or shrubs—that God whom no man's will resists when He wills to give salvation?"[116]

He Uses the Means of the Gospel

In John 6 we are taught to celebrate the Lord's kindness to us because *he uses the means of the gospel.* How were you born again? **As it hath pleased God, by the preaching of the gospel** (*per praedicationem Euangelii*), **to begin this work of grace in us.** Make no mistake about it, you were born again by the power of the Holy Spirit as we saw in connection with 3/4.3:

---

[115] Augustine, "On Rebuke and Grace," 5 (5:473). See also 25 (5:482).
[116] Augustine, "On Rebuke and Grace," 43 (5:489).

Truly, truly, I say to you, unless one is born of water and the Spirit, he cannot enter the kingdom of God. That which is born of the flesh is flesh, and that which is born of the Spirit is spirit.... The wind blows where it wishes, and you hear its sound, but you do not know where it comes from or where it goes. So it is with everyone who is born of the Spirit. (John 3:5, 6, 8)

Remember 1 Peter 1:

Since you have been born again, not of perishable seed but of imperishable, through the living and abiding word of God; for "All flesh is like grass and all its glory like the flower of grass. The grass withers, and the flower falls, but the word of the Lord remains forever." And this word is the good news that was preached to you. (1 Pet. 1:23)

Remember James 1:

Of his own will he brought us forth by the word of truth, that we should be a kind of firstfruits of his creatures. (James 1:18)

Just as God used the means of the Word, and in particular the gospel, to create faith in us to embrace Jesus, so he preserves, continues, and perfects that gracious work by the same. The translation we're using says:

And as it hath pleased God, by the preaching of the gospel, to begin this work of grace in us, so He preserves, continues, and perfects it by the hearing and reading of His *Word*, by meditation thereon, and by the exhortations, threatenings, and promises *thereof*, as well as by the use of the sacraments.

Notice the italicized words: *Word* and *thereof*, meaning, on the *Word*. The 2011 translation of the Christian Reformed Church gives a closer reading of the Latin text, especially in the latter half of this article:

And, just as it has pleased God to begin this work of grace in us by the proclamation of the gospel, so God preserves, continues, and completes this work by the hearing and reading of *the gospel*, by meditation on *it*, by *its* exhortations,

threats, and promises, and also by the use of the sacraments.[117]

The reason this is a better rendering is that the whole list of hearing,
reading, meditation, exhortations, threats, and promises (*auditum, lectionem,
meditationem, adhortationes, minas, promissa*) that God uses to preserve us are
linked back to the same means God used to regenerate us: **by the proclamation of the gospel** (*per praedicationem Euangelii*). These are linked with the
clause *ita per eiusdem*, "by means of the same," meaning, the same gospel. **By
the proclamation of the gospel** God has begun a work of grace in us **so
by means of the same** gospel he continues his work of grace in us to the
end.[118]

While it sounds "normal" to us that the gospel begins, preserves,
continues, and perfects God's work of grace in us and even that we are to
hear, read, meditate on, and embrace the promises of the gospel, to those of
us out of tune with seventeenth-century forms of speech, it sounds odd to
us that the gospel is described here as having **exhortations** and **threatenings**. Thus many translations like the one we're using as the baseline in this
book have tried to smooth this over by substituting "Word" in the place of
"gospel."

Yet this was standard fare in seventeenth-century Reformed orthodoxy. For example, immediately after the synod the theological faculty of
the University of Leiden held public disputations from 1620 to 1624
through the topics of theology. The theological faculty consisted of Johannes Polyander, Antonius Walaeus, Antonius Thysius, and Andreas Rivetus,
all of whom were delegates to the synod. In Disputation 22, "On the Gospel," presided over by Polyander, we read a pristine presentation of the
gospel. The word "gospel" generally means the promise of Christ but par-

---

[117] From the 2011 translation of the Christian Reformed Church. As cited at
https://www.crcna.org/welcome/beliefs/confessions/canons-dort (accessed October 4, 2018). See also Wilhelmus à Brakel, *The Christian's Reasonable Service*, trans.
Bartel Elshout, ed. Joel R. Beeke, 4 vols. (1995; repr., Grand Rapids, MI: Reformation Heritage Books, third printing 2007;), 4:276–77.

[118] See the discussion in Jones, *Antinomianism*, 47–49. For fuller treatments of law-
gospel issues, see "The Puritans on Law and Gospel," in Joel R. Beeke and Mark
Jones, *A Puritan Theology: Doctrine for Life* (Grand Rapids, MI: Reformation Heritage
Books, 2012), 321–33; Ryan M. McGraw, "The Threats of the Gospel: John Owen
on What the Law/Gospel Distinction Is Not," in *John Owen: Trajectories in Reformed
Orthodox Theology* (Cham, Switzerland: Palgrave Macmillan, 2017), 71–109.

ticularly refers to the manifestation of Christ in the flesh (Mark 1) and the proclamation of reconciliation with God on the basis of the death of Christ.[119] In fact, so zealous was the faculty to guard the proper use of "gospel" this disputation said, "The destruction of unbelievers, however, is not a goal of the Gospel; that is an unconnected outcome from elsewhere, from their sins."[120] Even "the evil consequences that come about by the guilt of depraved people from the preaching of the Gospel should not be numbered among its effects."[121] At the same time the proper use of "gospel" was affirmed and guarded, the *Synopsis* recognized that "the Gospel sometimes receives the distinguishing title of Law, because it also contains its own commands, promises, and warnings."[122] The *promises* of the gospel are obvious: justification and eternal life, citing Romans 1:17 and 1 John 2:25, respectively.[123] What about its commands and warnings? Its *commands* are repentance and faith. As Jesus said in Mark 1:15: "Repent and believe the Gospel." Repentance can either be legal or evangelical while faith is evangelical.[124] Finally, the gospel's *warnings* are the condemnation of unbelievers who do not obey Christ and the punishment of eternal death, citing John 3:18 and 36 as well as Hebrews 2:2–3.[125]

With this, we can go on to see how article 14 mentions three ways the gospel is used to **preserve[…], continue[…], and complete[…] this work** of God's grace.

First, *the gospel in public*: **by the hearing and reading of** *the gospel*. That's exactly what Peter celebrated in Jesus' bread of life discourse in John 6: the public preaching of Jesus. This public hearing and reading continued in the apostolic church as believers gathered to hear "the apostles' doctrine" (Acts 2:42) proclaimed. As Paul would tell Timothy: "Until I come, devote yourself to the public reading of Scripture, to exhortation, to teaching" (1 Tim. 4:13).

Second, *the gospel in private*: **by meditation on** *it*. The Lord commanded Joshua to meditate on the Book of the Law day and night (Josh.

---

[119] *Synopsis Purioris Theologiae: Volume 1*, 559.

[120] *Synopsis Purioris Theologiae: Volume 1*, 565.

[121] *Synopsis Purioris Theologiae: Volume 1*, 567.

[122] *Synopsis Purioris Theologiae: Volume 1*, 567.

[123] *Synopsis Purioris Theologiae: Volume 1*, 573.

[124] *Synopsis Purioris Theologiae: Volume 1*, 567.

[125] *Synopsis Purioris Theologiae: Volume 1*, 573.

1:8). The psalmist extols the man who meditates on the law day and night, which causes him to be like a tree planted by the waters (Ps. 1:2). In the great Psalm of the Word of God we read: "How can a young man keep his way pure? By guarding it according to your word" (Ps. 119:9). "I have stored up your word in my heart, that I might not sin against you" (Ps. 119:11). "Your word is a lamp to my feet and a light to my path" (Ps. 119:105).

Third, *the gospel in all its aspects*: **by *its* exhortations, threats, and promises**. As Paul said, "All Scripture"—not just the law, but the gospel; not just the gospel, but the law—"is breathed out by God and [therefore it is] profitable for teaching, for reproof, for correction, and for training in righteousness, that the man of God may be complete, equipped for every good work" (2 Tim. 3:16–17). We know the promise of gospel in John 3:16, but as our forefathers said above, how about the exhortations and threats that accompany the gospel message? Paul and Barnabas *exhorted* the congregations in Lystra, Iconium, and Antioch "to continue in the faith, and saying that through many tribulations we must enter the kingdom of God" (Acts 14:22). You are called by God to "work out your own salvation with fear and trembling" (Phil. 2:12), and this exhortation is the means by which this is caused. Jesus' proclamation that "God so loved the world...that whoever believed in him should not perish but have eternal life" (John 3:16) also included these *threats*: "whoever does not believe in condemned already" (John 3:18) and "whoever does not obey the Son shall not see life, but the wrath of God remains on him" (John 3:36). The apostolic writer to the Hebrew Christians also said, "Therefore we must pay much closer attention to what we have heard, lest we drift away from it. For since the message declared by angels proved to be reliable, and every transgression or disobedience received a just retribution, how shall we escape if we neglect such a great salvation?" (Heb. 2:1–3).

How is it helpful to exhort and even threaten or warn *Christians?* Herman Witsius (1636–1708) went on a generation later to say it like this: "These admonitions, promises, threatenings, and the like actions of God towards the elect, are so far from giving the least ground to conclude any thing against their perseverance, that, on the contrary, they are powerful means for their conservation [preservation]."[126] All these aspects of the ministry of the gospel are "powerful means for [your preservation]." Paul

---

[126] Witsius, *The Economy of the Covenants*, 2:77.

told Titus that it was by means of sharp rebuke "that they may be sound in the faith" (Titus 1:13). By means of disciplining us as his children, the writer to the Hebrews said this was "for our good, that we may share his holiness" because it "yields the peaceful fruit of righteousness" (Heb. 12:10, 11). When a believer is on a dangerous ledge, the warnings of Scripture call his or her back.[127]

He Uses the Means of the Sacraments

We celebrate our God's power through means. Not only does he preserve us by means of hearing his Word but also by expressing his preserving grace to all of our senses *through the sacraments*: **as well as by the use of the sacraments**. Like a parent, God doesn't just tell us he loves us; he shows us! It was Thomas Watson who said, "In the Word we hear God's voice, in the sacrament we have his kiss."[128]

In *baptism* we feel the Lord's grace of washing away all our sins. Every time you witness a baptism, remember your baptism, God's promise of grace to you, and your commitment to him by faith alone! In the *Lord's Supper* or Lord's Table or Communion we feast with our hands, eyes, noses, and mouths upon Jesus Christ our gracious Savior.

What a God of grace we have! He *planned* grace for me and you, Christ *purchased* us for it, the Holy Spirit *poured* it into our hearts, and this gracious triune God *preserves* through the means of Word and Sacrament.

Article 15

The carnal mind is unable to comprehend this doctrine of the perseverance of the saints and the certainty thereof, which God hath most abundantly revealed in His Word, for the glory of His Name, and the consolation of pious souls, and which He impresses upon the hearts of the faithful. Satan abhors it; the world ridicules it; the ignorant and hypocrite abuse, and heretics oppose it; but the spouse of Christ hath always most tenderly loved and constantly defended it as an inestimable treasure; and God, against whom neither counsel nor strength can prevail, will dispose her to continue this conduct to the end. Now, to this one God, Father, Son, and Holy Spirit, be honor and glory forever. Amen.

---

[127] Van Oosterzee, *Christian Dogmatics*, 665.

[128] Watson, *A Body of Divinity*, 21.

WHAT IS YOUR ATTITUDE TOWARD PERSEVERANCE?

As we come to the final article in the fifth point of doctrine, it takes the teaching of preservation/perseverance and applies it by connecting it to our need for assurance and comfort amid our struggles.

Article 15 speaks of the various attitudes toward this doctrine, but especially the attitude of those who are comforted by it: **this doctrine of the perseverance of the saints and the certainty thereof, which God hath most abundantly revealed in His Word, for the glory of His Name, and the consolation of pious souls... He impresses upon the hearts of the faithful**. The regenerated and converted believers have had a work of grace performed upon them by God. This causes a recognition that the perseverance of the saints is biblical, brings glory to our great God, and consoles the pious in their spiritual struggles. Our attitude is one of grateful humility for such a great benefit.

The Attitude of the Carnal

Moving from believer to unbeliever, the article says the attitude of the carnal or unregenerate mind is one of inability to understand this doctrine: **The carnal mind is unable to comprehend this doctrine of the perseverance of the saints and the certainty thereof**. As Paul says in 1 Corinthians 2:14, "The natural person does not accept the things of the Spirit of God, for they are folly to him, and he is not able to understand them because they are spiritually discerned."

The Attitude of Satan

Moving from human beings to spiritual beings, the article says of Satan: **Satan abhors** [this teaching]. He does so for obvious reasons. He abhors it because it means God triumphs in salvation. He abhors it because of what it does within the hearts of regenerated sinners: it causes us to be confident and to be dedicated to our gracious God.

The Attitude of the World

Going back to unbelievers, the article says the attitude of the world outside of Jesus Christ is to ridicule this doctrine: **the world ridicules** [this teaching].

The Attitude of the Ignorant and Hypocritical

The attitude of the ignorant and hypocrite within the church is to abuse it: **the ignorant and hypocrite abuse** [this teaching]. How so? By turning the certainty we have in Christ into certain sin.

The Attitude of the Heretic

What of heretics once in the church but now condemned outside it? Their attitude is to attack it: **heretics oppose** [this teaching].

The Attitude of the Bride

In contrast to the carnal, Satan, the world, the ignorant, the hypocritical, and the heretic, article 15 returns to the attitude of the bride of Christ: **the spouse of Christ hath always most tenderly loved and constantly defended it as an inestimable treasure**. Love and defense of this treasure are to be our outlook on this doctrine. Because of this, **God, against whom neither counsel nor strength can prevail, will dispose her to continue this conduct to the end**.

We see the glory of God and the consolation of the saints in 1 Peter. Peter writes to Christians in the context of their many anxieties (1 Pet. 5:7) and of their suffering at the hands of Satan (1 Pet. 5:8–9). In this context he writes of the perseverance of the saints and its connection with God's glory, saying, "The God of all grace, who has called you to his eternal glory in Christ, will himself restore, confirm, strengthen, and establish you. To him be the dominion forever and ever. Amen" (1 Pet. 5:10–11). And this is the doctrine that he turns to in order to console them: "The God of all grace, *who has called you* to his *eternal* glory in Christ, *will* himself restore, confirm, strengthen, and establish you" (1 Pet. 5:11). In the Epistle of Jude, he spoke of the glory of God, saying, "Now to him who is able *to keep you* from stumbling and *to present you* blameless before the presence of his glory with great joy, to the only God, our Savior, through Jesus Christ our Lord, be glory, majesty, dominion, and authority, before all time and now and forever. Amen" (vv. 24–25). This brings great consolation to those struggling with scoffers, who taught false doctrine and who lived ungodly lives, causing divisions in the church.

Now, to this one God, Father, Son, and Holy Spirit, be honor and glory forever. Amen.

VIII:
WHAT WE REJECT
REJECTION OF ERRORS 1-9

THE FINAL SET of rejections of errors by the orthodox Reformed at the Synod of Dort deals with the doctrine of the perseverance of the saints. We'll take them up one by one and comment on them briefly.

Rejection of Errors 1

That the perseverance of the true believers is not a fruit of election or a gift of God gained by the death of Christ, but a condition of the new covenant, which (as they declare) man before his decisive election and justification must fulfill through his free will.

For the Holy Scripture testifies that this follows out of election, and is given the elect in virtue of the death, the resurrection and intercession of Christ: "but the elect hath obtained it, and the rest were blinded" (Rom. 11:7). Likewise: "He that spared not His own Son, but delivered Him up for us all, how shall He not with Him also freely give us all things? Who shall lay any thing to the charge of God's elect? It is God that justifieth. Who is he that condemneth? It is Christ that died, yea rather, that is risen again, who is even at the right hand of God, who also maketh intercession for us. Who shall separate us from the love of Christ?" (Rom. 8:32–35).

The first rejected error of the Remonstrants is that perseverance is not a consequence of eternal election or the historical work of Christ, but a condition of final salvation: *that the perseverance of the true believers is not a fruit of election or a gift of God gained by the death of Christ, but a condition of the new covenant, which (as they declare) a person (homine) before his decisive election and justification must fulfill through his free will* (*libera voluntate*). In the background is what we learned earlier about the Remonstrants' various decrees of God in which there was "decisive" as well as "non-decisive" or conditional election (1.RE 2, 5). In contrast, the orthodox Reformed confessed an unchangeable and unconditional election on the basis of Scripture (CD 1.7). Also, in the background is the relation of perseverance to what we saw in 1.8, which said the believer could not totally fall from God's grace **since His counsel cannot be changed nor His promise fail, neither can the call according to His purpose be revoked, nor the merit, intercession and preservation of Christ be rendered ineffectual, nor the sealing of the Holy Spirit be frustrated or obliterated**. What this rejection shows us, among many things, is the interrelatedness of each of the Remonstrant as well as the Reformed doctrines. The doctrines of eternal and unchangeable election and the accomplishment of redemption at the cross in the first two points of doctrine are contrasted with the view in rejection 1. While the Reformed saw perseverance as flowing from these doctrines, the Remonstrants saw ultimate perseverance as a prior condition: through the means of exercising free will, a person fulfills the conditions of the new covenant and enters into a status of decisive election and final justification.

In response synod said, **Holy Scripture testifies that this** perseverance **follows out of election, and is given the elect in virtue of the death, the resurrection and intercession of Christ**. Two Scriptures were given as demonstration. First, Romans 11:7 and what it says about election. The overall context is Paul speaking of whether God has rejected his ancient covenant people since not all Israel believed Jesus was Messiah (11:1). Among them, though, Paul was evidence that "there is a remnant, chosen by grace" (11:5). In response he said, **"but the elect** [among the Israelites] **hath obtained it, and the rest were blinded."**[1] This is what he had said earlier: "Israel failed to obtain what it was seeking" (Rom. 11:7), meaning, salvation. The second text mentioned was Romans 8:32–35 dealing with the benefits of Christ's death. The synod cited Paul's great declaration of the believer's confidence:

> **He that spared not His own Son, but delivered Him up for us all, how shall He not with Him also freely give us all things? Who shall lay any thing to the**

---

[1] See *Dutch Annotations* on Romans 11:7.

> charge of God's elect? It is God that justifieth. Who is
> he that condemneth? It is Christ that died, yea rather,
> that is risen again, who is even at the right hand of
> God, who also maketh intercession for us. Who shall
> separate us from the love of Christ? (Rom. 8:32–35)

Because Christ died, rose again, and intercedes, God **freely give[s] us all things** pertaining to salvation. Note the connection between Paul's assurance and confidence of perseverance that ultimately nothing can **separate us from the love of Christ** and the work of Christ. These and other texts were commonplaces for Augustine so many centuries before to demonstrate the same doctrine.[2]

Rejection of Errors 2

That God does indeed provide the believer with sufficient powers to persevere and is ever ready to preserve these in him, if he will do his duty; but that though all things which are necessary to persevere in faith and which God will use to preserve faith are made use of, it even then ever depends on the pleasure of the will whether it will persevere or not.

For this idea contains an outspoken Pelagianism, and while it would make men free, it makes them robbers of God's honor, contrary to the prevailing agreement of the evangelical doctrine, which takes from man all cause of boasting and ascribes all the praise for this favor to the grace of God alone; and contrary to the apostle, who declares that it is God "Who shall also confirm you unto the end, that ye may be blameless in the day of our Lord Jesus Christ" (1 Cor. 1:8).

Rejection 2 picks up on the mention of free will in rejection 1, which doctrine we saw in greater detail in the third and fourth points of doctrine. The doctrine we reject is *that God does indeed provide the believer with sufficient powers to persevere* (*perseverandum*) *and is ever ready to preserve* (*conservare*) *these in him*. The issue with this language is its connection to what comes next: *if he will do his duty*. Again, ultimate perseverance was conditioned by the use of free will. The conclusion of this doctrine is stated this way: *but that though all things which are necessary to persevere* (*perseverandum*) *in faith and which God will use to preserve* (*conservandam*) *faith, are made use of, it even then ever depends on the pleasure of the*

---

[2] Augustine, "On Rebuke and Grace," 14–15 (5:477).

will (*voluntatis arbitrio*) *whether it will persevere or not persevere* (*ut perseveret, vel non perseveret*). Preservation and perseverance are dependent on the free choice of man.

Taking us back to our discussion of the Second Council of Orange, the rejection says: **For this** *sentence* (*sententia*) **contains** *plain* **Pelagianism** (*manifestum Pelagianismum*)**, and while it would make men free** (*liberos*)**, it makes them** *robbers of God's honor* (*sacrilegos;* sacrilegious). As a Reformed friend once told another friend who was defending the doctrine of free will, "Congratulations, you've just become the author of your own salvation!" How so? First, the synod said this doctrine was **contrary to the prevailing agreement of the evangelical doctrine** (*perpetuum evangeliæ doctrina; consensum*)**, which takes from man all cause of boasting and ascribes all the praise for this favor to the grace of God alone.** In the words of Paul's concluding words in 1 Corinthians 1: "Let the one who boasts, boast in the Lord" (1 Cor. 1:31). *Soli Deo Gloria:* to God alone be the glory! Second, the synod responded by saying this was **contrary to the apostle, who declares that it is** *God*—not your free will—**"Who shall also confirm you unto the end, that ye may be blameless in the day of our Lord Jesus Christ" (1 Cor. 1:8).** Note the subject of the verb: **God**.

Rejection of Errors 3

That the true believers and regenerate not only can fall from justifying faith and likewise from grace and salvation wholly and to the end, but indeed often do fall from this and are lost forever.

For this conception makes powerless the grace, justification, regeneration, and continued keeping by Christ, contrary to the expressed words of the apostle Paul: "That, while we were yet sinners, Christ died for us. Much more then, being now justified by His blood, we shall be saved from wrath through Him" (Rom. 5:8, 9). And contrary to the apostle John: "Whosoever is born of God doth not commit sin; for His seed remaineth in him: and he cannot sin, because he is born of God" (1 John 3:9). And also contrary to the words of Jesus Christ: "I give unto them eternal life; and they shall never perish, neither shall any man pluck them out of My hand. My Father, which gave them Me, is greater than all; and no man is able to pluck them out of My Father's hand" (John 10:28, 29).

Rejection 3 relates back to article 6, which stated that in the richness of God's mercy he does not allow true believers to lose his Spirit, forfeit their adoption or justification, or sin against the Holy Spirit so that they are lost forever. On the contrary, we reject the Remonstrant doctrine *that the true believers and regenerate not only can fall from justifying faith and likewise from grace and salvation wholly and to the end* (*totaliter et finaliter*), *but indeed often do fall from this and are lost forever.* They taught that falling away was not only hypothetically possible—**can**—but a reality—**do**. They taught falling was not only temporary but ultimately. They taught that falling away was not only partially but wholly.

In reply, the synod said **this conception makes powerless** three crucial biblical doctrines.

First, **the grace** *of* **justification** (*iustificationis gratiam*)**...contrary to the expressed words of the apostle Paul: "That, while we were yet sinners, Christ died for us. Much more then, being now justified by His blood, we shall be saved from wrath through Him" (Rom. 5:8–9).** Paul's logic is simple: if Christ died for us while we were sinners in this life we'll be saved from God's wrath in the life to come "since, therefore, we have now been justified" (Rom. 5:9).[3] In other words, if he died for sinners, will he not save justified sinners? The synod connects Paul's doctrines of justification to perseverance. There is no second stage of forensic justification. There is still future glorification, but justification is past.

Second, **the grace** *of* **regeneration** (*regenerationis gratiam*)**...contrary to the apostle John: "Whosoever is born** (γεγεννημένος)[4] **of God doth not commit sin; for His seed remaineth in him: and he cannot sin, because he is born** (γεγέννηται)[5] **of God" (1 John 3:9).** The past action of being born again has present power because the seed God used to give us new birth remains and will remain within us. Because it does we are not "intent on sin...giving not himself to an evil and sinful life; he lets not sin reign over him."[6] In a word: "to be regenerated, and to lead a sinful life are inconsistent."[7]

---

[3] δικαιωθέντες is an aorist passive participle. See *Dutch Annotations* on Romans 5:8–9.

[4] Perfect passive participle.

[5] Perfect passive indicative.

[6] *Dutch Annotations* on 1 John 3:6.

[7] *Dutch Annotations* on 1 John 3:9.

Third, citing a text we saw earlier in connection with 5.3, the synod said the Remonstrants' **conception makes powerless** the **continued keeping by Christ...contrary to the words of Jesus Christ: "I give unto them eternal life; and they shall never perish, neither shall any man pluck them out of My hand. My Father, which gave them Me, is greater than all; and no man is able to pluck them out of My Father's hand" (John 10:28–29).**

Rejection of Errors 4

That true believers and regenerate can sin the sin unto death or against the Holy Spirit.

Since the same apostle John, after having spoken in the fifth chapter of his first epistle, verses 16 and 17, of those who sin unto death and having forbidden to pray for them, immediately adds to this in verse 18: "We know that whosoever is born of God sinneth not (meaning a sin of that character); but he that is begotten of God keepeth himself, and that wicked one toucheth him not" (1 John 5:18).

The fourth rejection speaks to the issue of the blasphemy against the Holy Spirit (Matt. 12:22–32; Mark 3:22–30) and the sin that leads to death (1 John 5:16–17) in connection with 5.6 above. The Remonstrants taught *that true believers and regenerate can sin the sin unto death or against the Holy Spirit.*

In response to this teaching the synod cited the apostle John's words in 1 John 5:16–17 concerning **those who sin unto death.** Then the synod made, in my opinion, a brilliant exegetical and contextual point in complete contrast to the Remonstrants: **and having forbidden to pray for them, immediately adds to this in verse 18: "We know that whosoever is born of God sinneth not (meaning a sin of that character); but he that is begotten of God keepeth himself, and that wicked one toucheth him not" (1 John 5:18).** The **sin unto death** was committed by a group of people who were in the church and who made a public profession of faith in Jesus Christ. But those **born of God** (regenerated) do not sin, meaning in the context, *this* particular **sin unto death.**

Rejection of Errors 5

That without a special revelation we can have no certainty of future perseverance in this life.

For by this doctrine the sure comfort of the true believers is taken away in this life and the doubts of the papist are again introduced into the church, while the Holy Scriptures constantly deduce this assurance, not from a special and extraordinary revelation, but from the marks proper to the children of God and from the constant promises of God. So especially the apostle Paul: "Nor any other creature, shall be able to separate us from the love of God, which is in Christ Jesus our Lord" (Rom. 8:39). And John declares: "And he that keepeth His commandments dwelleth in Him, and He in him. And hereby we know that He abideth in us, by the Spirit which He hath given us" (1 John 3:24).

Rejection 5 takes us back to what we saw in 5.10 concerning the source of assurance. We reject the Remonstrant teaching *that without a special revelation* (*speciali revelatione*) *we can have no certainty of future perseverance in this life.* According to the Remonstrants, this **special** or **peculiar** (*peculiari*) **revelation** as 5.10 called it, could only come **contrary to, or independent** (*extra*; outside) **of the Word of God** (5.10).

The response of the synod was to see a connection between the Remonstrants and Rome: **For by this doctrine the sure comfort of the true believers is taken away in this life and the doubts of the papist** (*pontificiorum dubitatio*) **are again introduced into the church.**[8] The definitive statement of Roman Catholic doctrine vis-à-vis the Reformation teaching on grace was the Council of Trent. In its sixth session (June 21, 1546– January 13, 1547) it addressed grace, justification, and perseverance in the following points:

First, no believer should presume to have certain knowledge of his own predestination: "No one, so long as he lives in this mortal life, ought to be presumptuous about the deep mystery of divine predestination as to decide with certainty that he is definitely among the number of the predestined" (ch. 12). It is impossible for a believer, apart from a special revelation, to know if he or she has been chosen for salvation.

---

[8] On the doctrine of the Roman Catholic Council of Trent, see Berkouwer, *Faith and Perseverance*, 46–55.

Second, while believers cannot know with certainty their final perseverance—"Let no one feel assured of this gift with an absolute certitude"—at the same time "all ought to have most secure hope in the help of God" (ch. 13).

Third, it's anathema to presume to know this: "If anyone says that a man who has been reborn and justified is bound by faith to believe that he is certainly in the number of the predestined, let him be anathema" (canon 15); "If anyone says that he has absolute and infallible certitude that he will certainly have the great gift of final perseverance, without having learned this from a special revelation: let him be anathema" (canon 16).

Furthermore, the canons continue: **the Holy Scriptures constantly deduce this assurance, not from a special and extraordinary revelation, but from the marks proper to the children of God and from the constant promises of God**, which we saw in 1.12 and 5.10. They then quoted two apostolic passages.

The first is Romans 8:39 again: **"nor any other creature, shall be able to separate us from the love of God, which is in Christ Jesus our Lord" (Rom. 8:39)**. That's an already revealed promise, not a special, peculiar, or extrabiblical revelation to believers.

The second is from 1 John 3:24: **"And he that keepeth His commandments dwelleth in Him, and He in him,"** describing our intimate communion with Christ. **"And hereby we know that He abideth in us, by the Spirit which He hath given us."**[9]

Rejection of Errors 6

That the doctrine of the certainty of perseverance and of salvation from its own character and nature is a cause of indolence and is injurious to godliness, good morals, prayers and other holy exercises, but that on the contrary it is praiseworthy to doubt.

For these show that they do not know the power of divine grace and the working of the indwelling Holy Spirit. And they contradict the apostle John, who teaches the opposite with express words in his first epistle: "Beloved, now are we the sons of God, and it doth not yet appear what we shall be: but we know that, when He shall appear, we shall be like Him; for we shall see Him as He is. And every man that hath this hope in Him purifieth himself, even as He is pure" (1 John 3:2–3). Furthermore, these are contradicted by the example of the saints, both of the Old and the New

---

[9] *Dutch Annotations* on 1 John 3:24.

Testament, who though they were assured of their perseverance and salvation, were nevertheless constant in prayers and other exercises of godliness.

Rejection 6 takes us back to article 12 and the perennial objection to the preaching of God's free grace, as expressed by Paul's interlocutor: "Are we to continue in sin that grace may abound?" (Rom. 6:2). The Remonstrants agreed with the interlocutor against Paul *that the doctrine of the certainty of perseverance and of salvation from its own character and nature is a cause of indolence and is injurious to godliness, good morals, prayers and other holy exercises, but that on the contrary it is praiseworthy to doubt.*

The synod's reply was that **these show that they do not know** (*ignorare*) **the power** (*efficaciam*) **of divine grace and the working of the indwelling Holy Spirit**. Remember, a key issue between the Remonstrants and the orthodox Reformed was that the Remonstrants saw humanity's fallenness mostly in the mind while the orthodox saw it as mostly in the will. Therefore, grace was seen in the evidence of powerfully changed lives for the orthodox while for the Remonstrants it was seen in a change of mind.[10] The synod also said **they contradict the apostle John, who teaches the opposite with express words**:

> **Beloved, now are we the sons of God, and it doth not yet appear what we shall be: but we know that, when He shall appear, we shall be like Him; for we shall see Him as He is. And every man that hath this hope in Him purifieth himself, even as He is pure. (1 John 3:2–3)**

Now **we are** the children **of God**. While we do not yet know **what we shall be** in the resurrection, **we know** with true Christian assurance and hope that **when** Jesus **shall appear** again the second time **we shall be like Him** and **see Him as He is**. Knowing this with such confidence, we purify ourselves and

> do not abuse this hope, to sin the more freely thereupon, but seek[...] after this, that [we] may possess [our] body

---

[10] See the discussion in Goudriaan, "The Synod of Dordt on Arminian Anthropology," 81–106.

and soul, both which shall be so exceedingly glorified in purity and glory…setting before [ourselves] the example of Christ as a pattern of purity, to imitate the same, although this cannot be done perfectly in this life.[11]

The synod also responded by saying **furthermore, these are contradicted by the example of the saints, both of the Old and the New Testament, who though they were assured of their perseverance and salvation, were nevertheless constant in prayers and other exercises of godliness.** The list of these is innumerable and on every page of Scripture. For example, in Psalm 56 David said, "This I know, that God is for me" (v. 9). Yet, he pleaded with God for help against his enemies: "Be gracious to me, O God" (v. 1).

Rejection of Errors 7

That the faith of those who believe for a time does not differ from justifying and saving faith except only in duration.

For Christ Himself, in Matthew 13:20, Luke 8:13, and in other places, evidently notes, besides this duration, a threefold difference between those who believe only for a time and true believers, when He declares that the former receive the seed in stony ground, but the latter in the good ground or heart; that the former are without root, but the latter have a firm root; that the former are without fruit, but that the latter bring forth their fruit in various measure with constancy and steadfastness.

Rejection 7 deals with another recurring problem of Christian experience we've seen before in the canons: whether all faith is the same or whether there are distinctions between differing kinds of faith. The error rejected, therefore, was *that the faith of those who believe for a time does not differ from justifying and saving faith except only in duration.* The Remonstrants didn't distinguish temporary faith from justifying faith.

The synod's response was to quote and apply Matthew 13 and the parable of the sower. We saw this same text and application back in the third and fourth points of doctrine, article 9. The synod used this text again here in the context of the perseverance of the saints: **For Christ Himself,**

---

[11] *Dutch Annotations* on 1 John 3:2–3.

in Matthew 13:20, Luke 8:13, and in other places, evidently notes, besides this duration. The issue was not merely of the duration of faith but of the nature or character of faith. The synod made

> a threefold difference between those who believe only for a time and true believers, when He declares that the former receive the seed in stony ground, but the latter in the good ground or heart; that the former are without root, but the latter have a firm root; that the former are without fruit, but that the latter bring forth their fruit in various measure with constancy and steadfastness.

Rejection of Errors 8

That it is not absurd that one having lost his first regeneration, is again and even often born anew.

For these deny by this doctrine the incorruptibleness of the seed of God, whereby we are born again, contrary to the testimony of the apostle Peter: "Being born again, not of corruptible seed, but of incorruptible" (1 Peter 1:23)

Rejection 8 relates back to the nature of regeneration in the third and fourth points of doctrine. There we confessed that it is **denominated a new creation: a resurrection from the dead, a making alive, which God works in us without our aid** and **not inferior in efficacy to creation or the resurrection from the dead** (3/4.12). This rejection especially relates back to what we saw above in 5.7, which said God **preserves in them the incorruptible seed of regeneration from perishing or being totally lost**. In contrast, the Remonstrants said *it is not absurd that one having lost his first regeneration, is again and even often born anew.*

The response of the synod was consistent with article 7 just quoted: **For these deny by this doctrine the incorruptibleness of the seed of God** (*seminis Dei...incorruptibilitatem*), **whereby we are born again, contrary to the testimony of the apostle Peter: "Being born again, not of corruptible seed, but of incorruptible" (1 Peter 1:23)**. Because the Word of God is joined to the powerful Holy Spirit, who is given without regret or repentance by God, the seed that makes us alive and anew is not corruptible but incorruptible (φθαρτῆς ἀλλ' ἀφθάρτου).[12]

Rejection of Errors 9

That Christ has in no place prayed that believers should infallibly continue in faith.

For they contradict Christ Himself, who says: "I have prayed for thee (Simon), that thy faith fail not" (Luke 22:32); and the evangelist John, who declares that Christ has not prayed for the apostles only, but also for those who through their word would believe: "Holy Father, keep through Thine own name those whom Thou hast given Me," and: "I pray not that Thou shouldest take them out of the world, but that Thou shouldest keep them from the evil"; "Neither pray I for these alone, but for them also which shall believe on Me through their word" (John 17:11, 15, 20).

The final rejection of errors in relation to the preservation and perseverance of the saints relates to what we saw above in article 8 that Jesus' **merit, intercession and preservation** cannot **be rendered ineffectual.** Jesus prays for his particular people, and therefore they are preserved until the end of their lives unto eternity. On the contrary, because they denied that Christ died effectually for the elect, the Remonstrants taught *that Christ has in no place prayed that believers should infallibly continue in faith.* In response, the synod rejected this by offering up two biblical examples.

First, Jesus prayed for Peter in particular that he would be preserved and that he would persevere: **For they contradict Christ himself, who says: "I have prayed for thee (Simon), that thy faith fail not" (Luke 22:32).** Even with clear passages mentioned above like Romans 8:34, Hebrews 7:25, and 1 John 2:1, they said this. Augustine used Luke 22 to prove that perseverance was a gift: "For what did [Jesus] ask for him, but perseverance to the end?"[13] The fruit of Jesus' particular prayer for Peter is that he was restored (John 21:15–17), he powerfully preached in the power of the Spirit at Pentecost (Acts 2), and wrote two canonical letters to the ancient churches of Asia Minor. Augustine went on to say that Peter's perse-

---

[12] *Dutch Annotations* on 1 Peter 1:23.

[13] Augustine, "On Rebuke and Grace," 10 (5:475). He also cited Paul's prayers for the Philippians and Jude's for his hearers. Ibid., 10 (5:475–76).

verance, therefore, was not based in his free will else he could've contradicted Jesus' prayer for him and we know that can't happen since man's will is not stronger that God's.[14]

The second text the synod cited as proof that Jesus prayed for all believers' preservation and perseverance is in John 17. He did not only pray for his earliest disciples turned apostles: **the evangelist John, who declares that Christ has not prayed for the apostles only, but also for those who through their word would believe**. His prayer was thus:

> **"Holy Father, keep through Thine own name those whom Thou hast given Me," and: "I pray not that Thou shouldest take them out of the world, but that Thou shouldest keep them from the evil"; "Neither pray I for these alone, but for them also which shall believe on Me through their word." (John 17:11, 15, 20)**

---

[14] Augustine, "On Rebuke and Grace," 17, 45 (5:478, 489–90).

CONCLUSION

AT THE END of the articles and rejections the synod appended a conclusion, summarizing its doctrine, the errors it was responding to, and calling for unity among God's people. First was a summation of the whole:

> **And this is the perspicuous, simple, and *straightforward* (*ingenua*)[1] declaration of the orthodox doctrine respecting the five articles which have been controverted in the Belgic churches, and the rejection of the errors with which they have for some time been troubled. This doctrine the Synod judges to be drawn from the Word of God and to be agreeable to the confessions of the Reformed churches.**

Second, the synod gave a summation and rejection of the rumors and slanders by the Remonstrants,: **Hence it clearly appears that those of whom one could hardly expect it have shown no truth, equity, and charity at all in wishing to make the public believe.** The first slander was that the doctrines of predestination destroyed godliness and assurance:

> *That the doctrine of the Reformed churches concerning predestination, and the points annexed to it, by its own genius and necessary tendency, leads off the minds of people (hominum) from all piety and religion; that it is an opiate administered by the flesh and the devil, and the stronghold of Satan, where he lies in wait for all; and from which he wounds multitudes, and mortally strikes through many with the darts both of despair and security;*

---

[1] See "ingenuus, a, um," in Holyoak, *A Large Dictionary*, n.p.

375

The second slander was that predestination and the associated doctrines made God the author of sin as in other false religions:

> *that it makes God the author of sin, unjust, tyrannical, hypocritical; that it is nothing more than interpolated Stoicism, Manicheism, Libertinism, Islam (Turcismum);*[2]

The third slander was that predestination and the associated doctrines led to sinful self-assurance and spiritual laziness:

> *that it renders men carnally secure, since they are persuaded by it that nothing can hinder the salvation of the elect, let them live as they please; and therefore, that they may safely perpetrate every species of the most atrocious crimes; and that if the reprobate should even perform truly all the works of the saints, their obedience would not in the least contribute to their salvation;*

The fourth slander was that predestination and the associated doctrines, especially reprobation, caused serious spiritual damage:

> *that the same doctrine teaches that God, by a mere arbitrary act of His will, without the least respect or view to any sin, has predestinated the greatest part of the world to eternal damnation; and has created them for this very purpose; that in the same manner in which the election is the fountain and the cause of faith and good works, reprobation is the cause of unbelief and impiety; that many children of the faithful are torn guiltless from their mothers' breasts and tyrannically plunged into hell; so that neither baptism nor the prayers of the Church at their baptism, can at all profit by them;*

---

[2] The older translations rendered this "Turcism," meaning, the religion of the Turkic peoples (*Turcomanni*). More recent translations such as that of the Christian Reformed Church (2011) use "Mohammedanism." If we are to love our neighbors as ourselves, including those of other religions, then we need to speak of them in a way they would self-identify. Those who practice Islam do not consider themselves practitioners of "Turcism" or "Mohammedanism." H. A. R. Gibb, *Mohammedanism: An Historical Survey*, 2nd ed. (Oxford: Oxford University Press, 1970), 1: "Modern Muslims dislike the terms Mohammedan and Mohammedanism, which seem to them to carry the implication of worship of Mohammed, as Christian and Christianity imply the worship of Christ."

After these four rumors and slanders was this statement: "**and many other things of the same kind which the Reformed Churches not only do not acknowledge, but even detest with their whole soul.**" This is important because it means our doctrine is meant to build up godliness and assurance, guard the justice of God and the responsibility of man, stimulate spiritual zeal, and cause the church to pray in particular for its little ones.

Third, the synod issued a plea that those who disagree not base their judgments on accusations or personal positions of even the best theologians, but based on the public confessions of the churches:

> **Wherefore, this Synod of Dort, in the name of the Lord, *calls upon* (*invocant*)[3] as many as piously call upon the name of our Savior Jesus Christ, to judge of the faith of the Reformed Churches not from the *false accusations* (*calumniis*),[4] which on every side are heaped upon it; nor from the private expressions of a few among ancient and modern teachers, often dishonestly quoted or corrupted and wrested to a meaning quite foreign to their intention; but from the public confessions of the Churches themselves and from the declaration of the orthodox doctrine, confirmed by the unanimous consent of all and each of the members of the whole Synod.[5]**

In fact, in mentioned statements **often dishonestly quoted or corrupted and wrested to a meaning quite foreign to their intention,** the synod appeased those who desired a list of statements by men such as John Calvin and Johannes Piscator that were considered so scandalous.

Fourth, the delegates issued a warning about the seriousness of theological innuendo in the lives of God's people:

---

[3] See "invoco, as," in Holyoak, *A Large Dictionary*, n.p.

[4] See "calumnia, ae," in Holyoak, *A Large Dictionary*, n.p.

[5] One Synod delegate, Gisbertus Voetius, would later say, "I although I do not castigate Luther, Calvin, and other scholars along with their ungrateful students, I am not obliged to embrace all their utterances as common doctrine of our churches." Gisbertus Voetius, *Thersites heautontimorumenos hoc est, Remonstrantium hyperaspistes, catechesis, et liturgiae Germanicae, Gallicae, et Belgicae denuo insultrans, retusus* (Utrecht, 1635), 215. Cited in Beck, "'Expositio reverentialis,'" 127.

Moreover, the Synod warns false accusers (*calumnia-tores*) themselves to consider the terrible judgment of God which awaits them for bearing false witness against the confessions of so many churches, for distressing the consciences of the weak, and for laboring to render suspect the society of the truly faithful.

Fifth, the synod told ministers of the Word to preach, teach, and write in such a way on these doctrines that spiritual benefits resulted:

Finally, this Synod exhorts all their *fellow ministers* (*symmystas*)[6] in the gospel of Christ to conduct themselves piously and religiously in handling this doctrine, both in the universities and churches; to direct it, as well in discourse as in writing, to the glory of the divine Name, to holiness of life, and to the consolation of afflicted souls; to regulate, by the Scripture, according to the analogy of faith, not only their sentiments, but also their language; and to abstain from all those phrases which exceed the limits necessary to be observed in ascertaining the genuine sense of the holy Scriptures, and may furnish insolent sophists with a just pretext for violently assailing or even vilifying the doctrine of the Reformed churches.

Finally, this prayer was offered:

May Jesus Christ, the Son of God, who, seated at the Father's right hand, gives gifts to men, sanctify us in the truth, bring to the truth those who err, shut the mouths of the *false accusers* (*calumniatoribus*) of sound doctrine, and endue the faithful minister of His Word with the spirit of wisdom and discretion, that all their discourses may tend to the glory of God and the edification of those who hear them. Amen.

---

[6] Holyoak renders symmysta as "a Secretary or one of the Privy Council, a Fellow, a Fellow-Minister or Priest." See "symmysta, ae," in *A Large Dictionary*, n.p. Lewis and Short mention it's derived from the Greek, συμμύστης, and render it as "a fellow-priest, colleague in the priesthood." As cited at http://logeion.uchicago.edu/symmysta (accessed December 6, 2018). Bauer, Arndt, and Gingrich render συμμύστης as "one who has been initiated into the same mysteries, fellow initiate." *A Greek-English Lexicon of the New Testament and Other Early Christian Literature*, 778.

APPENDIX I:
THE REMONSTRANCE OF 1610[1]

Article 1

That God by an eternal and immutable decree has in Jesus Christ his Son determined before the foundation of the world to save out of the fallen sinful human race those in Christ, for Christ's sake, and through Christ who by the grace of the Holy Spirit shall believe in this his Son Jesus Christ and persevere in this faith and obedience of faith to the end; and on the other hand to leave the incorrigible and unbelieving in sin and under wrath and condemn (them) as alienate from Christ—according to the word of the holy gospel in John 3:36, "He that believeth on the Son hath eternal life, and whosoever is disobedient to the Son shall not see life, but the wrath of God abideth on him" and also other passages of the Scriptures.

Article 2

That in agreement with this Jesus Christ the Savior of the world died for all men and for every man, so that he merited reconciliation and forgiveness of sins for all through the death of the cross; yet so that no one actually enjoys this forgiveness of sins except the believer—also according to the word of the gospel of John 3:16: "God so loved the world that he gave his only-begotten Son that whosoever believeth in him shall not perish but have

---

[1] As cited in "The *Remonstrance* of 1610," appendix C in De Jong, *Crisis in the Reformed Churches*, 208–9.

380

eternal life." And in the first epistle of John 2:2: "He is the propitiation for our sins; and not only for ours, but also for the sins of the whole world."

Article 3

That man does not have saving faith of himself nor by the power of his own free will, since he in the state of apostasy and sin can not of and through himself think, will or do any good which is truly good (such as is especially saving faith); but that it is necessary that he be regenerated by God, in Christ, through his Holy Spirit, and renewed in understanding, affections or will, and all powers, in order that he may rightly understand, meditate upon, will, and perform that which is truly good, according to the word of Christ, John 15:5: "Without me ye can do nothing."

Article 4

That this grace of God is the commencement, progression, and completion of all good, also in so far that regenerate man cannot, apart from this prevenient or assisting, awakening, consequent and cooperating grace, think, will or do the good or resist any temptations to evil; so that all good works or activities which can be conceived must be ascribed to the grace of God in Christ. But with respect to the mode of this grace, it is not irresistible, since it is written concerning many that they have resisted the Holy Spirit. Acts 7 and elsewhere in many places.

Article 5

That those who are incorporated into Jesus Christ and thereby become partakers of his life-giving Spirit have abundant strength to strive against satan, sin, the world, and their own flesh and to obtain the victory; it being well understood (that this is) through the assistance of the grace of the Holy Spirit, and that Jesus Christ assists them through his Spirit in all temptations, extends the hand, and—if only they are prepared for warfare and desire his help and are not negligent—keeps them standing, so that by no cunning or power of satan can they be led astray or plucked out of Christ's hands, according to the word of Christ, John 10, "No one shall pluck them out of my hands." But whether they can through negligence fall away from the first principle of their life in Christ, again embrace the present world, depart from the pure doctrine once given to them, lose the good conscience, and neglect grace, must first be more carefully determined from the Holy Scriptures before we shall be able to teach this with the full persuasion of our heart.

Conclusion

These articles here set forth and taught the Remonstrants hold to be conformable to God's Word, edifying, and with respect to this matter sufficient unto salvation, so that it is neither necessary nor edifying to rise higher or to descend more deeply.

APPENDIX II:

THE OPINIONS OF THE REMONSTRANTS (1619)[1]

The Opinion of the Remonstrants regarding the first article, dealing with the decree of Predestination.

1.   God has not decided to elect anyone to eternal life, or to reject anyone from the same, prior to the decree to create him, without any consideration of preceding obedience or disobedience, according to His good pleasure, for the demonstration of the glory of His mercy and justice, or of His absolute power and dominion.

2.   Since the decree of God concerning both the salvation and perdition of each man is not a decree of the end absolutely intended, it follows that neither are such means subordinated to that same decree by which the elect and the reprobate are efficaciously and inevitably led to their final destination.

3.   Therefore God has not with this plan created in the one Adam all men in a state of rectitude, has not ordained the fall and the permission of it, has not withdrawn from Adam the grace which was necessary and sufficient, has not brought it about that the Gospel is preached and that men are externally called, does not confer on them any gifts of the Holy Spirit by means of which he leads some of them to life, but deprives others of the benefit of life, Christ, the Mediator, is not solely the executor of election, but also the foundation of that same decree of election: the reason why some are efficaciously called, justified, persevere in faith, and are glorified is

[1] As cited in "The Opinions of the Remonstrants," appendix H in De Jong, *Crisis in the Reformed Churches*, 222–29.

not that they have been absolutely elected to eternal life. That others are left in the fall, that Christ is not given to them, that they are either not called at all or not efficaciously called—these are not the reasons why they are absolutely rejected from eternal salvation.

4. God has not decreed to leave the greatest part of men in the fall, excluded from every hope of salvation, apart from intervening actual sins.

5. God has ordained that Christ should be a propitiation for the sins of the whole world, and by virtue of that decree He has determined to justify and to save those who believe in Him, and to provide for men means necessary and sufficient for faith in such a way as He knows to be in harmony with His wisdom and justice. But He has by no means determined, by virtue of an absolute decree, to give Christ the Mediator solely to the elect, and through an efficacious calling to bestow faith upon, justify, preserve in the faith and glorify them alone.

6. No one is rejected from life nor from the means sufficient for it by an absolute antecedent decree, so that the merit of Christ, calling, and all the gifts of the Spirit can be profitable to salvation for all, and truly are, unless they themselves by the abuse of these gifts pervert them to their own perdition; but to unbelief, to impiety, and to sins, a means and causes of damnation, no one is predestined.

7. The election of particular persons is decisive, out of consideration of faith in Jesus Christ and of perseverance; not, however, apart from a consideration of faith and perseverance in the true faith, as a condition prerequisite for electing.

8. Rejection from eternal life is made on the basis of a consideration of antecedent unbelief and perseverance in unbelief; not, however, apart from a consideration of antecedent unbelief and perseverance in unbelief.

9. All the children of believers are sanctified in Christ, so that no one of them who leaves this life before the use of reason will perish. By no means, however, are to be considered among the number of the reprobate certain children of believers who leave this life in infancy before they have committed any actual sin in their own persons, so that neither the holy bath of baptism nor the prayers of the church for them in any way be profitable for their salvation.

10. No children of believers who have been baptized in the name of the Father, the Son, and the Holy Spirit, living in the state of infancy, are reckoned among the reprobate by an absolute decree.

The Opinion of the Remonstrants regarding the second article, which deals with the universality of the merit of the death of Christ.

1. The price of redemption which Christ offered to God the Father is not only in itself and by itself sufficient for the redemption of the whole human race but has also been paid for all men and for every man, according to the decree, will, and the grace of God the Father; therefore no one is absolutely excluded from participation in the fruits of Christ's death by an absolute and antecedent decree of God.

2. Christ has, by the merit of his death, so reconciled God the Father to the whole human race that the Father, on account of that merit, without giving up His righteousness and truth, has been able and has willed to make and confirm a new covenant of grace with sinners and men liable to damnation.

3. Though Christ has merited reconciliation with God and remission of sins for all men and for every man, yet no one, according to the pact of the new and gracious covenant, becomes a true partaker of the benefits obtained by the death of Christ in any other way than by faith; nor are sins forgiven to sinning men before they actually and truly believe in Christ.

4. Only those are obliged to believe that Christ died for them for whom Christ has died. The reprobates, however, as they are called, for whom Christ has not died, ore not obligated to such faith, nor can they be justly condemned on account of the contrary refusal to believe this. In fact, if there should be such reprobates, they would be obliged to believe that Christ has not died for them.

The Opinion of the Remonstrants regarding the third and fourth articles, concerning the grace of God and the conversion of man.

1. Man does not have saving faith of himself, nor out of the powers of his free will, since in the state of sin he is able of himself and by himself neither to think, will, or do any good (which would indeed to be saving good, the most prominent of which is saving faith). It is necessary therefore that by God in Christ through His Holy Spirit he be regenerated and re-

newed in intellect, affections, will, and in all his powers, so that he might be able to understand, reflect upon, will and carry out the good things which pertain to salvation.

2. We hold, however, that the grace of God is not only the beginning but also the progression and the completion of every good, so much so that even the regenerate himself is unable to think, will, or do the good, or to resist any temptations to evil, apart from that preceding or prevenient, awakening, following and cooperating grace. Hence all good works and actions which anyone by cogitation is able to comprehend are to be ascribed to the grace of God.

3. Yet we do not believe that all zeal, care, and diligence applied to the obtaining of salvation before faith itself and the Spirit of renewal are vain and ineffectual—indeed, rather harmful to man than useful and fruitful. On the contrary, we hold that to hear the Word of God, to be sorry for sins committed, to desire saving grace and the Spirit of renewal (none of which things man is able to do without grace) are not only not harmful and useless, but rather most useful and most necessary for the obtaining of faith and of the Spirit of renewal.

4. The will in the fallen state, before calling, does not have the power and the freedom to will any saving good. And therefore we deny that the freedom to will saving good as well as evil is present to the will in every state.

5. The efficacious grace by which anyone is converted is not irresistible; and though God so influences the will by the word and the internal operation of His Spirit that he both confers the strength to believe or supernatural powers, and actually causes man to believe—yet man is able of himself to despise that grace and not to believe, and therefore to perish through his own fault.

6. Although according to the most free will of God the disparity of divine grace is very great, nevertheless, the Holy Spirit confers, or is ready to confer, as much grace to all men and to each man to whom the Word of God is preached as is sufficient for promoting the conversion of men in its steps. Therefore sufficient grace for faith and conversion falls to the lot not only of those whom God is said to will to save according to the decree of absolute election, but also of those who are not actually converted.

7. Man is able through the grace of the Holy Spirit to do more good than he actually does, and to avoid more evil than he actually avoids; and

we do not believe that God simply does not will that man should do more good than he does and avoid more evil than he does avoid, and that God has decreed precisely from eternity that both should so happen.

8. Whomever God calls to salvation, he calls seriously, that is, with a sincere and completely unhypocritical intention and will to save; nor do we assent to the opinion of those who hold that God calls certain ones externally whom He does not will to call internally, that is, as truly converted, even before the grace of calling has been rejected.

9. There is not in God a secret will which so contradicts the will of the same revealed in the Word that according to it (that is, the secret will) He does not will the conversion and salvation of the greatest part of those whom He seriously calls and invites by the Word of the Gospel and by His revealed will; and we do not here, as some say, acknowledge in God a holy simulation, or a double person.

10. Nor do we believe that God calls the reprobate, as they are called, to these ends: that He should the more harden them, or take away excuse, or punish them the more severely, or display their inability; nor, however, that they should be converted, should believe, and should be saved.

11. It is not true that all things, not only good but also bad, necessarily occur, from the power and efficacy of the secret will or decree of God, and that indeed those who sin, out of consideration of the decree of God, are not able to sin; that God wills to determine and to bring about the sins of men, their insane, foolish, and cruel works, and the sacrilegious blasphemy of His name—in fact, to move the tongues of men to blasphemy, and so on.

12. To us the following is false and horrible: that God impels men to sins which He openly prohibits; that those who sin do not act contrary to the will of God properly named; that what is unrighteous (that is, what is contrary to the will of God properly named; that what is unrighteous (that is, what is contrary to His precept) is in agreement with the will of God; indeed, that it is truly a capital crime to do the will of God.

The Opinion of the Remonstrants with respect to the fifth article, which concerns Perseverance.

1. The perseverance of believers in the faith is not an effect of the absolute decree by which God is said to have chosen singular persons defined by no condition of obedience.

2. God provides true believers with as much grace and supernatural powers as He judges, according to His infinite wisdom, to be sufficient for persevering and for overcoming the temptations of the devil, the flesh, and the world; it is never charged to God's account that they do not persevere.

3. True believers call fall from true faith and can fall into such sins as cannot be consistent with true and justifying faith; not only is it possible for this to happen, but it even happens frequently.

4. True believers are able to fall through their own fault into shameful and atrocious deeds, to persevere and to die in them; and therefore finally to fall and to perish.

5. Nevertheless we do not believe that true believers, though they may sometimes fall into grave sins which are vexing to their consciences, immediately fall out of every hope of repentance; but we acknowledge that it can happen that God, according to the multitude of His mercies, may recall them through His grace to repentance; in fact, we believe that this happens not infrequently, although we cannot be persuaded that this will certainly and indubitably happen.

6. The following dogmas, therefore, which by public writings are being scattered among the people, we reject with our whole mind and heart as harmful to piety and good morals: namely, 1) True believers are not able to sin deliberately, but only out of ignorance and weakness. 2) True believers through no sins can fall out of the grace of God. 3) A thousand sins, even all the sins of the whole world, are not able to render election invalid. 4) To believers and to the elect no sins, however great and grave they can be, are imputed; but all present and future sins have already been remitted. 5) True believers, having fallen into destructive heresies, into grave and most atrocious sins, like adultery and homicide, on account of which the church, after the justification of Christ, is compelled to testify that it is not able to tolerate them in its external communion and that they will have no part in the kingdom of Christ unless they are converted, nevertheless are not able to fall from faith totally and finally.

7. A true believer, as for the present time he can be certain about his faith and the integrity of his conscience, and thus also concerning his salvation and the saving benevolence of God toward him, for that time can be and ought to be certain; and on this point we reject the pontifical opinion.

8. A true believer can and ought indeed to be certain for the future that he is able, by diligent watchfulness, through prayers, and through other holy exercises, to persevere in true faith, and he ought also to be certain that divine grace for persevering will never be lacking; but we do not see how he can be certain that he will never afterwards be remiss in his duty but that he will persevere in faith and in those works of piety and love which are fitting for a believer in this school of Christian warfare; neither do we deem it necessary that concerning this thing a believer should be certain.

BIBLIOGRAPHY

Primary Sources

à Brakel, Wilhelmus. *The Christian's Reasonable Service.* Translated by Bartel Elshout. Edited by Joel R. Beeke. 4 vols. 1995. Reprint, Grand Rapids, MI: Reformation Heritage Books, third printing 2007.

Acta of the Synod of Dordt: Acta et Documenta Synodi Nationalis Dordrechtanae (1618–1619): Volume 1. Edited by Donald Sinnema, Christian Moser, and Herman J. Selderhuis. Göttingen, Germany: Vandenhoeck & Ruprecht, 2015.

Acta Synodi Nationalis…Dordrechti habitae. Lugduni Batavorum, 1620. https://books.google.com/books?id=2M5DAAAAcAAJ&printsec=frontcover#v=onepage&q&f=false. Accessed August 9, 2018.

Ambrose. "On the Death of Satyrus." In *Nicene and Post-Nicene Fathers: Second Series*, Vol. 10. 1896. Reprint, Peabody, MA: Hendrickson, fourth printing 2004.

Anselm of Canterbury: The Major Works. Edited by Brian Davies and G. R. Evans, Oxford World's Classics. Oxford: Oxford University Press, 1998.

Aquinas, Thomas. *Catena Aurea: Commentary on the Four Gospels Collected out of the Works of the Fathers*, St. Matthew: Volume I, Part I. Oxford: John Henry Parker, 1841.

————. *Catena Aurea: Commentary on the Four Gospels Collected out of the Works of the Fathers*, St. Matthew: Volume I, Part II. Oxford: John Henry Parker, 1841.

————. *Catena Aurea: Commentary on the Four Gospels Collected out of the Works of the Fathers*, St. Matthew: Volume I, Part III. Oxford: John Henry Parker, 1842.

————. *Catena Aurea: Commentary on the Four Gospels Collected out of the Works of the Fathers*, St. Luke: Volume III, Part I. Oxford: John Henry Parker, 1843.

————. *Catena Aurea: Commentary on the Four Gospels Collected out of the Works of the Fathers*, St. John: Volume IV, Part I. Oxford: John Henry Parker, 1845.

————. *Catena Aurea: Commentary on the Four Gospels Collected out of the Works of the Fathers*, St. John: Volume IV, Part II. Oxford: John Henry Parker, 1845.

————. *St. Thomas Aquinas: Summa Theologica*. Translated by Fathers of the English Dominican Province. 5 vols. 1948. Reprint, Notre Dame, IN: Christian Classics, 1981.

The Arminian Confession of 1621. Translated and edited by Mark A. Ellis. Princeton Theological Monograph Series 51. Eugene, OR: Pickwick, 2005.

The Articles of the Synod of Dort. Translated by Thomas Scott. Philadelphia: Presbyterian Board of Publication, 1856.

Arminius, James. *Apologia…Arminii adversus Articulos*, in *Opera Theologicia*. Leiden: Godefridus Basson, 1629.

————. "The Apology or Defence against Thirty-One Theological Articles." In *The Works of James Arminius: Volume 2*. Translated by James Nichols, 1–79. 1828. Reprint, Grand Rapids, MI: Baker Books, 1999.

————. "Dissertation on the True and Genuine Sense of the Seventh Chapter of the Epistle to the Romans." In *The Works of James Arminius: Volume 2*. Translated by James Nichols, 471–683. 1828. Reprint, Grand Rapids, MI: Baker Books, 1999.

————. *Examen Libelli Perkinsiani de Praedestinationis Ordine et Modo*, in *Opera Theologicia*. Leiden: Godefridus Basson, 1629.

————. *Examen modestum libelli*. Leiden, 1612.

————. "Friendly Conference with Dr. F. Junius." In *The Works of James Arminius: Volume 3*. Translated by William Nichols, 1–235. 1875. Reprint, Grand Rapids, MI: Baker Books, 1999.

————. "Modest Examination of a Pamphlet, Which That Very Learned Divine, Dr. William Perkins, Published Some Years Ago, on the Mode and Order of Predestination, and on the Amplitude of Divine Grace." In *The Works of James Arminius: Volume 3*. Translated by William Nichols, 249–484. 1875. Reprint, Grand Rapids, MI: Baker Books, 1999.

————. "Orations." In *The Works of James Arminius: Volume 1*. Translated by James Nichols, 321–401. 1825; repr., Grand Rapids, MI: Baker Books, 1999.

Augustine. *Confessions: Books 9–13*. Edited and translated by Carolyn J.-B. Hammond. Loeb Classical Library 27. Cambridge, MA: Harvard University Press, 2016.

————. *The Enchiridion on Faith, Hope, and Love*. Translated by J. F. Shaw. Edited by Henry Paolucci. Chicago: Regnery Gateway, 1961.

————. "Homilies on the First Epistle of John." In *Nicene and Post-Nicene Fathers: First Series*, Vol. 7. 1888. Reprint, Peabody, MA: Hendrickson, fourth printing 2004.

————. "On Rebuke and Grace." In *Nicene and Post-Nicene Fathers: First Series*, Vol. 5. 1887. Reprint, Peabody, MA: Hendrickson, fourth printing 2004.

————. "On the Gift of Perseverance." In *Nicene and Post-Nicene Fathers: First Series*, Vol. 5. 1887. Reprint, Peabody, MA: Hendrickson, fourth printing 2004.

————. "On the Predestination of the Saints." In *Nicene and Post-Nicene Fathers: First Series*, Vol. 5. 1887. Reprint, Peabody, MA: Hendrickson, fourth printing 2004.

————. "Tractates on the Gospel of John," in *Nicene and Post-Nicene Fathers: First Series*, Vol. 7. 1888. Reprint, Peabody, MA: Hendrickson, fourth printing 2004.

Baxter, Richard. *Reliquiae Baxterianae*. London, 1696.

Bertius, Petrus. *Scripta Adversaria Collationis Hagiensis*. Lugduni Batavorum, 1615.

Biesterveld, P., and H. H. Kuyper, *Ecclesiastical Manual*. Translated by Richard R. De Ridder. Grand Rapids, MI: Calvin Theological Seminary, 1982.

The Book of Common Prayer. 1662. Reprint, Cambridge: Cambridge University Press, 2012.

Boston, Thomas. "Why the Lord Suffereth Sin to Remain in the Regenerate?" In *The Whole Works of the Larte Reverend Thomas Boston of Ettrick: Sermons and Discourses on Several Important Subjects in Divinity*. Edited by Samuel M'Millan, 6:110–24. Aberdeen, Scotland: George and Robert King, 1849.

The British Delegation and the Synod of Dort (1618–1619). Edited by Anthony Milton. Church of England Record Society 13. Woodbridge, UK: Boydell, 2005.

Calvin, John. *The Acts of the Apostles, Volume II*. Translated by John W. Fraser. Edited by David W. Torrance and Thomas F. Torrance. Calvin's New Testament Commentaries 7. 1966. Reprint, Grand Rapids, MI: Eerdmans, 1973.

———. *Commentaries on the Last Four Books of Moses Arranged in the Form of a Harmony: Volume 1.* Translated by Charles William Bingham. Calvin's Commentaries 2. 1852–1855. Reprint, Grand Rapids, MI: Baker Books House, 1996.

———. *Commentary on the Book of Psalms: Volume 1.* Translated by James Anderson. Calvin's Commentaries 4. Reprint, Grand Rapids, MI: Baker Book House, 1996.

———. *The Epistles of Paul the Apostle to the Galatians, Ephesians, Philippians and Colossians.* Translated by T. H. L. Parker. Edited by David W. Torrance and Thomas F. Torrance. Calvin's New Testament Commentaries 11. 1965. Reprint, Grand Rapids, MI: Eerdmans, 1972.

———. *The Epistles of Paul the Apostle to the Romans and to the Thessalonians.* Translated by Ross Mackenzie. Edited by David W. Torrance and Thomas F. Torrance. Calvin's New Testament Commentaries 8. Grand Rapids, MI: Eerdmans, 1961.

———. *The Gospel according to St. John 1–10.* Translated by T. H. L. Parker. Edited by David W. Torrance and Thomas F. Torrance. Calvin's Commentaries 4. Grand Rapids, MI: Eerdmans, 1959.

———. *Institutes of the Christian Religion.* Edited by John T. McNeill. Translated by Ford Lewis Battles. 2 vols. Philadelphia: Westminster, 1960.

———. *Institutes of the Christian Religion.* Translated by Robert White. Edinburgh: Banner of Truth Trust, 2014.

———. *The Second Epistle of Paul the Apostle to the Corinthians and the Epistles to Timothy, Titus, and Philemon.* Translated by T. A. Smail. Edited by David W. Torrance and Thomas F. Torrance. Calvin's Commentaries 10. Grand Rapids, MI: Eerdmans, 1964.

———. *Sermons on the Epistle to the Ephesians.* Translated by Arthur Golding. 1577. Reprint, Edinburgh: Banner of Truth, 1987.

————. "To a Gentleman of Provence." In *Selected Works of John Calvin: Tracts & Letters*, edited by Jules Bonnet, 6:71–74. Translated by Marcus Robert Gilchrist. 7 vols. Grand Rapids, MI: Baker Book House, 1983.

————. "A Treatise on the Eternal Predestination of God." In *Calvin's Calvinism: Treatise on the Eternal Predestination of God & the Secret Providence of God*. Translated by Henry Cole. 1856. Reprint, Grand Rapids, MI: Reformed Free Publishing Association, 1987.

The Canons and Decrees of the Sacred and Oecumenical Council of Trent. Translated by J. Waterworth. London: C. Dolman, 1848.

"Canons of the Council of Carthage May 1, 418." http://www.seanmultimedia.com/Pie_Council_Of_Carthage_May _1_418.html. Accessed May 9, 2018.

Carleton, George. "An Oration Made at the Hage, Before the Prince of Orange, and the Assembly of the High and Mighty Lords, the States General of the United Provinces." London, 1619.

Chrysostom, John. *The Homilies of S. John Chrysostom Archbishop of Constantinople on the Gospel of St. Matthew: Part I, Homilies I–XXV*. Translated by Frederic Field. London: Walter Smith, 1885.

The Creeds of Christendom: Volume 1, The History of Creeds. Edited by Philip Schaff. Revised by David S. Schaff. 1931. Reprint, Grand Rapids, MI: Baker Books, 1993.

Cunningham, William. *The Reformers: And the Theology of the Reformation*. In *Collected Works: Vol. 1*. Edinburgh: T&T Clark, 1862.

Davenant, John. *A Dissertation on the Death of Christ, as to Its Extent and Special Benefits*. In *An Exposition of the Epistle of St. Paul to the Colossians*. 2 vols.. Translated by Josiah Allport. London: Hamilton, Adams, 1832.

————. *Animadversions written by the Right Reverend Father in God, John Lord Bishop of Sarisbury, upon a Treatise intitled Gods love to Mankinde*. London, 1641.

De Moor, Bernardinus. *Continuous Commentary on Johannes Marckius' Didactico-Elenctic Compendium of Christian Theology: Volume 1, Concerning the Word and Definition of Theology.* Translated by Steven Dilday. Culpeper, VA: L&G Reformation Translation Center, 2014.

De Nederlandse belijdenisgeschriften. Edited by J. N. Bakhuizen van den Brink. 2nd ed. Amsterdam: Ton Bolland, 1976.

Dennison, James T., Jr., ed. *Reformed Confessions of the 16th and 17th Centuries in English Translation: Volume 2, 1552–1566.* Grand Rapids, MI: Reformation Heritage Books, 2010.

Early Sessions of the Synod of Dort: Acta et Documenta Synodi Nationalis Dordrechtanae (1618–1619): Volume II/2. Edited by Donald Sinnema, Christian Moser, and Herman J. Selderhuis. Göttingen, Germany: Vandenhoeck & Ruprecht, 2018.

Episcopius, Simon. *The Confession or Declaration of the…Remonstrants.* London, 1676.

Gottschalk and a Medieval Predestination Controversy: Texts Translated from the Latin. Edited and translated by Victor Genke & Francis X. Gumerlock. Mediaeval Philosophical Texts in Translation 47. Milwaukee, WI: Marquette University Press, 2010.

Gunter, W. Stephen. *Arminius and His Declaration of Sentiments: An Annotated Translation with Introduction and Theological Commentary.* Waco, TX: Baylor University Press, 2012.

Hales, John. *Golden Remains of the Ever Memorable Mr. John Hales.* 2nd ed. London: Newcomb, 1673.

Hall, Joseph. *The Reconciler, or An epistle pacificatorie of the seeming differences of opinion concerning the true being and visibilitie of the Roman Church Enlarged with the addition of letters of resolution, for that purpose, from some famous divines of our Church.* London: Printed for Nath: Butter, 1629).

Henry, Matthew. *Commentary on the Whole Bible.* 1991. Reprint, Peabody, MA: Hendrickson, eighth printing 1997.

Hommius, Festus. *Specimen controversiarum Belgicarum*. Leiden, 1618. https://books.google.com/books?id=1HhJAAAAcAAJ&printsec =frontcover#v=onepage&q&f=false. Accessed July 25, 2018.

Jerome. *Commentary on Matthew*. Translated by Thomas P. Scheck. Fathers of the Church: A New Translation. Vol. 117. Washington, DC: Catholic University of America Press, 2008.

Junius, Franciscus. *The Mosaic Polity*. Translated by Todd M. Rester. Edited by Andrew M. McGinnis. Sources in Early Modern Economics, Ethics, and Law. Grand Rapids, MI: Christian's Library, 2015.

———. *A Treatise on True Theology*. Translated by David C. Noe. Grand Rapids, MI: Reformation Heritage Books, 2014.

Lombard, Peter. *The Sentences, Book 1: The Mystery of the Trinity*. Translated by Giulio Silano. Mediaeval Sources in Translation 42. Toronto: Pontifical Institute of Mediaeval Studies, 2007.

———. *The Sentences, Book 2: On Creation*. Translated by Giulio Silano. Mediaeval Sources in Translation 43. Toronto: Pontifical Institute of Mediaeval Studies, 2008.

———. *The Sentences, Book 3: On the Incarnation of the Word*. 4 vols. Toronto: Pontifical Institute of Medieval Studies, 2008.

Luther, Martin. *Martin Luther: Hymns, Ballads, Chants, Truth* (4-CD set; St. Louis, MO: Concordia, 2004).

———. "Sermons on the Second Epistle of St. Peter." In *Luther's Works 30: The Catholic Epistles*, edited by Jaroslav Pelikan. Translated by Martin H. Bertram. St. Louis, MO: Concordia, 1967.

———. *What Luther Says: Volume 1*. Edited by Ewald M. Plass. St. Louis, MO: Concordia, 1959.

Manton, Thomas. "Sermons upon the Eighth Chapter to the Romans." In *The Works of Thomas Manton: Volume 12*. Reprint, Birmingham, AL: Solid Ground Christian Books, 2008.

———. "Sermons upon the Seventeenth Chapter of St. John." In *The Works of Thomas Manton: Volume 11*. Reprint, Birmingham, AL: Solid Ground Christian Books, 2008.

Martyr, Justin. "First Apology." In *Ante-Nicene Fathers: Volume 1*. Edited by Alexander Roberts and James Donaldson. 1885. Reprint, Peabody, MA: Hendrickson, fourth printing 2004.

The Missing Public Disputations of Jacobus Arminius: Introduction, Text, and Notes. Edited by Keith D. Stanglin. Brill's Series in Church History 47. Leiden: Brill, 2010.

"The Opinions of the Remonstrants." Appendix H in De Jong, *Crisis in the Reformed Churches*, 221–29.

Owen, John. "Christologia." In *The Works of John Owen*, edited by William H. Goold, 16 vols., 1:1–272. 1850–1853. Reprint, Edinburgh: Banner of Truth, fifth printing 1993.

———. "The Nature of Apostasy from the Profession of the Gospel and the Punishment of Apostates Declared." In *The Works of John Owen*, edited by William H. Goold, 7:1–259. 16 vols. Edinburgh: Banner of Truth, 1965.

———. "Of the Mortification of Sin in Believers." In *The Works of John Owen*, edited by William H. Goold, 6:1–86. 16 vols. 1850–1853. Reprint, Edinburgh: Banner of Truth, fifth printing 1993.

———. "Salus Electorum, Sanguis Jesu; or, The Death of Death in the Death of Christ." In *The Works of John Owen*, edited by William H. Goold, 10:139–479, 16 vols. 1850–1853. Reprint, Edinburgh: Banner of Truth, fifth printing 1993.

Paraeus, David. "Epitome of Arminianisme: or, The Examination of the Five Articles of the Remonstrants, in the Netherlands." In *The Summe of Christian Religion, Delivered by Zacharias Ursinus*. Translated by A. R., 817–44. London, Printed by James Young, 1645.

Perkins, William. "A Christian and Plain Treatise of the Manner and Order of Predestination, and of the Largeness of God's Grace." In *The*

Workes of that Famous and Worthy Minister of Christ in the University of Cambridge M. William Perkins: Volume 2. Translated by Francis Cacot and Thomas Tuke. London: John Kegatt, 1631.

Pictet, Benedict. *Christian Theology.* Translated by Frederick Reyroux. Philadelphia: Presbyterian Board of Publication, 1845.

Poole, Matthew. *A Commentary on the Holy Bible, Volume I: Genesis–Job.* Peabody, MA: Hendrickson, 2008.

Prosper of Aquitaine: Defense of St. Augustine. Translated by P. De Letter. Ancient Christian Writers 32. New York: Newman, 1963.

Rees, B. R. *Pelagius: Life and Letters.* 1988, 1991. Reprint, Woodbridge, UK: Boydell, 1998.

"The *Remonstrance* of 1610." Appendix C in De Jong, *Crisis in the Reformed Churches*, 207–9.

Roberts, T. R. "A Translation and Critical Edition of Ratramnus of Corbie's *De Predestinatione Dei*." PhD diss., University of Missouri–Columbia, 1977.

Synopsis Purioris Theologiae/Synopsis of a Purer Theology: Volume 2. Edited by Henk van den Belt. Translated by Riemer A. Faber. Leiden: Brill, 2016.

Ursinus, Zacharias. *The Commentary of Dr. Zacharias Ursinus on the Heidelberg Catechism.* Translated by G. W. Williard. 1852. Reprint, Phillipsburg, NJ: P&R, 1985.

Voetius, Gisbertus. *Selectarum Disputationum Theologicarum: Pars Prima.* Utrecht: Joannem à Waesberge, 1648.

————. *Thersites heautontimorumenos hoc est, Remonstrantium hyperaspistes, catechesis, et liturgiae Germanicae, Gallicae, et Belgicae denuo insultrans, retusus.* Utrecht, 1635.

Voetius, Gisbertus, and Johannes Hoornbeeck. *Spiritual Desertion.* Translated by John Vriend and Harry Boonstra. Edited by M. Eugene Oosterhaven. Classics of Reformed Spirituality. Grand Rapids, MI: Baker Academic, 2003.

Watson, Thomas. *A Body of Divinity*. 1692. Reprint, Edinburgh: Banner of Truth Trust, 2000.

Witsius, Herman. *The Economy of the Covenants between God and Man: Comprehending a Complete Body of Divinity*. Translated by William Crookshank. 2 vols. 1822. Reprint, Escondido, CA: den Dulk Foundation, 1990.

Woods, F. H. *Canons of the Second Council of Orange, A.D. 529*. Oxford: James Thornton, 1882.

The Works of James Arminius. Translated by James Nichols and William Nichols. 3 vols. 1828. Reprint, Grand Rapids, MI: Baker Books, 1999.

Secondary Sources

A Faith Worth Teaching: The Heidelberg Catechism's Enduring Heritage. Edited by Jon D. Payne and Sebastian Heck. Grand Rapids, MI: Reformation Heritage Books, 2013.

A Greek-English Lexicon of the New Testament and Other Early Christian Literature. Translated by William F. Arndt and F. Wilbur Gingrich. 2nd ed. 1958. Reprint, Chicago: University of Chicago Press, 1979.

"An Assemblies of God Response to Reformed Theology (Adopted by the General Presbytery in Session August 1 & 3, 2015)." https://ag.org/Beliefs/Topics-Index/Reformed-Theology-Response-of-the-AG-Position-Paper. Accessed August 2, 2018.

Appold, Kenneth G. *Abraham Calov's Doctrine of Vocatio in its Systematic Context*. Tübingen: Mohr Siebeck, 1998.

Arminius, Arminianism, and Europe: Jacobus Arminius (1559/60–1609). Edited by Th. Marius van Leeuwen, Keith D. Stanglin, and Marijke Tolsma. Brill's Series in Church History 39. Leiden: Brill, 2009.

Armstrong, Brian G. *Calvinism and the Amyraut Heresy: Protestant Scholasticism and Humanism in Seventeenth-Century France.* 1969. Reprint, Eugene, OR: Wipf & Stock, 2004.

"Assurance of Salvation (Adopted by the General Presbytery in Session August 5 & 7, 2017)." https://ag.org/Beliefs/Topics-Index/Assurance-Of-Salvation. Accessed August 2, 2018.

Baars, A. "The 'Appropriation of Salvation' in the Creeds: An Overview (Part 1)." *Clarion* 46, no. 24 (November 28, 1997): 528–31.

———. "The 'Appropriation of Salvation' in the Creeds: An Overview (Part 2)." *Clarion*, December 1997, 566–68.

Backus, Irena, and Aza Goudriaan. "'Semipelagianism': The Origins of the Term and Its Passage into the History of Heresy." *Journal of Ecclesiastical History* 65, no. 1 (January 2014): 25–46.

Bangs, Carl. *Arminius: A Study in the Dutch Reformation.* Nashville, TN: Abingdon, 1971.

Barrett, Matthew. *The Grace of Godliness: An Introduction to Doctrine and Piety in the Canons of Dort.* Kitchener, ON: Joshua, 2013.

Bavinck, Herman. *Saved by Grace: The Holy Spirit's Work in Calling and Regeneration.* Translated by Nelson D. Kloosterman. Edited by J. Mark Beach. Grand Rapids, MI: Reformation Heritage Books, 2008.

Beach, J. Mark. "Some Observations about the *Three Forms of Unity* and the Doctrine of the Covenant of Works." *Mid-America Journal of Theology* 21 (2010): 103–19.

Beale, G. K. *The Book of Revelation: A Commentary on the Greek Text.* Grand Rapids, MI: Eerdmans, 1999.

Beck, Andreas J. "'Expositio reverentialis': Gisbertus Voetius's (1589–1676) Relationship with John Calvin." *Church History and Religious Culture* 91, nos. 1–2 (2011): 121–33.

———. "Reformed Confessions and Scholasticism: Diversity and Harmony." *Perichoresis* 14, no. 3 (2016): 17–43.

Beeke, Joel R. *Debated Issues in Sovereign Predestination: Early Lutheran Predestination, Calvinian Reprobation, and Variations in Genevan Lapsarianism.* Reformed Historical Theology 42. Göttingen, Germany: Vandenhoeck & Ruprecht, 2017.

Beeke, Joel R., and Mark Jones. "The Puritans on Law and Gospel." In *A Puritan Theology: Doctrine for Life*, 321–33. Grand Rapids, MI: Reformation Heritage Books, 2012.

Beets, Henry. *The Reformed Confession Explained.* Grand Rapids, MI: Eerdmans, 1929.

Bell, Rob. *Velvet Elvis: Repainting the Christian Faith.* Grand Rapids, MI: Zondervan, 2005.

Berkhof, Louis. *The Assurance of Faith: The Firm Foundation of Christian Hope.* 1939. Reprint, Birmingham, AL: Solid Ground Christian Books, 2004.

————. *Systematic Theology.* 4th rev. ed. Grand Rapids, MI: Eerdmans, 1994. First published 1941.

Berkouwer, G. C. *Faith and Perseverance.* Translated by Robert D. Knudsen. Studies in Dogmatics. 1958. Grand Rapids, MI: Eerdmans, second printing 1973.

————. *Faith and Sanctification.* Translated by John Vriend. Studies in Dogmatics. 1952. Grand Rapids, MI: Eerdmans, fifth printing 1972.

Beyer, Jürgen, and Leigh T. I. Penman. "The Petitions of 'A Supposed Prophetesse.' The Lübeck Letters of Anna Walker and Their Significance for the Synod of Dordt. A Linguistic and Contextual Analysis." In Goudriaan and van Lieburg, *Revisiting the Synod of Dordt*, 107–33.

Beyond Calvin: Essays on the Diversity of the Reformed Tradition. Edited by W. Brad Littlejohn and Jonathan Tomes. Proceedings of the 4th Annual Convivium Irenicum. Lincoln, NE: Davenant Trust, 2017.

Bierma, Lyle D. *The Theology of the Heidelberg Catechism: A Reformation Synthesis.* Columbia Series in Reformed Theology. Louisville, KY: Westminster John Knox, 2013.

Bischof, Janika. "The Printed *Acta Synodi Nationalis Dordrechti* as a Networking Tool." In *Material Moments in Book Cultures: Essays in Honour of Gabriele Müller-Oberhäuser*, edited by Simon Rosenberg and Sandra Simon, 177–87. Frankfurt am Main: Peter Lang, 2014.

Blacketer, Raymond A. "Definite Atonement in Historical Perspective." In *The Glory of the Atonement, Biblical, Historical & Practical Perspectives: Essays in Honor of Roger Nicole*, 304–23. Downers Grove, IL: IVP Academic, 2004.

———. "The Three Points in Most Parts Reformed: A Reexamination of the So-Called Well-Meant Offer of Salvation." *Calvin Theological Journal* 35 (2000): 37–65.

Blei, Karel. *The Netherlands Reformed Church, 1571–2005.* Translated by Allan J. Janssen. Grand Rapids, MI: Eerdmans, 2006.

Boer, Harry R. *The Doctrine of Reprobation in the Christian Reformed Church.* Grand Rapids, MI: Eerdmans, 1983.

Brandt, Casper. *The Life of James Arminius, D.D..* Translated by John Guthrie. London: Ward,1854.

Brandt, Gerard. *The History of the Reformation and other ecclesiastical transactions in and about the Low-Countries.* 4 vols. London, 1720–1723.

Brown, Peter. *Augustine of Hippo: A Biography.* Rev. ed. Berkeley: University of California Press, 2000.

Bryson, George. *The Five Points of Calvinism: Weighed and Found Wanting.* Costa Mesa, CA: Word for Today, 1996.

Cameron, Euan. *The European Reformation.* Oxford: Clarendon, 1991.

Carey, William. *An Enquiry into the Obligations of Christians, to Use Means for the Conversion of the Heathens.* Leicester, UK: Ann Ireland, 1792.

Carson, D. A. *The Difficult Doctrine of the Love of God.* Wheaton, IL: Crossway Books, 2000.

———. *The Gospel according to John.* Grand Rapids, MI: Eerdmans, 1991.

Chafer, Lewis Sperry. *Salvation.* New York: Charles C. Cook, 1917.

Cranfield, C. E. B. *A Critical and Exegetical Commentary on the Epistle to the Romans,* 2 vols. 1979. Reprint, London: T&T Clark, 2004.

Daniell, David. *The Bible in English: Its History and Influence.* New Haven, CT: Yale University Press, 2003.

Davids, Peter H. *The First Epistle of Peter.* New International Commentary on the New Testament. Grand Rapids, MI: Eerdmans, 1990.

Davis, John Jefferson. "The Perseverance of the Saints: A History of the Doctrine." *Journal of the Evangelical Theological Society* 34, no. 2 (June 1991): 213–28.

de Boer, Erik A. "'O, Ye Women, Think of Thy Innocent Children, When They Die Young!' The Canons of Dordt (First Head, Article Seventeen) between Polemic and Pastoral Theology." In Goudriaan and van Lieburg, *Revisiting the Synod of Dordt,* 261–90.

De Jong, Peter Y., ed. *Crisis in the Reformed Churches: Essays in Commemoration of the Great Synod of Dort, 1618–1619.* Grand Rapids, MI: Reformed Fellowship, 1968.

———. "The Rise of the Reformed Churches in the Netherlands." In De Jong, *Crisis in the Reformed Churches,* 1–21.

DeKoster vs. Boer: Debate; A Debate Originally Given at the Request of the Men's Christian Fellowship of the 3rd Christian Reformed Church of Kalamazoo, Michigan, March 7, 1979. Blue Island, IL: Paracletos, 1979.

den Boer, William. "Defense or Deviation? A Re-examination of Arminius' Motives to Deviate from the 'Mainstream' Reformed Theology." In Goudriaan and van Lieburg, *Revisiting the Synod of Dordt,* 23–47.

————. *God's Twofold Love: The Theology of Arminius (1559–1609)*. Translated by Albert Gootjes. Reformed Historical Theology 14. Göttingen, Germany: Vandenhoeck & Ruprecht, 2010.

de Witt, John R. "The Arminian Conflict and the Synod of Dort." In *Puritan Papers: Volume 5, 1968–1969*, edited by J. I. Packer, 3–23. Phillipsburg, NJ: P&R, 2005.

Drawn into Controversie: Reformed Theological Diversity with Seventeenth-Century British Puritanism. Edited by Michael A. G. Haykin and Mark Jones. Göttingen, Germany: Vandenhoeck & Ruprecht, 2011.

Drobner, Hubertus R. *The Fathers of the Church: A Comprehensive Introduction*. Translated by Siegrief S. Schatzmann. Peabody, MA: Hendrickson, 2007.

Duke, Alastair. *Reformation and Revolt in the Low Countries*. London: Hambledon and London, 2003.

Fata, Márta. "The Kingdom of Hungary and Principality of Transylvania." In *A Companion to the Reformation in Central Europe*, edited by Howard Louthan and Graeme Murdock, 92–120. Brill's Companions to the Christian Tradition 61. Leiden: Brill, 2015.

Feenstra, Peter G. *Unspeakable Comfort: A Commentary on the Canons of Dort*. Winnipeg: Premier, 1997.

Fesko, J. V. *Diversity within the Reformed Tradition: Supra- and Infralapsarianism in Calvin, Dort, and Westminster*. Greenville, SC: Reformed Academic Press, 2001.

————. *The Theology of the Westminster Standards: Historical Context and Theological Insights*. Wheaton, IL: Crossway, 2014.

Fornerod, Nicolas. "'The Canons of the Synod Has Shot Off the Advocate's Head': A Reappraisal of the Genevan Delegation at the Synod of Dordt." In Goudriaan and van Lieburg, *Revisiting the Synod of Dordt*, 181–215.

Foster, Herbert Darling. "Liberal Calvinism: The Remonstrants at the Synod of Dort in 1618." *Harvard Theological Review* 16, no. 1 (January 1923): 1–37.

Gatiss, Lee. "Abundant Sufficiency and Intentional Efficacy: Particular Redemption at the Synod of Dort." *Unio Cum Christo* 4, no. 2 (October 2018): 145–61.

———. *For Us and for Our Salvation: "Limited Atonement" in the Bible, Doctrine, History, and Ministry*. London: Latimer Trust, 2012.

———. "Grace Tasted Death for All: Thomas Aquinas on Hebrews 2.9." *Tyndale Bulletin* 62, no. 2 (2012): 217–37.

Gazal, Andre. "George Carleton's Reformed Doctrine of Episcopal Authority at the Synod of Dort." In *Beyond Calvin: Essays on the Diversity of the Reformed Tradition*, edited by W. Bradford Littlejohn and Jonathan Tomes, 107–26. Lincoln, NE: Davenant Trust, 2017.

Gibb, H. A. R. *Mohammedanism: An Historical Survey*. Second edition. Oxford: Oxford University Press, 1970).

Godfrey, W. Robert. "Calvin and Calvinism in The Netherlands." In *John Calvin: His Influence in the Western World*, edited by W. Stanford Reid, 95–120. Grand Rapids, MI: Zondervan, 1982.

———. "Canons From Dort." In *Reformation Sketches*, 123–32. Phillipsburg, NJ: P&R, 2003.

———. "Did the Canons Misfire?" *Outlook* 26, no. 6 (June 1976): 18–21.

———. "Election and Covenant: The Synod of Dort and Children Dying in Infancy." Unpublished.

———. "John Hales' Good-Night to John Calvin." In *Protestant Scholasticism: Essays in Reassessment*, edited by Carl R. Trueman and R. Scott Clark, 165–80. Carlisle, UK: Paternoster, 1999.

———. "Popular and Catholic: The *Modus Docendi* of the Canons of Dordt." In Goudriaan and van Lieburg, *Revisiting the Synod of Dordt*, 243–60.

————. "Reprobation—the Critics and the Canons." *Outlook* 26, no. 9 (September 1976): 2–5.

————. *Reformation Sketches.* Phillipsburg, NJ: P&R, 2003.

————. "Reformed Thought on the Extent of the Atonement to 1618." *Westminster Theological Journal* 37, no. 2 (Winter 1975): 133–71.

————. "Subscription in the Dutch Reformed Tradition." In *The Practice of Confessional Subscription*, edited by David W. Hall, 67–75. Oak Ridge, TN: Covenant Foundation, 2001.

————. "Tensions within International Calvinism: The Debate on the Atonement at the Synod of Dordt 1618–1619." PhD diss., Stanford University, 1974.

————. "Who Was Arminius?" *Modern Reformation* 1, no. 3 (May/June 1992): 6–7.

Gootjes, N. H. "Can Parents Be Sure? Background and Meaning of Canons of Dort I, 17 (1)." *Clarion: The Canadian Reformed Magazine* 44, no. 20 (October 6, 1995): 464–65.

————. "Can Parents Be Sure? Background and Meaning of Canons of Dort I, 17 (2)." *Clarion: The Canadian Reformed Magazine* 44, no. 21 (October 20, 1995): 481–83.

Goudriaan, Aza. "Justification by Faith and the Early Arminian Controversy." In *Scholasticism Reformed: Essays in Honor of Willem J. van Asselt*, edited by Maarten Wisse, Marcel Sarot, and Willemien Otten, 155–78. Leiden: Brill, 2010.

————. *Reformed Orthodoxy and Philosophy, 1625–1750. Gisbertus Voetius, Petrus van Mastricht, and Anthonius Driessen.* Brill's Series in Church History 26. Leiden: Brill, 2006.

————. "The Synod of Dordt on Arminian Anthropology." In Goudriaan and van Lieburg, *Revisiting the Synod of Dordt*, 81–106.

Goudriaan, Aza, and Fred van Lieburg, eds. *Revisiting the Synod of Dordt (1618–1619)*. Brill's Series in Church History 49. Leiden: Brill, 2011.

Haley, K. H. D. *The Dutch in the Seventeenth Century*. New York: Harcourt Brace Jovanovich, 1972.

Hall, Basil. "Calvin against the Calvinists." In *John Calvin*, edited by G. E. Duffield, 19–37. Grand Rapids, MI: Eerdmans, 1968.

Hamilton, Ian. "Winsome Calvinism." *Banner of Truth* 526 (2007): 1–5.

Haykin, Michael A. G., and C. Jeffrey Robinson Sr. *To the Ends of the Earth: Calvin's Missional Vision and Legacy*. Wheaton, IL: Crossway, 2014.

Hefele, Charles Joseph. *A History of the Councils of the Church from the Original Documents: Volume 4, A.D. 451 to A.D. 680*. Translated by William R. Clark. Edinburgh: T&T Clark, 1895.

Hendriksen, William. *Romans*. New Testament Commentary. 1980, 1981. Grand Rapids, MI: Baker Book House, sixth printing 1989.

Henzel, Ján. "When Conversion Is Joy and Death Victory: Historical Foundations of the Doctrine of Perseverance." *Tyndale Bulletin* 54, no. 2 (2003): 123–48.

Heppe, Heinrich. *Reformed Dogmatics*. Edited by Ernst Bizer. Translated by G. T. Thomson. London: George Allen & Unwin, 1950.

Hodge, Charles. *Systematic Theology*. 3 vols. Reprint, Grand Rapids, MI: Eerdmans, 1995.

Hoekema, Anthony. "The Missionary Focus of the Canons of Dort." *Calvin Theological Journal*, November 1972, 209–20.

Hoeksema, Herman. *Believers and Their Seed*. Translated by Homer C. Hoeksema. 1971. Reprint, Grand Rapids, MI: Reformed Free Publishing Association, 1977.

———. *Reformed Dogmatics: Volume 2*. 2nd ed. Jenison, MI: Reformed Free Publishing Association, 2005.

———. *Predestination: The Heart of the Gospel.* Grand Rapids, MI: Radio Committee of the First Protestant Reformed Church, 1949.

Hoeksema, Homer C. *The Voice of Our Fathers.* Grand Rapids, MI: Reformed Free Publishing Association, 1980.

Holcomb, Justin S. *Know the Creeds and Councils.* Grand Rapids, MI: Zondervan, 2014.

Holyoak, Thomas. *A Large Dictionary: In Three Parts.* London: Printed by W. Rawlins for G. Sawbridge et al., 1677.

Horton, Michael S. *Covenant and Salvation: Union with Christ.* Louisville, KY: Westminster John Knox, 2007.

Huijgen, Arnold. "The Theology of the Canons of Dort: A Reassessment after Four Hundred Years." *Unio Cum Christo* 4, no. 2 (October 2018): 111–28.

Hunt, Dave. *What Love Is This? Calvinism's Misrepresentation of God.* Sisters, OR: Loyal, 2002.

Hyde, Daniel R. *Content Yet Contending: Jude.* Welwyn Garden City, UK: EP Books, 2017.

———. *From the Pen of Pastor Paul: 1–2 Thessalonians.* Welwyn Garden City, UK: EP Books, 2015.

———. *God in Our Midst: The Tabernacle and Our Relationship with God.* Orlando, FL: Reformation Trust, 2012.

———. *The Good Confession: An Exploration of the Christian Faith.* Eugene, OR: Wipf & Stock, 2006.

———. "Handling a High Mystery: The Westminster Confession on Preaching Predestination." *Puritan Reformed Journal* 2, no. 2 (June 2010): 235–58.

———. *In Defense of the Descent: A Response to Contemporary Critics.* Explorations in Reformed Confessional Theology. Grand Rapids, MI: Reformation Heritage Books, 2010.

————. *Jesus Loves the Little Children: Why We Baptize Children.* 2006. Grandville, MI: Reformed Fellowship, second printing 2012.

————. "Ministering after Miscarriages." Audio file, 42:11. https://www.sermonaudio.com/sermoninfo.asp?SID=28111739547. Accessed August 9, 2018.

————. "The Principle and Practice of Preaching in the Heidelberg Catechism." *Puritan Reformed Journal* 1, no. 1 (January 2009): 97–117.

————. "*Regulae de Observatione Sabbathi*: The Synod of Dort's (1618–19) Deliverance on the Sabbath." *Puritan Reformed Journal* 4, no. 1 (January 2012): 161–83.

————. *Welcome to a Reformed Church: A Guide for Pilgrims.* 2010. Orlando, FL: Reformation Trust, eighth printing 2017.

————. *With Heart and Mouth: An Exposition of the Belgic Confession.* Grandville, MI: Reformed Fellowship, 2008.

Israel, Jonathan I. *The Dutch Republic: Its Rise, Greatness, and Fall 1477–1806.* 1995. Reprint, Oxford: Clarendon, 1997.

Jones, Mark. *Antinomianism: Reformed Theology's Unwelcome Guest?* Phillipsburg, NJ: P&R, 2013.

Kelly, J. N. D. *Early Christian Doctrines.* 1960. Rev. ed., New York: HarperSanFrancisco, 1978.

King, Martin Luther, Jr. "What Is Man?" http://mlk-kpp01.stanford.edu/primarydocuments/Vol6/11July1954WhatIsMan.pdf. Accessed August 9, 2018.

Kistemaker, Simon. "Leading Figures at the Synod of Dort." In De Jong, *Crisis in the Reformed Churches*, 39–51.

Klooster, Fred H. "The Doctrinal Deliverances of Dort." In De Jong, *Crisis in the Reformed Churches*, 52–94.

Knapp, Henry. "Augustine and Owen on Perseverance." *Westminster Theological Journal* 62, no. 1 (Spring 2000): 65–87.

Köstlin, Julius. *The Theology of Luther in Its Historical Development and Inner Harmony.* Translated by Charles E. Hay. 2 vols. Philadelphia: Lutheran Publication Society, 1897.

Krop, Henri A. "Philosophy and the Synod of Dordt: Aristotelianism, Humanism, and the Case against Arianism." In Goudriaan and van Lieburg, *Revisiting the Synod of Dordt,* 49–79.

Lane, A. N. S. "Did Calvin Believe in Freewill?" *Vox Evangelica* 12 (1981): 72–90.

Letham, Robert. *The Westminster Assembly: Readings Its Theology in Historical Context.* Phillipsburg, NJ: P&R, 2009.

Levering, Matthew. *The Theology of Augustine: An Introductory Guide to His Most Important Works.* Grand Rapids, MI: Baker Academic, 2013.

Littlejohn, W. Bradford. *The Two Kingdoms: A Guide for the Perplexed,* Davenant Guides. Lincoln, NE: Davenant Trust, 2017.

Lynch, Michael. "Confessional Orthodoxy and Hypothetical Universalism: Another Look at the Westminster Confession of Faith." In *Beyond Calvin: Essays on the Diversity of the Reformed Tradition,* edited by W. Bradford Littlejohn and Jonathan Tomes, 127–48. Lincoln, NE: Davenant Trust, 2017.

Maag, Karin. "Impact amid Absence: The Synod of Dordt and the French Huguenots." *In die Skriflig* 52, no. 2 (2018): a2340. https://doi.org/10.4102/ids.v52i2.2340.

Machen, J. Gresham. *The Christian View of Man.* Edinburgh: Banner of Truth Trust, 1984.

Martin, Al. "The Practical Implications of Calvinism." BannerofTruth.org. https://banneroftruth.org/us/resources/articles/2002/the-practical-implications-of-calvinism. Accessed May 9, 2018.

Mathisen, Ralph W. "Caesarius of Arles, Prevenient Grace, and the Second Council of Orange." In *Grace for Grace: The Debates after Augustine and Pelagius,* edited by Alexander Y. Hwang, Brian J. Matz, and Augustine Casiday, 208–34. Washington, DC: Catholic University of America Press, 2014.

MacCulloch, Diarmaid. *The Reformation: A History*. New York: Penguin, 2003.

McComish, William A. *The Epigones: A Study of the Theology of the Genevan Academy at the Time of the Synod of Dort, with Special Reference to Giovanni Diodati*. Princeton Theological Monograph Series 13. Eugene, OR: Pickwick, 1989.

McGraw, Ryan M. *Knowing the Trinity: Practical Thoughts for Daily Life*. Lancaster, PA: Alliance of Confessing Evangelicals, 2017.

———. "The Threats of the Gospel: John Owen on What the Law/Gospel Distinction Is Not." In *John Owen: Trajectories in Reformed Orthodox Theology*, 71–109. Cham, Switzerland: Palgrave Macmillan, 2017.

Milton, Anthony. "A Distorting Mirror: The Hales and Balcanquahal Letters and the Synod of Dordt." In Goudriaan and van Lieburg, *Revisiting the Synod of Dordt*, 135–61.

Moore, Jonathan D. "James Ussher's Influence on the Synod of Dort." In Goudriaan and van Lieburg, *Revisiting the Synod of Dordt*, 163–79.

Morris, Leon. *The Epistle to the Romans*. Grand Rapids, MI: Eerdmans, 1988.

———. *The Gospel according to John*. New International Commentary on the New Testament. 1971. Reprint, Grand Rapids, MI: Eerdmans, 1989.

Muller, Richard A. "Arminius and Arminianism." In *The Dictionary of Historical Theology*, edited by Trevor A. Hart, 33–36. Grand Rapids, MI: Eerdmans, 2000.

———. "Arminius and the Reformed Tradition." *Westminster Theological Journal* 70, no. 1 (Spring 2008): 19–48.

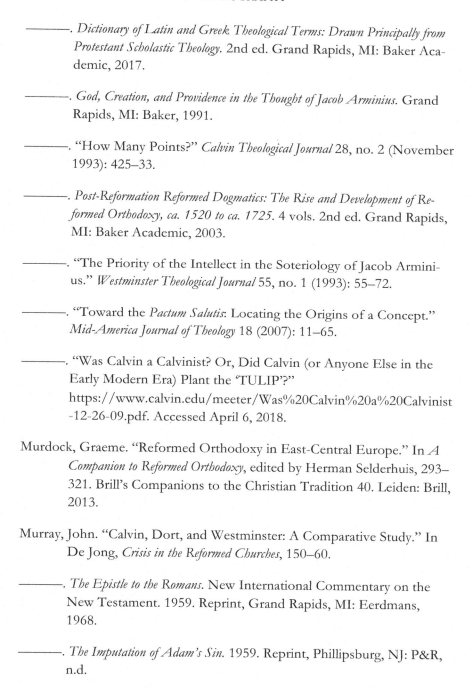

———. *Dictionary of Latin and Greek Theological Terms: Drawn Principally from Protestant Scholastic Theology*. 2nd ed. Grand Rapids, MI: Baker Academic, 2017.

———. *God, Creation, and Providence in the Thought of Jacob Arminius*. Grand Rapids, MI: Baker, 1991.

———. "How Many Points?" *Calvin Theological Journal* 28, no. 2 (November 1993): 425–33.

———. *Post-Reformation Reformed Dogmatics: The Rise and Development of Reformed Orthodoxy, ca. 1520 to ca. 1725*. 4 vols. 2nd ed. Grand Rapids, MI: Baker Academic, 2003.

———. "The Priority of the Intellect in the Soteriology of Jacob Arminius." *Westminster Theological Journal* 55, no. 1 (1993): 55–72.

———. "Toward the *Pactum Salutis*: Locating the Origins of a Concept." *Mid-America Journal of Theology* 18 (2007): 11–65.

———. "Was Calvin a Calvinist? Or, Did Calvin (or Anyone Else in the Early Modern Era) Plant the 'TULIP'?" https://www.calvin.edu/meeter/Was%20Calvin%20a%20Calvinist-12-26-09.pdf. Accessed April 6, 2018.

Murdock, Graeme. "Reformed Orthodoxy in East-Central Europe." In *A Companion to Reformed Orthodoxy*, edited by Herman Selderhuis, 293–321. Brill's Companions to the Christian Tradition 40. Leiden: Brill, 2013.

Murray, John. "Calvin, Dort, and Westminster: A Comparative Study." In De Jong, *Crisis in the Reformed Churches*, 150–60.

———. *The Epistle to the Romans*. New International Commentary on the New Testament. 1959. Reprint, Grand Rapids, MI: Eerdmans, 1968.

———. *The Imputation of Adam's Sin*. 1959. Reprint, Phillipsburg, NJ: P&R, n.d.

———. "Paul's Use of 'Nomos.'" In *Collected Writings of John Murray: Volume 4, Studies in Theology*, 133–41. Edinburgh: Banner of Truth, 1982.

Nineham, D. E. "Gottschalk of Orbais: Reactionary or Precursor of the Reformation?," *Journal of Ecclesiastical History* 40 (1989): 1–18.

1980 Acts of Synod. Grand Rapids, MI: Board of Publication of the Christian Reformed Church, 1980.

Oberman, Heiko A. *The Dawn of the Reformation: Essays in Late Medieval and Early Reformation Thought*. 1986. Reprint, Grand Rapids, MI: Eerdmans, 1992.

———. *Forerunners of the Reformation: The Shape of Late Medieval Thoughts Illustrated by Key Documents*. Translated by Paul L. Nyhus. New York: Holt, Rinehart and Winston, 1966.

———. *The Harvest of Medieval Theology: Gabriel Biel and Late Medieval Nominalism*. 1963. Rev. ed., Grand Rapids, MI: Eerdmans, 1967.

———. *Masters of the Reformation: The Emergence of a New Intellectual Climate in Europe*. Cambridge: Cambridge University Press, 1981.

———. *The Two Reformations: The Journey from the Last Days to the New World*. New Haven, CT: Yale University Press, 2003.

Packer, J. I. "The Love of God: Universal and Particular." In *Still Sovereign: Contemporary Perspectives on Election, Foreknowledge, and Grace*, edited by Thomas Schreiner and Bruce Ware, 277–91. Grand Rapids, MI: Baker, 2000.

Péter, Katalin. *Studies on the History of the Reformation in Hungary and Transylvania*. Edited by Gabriella Erdélyi. Refo500 Academic Studies 45. Göttingen, Germany: Vandenhoeck & Ruprecht, 2018.

Petersen, Henry. *The Canons of Dort: A Study Guide*. Grand Rapids, MI: Baker Book House, 1968.

Petersen, Leif Inge Ree. *Siege Warfare and Military Organization in the Successor States (400–800 AD): Byzantium, the West and Islam*. Leiden: Brill, 2013.

Platt, John. "Eirenical Anglicans at the Synod of Dort." In *Reform and Reformation: England and the Continent c. 1500–1750.* edited by D. Baker. Oxford: Blackwell, 1979.

———. *Reformed Thought and Scholasticism: The Arguments for the Existence of God in Dutch Theology, 1575–1650.* Leiden: Brill, 1982.

Praasma, Louis. "The Background of the Arminian Controversy (1586–1618)." In De Jong, *Crisis in the Reformed Churches,* 22–38.

Pronk, Cornelis. *Expository Sermons on the Canons of Dort.* St. Thomas, ON: Free Reformed, 1999.

Psalter Hymnal. Grand Rapids, MI: Board of Publications of the Christian Reformed Church, 1976.

Registers of the Consistory of Geneva in the Time of Calvin, Volume 1: 1542–1544. Edited by Robert M. Kingdon, Thomas A. Lambert, and Isabella M. Watt. Translated by M. Wallace McDonald. 1996. Reprint, Grand Rapids, MI: Eerdmans, 2000.

"Report 30: Committee on Dr. Harry Boer's Confessional-Revision Gravamen." in *1980 Acts of Synod,* 486–558. Grand Rapids, MI: Board of Publication of the Christian Reformed Church, 1980.

Richards, James. *Lectures on Mental Philosophy and Theology.* New York: M. W. Dodd, 1846.

Ridderbos, Herman. *The Gospel of John: A Theological Commentary.* Translated by John Vriend. Grand Rapids, MI: Eerdmans, 1997.

———. *Paul: An Outline of His Theology.* Translated by John Richard De Witt. 1966. Reprint, Grand Rapids, MI: Eerdmans, 1975.

Rogers, Jack, and Donald McKim. *The Authority and Interpretation of the Bible: An Historical Approach.* San Francisco: Harper and Row, 1979.

Ryle, J. C. *Holiness: Its Nature, Hindrances, Difficulties, & Roots.* 1879. Reprint, Moscow, ID: Charles Nolan, 2001.

Schreiner, Thomas R. *Romans*. Baker Exegetical Commentary on the New Testament. Grand Rapids, MI: Baker Books, 1998.

Sinnema, Donald W. "Are the Canons of Dordt a True Reflection of Calvin's View of Predestination?" *In die Skriflig* 52, no. 2 (2018): a2347. https://doi.org/10.4102/ids.v52i2.2347.

———. "Calvin and the Canons of Dordt (1619)." *Church History and Religious Culture* 91, nos. 1–2 (2011): 87–103.

———. "The Canons of Dordt: From Judgment on Arminianism to Confessional Standard." In Goudriaan and van Lieburg, *Revisiting the Synod of Dordt*, 313–33.

———. "The Distinction between Scholastic and Popular: Andreas Hyperius and Reformed Scholasticism." In *Protestant Scholasticism: Essays in Reassessment*, edited by Carl R. Trueman and R. S. Clark, 127–43. Carlisle, UK: Paternoster, 1999.

———. "The Drafting of the Canons of Dordt: A Preliminary Survey of Early Drafts and Related Documents." In Goudriaan and van Lieburg, *Revisiting the Synod of Dordt*, 291–311.

———. "The French Reformed Churches, Arminianism, and the Synod of Dort (1618–1619)." In *The Theology of the French Reformed Churches: From Henri IV to the Revocation of the Edict of Nantes*, edited by Martin I. Klauber, 98–136. Grand Rapids, MI: Reformation Heritage Books, 2014.

———. "The Issue of Reprobation at the Synod of Dort (1618–1619) in the Light of the History of This Doctrine." PhD diss., University of St Michael's College, 1985.

———. "Reformed Scholasticism and the Synod of Dort (1618–19)." In *John Calvin's Institutes: His Opus Magnum*, edited by B. J. Van de Walt. Potchefstroom, South Africa: Potchefstroom University for Christian Higher Education, 1986.

Smith, Chuck. *Calvinism, Arminianism, and the Word of God: A Calvary Chapel Perspective*. Costa Mesa, CA: Word for Today, 2005.

Sproul, R. C. *Surprised by Suffering.* Wheaton, IL: Tyndale House, 1988.

Spurgeon, C. H. "Misrepresentations of True Calvinism Cleared Away." https://www.spurgeongems.org/vols7-9/chs002.pdf. Accessed May 9, 2018.

―――. "The Perseverance of the Saints." https://www.spurgeongems.org/vols13-15/chs872.pdf. Accessed August 6, 2018.

Stanglin, Keith D. *Arminius on the Assurance of Salvation: The Context, Roots, and Shape of the Leiden Debate, 1603–1609.* Brill's Series in Church History 27. Leiden: Brill, 2009.

Stanglin, Keith D., and Thomas H. McCall. *Jacob Arminius: Theologian of Grace.* Oxford: Oxford University Press, 2012.

Steinmetz, David C. *Luther and Staupitz: An Essay in the Intellectual Origins of the Protestant Reformation.* Durham, NC: Duke University Press, 1980.

―――. *Reformers in the Wings: From Geiler von Kaysersberg to Theodore Beza.* 2nd ed. Oxford: Oxford University Press, 2001.

Stewart, Kenneth J. *Ten Myths about Calvinism: Recovering the Breadth of the Reformed Tradition.* Downers Grove, IL: IVP Academic, 2011.

Stone, Lawrence. *The Family, Sex and Marriage in England 1500–1800.* 1977. Rev. ed., Harmondsworth, UK: Penguin, 1985.

Strehle, Stephen. "The Extent of the Atonement and the Synod of Dort." *Westminster Theological Journal* 51, no.1 (Spring 1989): 1–23.

The New Scofield Reference Bible. Edited by C. I. Scofield. New York: Oxford University, 1967).

Thomas, G. Michael. *The Extent of the Atonement: A Dilemma for Reformed Theology from Calvin to the Consensus (1536–1675).* Carlisle, UK: Paternoster, 1997.

Todd, Margo. "Justifying God: The Calvinisms of the British Delegation to the Synod of Dort." *Archiv für Reformationsgeschichte* 96 (2005): 272–89.

Trueman, Carl R. *The Creedal Imperative.* Wheaton, IL: Crossway, 2012.

van Asselt, W. J. "No Dordt without Scholasticism: Willem Verboom on the Canons of Dordt." *Church History and Religious Culture* 87, no. 2 (2007): 203–10.

Van Bruggen, Jakob. *Paul: Pioneer for Israel's Messiah.* Translated by Ed M. van der Maas. 2001. Reprint, Phillipsburg, NJ: P&R, 2005.

van den Berg, Johannes. "The Synod of Dort in the Balance." In *Religious Currents and Cross-Currents: Essays on Early Modern Protestantism and the Protestant Enlightenment,* edited by Jan de Bruijn, Pieter Nanne Holtrop, and Ernestine G. E. Van Der Wall, 1–17. Leiden: Brill, 1999.

Vander Gugten, S. "The Arminian Controversy and the Synod of Dort." http://www.spindleworks.com/library/vandergugten/arminian_c.htm#6. Accessed November 4, 2013.

van der Westhuizen, Henco. "The Trinity in the Canons of Dordt?" *In die Skriflig* 52, no. 2. https://doi.org/10.4102/ids.v52i2.2338.

VanDoodewaard, William. "Remonstrants, Contra-Remonstrants, and the Synod of Dort (1618–1619): The Religious History of the Early Dutch Republic." *Puritan Reformed Journal* 4, no. 1 (January 2002): 135–60.

Van der Pol, Frank, ed. *The Doctrine of Election in Reformed Perspective: Historical and Theological Investigations of the Synod of Dordt 1618–1619.* Refo500 Academic Studies 51. Göttingen, Germany: Vandenhoeck & Ruprecht, 2019.

van Genderen, J., and W. H. Velema. *Concise Reformed Dogmatics.* Translated by Gerrit Bilkes and Ed M. van der Maas. Phillipsburg, NJ: P&R, 2008.

van Lieburg, Fred. "Gisbertus Samuels: A Reformed Minister Sentences by the Synod of Zeeland in 1591 for His Opinions on Predestination." In Goudriaan and van Lieburg, *Revisiting the Synod of Dordt*, 1–22.

———. "The Public Gallery of the Dordt Synod." Synod of Dordt Conference, Calvin Theological Seminary, September 14–15, 2018. https://vimeo.com/291164865.

———. *The Synod of Dordrecht 1618–1619.* Translated by Dick Swier. Edited by Herman A. van Duinen and Cees Esseboom. Dordrecht: Stichting Historisch Platform Dordrecht, 2017.

van Oosterzee, J. J. *Christian Dogmatics: A Text Book for Academical Instruction and Private Study.* Translated by John Watson Watson and Maurice J. Evans. 1870. 5th ed., London: Hodder and Stoughton, 1891.

Van Vliet, Jason. "Election: The Father's Decision to Adopt." *Unio Cum Christo* 4, no. 2 (October 2018): 129–43.

Venema, Cornelis P. *But for the Grace of God: An Exposition of the Canons of Dort.* Grand Rapids, MI: Reformed Fellowship, 1994.

———. *By His Spirit and Word: How Christ Builds His Church.* Grandville, MI: Reformed Fellowship, 2015.

———. "The Election and Salvation of the Children of Believers Who Die in Infancy: A Study of Article I/17 of the Canons of Dort." *Mid-America Journal of Theology* 17 (2006): 57–100.

Verboom, Wim. "The Christology in the *Heidelberg Catechism* and in the *Canones of Dordt.*" In *Strangers and Pilgrims on Earth: Essays in Honor of Abraham van de Beek,* edited by E. Van der Borght and P. van Geest, 115–28. Studies in Reformed Theology 22. Leiden: Brill, 2012.

Vos, Geerhardus. "The Scriptural Doctrine of the Love of God." In *Redemptive History and Biblical Interpretation: The Shorter Writings of Geerhardus Vos,* 425–57. Phillipsburg, NJ: P&R, 1980.

Wallace, Daniel B. *Greek Grammar beyond the Basics: An Exegetical Syntax of the New Testament.* Grand Rapids, MI: Zondervan, 1996.

Warfield, B. B. "The Development of the Doctrine of Infant Salvation." In *Studies in Theology: The Works of Benjamin B. Warfield*, 10 vols., 9:411–44. 1932; repr., Grand Rapids, MI: Baker Book House, 2000.

Weaver, Rebecca Harden. *Divine Grace and Human Agency: A Study of the Semi-Pelagian Controversy*, Patristic Monographs Series 15. Macon, GA: Mercer University Press, 1996.

———. Introduction to *Grace for Grace: The Debates after Augustine and Pelagius*, edited by Alexander Y. Hwang, Brian J. Matz, and Augustine Casiday, xi–xxvi. Washington, DC: Catholic University of America Press, 2014.

Wright, David F. "Augustine and Augustinianism." In *New Dictionary of Theology*, edited by Sinclair B. Ferguson, David F. Wright, and J. I. Packer, 58–63. Downers Grove, IL: InterVarsity, 1988.

———. "Pelagianism." In *New Dictionary of Theology*, edited by Sinclair B. Ferguson, David F. Wright, and J. I. Packer, 499–501. Downers Grove, IL: InterVarsity, 1988.

Wuest, Kenneth S. "Bypaths in the Greek New Testament." In *Wuest's Word Studies from the Greek New Testament: Volume 3*. 1940. Reprint, Grand Rapids, MI: Eerdmans, 2004.

ABOUT THE DAVENANT INSTITUTE

The Davenant Institute aims to retrieve the riches of classical Protestantism in order to renew and build up the contemporary church: building networks of friendship and collaboration among evangelical scholars committed to Protestant resourcement, publishing resources old and new, and offering training and discipleship for Christians thirsting after wisdom.

We are a nonprofit organization supported by your tax-deductible gifts. Learn more about us, and donate, at www.davenantinstitute.org.

Made in the USA
Coppell, TX
17 January 2023

11261422R10243